Vasant
Kaiwar and
Sucheta
Mazumdar,
editors

# of Modernity

Essays on Race, Orient, Nation

© 2003 Duke University Press
All rights reserved
Printed in the United States of
America on acid-free paper ∞
Designed by Rebecca Giménez
Typeset in Sabon with Helvetica
Display by Keystone Typesetting
Library of Congress Cataloging-in-
Publication Data appear on the
last printed page of this book.

Contents

Acknowledgments

The origins of this volume go back to two debates that have especially engaged us in the last decade: the crisis of area studies and the crisis of ethnic studies. By the 1990s, both fields, born almost in tandem but coming of age in very separate spheres, were being challenged to confront the cultural and political manifestations of global capitalism by their internal membership as well as by those working outside the self-defined perimeters of these sites of scholarly investigation. This book is the product of the dialogue between the two fields that we have been privileged to be part of. In addition to comments by colleagues on our individual essays that we have acknowledged below, here we wish to thank various conference and workshop organizers who have provided us with opportunities over the years to present our exploratory work and to benefit from the comments of the participants. In particular:

The annual conference of the Association of Asian American Studies at Cornell in 1993, organized by Gary Okihiro, which fostered a broader debate within American Studies; William Martin, Gloria Waite, and Michael West of the Current Affairs Committee for sponsoring a cross-borders session at the 1996 annual meeting of the Association of African Studies; Joseph Elder for enthusiastically supporting a special conference on globalization at the annual 1997 South Asia conference at the University of Wisconsin, Madison; Mohamad Tavakoli-Targhi, Reza Sheikholeslami, and

Homa Katouzian for creating a dialogue between Iranian Studies and South Asian Studies at the 1998 conference "The Coming of Modernity to Qajar Iran" at St. Anthony's College, Oxford; Emilio Pantojas Garcia for helping link Asian and Caribbean perspectives through the 1998 conference "Colonial Plantations to Global Peripheries" at the University of Puerto Rico, San Juan; and Jean-Luc Racine for encouraging scholars of South Asia politics to look beyond the homeland and consider dimensions of diaspora studies at the Maison des Sciences de l'Homme 2001 workshop "India, Discussing New Parameters."

The editors would like to acknowledge the support of Rob Sikorski, executive director at the Center for International Studies, for funding a two-year faculty seminar at Duke University on International Migration (1996–98) that allowed us to learn much about Caribbean, Asian, and African migrations, explore issues of development, globalization, and politics, and rethink area studies.

The editors are most grateful to the two anonymous readers of this manuscript for their very helpful comments, the contributors for their good cheer and hard work in bringing this manuscript to its final form, and Ken Wissoker at Duke University Press for his enthusiastic support of this project. We are grateful to Petra Dreiser and Pamela Morrison for their editing. Last but not least, we received invaluable help in compiling the bibliography from David Pizzo and in producing the final copy from Denise Rippenhagen.

Earlier versions of the following chapters were published as articles in *Comparative Studies of South Asia, Africa, and the Middle East*: Michael West, "An Anticolonial International? Indians, India, and Africans in British Central Africa," which appeared under the title, "Indians, India, and Race and Nationalism in British Central Africa," 14.2 (1994): 86–108; Neville Alexander, " 'The Moment of Manoeuvre': 'Race,' Ethnicity, and Nation in Postapartheid South Africa," 15.1 (1995): 5–11; A. R. Venkatachalapathy, "Coining Words: Language and Politics in Late Colonial Tamilnadu," 15.2 (1995): 120–32; Mohamad Tavakoli-Targhi, "Orientalism's Genesis Amnesia," 16.1 (1996): 1–14; and Andrew E. Barnes, "Aryanizing Projects, African 'Collaborators,' and Colonial Transcripts," 17.2 (1997): 46–61. Those articles have been reworked with comments from the readers and editors.

Vasant Kaiwar and Sucheta Mazumdar

Introduction

■ The essays in this collection explore aspects of modernity in South Asia, the Middle East, and Africa generated by the triangulation of romantic racialism, Orientalism, and nationalism, as well as their specific approaches to issues of time and space in the construction of "indigenous" modernist projects. In recent decades, a renewed, profound ambiguity about the processes, experiences, and results of capitalist modernization has emerged, even as the "premodern" has, in some cases, been thoroughly consigned to the museum of history.[1] In this context, assessments of modernity — which we define, drawing on elements from Jameson and Berman,[2] as the experiences of incomplete capitalist modernization and attempts to make sense of it or to tap into its rich potentialities while avoiding its pitfalls — have become a crucial arena of contention.[3] The sense of crisis that the encounter with global capitalism, via the agency of colonial and imperial powers, first provoked during the colonial period — and now recapitulates in new forms with structural adjustment and related policies — has also produced an enormously productive reworking of the ideological and political resources afforded by the trio of forces mentioned above, whose advent coincides with the moment of capital's comprehensive encircling of the globe, for the ends of political and cultural renewal.

While the essays in this volume do not directly investigate the political-economic processes that brought about a "Third World" or the universalizing impact of capital through the production and worldwide circulation of commodities that ties different regions of the world into a single economic framework, vastly expands the range of common media of exchange, and subjects disparate labor processes to a common value framework,[4] this perspective is implicit in the historical documentation, analysis, and interpretation of the contours of modernity in South Asia, the Middle East, and Africa. After all, while modernity may be a universal and inescapable condition of the age of capital, its lineaments differ considerably according to one's location in the global division of labor and in the hierarchy of global power.

This uneven geography is crucial to understanding the sources of people's complementary-contradictory and tension-laden impulses, those incompatible interpretations of life's possibilities and limits, which they entertain even as they seek to bring order to the apparent disappearance of fixed signposts of all kinds by marking, categorizing, and demarcating new points of reference that might aid them in navigating modernity's challenges. Conceptualizing an antinomy — following Fredric Jameson — as the statement of two propositions "radically, indeed absolutely incompatible," but which in their opposition fail to recognize certain common points of departure, we suggest that the complexities of modernity are best understood by examining its antinomies, at the core of which lie a compact set of ideas about the nature of economics, cultures, nations, identity, and alterity.[5] Notions of time as that which precedes but anticipates "modernization," no less than the time of modernization itself, and space, as the physical horizon of communities and nations, frame critical facets of modernity. At the same time, this compact set of ideas has resulted in different and quite incompatible totalizing schemes — a sign, one might say, that the points of departure are themselves subject to "genesis amnesia."[6]

The attempt to construct secular histories, in which time, like value, constitutes a universal categorial referent, is arguably part and parcel of modernity. Premodern chronicles typically linked the specific group to which a particular chronicle applied to a personal deity or a savior, or told the story of secular rulers as analogues of the divine. With the advent of modernity, large horizontal linkages (*Volk*, "race," etc.) began to replace smaller vertical ones within a purely secular notion of space.[7] Simultaneously, clocked, calendrical time came to substitute cosmological notions of time.[8] History became quintessentially the discipline of this novel kind of time, with "scientific" pretensions,[9] even as science-articulated notions of race and politics began to grapple with "community" beyond the local.

Secular history, not as a mere chronicle of kings, queens, and saints, but as the "biography of a people," at least theoretically presents a more democratic or populist notion. Such a biography is traceable through a people's archive of achievements as manifested in archaeological, monumental, and documentary records, the story assuming heroic and epic proportions through sagas of migrations, wars, invasions, and conquests. Such history could also serve as a record of collective achievement, an invaluable resource for nationalist movements. The academic disciplines—philology, anthropology, and sociology in particular—that emerged in the second half of the nineteenth century out of the breakup of the "master" discipline of political economy,[10] produced "scientific" categories and significant bodies of thought that reduced apparently disparate phenomena to a few universal simples, while paradoxically aiding in the construction of locality that broke up the immanent universalism of the global capitalist system. It is the uneven geography of capitalist modernization, we argue, together with the elaboration of secular modes of thought grounded in the academic disciplines of time and space, that crystallized the dialectical tension between the universal and the particular. These developments are of great importance and form primary avenues of exploration in this volume.

In the pages that follow, we consider three critical categories—race, Orient, and nation—which, we contend, have become thoroughly imbricated with each other in the making of modernity. Both in their separate manifestations and together they have proven central to the particularization of modernity. While race mapped the coordinates of a world of visible and measurable difference, Orientalism arose as a powerful autonomous ideology positing culturally separate but mutually constituting worlds. European colonial control made for an important mediation in giving Orientalism a material manifestation via the rules of reproduction of colonial administration. Orientalism, in turn, constituted a notable component of anticolonial nationalism.[11] Orientalism's myths have become central to identity politics in the postcolonial world, while nationalism, in turn, has become the great abstraction able to subsume previously autonomous projects within its gravitational field. The concept of nation provided voice and shape to certain universalist goals, such as the emancipation from colonial shackles and limits, self-determination, and so on. It has often also served to contain explosive tensions—those of class, for example—within the institutional frameworks of newly formed states that expressed, through their particularist mythographies, notions of racial destiny and community.

"Real life" experiences of dislocation, migration, and alienation were—to no one's enduring satisfaction—smoothed away through submersion within the ontological structure of a community of fate and predestination.

All three categories operated not only to divide "us" from "them" but also, in their dialectically antithetical mode, as important avenues of solidarity. Equally, they express attempts to categorize and describe the world in an economical framework and to reduce the welter of reality to an easily transportable conceptual order. Their implicit universalism proved important to achieving this end, so that empirical complexity could often be dealt with through fairly straightforward deductive exercises. Thus universalist ambitions underlie every exercise in particularization, as they are part and parcel of global schemes of understanding the world that capitalism shapes. The universal and the particular appear not so much opposed as bound together in the unfolding of the process of which modernity itself is both a creation and an expression; the tensions implicit in this process give rise to some of the central antinomies of modernity.

Marx's vision of modernity, for example, sprang from a radical universalism that saw the meltdown of the ancien régime and the many small communities sustaining a traditional way of life as the precondition for the reconstruction of production, distribution, and indeed of human community itself. Other voices have maintained that the "breakdown of communities, the psychic isolation of the individual, mass impoverishment and class polarization, cultural creativity springing from desperate moral and spiritual anarchy" constitute a parochial Western experience at best and that areas outside the heartland of capitalism could at least hope to avoid its economic and psychic turmoil.[12] Recent experience suggests how illusory those hopes might be. But what is important is the passion invested precisely in stating and restating that alternative possibility, even when the social and human costs have, at times, proven prohibitive.

An Overview

The origins of this volume go back to that period when political events like the Iranian Revolution, the rise to power of the Hindu Right in India, the long struggle against apartheid, the comprehensive breakdown of modernization projects and the beginnings of structural adjustment policies in the "Third World" engaged many of us. These issues generated conversations with colleagues across disciplinary boundaries, while challenging us to rethink the established frames of national and regional area studies that had by and large excluded dialogue among people with shared histories of colonialism, capitalism, and modernity, the knowledge of which, it seems, had become a casualty of nationalist educational schemes remaining mostly entrapped in racialized and Orientalist frameworks.

Several of the essays in this volume were first published, in earlier versions, in *South Asia Bulletin*, a journal founded twenty years ago, and later, in 1993, expanded and renamed *Comparative Studies of South Asia, Africa, and the Middle East*. The journal itself grew out of our efforts to transcend the limited and limiting frameworks of knowledge produced within the coordinates of race, Orient, and nation and to develop a comparative and more comprehensive perspective of the forces that have shaped our contemporary realities.

Although the political events of the late 1970s and early 1980s first drew us into dialogue, the subsequent, visibly intensified reach of global capital and the transformations that occurred in its wake constitute the real genesis of this volume, providing the spur to reworking several of the essays and writing new ones. Ironically enough, much of the thinking about the modern and the postmodern since the 1980s has disengaged from closer investigations of the systemic dimensions of late capitalism.[13] The rise to prominence of models of inquiry that foregrounded the local, and led a retreat into particularism and neonationalist cultural politics, seemed to offer limited avenues for understanding the tenacity, universality, and relevance to our time of certain concepts quintessentially modern and permeating the globe like the economic system itself. This is not to suggest that global capitalism, and the transnationalization of some aspects of culture, produce a "flat, uniform cosmopolitanism."[14] This volume meets the challenge to show that people do make history — with very specific and varied outcomes at that — constrained in part by political-economic realities, but also in part by the categories they marshal in doing so.

Continuity, tradition, and antiquity provide important symbolic resources to modernizing cultural and political projects in South Asia, Africa, and the Middle East. The essays in this volume explore the ways in which romantic racialism, Orientalism, and nationalism — first articulated in their characteristic academic and political forms in Western Europe — have been indispensable to those projects in the rest of the world as well, particularly when the dominance of the West is questioned. The polemics that issue from these projects then feed into the further constructions of cultural authenticity, political autonomy, and anti-Westernism. Global categories — spanning vast secular continuities of time and space — are apparently indispensable to the outgrowth of local particularisms.

The chapters by Vasant Kaiwar, Andrew Barnes, Mohamad Tavakoli-Targhi, A.R. Venkatachalapathy, and Michael O. West show how these categories were deployed in the colonial and immediate postcolonial period. Romantic racialism and first-generation Orientalism — products of the revolutionary upheavals of the late eighteenth and early nineteenth century in Europe's disruptive encounter with modernization — were, Kaiwar maintains, as much manifestations of a crisis of confidence among sections of the European aristocracy and bourgeoisie, as a self-confident projection of European economic and epistemic power. They created the rich philological, historical, and social-scientific disciplinary resources that gave rise to unpredictable but powerful ideological currents in India, when colonial subjects appropriated the metropolitan categories and discourses to formulate arguments for parity with, or superiority to, their colonizers, and to construct hierarchies within the project of decolonization. These hierarchies — involving novel forms of resignifying socioeconomic and ascriptive differences (e.g., the racialization of caste) and spatialization (north-south, Aryan/insider-Muslim/outsider) — Kaiwar contends, have set in place powerful foundational myths of Indian nationalism and central elements of bourgeois culture in India.

Tavakoli-Targhi argues that Orientalism resulted from a dialogue and partnership between Indo-Iranian and European scholars, but that this collaboration became subject to systematic amnesia in the course of the nineteenth century, not only in Europe, where it might be understandable, but also in India and Iran, where it is harder to account for. This amnesia could take hold not simply because Europeans suppressed the knowledge of such collaboration, as Tavakoli-Targhi suggests, but also because Orientalism was, during this period, incorporated into the domain of racism and became a discourse of the inferiorization and marginalization of the "Orient." This notion, playing into the world of nationalist scholarship in Iran and India, has produced a second amnesia about a common Indo-Persian world of scholarship that lasted into the twentieth century and has also led to the rival disparagement of scholarship and aptitude, recapturing in subaltern register the racism of the colonizers.

Barnes's chapter illustrates one of the more eccentric, and seemingly preposterous, uses of the Aryan myth to work out "collaborative" relations between British colonizers and the indigenous elites of northern Nigeria. However, the categories of Aryan and Other (Semite, Dravidian, etc.) provided important discursive and political resources for colonial policy-makers in search of collaborators in a regionally specific project of indirect rule. Additionally, it resonated powerfully with metropolitan interlocutors for whom colonial projects made sense only within universalizing categories. These categories also colored the collaborators' responses, even as they tried to adapt to the racial, and racist, stereotypes being fabricated for their benefit. As Barnes illustrates, imputed racial affinity with likely collaborators did nothing to disturb, and much to sustain, a radically simplified racial grid that operated moreover as a powerful sign of the colonizers' dominance.

All three chapters develop the idea that the contours of cultural and identity politics did not simply originate in metropolitan centers to get adopted wholesale in the colonies. Colonial modernisms emerge via the active appropriation of, or resistance to, far-reaching European ideas and/or active participation in the construction of the outlines, at least, of Orientalism and racialized knowledge. Over time, these ideas become indigenized and acquire, for all practical purposes, a completely "Third Worldist" patina, giving rise to a further, more potent amnesia, whose consequences are still with us.

The mobilization of the combination of romantic racialism, Orientalism, and nationalism in the provincial theater of Tamil identity politics in southern India is the subject of Venkatachalapathy's essay. It makes clear the hegemonic position those categories had attained by the late nineteenth century, ironically to the very extent to which they predominated in counterhegemonic arguments. As Indian nationalism appropriated the Aryan myth of an unbroken linguistic/cultural antiquity to articulate a position of moral, if not material, parity with the colonial rulers, so Tamil discourse invented a Dravidian particularism (vis-à-vis Aryan universalism), whose success was preconditioned as much by the establishment of the antiquity of Tamil as by the fusion of race, territory, and language in Tamil-Dravidian discourse.

This fusion of race and territory, if not language, in counterhegemonic politics is further underlined in West's chapter on British Central Africa, via the African challenge to both white and South Asian settlers. West's consideration of the role that India and Indian settlers in British Central Africa played during the decolonization process, balanced by his consideration of the fragile position of the Indian settlers following independence as a result of their exoticization and self-exoticization, illustrates the ongoing tension between the civic-universal and the ethnic-particular in all nationalist movements. There is also a universal element in the recovery, or indeed "discovery" given the dismissive attitude of the colonizers to local history, of an indigenous antiquity to legitimize nationalist projects — witness the names (Zimbabwe, Zambia, Malawi) of the successor states of the erstwhile British Central Africa.

The next set of essays by Neville Alexander, Minoo Moallem, and Sucheta Mazumdar move into the terrain of postcolonial identity politics and nationalism. While much did change in the post-1945 period with decolonization, the establishment of new nation-states, and the ensuing new forms of identity politics, these essays underscore the necessity of interpreting local developments within the larger forces outlined above.

Alexander's chapter continues the consideration of the tension between the civic-universal and the ethnic-particular in South Africa, a country undergoing profound, certainly irreversible, change. Generally, such moments seem to provide the best opportunity to challenge ascriptive identities and boundaries, which in more "normal" times appear both natural and insuperable. Alexander calls for transformative politics as a precondition for a new core culture that would create unity while recognizing diversity, and nation building untainted by xenophobia. Yet the precise lines along which diversity will be formulated in South Africa remain problematic. Postapartheid South Africa has affirmed once again the strength of the racialist discourse that over generations tribalized the African population and exoticized the South Asians as alien to the soil of Africa, while reserving a universal position for white settlers. Indeed, the reinvigoration of South Asian identity politics, not to mention tribal identities, underlines the continuation of the politics of subalternity.

The final two essays, by Moallem and Mazumdar, confront us directly with historical continuities and disruptions in the mobilization of racism, Orientalism, and nationalism in the post–World War II period. In some senses, there is continuity with the first three chapters of the volume in the language of blood and soil, describing a world rich in racial and cultural symbolism that continues to form the bases of identity politics and nationalism. Indeed, some romantic themes survive the crucial decades of decolonization and postcolonial nation building. But, on closer examination, much has changed: the post-1945 transformations of capitalism, par-

ticularly in the sphere of communication technologies; the deepening medi-
atization of the world, which furthers the conquest of space by time; and
the more streamlined character of U.S. imperialism, replacing the multiple
ramshackle colonialisms of the pre-1945 period. They have all contributed
to the sharp juxtaposition of rich and poor countries and the commodification of everything in a vast global consumerism, which includes the transnationalization and consumption of religious and cultural symbols and the
near complete collapse of any alternative to "the blank passage of time."[15]

In this context, the Khomeini regime's attempt in Iran to construct a
social order based on the rejection of capitalism and its associated consumerism appears to have tapped important sources of mass discontent. Islamic
fundamentalism attempts a national renovation constructed around powerful elements of Islamic theology and an essentialized and reified version
of Iranian history and culture, with the segregation of gender roles based on
notions of martyrdom and veiling playing a visible public role — all components of what Moallem calls an Islamic ethnicity. On a larger view, however, the heroic fundamentalist vision of an alternative modernity has ex-
cited such considerable opposition that, coupled with its own uncertain
achievements, it raises questions of the limitations of a largely reactive and
self-exoticizing approach to dealing with the challenges posed by global
capital in our epoch.

In a similar vein, Mazumdar describes the identity crises of Hindu Indian immigrants in the United States and their attempts to come to grips
with their double alienation, physically from the country of their birth, and
culturally from their adopted country. Examining two distinct periods of
Indian immigration — the 1920s and the 1990s — Mazumdar notes that the
immigrants' specific uses of the discourses of race, Orientalism, and nationalism was, and is, designed to place them on par with "whites" while
raising them above all other "people of color." This strategy has been
further bolstered by the busy global shuttling of the "apostles of purity,"
who work to channel nostalgia into political energy and commitment — in
full concordance with the agendas of right-wing Hindu chauvinism in India
and radically at odds with the evolving cultural fusions in the United States
and with both popular anticommunalism and the secularist worldview of
significant sections of the intelligentsia in India.

The final essay, by Kaiwar and Mazumdar, explores — through the categories of race, Orient, and nation — some central aspects of modernity.
Large, unified, and mappable categories have been the means of organizing

the motley populations of the world into races, cultures, nations, and civilizations. This procedure corresponds to the ambition of the capitalist system to reduce the welter of local measures of time, distance, space, mass, and so on, to a universal standard. However, the authors maintain, the categories that have sought to group human populations have remained immensely flexible, allowing them to be appropriated, reinterpreted, and recast in local terms. This paradoxical combination of universality and particularity has endowed them with immense symbolic range, great longevity, and continued vitality. The essay iterates the importance of history, not only in being able to locate the categories themselves in their dynamic unfolding over time and space, but also in showing the various moments in which they are mobilized for large-scale political and cultural projects.

"Asia," "Africa," and the "Islamic World" may have engaged "Europe" in the processes of the construction of their modernity, even as "Europe" appropriated "Asia" for the same reason. In each case it is worth noting, however, that the Orientalist fascination with the antiquity and cultural richness of Asia and the Islamic world faded out in Europe itself in the course of the nineteenth century, leaving powerful legacies in parts of the colonies and ex-colonies, where as yet uncompleted national and regional projects freely appropriate the romantic inspiration of the "Oriental Renaissance," racialist stereotypes, and nationalist ideology for identity and cultural politics. Insofar as Orientalism survives in the West in this postmodern moment, it is as a form of racism, yoked to post–World War II modernization theories and the supposed incapacity of the ex-colonial world of South Asia, Africa, and the Middle East to respond to new political and economic challenges.[16]

As a response, many of the countries in those regions have proposed a culturalist alternative to modernization in the form of a "third way" — for example, Hindutva or Islamic fundamentalism — that would bring about a modern sense of community and representation without the meltdown of all old forms implied by capitalism in full flow. In reality, these efforts merely perpetuate in new forms the cultural and economic asymmetry that first arose with the vast differences in the respective capacities of the colonizers and the colonized to project both political and epistemic power. Many — if not all — of the radically different and irreconcilable assessments of the nature of economic development, political community, and cultural hegemony of our time continue to fall along that divide, sustained and continually renewed by the uneven geography of global capitalism.

Notes

1. For some incisive attempts to link modernity (and postmodernity) with the multiple dislocations produced by capitalism, see Perry Anderson, "Modernity and Revolution," in Cary Nelson and Lawrence Grossberg, eds., *Marxism and the Interpretation of Culture* (Urbana: University of Illinois Press, 1988), 317–33; Perry Anderson, *The Origins of Postmodernity* (London: Verso, 1998); Marshall Berman, *All That Is Solid Melts into Air: The Experience of Modernity* (New York: Simon and Schuster, 1982); Arif Dirlik, "The Postcolonial Aura: Third World Criticism in the Age of Global Capitalism," *Critical Inquiry* 20.2 (1994): 328–56; Fredric Jameson, *Postmodernism, or, The Cultural Logic of Late Capitalism* (Durham, N.C.: Duke University Press, 1991); David Harvey, *The Condition of Postmodernity: An Enquiry into the Origins of Cultural Change* (Oxford: Blackwell, 1990); Derek Sayer, *Capitalism and Modernity: An Excursus on Marx and Weber* (London: Routledge, 1991).

2. Jameson, *Postmodernism,* esp. 304–11, 366; Berman, *All That Is Solid Melts into Air,* 6–7, 15.

3. A casual search reveals well over a thousand monographs on the subject, the vast majority published within the last decade. A search of periodical literature would readily triple the figure.

4. For two very interesting expositions of the notion of value under capitalism, see Isaak Illich Rubin, *Essays on Marx's Theory of Value,* trans. Miloš Samardžija and Fredy Perlman (Montreal: Black Rose, 1973); and Moishe Postone, *Time, Labor, and Social Domination: A Reinterpretation of Marx's Critical Theory* (Cambridge: Cambridge University Press, 1993).

5. Fredric Jameson, "The Antinomies of Postmodernity," in *The Seeds of Time* (New York: Columbia University Press, 1994), 1. Jameson argues that the notion of antinomy is more suited to the postmodern moment (defined historically as the moment when modernization gradually eliminates from the socioscape all aspects of the premodern), whereas contradiction, which holds open the dialectical possibility of the reconciliation of opposing propositions, is more suited to the modern moment (2).

6. See Mohamad Tavakoli-Targhi's essay, "Orientalism's Genesis Amnesia," in this volume.

7. *Race* is placed in quotation marks because while widely used in everyday language as a descriptor of otherness, it is no longer accepted as objectively designating difference. In subsequent uses, we shall not use quotation marks with the word, though this tension between popular usage of the term and its erstwhile "scientific" uses needs to be remembered throughout.

8. Benedict Anderson, *Imagined Communities: Reflections on the Origin and Spread of Nationalism* (London: Verso, 1991), 24.

9. See, for example, Fernand Braudel, "History and the Social Sciences: The Longue Durée," in *On History,* trans. Sarah Matthews (Chicago: University of Chicago Press, 1980).

10. Eric R. Wolf, *Europe and the People without History* (Berkeley: University of California Press, 1982), 8.

11. A point well made by several authors in Carol A. Breckenridge and Peter van der Veer, eds., *Orientalism and the Postcolonial Predicament: Perspectives on South Asia* (Philadelphia: University of Pennsylvania Press, 1993). See, in particular, the essays by Arjun Appadurai, Nicholas Dirks, and David Ludden.

12. Berman, *All That Is Solid Melts into Air,* 124.

13. P. Anderson, *The Origins of Postmodernity* and Jameson, *Postmodernism,* define the postmodern as a historical stage when the capitalist system has completed the "modernization" of economy and society, and vestiges of the premodern, and nature itself, have been rendered residual in the core countries of capitalism. The global ramifications of this momentous transformation — operating via time-space compression and the uneven and combined development of economy, culture, and politics — might then produce facets of postmodernism in societies whose economies are arguably still in a modernist phase. On uneven and combined development of culture and economy, see the concluding pages of P. Anderson's *The Origins of Postmodernity.* A related concept — time-space compression — developed in Harvey, *The Condition of Postmodernity,* is important to understanding the rejection of historical perspective so common to non-/anti-Marxist writings on the subject.

14. The phrase is Otto Bauer's, quoted in Benedict Anderson, Introduction to Gopal Balakrishnan, ed., *Mapping the Nation* (London: Verso, 1996), 4.

15. P. Anderson, "Modernity and Revolution," 332.

16. Modernization theories themselves draw on earlier utilitarian notions without quite acknowledging their intellectual debt. See Michael Adas, *Machines as the Measure of Men: Science, Technology, and Ideologies of Western Dominance* (Ithaca, N.Y.: Cornell University Press, 1989), 402–18.

Vasant Kaiwar

The Aryan Model of History and the Oriental
Renaissance: The Politics of Identity in an Age of
Revolutions, Colonialism, and Nationalism

In a period before all historical knowledge, which is lost in the darkness of time, a whole race, destined by Providence to reign one day supreme over the entire earth, grew up slowly in the primitive cradle, preparing for a brilliant future. Favored above all others by nobility of blood and the gift of intelligence, in a natural setting which was beautiful but harsh and which yielded up its riches without lavishing them, this race was destined from the outset to create by its labors the basis of a lasting industrial organization, which would raise it above the elementary necessities of life. . . . This was the race of the Aryas, who were endowed from the very beginning with the very qualities that the Hebrews lacked to become the civilizers of the world.—Adolphe Pictet, *Les origines indo-européennes ou les Aryas primitifs: Essai de paléontologie linguistique* (1877)

■ This essay traces the formulation and unfolding of the Aryan model of history and the Oriental Renaissance via the mobilization of an array of newly developing sciences and disciplines in the course of the nineteenth century in Europe and India. Their initial articulation and subsequent reception in Europe had much to do with devising "scientific" and academic underpinnings for so many of the social and political agendas that grew out of the aftermath of the Industrial and French Revolutions, upholding the triumphalism and imperialism that accompanied the formation of European modernity, and — momentarily and paradoxically — sustaining the romantic rejection of the bourgeois notion of progress. Turning to India, the other "beneficiary" of the Aryan model of history and the Oriental Renaissance — where a similar imbrication of "science" and politics acted as a powerful catalytic agent in the formation of a nationalist consciousness, particularly in enabling the colonized to articulate claims for equality and parity with the colonizers — the essay concludes by exploring how this model, via the notion of an autochthonous Aryan-Hindu culture overlaid and corrupted by an invading Islam, contributed to the growth of a right-wing exclusivist Hindu nationalism to this day.

The Aryan model of history and the Oriental Renaissance illustrate some of the paradoxes and antinomies that accompany the development of modernity. Formulated in the nineteenth century, "the heyday of positivism and scientism," as Jean-Pierre Vernant puts it, they constituted arenas of research steeped in a profound knowledge of Hebrew, Sanskrit, and the European classical languages, "fortified by comparative study of linguistic data, mythology, and religion and shaped by efforts to relate linguistic structures, forms of thought, and features of civilization." As such, they gave rise, in fact, to a "tissue of scholarly myths," "fantasies of the social imagination at every level."[1] Developed in an age of profound social upheaval, flux, and change associated with revolutions, colonialism, and nationalism, they seem to have maintained their salience precisely by positing transhistorical continuities linked to the notions of race and culture, the latter interpreted in this model as the unique traces of a particular race or people endowed with faculties other races or peoples lacked.

Critical to the paradoxical association between secular discontinuities in the realms of politics and economy on the one hand, and the supposed continuities in the realm of culture around which the Aryan model of history and the Oriental Renaissance are built, is the notion of history as the "biography of a people" and of a relatively unchanging essence underlying historical processes.[2] As such, both crucially mediated the incorporation of racial doctrine and Orientalist ideas into the writing of world history. Their contemporary survival, postdating the demise of romanticism and even the heyday of Orientalism and racism, is explainable sometimes by their fit with new political agendas, as in India, and sometimes by the inertial weight of the bodies of knowledge developed in the nineteenth and early twentieth centuries.[3]

The sheer modernity of the Aryan model and the Oriental Renaissance is signaled by their fundamental secularization and globalization of space and time and from their profound debt to the sciences and disciplines of anthropology, archaeology, biology, philology, and linguistics. Physical and linguistic similarities and differences — established not by impressionistic accounts, but by the scientific study of skulls and facial angles, not to mention the structural properties of languages — became ways to track global migrations and diaspora and to establish connections across vast expanses of time and space. The study of Indo-European languages across the whole space of Europe and southwest and south Asia established the idea of the diffusion of the master culture and civilization of the Aryans from a central homeland.[4] In this model, Greece and India served as the opposing poles of the dialectic of world history. Both were neatly detached from their local contexts and attached to a central diasporic model, with classical Greece anchoring a triumphalist account of European history, and India — after a brief romantic flirtation with the notion of an Oriental Renaissance — illustrating a story of decline and degeneration, except in India itself, where the Aryan model and the ideas generated by the Oriental Renaissance could be mobilized behind conservative agendas of a national renaissance. The imbrication of Greece and India in the local geographies of the Mediterranean and maritime South Asia became subjects of profound amnesia, eclipsed by their exemplary status in a triumphalist world historiography.

Greece and the Aryan Model of History

All the peoples of Europe and, to begin with, those which were originally related and which gained supremacy at the cost of many wanderings and dangers, emigrated from Asia in the remote past. They were propelled from East to West by an irresistible instinct, the real cause of which is unknown to us. . . . The vocation and courage of those peoples, which were originally related and destined to rise to such heights, is shown by the fact that European history was almost entirely made by them.—Jakob Grimm, *Geschichte der deutschen Sprache* (1868)

It may seem odd that such metaphysical notions should ever have gained currency, but race, for all its supposed scientific rootedness in physical anthropology, easily shaded into vast romantic dreams of an Asian *Urheimat* (original homeland) for modern Europeans. Barthold Niebuhr (1776–1831), the "founder of critical-genetic historiography," stated the racist manifesto of history in the early nineteenth century: "Race is one of the most important elements of history still remaining to be examined — that which is, in truth, the very first basis upon which all history is reared and the first principle upon which it must proceed."[5] When, from about the late eighteenth century onward, this notion combined with populist romanticism, in which the *Volk* (people) or the *Gemeinschaft* (community) are seen as the sources of cultural vitality, distinctiveness, and historical continuity,[6] the foundations of a romantic-racialist view of history — in which categorically different peoples each develop their own history, not according to material circumstances and interactions between social classes and empires or nations, but according to some genetic or cultural potential laid down at the outset — were in place.

History could no longer be mainly or exclusively a chronicle of wars and the achievements of monarchs and dynasties, but emerged, as noted, as the biography of a people. This is an interesting concept because it personifies a civilization, or a nation, and makes it legitimate to look for its beginnings. Taking into account the exalted view Europeans began to develop of their own civilization, it translated into nothing less than a search for the origins of the vigorous European genius. A number of epics, real and fabricated, not to mention volumes of folktales of medieval Scotland and Germany, were published, but apparently this did not prove sufficiently heroic. The search for the first expression of the German — and European — genius would lead via Homer and the classical Greeks to the discovery of modern Europe's origin in ancient Greece, although it would not end there, as we shall see. This idea would come into its own in the 1820s during the Greek war of independence against the Ottoman Empire. In this context the poet Shelley declared: "We are all Greeks. . . . Our laws, our literature, our religion, our arts all have their roots in Greece."[7] Throughout Western Europe, the Greek war of independence was viewed as a struggle between European youthful vigor and Asiatic and African decadence, corruption, and cruelty. Turkish rule over European populations was seen as unnatural, a reversal of the natural order in which an inferior race ruled over a superior one.[8]

In fact, most northern Europeans, like Joseph Arthur de Gobineau (1816–82), viewed the Greeks of their day as no more than degenerate brigands. He attributed the decline of Greek civilization from the heights it had reached in antiquity to racial admixtures: "Hellenes — Aryans modified by yellow elements but with a great preponderance of the white essence and some Semitic affinities; Aborigines — Slavo-Celtic peoples saturated with yellow elements; Thracians — Aryans mixed with Celts and Slavs; Phoenicians — Black Hamites; Arabs and Hebrews — very mixed Semites; Philistines — Semites perhaps of purer stock; Libyans — almost black Hamites; Cretans and other islanders — Semites more or less resembling the Philistines."[9] It was the Greeks of classical antiquity that nineteenth-century Europeans wanted to appropriate as their ancestors. Accordingly, a certain critical "requirement" was placed on the Greeks. They had to be northern people with a capacity for civilization and conquest, and they needed to be "wholly independent" of their Semitic and African Mediterranean contemporaries.[10] As Wilhelm von Humboldt (1767–1835) put it: "We fail entirely to recognize our relationship to them [the Greeks] if we dare to apply the standards to them that we apply to the rest of world history . . . in the Greeks alone we find the ideal of that which we would like to be and produce . . . from the Greeks we take something more than earthly — almost Godlike."[11]

An organic northern image of the Greeks formed the core of the new science of antiquity (*Altertumswissenschaft*). The northern picture of the Greeks that emerged proved integral to the Aryan model, and its elements were assembled from the 1820s by, among others, Karl Otfried Müller at the University of Göttingen.[12] Müller developed his model according to certain a priori criteria: if cults, myths, or names were found in Greece and the Near East, they must be Greek; if similar features were found in the north and south of the country, then they must come from the north; and if cults were found in Greece and the Aegean, then they must be local and not of foreign origin. The north to south transmission of culture was paradigmatic requiring no evidence, but Müller insisted that any argument for transplantation of Egyptian myths, for example, had to meet strict criteria of "proof."[13]

Two developments in the course of the nineteenth century enabled the transition from the inchoate romantic racialism of the late eighteenth and early nineteenth century to a more "scientific," if dogmatic, model of racial diaspora and diffusionism central to the Aryan model of history: the development of the notion of the Indo-European language family and that of the notion of the Aryan race. The fact that Greek was undoubtedly an Indo-European language — and the conflation of language and race, quite common among proponents of Aryanist theories — made a plausible case for attaching the Greeks to the Aryan race. The supposed early attestation of a northern "invasion" into India, which became all the rage among the Aryanists for a while,[14] could be quietly transplanted to Greece to provide an overall model whereby a northern (presumably Nordiclike) race moved south to plant the seeds of its civilization among the barbarous people living in southern climes. The absence of any sort of attestation of such a conquest in the Greek case did not apparently bother either Müller or his successors. Once they had linked a north-south transmission of civilization to racial essences, given the general environment, the elaboration of a racialist historiography was simply a matter of time and detail.

The Curtius brothers, Ernst (1814–96) and Georg (1820–85), took on this task. Georg Curtius elaborated via comparative etymology an understanding of the development of Indo-Germanic languages from an ancestral tongue now lost. As he put it in his *Principles of Comparative Etymology*: "The several languages of the Indo-Germanic stock may to a certain extent be compared to so many copies of the lost original MS. Not one presents us with a faithful copy of the original text. . . . Each copy has its peculiar, regularly recurring blunders, but the copies mutually correct each other."[15] Armed with this idea, he systematically applied Indo-European linguistics to Greek, setting out the "regular and elegant sound shifts according to which much of Greek can be derived from a hypothetical proto-Indo-European."[16] Ernst Curtius developed the historical side of the Aryan model, describing two migrations, the crucial one, for our purposes, being to the north of Greece, where the pure Greek language developed in mountainous terrain and without contact or mixing with the indigenous population. These resolute migrants were the Dorians, the ancestors of the Spartans, the preferred Greeks. According to Friedrich Schlegel (1772–1829), the Dorians were the older, purer, more truly Hellenic people responsible for the Greek spirit, music, and gymnastics. They originated in the north, possibly in Germany![17] The second migration came via Anatolia (in modern Turkey) to Ionia, whence came the Ionian Athenians, more easily orientalized. Ernst Curtius was ecstatic about the Greek language:

> The people which knew in so peculiar a manner how to develop the common treasure of the Indo-Germanic language was . . . the Hellenes. Their first historic deed is the development of this language, and this deed is an artistic one. For above all its sister-tongues the Greek must be regarded as a work of art. . . . If the grammar of their language were the only thing remaining to us of the Hellenes, it would serve as a full and valid testimony to the extraordinary natural gifts of this people. . . . The whole language resembles the body of a trained athlete, in which every muscle, every sinew is developed into full play, where there is no trace of tumidity or of inert material, and all is power and life.[18]

This "pure" language, of course, had to develop fully in the mountains before descending to the plains, because as Curtius explained, "One class of sounds is wont to predominate on the hills, another in the valley, and again another in the plains."[19] The Greek language on which so much of the new historiography rested could not, almost by definition, be a maritime, Mediterranean language.

Distancing Greece from the Other Mediterranean World

The Aryan model was also concerned, up to the 1860s, with removing traces of "Egyptomania" from Greek history. From the 1860s onward, a more extreme version developed with the intent of removing as well the Phoenician influence on Greece.[20] As the Greeks were raised to the level of divinity, their Mediterranean neighbors had to be lowered, not very gently, into subhuman depths. As early as 1730, Bishop William Warburton argued in his book *The Divine Legation of Moses* that though Pythagoras studied in Egypt for twenty-one years, he set out his theorems only on returning to Greece. He inferred from this the Egyptians' inability to hypothesize, a canon that apparently survives to this day.[21] Two centuries later, J.-P. Lauer maintained that Egyptian priests had built up a store of practical and technical knowledge by postfact discoveries of "chance qualities that had remained totally unsuspected by their creators."[22] He held that the historic role of the Egyptians through the 3,000 years of their history was to pave the way for Greek scholars like Thales, Pythagoras, and Plato, who came to study at the school in Alexandria armed with the Greek philosophic spirit and thus able to transform the technical positivism of the Egyptians into genuine science.[23]

Egyptian religion was seen as no more than zoolatry (worship of animals). The French Egyptologist Maspero argued that Egypt held most of its myths in common with the "most savage tribes of the Old and New World."[24] The English Egyptologist Wallis Budge maintained that the Egyptian language did not have the vocabulary to express subtle metaphysical, much less philosophical, speculations: "Even an Egyptian priest of the highest intellectual attainments would have been unable to render a treatise of Aristotle into language which his brother priests, without teaching, could understand. The mere construction of the language would make such a thing impossible, to say nothing of the ideas of the great Greek philosopher, which belong to a domain of thought and culture wholly foreign to the Egyptian."[25]

Those who saw Egypt as having produced an adequate, if not great, civilization, tended to think of Egypt as in some way "oriental."[26] Others, particularly sensitive to the ancient argument that Egypt had civilized "sacred Hellas," damned Egypt by showing how utterly barren its culture was, and made doubly sure that the charge stuck by linking the Egyptians with central Africa, as Maspero did:

> Time, which has done so much harm to other nations, has shown itself most favorable to the Egyptians. It has spared their tombs, their temples, their statues and . . . it has led us in such a way that we judge them by the most beautiful and the prettiest of the things which they made, and has at length caused us to place their civilization on the same footing as that of the Romans and the Greeks. But if it be looked at more nearly, the point of view changes . . . Thothmes III and Rameses II resemble Mtesa of Central Africa more than they do Alexander or Caesar.[27]

The acceptance of Phoenician influence on Greece lasted a little longer. Ernest Renan (1823–92), the founder of Phoenician studies, felt that Semites had good qualities, some of which they shared with the English (!), such as "a great uprightness of mind and an enviable simplicity of heart, an exquisite sentiment of morality."[28] The downfall of the Phoenicians coincided with the rise of racial anti-Semitism in Western Europe.[29] The first wave of racial anti-Semitism coincided with the late nineteenth-century mass migration of Jews from Eastern Europe to the West, and it crystallized around the notorious Dreyfus Affair in France. As is well known, Jews were used as scapegoats for the sufferings of the working class and the peasantry, and in building xenophobic cross-class alliances.[30] The second wave of racial anti-Semitism in the 1920s and 1930s started with the supposed role of Jews in the Bolshevik Revolution and international communism.[31] Emile Burnouf used the craniological argument to establish Jewish inferiority: "He [the Jew] belongs to the occipetal races . . . those whose hinder parts of the head are more developed than the front. . . . At [fifteen or sixteen] the divisions of the skull which contain the organs of intelligence are already joined, and in some cases welded together. From that period the growth of the brain is arrested."[32]

S. A. Cook's chapter on the Semites in the 1924 edition of *The Cambridge Ancient History* referred to their extremes of optimism and pessimism, asceticism and sensuality, and absence of civic or national loyalty or concern for the ethical value of actions. Personal feeling, rather than common sense, plan, or morality served as their source of action.[33] Gobineau had earlier referred to the "hideous religious rites" of the Phoenicians, including prostitution and child sacrifice, which the "white race has never practised."[34] Flaubert's *Salammbô* turned this theme into a novel of the horrors of racial mixing, vice, and cruelty. Bernal sums up the reasons for *Salammbô*'s success:

> When Flaubert had tried to portray French bourgeois life realistically in *Madame Bovary,* his book had been mutilated by the publisher and he was put on trial for "outraging public morals." *Salammbô* was far more scabrous in every respect, but this time it made Flaubert the lion of Parisian high society. . . . Flaubert had hit a literary jackpot; his "realism" applied to the "Orient" allowed readers to get their sexual and sadistic thrills, while maintaining their sense of innate and categoric superiority as white Christians. It also increased the urgency of France's *mission civilisatrice* to save the peoples of other continents from their own cruelty and wickedness.[35]

Historians were no longer prepared to admit any deep Phoenician presence or influence in ancient Europe, particularly in divine Hellas. Adolf Holm in the 1880s referred to the "existence of mere settlements of Phoenicians in Greece" and added that "their influence was inconsiderable."[36] J. B. Bury in his *History of Greece* (1900) amplified this suggestion with the benefit of blood and soil imagery: "The Phoenicians doubtless had marts here and there on coast and island, but there is no reason to think that Canaanites ever made homes for themselves on Greek *soil* or introduced Semitic *blood* into the population of Greece."[37]

With their racial nature and character established, Phoenicians and Jews could be subject to utter humiliation. Robert Knox, the anatomist, writing in the 1860s described "the Jew" as a "sterile hybrid," with "no ear for music, no love for science or literature."[38] Two decades later, a writer in the *American Journal of Archaeology* evaluated Phoenician cultural achievements in equally unflattering terms: "The Phoenicians, so far as we know, did not bring a single fructifying idea into the world. . . . Their archaeology, sculpture, painting were of the most unimaginative sort. Their religion, so far as we know it, was entirely an appeal to the senses."[39]

Renan, who we have seen expressing the odd sympathetic view of Semites above, nonetheless thought the Semitic languages, no less than Egyptian, unsuitable to "all philosophical and all purely intellectual speculation.

... Almost denuded of syntax, lacking any varieties of construction, without the conjunctions which establish such delicate relations between the elements of thought," Semitic languages were suitable for the "eloquent inspirations of seers," but not for philosophy. Naturally, the Semites had "no mythology, no epic, no science, no philosophy, no fiction, no plastic arts, no civil life."[40] The Semitic language reached its heights in expressing the immutable. This was regarded as an objective linguistic fact, matching the image of the Hebrew people as unchangeable and "impervious to history," in contrast, of course, to the Aryans. As with the structure of the Indo-European languages, especially Greek, which expressed so sensitively the northern spirit of the people who developed it, so the Semitic languages functioned as a perfect mirror of the soul of a people dominated by desert landscapes.[41] Gordon Childe, writing in the 1920s, echoed some of these sentiments. The Indo-European languages, and their parent speech, were "exceptionally delicate and flexible instruments of thought." It followed therefore that "Aryans must have been gifted with exceptional mental endowments." Childe invites us to examine the "dignified narrative carved by [the Aryan] Darius on a rock at Behistun," contrasted with the "bombastic and blatant self-glorification of the inscriptions of Ashurbanipal or Nebuchednazzar."[42] The "science" of comparative philology appears firmly rooted in racist triumphalism.

Christianity, too, had to be rescued from its Semitic roots. Thus, Renan stated, there was nothing "Jewish about Jesus." Christianity was less purely Semitic than Judaism or Islam; it became the least monotheistic of the three revealed religions that originated in the eastern Mediterranean. If Christianity thus transcended the limits of the Semitic spirit, it did so because it adopted the spirit of the people it converted—namely the Aryans. In his inaugural lecture at the Collège de France, Renan clarified his position: "The victory of Christianity was not secure until it completely broke out of its Jewish shell and again became what it had been in the exalted consciousness of its founder, a creation *free from the narrow bonds of the Semitic spirit*."[43] "Originally Jewish to the core," Christianity over time "rid itself of nearly everything it took from the race, so that those who consider *Christianity to be the Aryan religion par excellence* are in many respects correct."[44] In this sense, for Renan, the continuation of Judaism was, portentously enough, Islam, not Christianity. His view of Christianity was widely echoed in the Europe of the latter half of the nineteenth and early twentieth century.

The twentieth-century Belgian scholar Guy Bunnens spells out the political motivation underpinning much comparative philology and the historiography it supported:

> In reading their work, one cannot help thinking that these authors were not always motivated by scientific objectivity alone. [They] insisted on reserving a place in the most distant past for the peoples who dominated world politics in their own period: that is to say, for the Europeans. They maintained that it was unbelievable that nations so important today should have played no role in the past. It was necessary therefore to "assert the rights of Europe over Asia." The historical background at the end of the nineteenth and beginning of the twentieth centuries explains these new theories. For this was an epoch when the colonialism of the Europeans was triumphant. . . . The end of the nineteenth century [also] saw a great current of anti-Semitism in Europe, particularly in Germany and France.[45]

It should be clear that, from the outset, the Aryan model of classical antiquity, and the simultaneous recasting of Africa and Asia as Europe's categorical inferior, wore the stigmata of racism.[46] As Eric Hobsbawm observes: "Racism pervades the thought of our period to an extent hard to appreciate today, and not always easy to understand."[47] However, it is important to emphasize, in keeping with the preoccupations of many of the influential founders of comparative philology, that the meaning of the term *race* itself changed in the course of the nineteenth century, becoming "a matter of language, religion, laws, and customs, more than blood."[48]

India and the Oriental Renaissance

At its starting point in India, the birthplace of races and of religions, the womb of the world.—Jules Michelet, *Sélections* (1946)

When among the ruins of the ancien régime, Adam died as a universal ancestor, first scientists and then philosophers affiliated Christian peoples to other patriarchs, and these were no longer Biblical but Indian.—Léon Poliakov, *The Aryan Myth: A History of Racist and Nationalist Ideas in Europe* (1974)

The Aryan model of history in the nineteenth century had two main pillars, one Greek, one Indian. Ancient north India, the Aryavarta of the romantic imagination, had to be categorically separated from south India and its involvement in the maritime world of the Indian Ocean with its mélange of "inferior" cultures and races, just as classical Greece had to be insulated from the Mediterranean world of Semites and North Africans. The Aryan model of Indian history served to establish the ancient origin of the Aryan peoples (or race) in central Asia, their migrations first into Iran and India and subsequently into Europe. Raymond Schwab notes in his *Oriental Renaissance* that the effect of the Oriental Renaissance — that is, the "discovery" of the ancient texts of India and other "Oriental" cultures and their anticipated contribution to a new post–French Revolution revival of European civilization — was to undermine the barriers raised between the "West" and the "East."[49] However, he remarks, the partition was dismantled in accordance with "special interests and controversies, intellectual, spiritual or political in the West itself." The "Orient" was drawn into polemics, "pushed towards the right or the left, the top or the bottom of the map, depending on the . . . disposition of those who invoked it." While nineteenth-century romantics saw India as the "schoolmistress of the human race," others had a less flattering opinion of its civilization.[50] Whatever the longer-term outcomes of this fascination with India, there is no question that the ancient writings translated into European languages by the Orientalists (pioneered by the arrival in India of Anquetil-Duperron in 1754 and William Jones in 1783) played a major, indeed seminal, role in unlocking the linguistic and historic information hitherto inaccessible, or not fully accessible, to European scholars.[51] Schwab proclaims rather extravagantly that the pioneering linguistic work of the British Orientalists and their German romantic counterparts made the world, for the first time in human history, "a whole." Suddenly the "partial humanism" of the classics — confined to the Greek and Latin spheres — grew into the "integral humanism" that "today seems natural to us."[52]

British Orientalists and German romantics mainly, but with contributions from their French counterparts and native informants and collaborators, played a major role in constructing the Aryan model of Indian history as a narrative of heroic invasions, migrations, and settlements of an Aryan stock (or race) that not only founded kingdoms and empires but also developed a great philosophy and literature which, translated into modern European languages and made suitable for modern sensibilities, were expected to contribute to the revitalization of the West. Schwab divides the most creative period of European Orientalism from the 1780s to the 1890s into three periods:

1. 1785–1825: A period shortly after the founding of the Asiatic Society of Calcutta, a period of "philological and literary romanticism," associated with the names of William Jones and Friedrich Schlegel; an era of "approximations; the data retain[ing] an arbitrary quality." "Primitive" poetry continued to be discussed on the basis of the very partial glimpses of the Vedas and the epics, while the idea of a "mother language" continued to be based "on the mysticism of the linguists."[53] Misleading as were, for example, some of Schlegel's generalizations, this was also an exciting and heady period when European scholars of the "Orient" felt that they were on the verge of discoveries that would transform not only history but the direction of world civilization.

2. 1830s–1850s: A period of more rigorous linguistic research involving the study of linguistic structure and grammar by, among others, Franz Bopp and Eugène Burnouf.[54] It established the notion of an Indo-European language family as part of linguistic science, rather than as a vague longing for an extra-European Urheimat. Schwab records that during this period the British primacy in the field faded to be replaced by the German. The frameworks and processes "became those of a science."[55]

3. 1855–1890s: Sanskrit came to be taught at the Ecole des Hautes Etudes and at the University of Oxford, even as the British shed their utilitarian visions of transforming India and settled into the mature phase of colonial rule. Abel Bergaigne completed the break with the "fetishism" that regarded the Vedas as the Bible of the Aryan peoples. Auguste Barth replaced the notion of the Vedas as primitive collective poetry with the idea that it constituted the ritual poetry of an elite priestly circle.[56] Orientalism settled into a more institutionalized phase. Sanskrit became a rather limited specialization: it was taught only to those who wished to teach it. The specialty "became cloistered."[57] The Brahmans of India apparently had their secular counterparts in Europe. After 1875, Schwab feels there were no more fundamental breakthroughs, at least within the Orientalist framework. Orientalism entered a phase when specializations developed, and scholars of India, mainly philologists, philosophers, and historians, began to "analyze their acquisitions more thoroughly."[58] By the closing decades of the nineteenth century, a great revival of interest in Europe's classical antiquity had more or less completely eclipsed India in the popular, if not scholarly, educational curriculum.

Although the pioneering linguistic efforts came from the English Oriental-ists—among them William Jones, William Colebrooke, and Horace Hy-man Wilson—the philosophical, indeed metaphysical, elements of the Ori-ental Renaissance were developed among the German romantics. Friedrich Schlegel, whom Léon Poliakov calls "the real founder of the Aryan myth," perhaps articulated its idealistic side.[59] In 1800, even before learning San-skrit, he announced: "We must seek the supreme romanticism in the Ori-ent."[60] In 1808, having learned the ancient language, he made explicit the program of the Oriental Renaissance in his *Über die Sprache und die Weis-heit der Indier: Ein Beitrag zur Begründung der Altertumskunde* [On the speech and wisdom of the Indians] (1808):

> May Indic Studies find as many disciples and protectors as Germany and Italy saw spring up in such great numbers for Greek studies in the fif-teenth and sixteenth centuries.... The Renaissance of antiquity promptly transformed and rejuvenated all the sciences; we might add that it rejuve-nated and transformed the world. We could even say that the effect of Indic studies, if these enterprises were taken up and introduced into learned circles with the same energy today, would be no less far-reach-ing.[61]

Schopenhauer echoed that sentiment: "Sanskrit literature will be no less influential for our time than Greek literature was in the fifteenth century for the Renaissance."[62] German romantics hoped that a renaissance in philoso-phy, poetry, and art would accompany the European "discovery" of San-skrit, one no less significant than the earlier Renaissance ushered in by the "discovery" of Greek philosophy and sciences. It is in this sense that the term *Oriental Renaissance* is appropriate. Notably absent in Schlegel's nar-rative is the Enlightenment, doubly damned for being both French and revolutionary.

This romantic credo produced the most extravagant claims. Johann Gottfried Herder (1744–1803) could claim India as the fatherland of the human race in its infancy. Wilhelm von Humboldt thanked God for having allowed him to live long enough to read Georg Forster's translation of *Sakontala* [Shakuntala] (1791),[63] and Goethe, who would later turn against these Indic extravagances, rhapsodized in 1791: "When I mention *Sakon-tala*, everything is said."[64] In this view, it not only became possible to discover a single mythology shared by the entire Aryan world, with its roots in the deep antiquity of the Indo-Iranian Orient, but monotheistic religion itself had its pre-Christian roots in the ancient past of India: "The single truth, now clear to the Christians, had been known and preserved even among remote and unbelieving peoples by the sacerdotal families who allowed this truth to be perceived by the masses only through the veil of legends."[65] Karl Hillebrand attempted to fuse all the legends of India, Greece, Scandinavia, and Persia into a universal religion that would "regenerate a world distracted by rationalism."[66] These notions were romantic in another sense: for India was not just the past (the greatness revealed in the infancy of the human race) but also the future (a source of enrichment to the human race led by Germany in a determinedly anti-Enlightenment direction). For Baron Ferdinand von Eckstein, India could be claimed along with Persia and Greece as the precursors of the German gothic, that is, the Germanic Middle Ages: "Homer was the base, India and Persia the two lateral sides of the pyramid whose peak was the German Middle Ages." Elsewhere he wrote: "All Europe, which was formerly Latin, is now Germanic, for the peoples of the North established all the southern empires."[67]

The antinomies of German romanticism are revealed precisely here: one stream of German romantics undertook the study of all human matters with "the illusion, the purpose, of placing all in one" — "in the convenient vocabulary of short German particles it would seem that 'Ur' was the key to 'sym,' which intruded itself everywhere"; the other found a way to "insert their ethnic interests into the very concept of the Renaissance."[68] German nationalism and Aryan mythography had converged to produce not only the putative outlines of a master race but one which rejected the French Enlightenment for the "mist-enveloped" regions of universal religion and primitive poetry. As Edmond Vermeil wrote, "Romanticism had declared war on those fraternal enemies, Roman Catholicism and the Enlightenment."[69]

Elsewhere, Adolphe Pictet (1799–1875), who combined an eminently modern interest in mathematics and ballistics with a mystical interest in the far reaches of mythological time in search of primitive Aryans, embarked on a journey of "linguistic paleontology" with a view to reviving Indo-European memories in a Christian Europe looking for an even brighter future.[70] Many of his contemporaries launched similar projects, hoping to bring to life an Indian temporality that would tell of the origins of a long-forgotten Aryan territory, the primitive homeland of "Western man in search of legitimation."[71] One of the many functions of Indo-European research was, as Olender suggests, to provide answers to questions that became urgent in the nineteenth century, questions pertaining to "the origins and vocation of a Western world in search of a national, political, and religious identity."[72] As Houston Stewart Chamberlain (1855–1927), the celebrated Anglo-German race theorist, was to put it so clearly: "Indology must help us fix our sights more clearly on the goals of our culture. A great humanistic task has fallen to our lot to accomplish; and thereto is Aryan India summoned."[73] In the age of revolutions, counterrevolutions, and competitive nation building, India, it seems, had come to serve quintessentially European purposes.

Even if the original point of the Oriental Renaissance had been the "absolute equality of all races and ages," it did not, as we have seen, long remain in that mode of generous thought. Very soon, it became embroiled in the racialism (with racist historiography as a leading element) of the time. The primitive, once regarded as "ancestral in time" could easily be switched to meaning "lower in scale."[74] The unholy trinity of biology, philology, and history worked against the German romantic exaltation of India. Felicité Robert de Lammenais and Gobineau elaborated the implications of this triad of forces. Lammenais, while celebrating India in the most unrealistic terms ("It is particularly from the Orient, the cradle of religion, the arts and the sciences, that this primitive tradition that we insist upon must be drawn. It is from here that it has passed to all peoples"), could nonetheless also state: "With the Indians, as with all other peoples on earth, one can recognize, underneath the most bizarre fiction and fable, *a cult that was originally pure* and that became corrupted only through the course of time."[75] Gobineau removed even this concession — "as with all peoples on earth" — interpolating "the arsenal of ethnic propaganda" into Oriental studies and openly paving the way for the "partisan exploitation of historical philosophy."[76] To put it bluntly, continental Orientalism had now openly acknowledged its allegiance to racialist thought (and organization of knowledge), a potentiality inherent in it from the outset. In his *Les religions et les philosophies dans l'Asie centrale* (1865), Gobineau spelt out his theory of racial degeneration: "The languages of the white race are no more Hindu than Celtic. . . . Long before they arrived in India, the Aryans ceased to have anything in common with the nations that were to become European."[77] In the final book of *Essai sur l'inégalité des races humaines,* entitled "The Capacity of the Native German Races," Gobineau concluded that the Germanic Aryans were sacred, the race of the lords of the earth. He consigned their Indian counterparts, with whom Schlegel and others had sought to align themselves in an antiquity long predating the classical antiquity of Mediterranean Europe, to a lower rank. Schwab concludes, "Now, against the Declaration of the Equality of the rights of all people [the doctrine of the French Revolution], which had stirred nations everywhere . . . they [Gobineau, Schopenhauer, Wagner, and Nietzsche] could oppose, and soon substitute, something that had *philosophy and science on its side* . . . the Declaration of Inequality. . . . It was enough to make the Oriental Renaissance stand for the opposite of its content and justification."[78] Max Müller might well note in his Oxford *Lectures on the Science of Language* (1861) that "confusing the history of languages with the history of races falsified everything," but powerful forces opposed him. The tidal wave of ethnicity and racialism was to sweep aside such distinctions.

With the adherents of Greece ranged against the adherents of Vedic India, it became a simple matter to reverse the exalted fictions of an earlier generation. Even in the 1830s the partisans of Greece, Niebuhr and Karl Otfried Müller, objected to the tyranny of Orientalist theories that claimed to have traced the origin of Greek thought to India.[79] By the 1850s, Ernest Renan had discredited the cliché that the Vedas were the "Aryan Bible." While he considered the poetry of the Vedas "admirable," he noted that it could never replace the biblical psalms.[80] And by 1884, in the preface to *Shakuntala*, Bergaigne was to be even more forthright: "In general the initial enthusiasm that greeted the discovery of Sanskrit has now been abandoned. . . . The literature presently attracts, almost exclusively, scholars, philologists, archaeologists and religious historians."[81] Schlegel's call, made in the heyday of romanticism, to introduce Sanskrit into the German educational curriculum did not happen. Arguably, the Oriental Renaissance had been a manifestation — if a transient one — of a crisis in European modernity.

The postrevolutionary bourgeoisie of Europe preferred to fortify itself behind Greek (and Latin) ramparts. When the crisis provoked by the French Revolution and its aftershocks passed, and a newly self-confident bourgeoisie began its own process of global expansion under the aegis of science and technology, the enthusiasms of an earlier generation seemed quaint. The German *Bildung* that Bernal discusses in *Black Athena* was not about religious discovery but about more secular ends. For Indians, on the other hand, the legacies of Orientalism have had an enduring significance. As British colonial rule fastened itself ever more firmly on the Indian subcontinent, a new class of English-educated Indian literati began to comb European literature for models of self-development. Their educational curriculum and identity politics internalized the philosophical speculations of German romantics as religion and dogma, and the Aryan historiography as a sign of past and future greatness. In the latter enterprise, ironically, British historians helped them. Self-Orientalization completed the colonized's entrapment.

British Orientalism and Indian History

The orientation and tasks of British Orientalism differed rather markedly from those of German romanticism. German Orientalist scholarship was influenced both by its lack of direct involvement in India and by the hostility of German romanticism to French rationalism and English empiricism, leading, in fact, to a kind of anti-Westernism. The British Orientalists, on the other hand, were often empire builders. Warren Hastings and William Jones may serve as but two well-known examples. Early colonial administrators appointed "fact-finding" teams to amass a wealth of local knowledge for the purposes of discovering authentic local customs, practices, legal norms, and so on. Mastery of language would hold the key to dominion, at least initially.

Hastings summoned Brahmans versed in the Shastras from all parts of India to supply the East India Company with the most authentic texts of the Hindu laws. Translated from Sanskrit into Persian and later into English by Nathaniel Brassey Halhed,[82] these regulations became the basis of the Company's law courts, and they passed into the legal framework even after the dissolution of the East India Company. The task of the British administrators at this time was to disentangle "Indic thought from its Islamic overlay," that is, to fashion a Hindu code of laws. The Brahmans who answered Hastings's call may have hoped for a partnership in empire, if not true universality of culture, but most British civil servants went to India not "to gain knowledge of a new world or its mode of existence but to maintain British prestige or complete a useful phase in their careers."[83] Even as a fashion for Orientalism overtook Continental salons and intellectual journals, British civil servants were painting a rather different, and unflattering, portrait of their Indian subjects, a tendency that became all the more pronounced as the nineteenth century wore on.

Ironically, too, it was precisely British writers who carried over the myth of the all-conquering Aryan peoples — or Aryan race, once racialist thought had established itself — from the realms of philosophy and religious studies into those of history and anthropology. While German scholars may have believed that the Aryans migrated in waves from India, the ancient Urheimat of the master race, British historians developed the notion of an extra-Indian homeland from which the race spread into Western Europe as well as into Persia and India. But, as we shall see, regardless of whether the Aryans emerged as autochthonous or foreign, the Aryan model of history has assumed something of a paradigmatic status in Indian historiography.[84]

Vincent Smith's *Oxford History of India,* first published in 1919 and a standard textbook in the curriculum for Indian civil servants and in Indian higher education, states the Aryan model of history in clear, unambiguous terms.[85] He takes as his point of departure the undisputed dominance of the Aryan north over the rest of India, implying clearly the superiority of the Aryan invaders of the second millennium B.C. over the dark-skinned "aborigines." In Smith's words:

> From the Vedic hymns it has been possible to piece together a reasonably coherent picture of the Aryan invaders on their first impact with the black, noseless (flat-nosed) *dasyus* who comprised their native opponents and subjects. The archetype of the invaders was their war god, Indra; like him, the Aryan hero was strong, bearded, of mighty appetite, and a great drinker of the divine liquid, soma, a drink of unknown composition but *equivalent to the nectar of the Greek world.*[86]

In light of the geographic range of validity the Aryan model posited, the comparison with the Greeks is significant. Smith continues: "The picture [is] of an essentially mobile society of a kind typical of the heroic age in other lands — in Homeric Greece, for example, and in the Celtic West. It is that of a warrior aristocracy, interested in feeding and fighting but little concerned with its humbler foot-slogging peasantry." Naturally, the Aryans would come to dominate the political landscape: "Usually the northern plains, the Aryavarta of the Hindu period, and the Hindustan of more recent times, have been the seat of the principal empires and the scene of the events most interesting to the outer world. . . . The open nature of the country, easily accessible to *martial invaders from the north-west,* has given frequent occasion for the formation of powerful kingdoms ruled by vigorous foreigners."[87]

On the other hand, "the peninsular, tropical section of India, isolated from the rest of the world by its position and in contact with other countries only by sea-borne commerce, has pursued its own course, little noticed by and caring little for foreigners." The contradiction in the above statement, the isolation of the south in "contact with other countries *only* by sea-borne commerce," could have been sustained only in the context of a powerful model valorizing the martial races who lived on the land and loved it, as opposed to the effete seafaring peoples crisscrossing the oceans but unable really to build empires or produce technology and philosophy. Smith continues: "No southern power could ever succeed in mastering the north, but the more ambitious rulers of Aryavarta or Hindustan often have extended their sway far beyond the dividing line of the Narbada."[88] Smith engages in a fanciful construction of the survival of historical (racial) memory in south India, quoting from a contemporary source to the effect that the hatred that existed between the early Dravidians (presumably the Dasas and Dasyus of the Vedic literature) and Aryans is still preserved by a low-ranked caste in Malabar, who apparently plaster their huts with cow dung to remove the pollution caused by the entrance of a Brahman.[89]

In another bow to events closer to his time, Smith points out the moral of the north-south divide should someone have missed it: "When Dupleix [the governor of the French East India Company] in the eighteenth century dreamed of a Franco-Indian empire with its base in the peninsula he was bound to fail. The success of the English was dependent on their acquisition of rich Bengal and the Gangetic waterway."[90] In other words, the English as the natural successors to the real India, Aryavarta, had to prevail whereas Dupleix, attempting to carve out a maritime empire from the south, was doomed from the inception.

Another widely circulated text — *A Short History of India,* first published in 1936 by William Moreland (who started his career as a member of the Indian Civil Service) and Atul Chandra Chatterjee — recapitulates some of the commonplace themes of Indian civilization in its formative stage as being the work of Aryan settlers who were "normally at war with the 'black-skinned Dasyus' who may reasonably be identified with the peoples speaking Dravidian languages."[91] Moreland and Chatterjee prefer the term *settlers* to that of *invaders* and embellish their account with ideas borrowed from colonial anthropology: one on the family, the other on race consciousness. The "Aryan family" was presented as a virtuous monogamous patriarchy: "An Aryan tribe was composed of families, never polyandrous and usually monogamous, in which the father held a patriarchal position, and the mother an honorable but subordinate position."[92] This idea, already stated by Renan as a characteristic of Aryans, was not particularly original.[93] Moreland and Chatterjee continue: "There is no hint of city life . . . and it has been conjectured that at this period each family lived apart and that the village, which is still the unit of population, arose as the family multiplied."[94] This attitude resembles the völkisch ideology that became popular in Germany at the turn of the twentieth century, when broad political and economic changes and the anti-Semitism associated with them produced an outburst of ruralist romanticism allied to Aryan notions of superiority.[95] The rural patriarchal, nuclear family as the unit of economic and cultural dynamism, a staple of Eurocentric historiography, underwent an apparently seamless transfer to Indian history. The extrapolation of similarities in family structure usually meant to indicate a similar racial type and, hence, developmental potential. Despite much change in the decades since its heyday, that notion apparently retains its appeal to this day.[96]

Moreland and Chatterjee develop the issue of race consciousness via the notion of tribal solidarity: "The tribe was ruled by a king, whose position was usually, if not always, hereditary and there was a council, apparently composed of the heads of families"; "apart from the tribesmen there were numerous slaves, consisting of prisoners of war."[97] This, in itself, would be rather unremarkable, had readers not already learned that the fair-skinned Aryans were frequently, if not incessantly, at war with the dark-skinned Dasas and Dasyus. We must presume that the Aryans preferred to enslave rather than annihilate the latter outright. Moreland and Chatterjee quote an unknown historian as apparently saying of the Aryan of the Rigveda that he "was a white man and proud of it."[98] Thus Indian society in its formative stages was subject to the direction and control of light-skinned patriarchs. Once again, ancient and modern history conspired to place white males at the top of the ruling hierarchy.

Much of the Aryan model survives intact in A. L. Basham's *The Wonder That Was India*, first published in 1954, including the retrojection of a notion of racial purity onto ancient peoples:[99]

Even in the earliest hymns [of the *Rigveda*] we read of the *ksatra*, the nobility, and the *vis*, the ordinary tribesmen, and the records of several other early Indo-European peoples suggest that a tribal aristocracy was a feature of Indo-European society even before the tribes migrated from their original home. As they settled among the darker aboriginals, the

Aryans seem to have laid greater stress than before on *purity of blood,* and class divisions hardened, to exclude those Dasas who found a place on the fringes of Aryan society, and those Aryans who had intermarried with the Dasas and adopted their ways. . . .

The four classes . . . were crystallizing throughout the period of the Rig Veda. They have survived to the present day. The Sanskrit word used for them, *varna,* means "colour," and itself indicates their origin in the development of the old tribal class structure in contact with people of different complexion and alien culture.[100]

The upshot of this kind of reasoning is that the elite of the Aryan diaspora in Europe, encountering aboriginal populations of roughly similar color, did not have to devise the draconian sanctions of the varna system, but in India, encountering an "inferior" (that is, darker) race, had to resort to extreme measures of segregation and social sanction. It is not clear in Basham's account whether the Dravidians, whom the Aryans vanquished en route to establishing their hegemony in India, are proto-Australoid aborigines or a mixture of the latter with Mediterranean peoples.[101] In either case, their racial composition and position in the varna hierarchy is distinctly lower than that of the Aryan peoples, who were of the same stock as northern Europeans. In later writings, Basham is more circumspect. In his introductory essay to the edited volume, *Aryan and Non-Aryan in India,* published in 1979, he notes:

In our study of Aryan and non-Aryan in India, we are not in search of *racial survivals.* There is no question here of tracing how a tall, upstanding, extroverted *race* of Proto-Nordics was *corrupted and polluted* by the blood of darker subtropical peoples to become the contemporary Indians, and I am sure none of the organizers of this conference had anything like this in mind. Rather, we are tracing the progress and development of ancient Indo-European cultural and religious traditions, already much modified in their Indo-Iranian form, under the impact of new geographic and climatic conditions.[102]

Despite its disclaimers, this statement eloquently enough tells us what the Aryan model of history was all about—race and blood, corruption and pollution through miscegenation. The very title of the collection, *Aryan and Non-Aryan,* gives testimony to the perduring legacy of the Aryan model of history, now shorn of its metaphysical attachments to racial purity, but nonetheless retaining a kind of diasporic and cultural content. The real story of Indian history, if we are to take Basham literally, is a variation of an Indo-Iranian modification of the authentic Indo-European (Aryan) culture via contact with the indigenes of the subcontinent. By extension, the Aryan model of history upholds the story of the original Aryan stock's global diaspora and its world-conquering ways.

Mortimer Wheeler's *Civilizations of the Indus Valley and Beyond* (originally published in 1961) devotes six out of seven chapters to northern, and one chapter to eastern, central, and southern India.[103] He states explicitly that civilization came to southern India when the Mauryan dynasty (an Indo-Greek dynasty) took its empire-building skills and religion (Buddhism) to the south. Contacts with the northwest regions beyond the subcontinent are, by definition, civilizing, whether incoming Aryans of the second millennium B.C.E. or Greeks of the third century B.C.E. established them. Wheeler concludes: "The picture of gradual pervasion from north to south is a logical and integral one."[104]

This theme of northern Aryan colonization of south India was a recurrent motif of Aryanist historiography. In his 1918 lectures as Carmichael Professor of Ancient Indian History and Culture at the University of Calcutta, Devadatta Ramakrishna Bhandarkar draws on Sanskrit texts to construct his account of the Aryan conquest and settlement of south India. It has the civilizing of the Dravidians take place through the usual means of the conquerors imposing their civilization on the conquered, but also by the missionary activities of the Rishis, who in the process impose their language on the aboriginal population.[105] Bhandarkar quotes Sir George Grierson, "an eminent linguist" of his day, to the effect that

> when an Aryan tongue comes into contact with an uncivilized aboriginal one, it is invariably the latter which goes to the wall. The Aryan does not attempt to speak it, and the necessities of intercourse compel the aborigine to use a broken "pigeon" [*sic*] form of the language of a superior civilisation. As generations pass this mixed jargon more and more approximates to its model, and in process of time the old aboriginal language is forgotten and dies a natural death.[106]

What this does not explain is, of course, the survival of so-called non-Aryan languages in southern India. After several convoluted pages of argument, Bhandarkar gives up his attempt, merely noting: "And, I therefore, leave it to Dravidian scholars to tackle this most interesting but also most bewildering problem."[107] Bewildering, that is, from the point of view of Aryan diffusionist theories of history. Radhakumud Mookerji similarly attributes the unity of Bharatvarsha — the ancient term signifying the symbolic unity of the Indian subcontinent — to the Aryan genius.[108] Bharatvarsha, as he puts it, is another name for "Aryanised India, the congenial fertile soil where Aryan culture planted itself and attained its fruition, the chosen abode which the *pioneers of human civilisation* adopted as the scene of their labours for the proper expression of their particular genius."[109]

Other Indian historians, in taking over the Aryan model, supplied gory details to the story of conquest and settlement. Abinas Chandra Das's *Rig-vedic India,* for instance, first published in 1921 and reprinted as recently as 1971, brought a liquidationist note to the Aryan expansion on the subcontinent. He argued that the Aryan expansion had led to massacres of the Dasas and Dasyus in order to "create an altogether new and peaceful atmosphere in the country, conducive to their mental, moral, and spiritual growth and development according to their own standard of excellence. In this they were eminently successful in the long run, the discordant elements having been purged out of the country."[110] This genocidal note is quite precocious, considering that it would still be many years before European fascists visualized anything like a final solution to their "Jewish problem." Writing more than a generation later, in 1956, P. L. Bhargava in his *India in the Vedic Age* retains the master race motif: "The foundation of the civilization of India was truly laid in the glorious epoch when the people who called themselves Aryas colonised one district after another of the country, turning forests infested by wild beasts into merry villages, converting tracts laden with thorny bushes and shrubs into green fields, and sanctifying the atmosphere with the music of their inspired hymns."[111] In their later expansion into the "tribal" regions of the south and east, these same jolly Aryans encountered and liquidated those aboriginal tribes who refused Aryan hegemony.[112]

Clearly, several generations of linguistic, historical, and philosophical research, analysis, and speculation have left a major legacy of scholarship that has shaped the fabrication of India in the historical imagination. At a minimum, several notions became virtual clichés in the writings of British and Indian historians: the notion of India as the eastern extension of the Aryan people, and the Aryan model of history as a narrative of invaders, or migrants, who brought technology, linguistic refinement, and philosophy from central Asia or southern Russia to the subcontinent and were, where necessary, unafraid to employ techniques of ethnic cleansing against inferior races. The Aryan-Dravidian divide in India has been posited as a racial divide between light-skinned northerners and dark-skinned southerners, with the former, naturally, prevailing at every level. This, in turn, has generated other myths of the lower-caste people in north India, and those of south India, as the aboriginal Dravidian peoples.[113] In the Aryan model, civilization invariably flows from north to south, with the most important migrations being land-based rather than maritime (similar to the Greek version of the Aryan model). In its kindest, gentlest form, it is a relatively peaceful expansion of the superior race, borrowing elements of inferior aboriginal civilizations; at its worst, it becomes an anticipation of twentieth-century race war and genocide. In the examples cited above, the Dasas and Dasyus stand as the enemies of Aryan civilization. However, the category of enemy was a fungible one; later historiography could turn Muslims, for example, into Aryan civilization's adversaries.

Another enduring legacy of the Aryan model of history is the division of Indian history into Hindu, Muslim, and British periods (corresponding to the ancient, medieval, and modern periods of European history), established originally by British and later by nationalist historians. The ulterior political motive was to demarcate the Hindu golden age from a long Muslim (i.e., alien) interregnum. This division originally served a polemical purpose for the British, who claimed that they were in India to restore the glories of ancient India by liberating India from Muslim rule. The acceptance of the Aryan model involves some curious occlusions and amnesia:

First, India as demarcated in colonial and nationalist historiography for the most part coincides with the boundaries of British India. Right-wing historians occasionally imagine a "greater India" to include Afghanistan and Southeast Asia. The fundamental unity of India, going back to ancient times, has constituted an unquestionable ingredient of Aryanist historiography, with the invading/migrating Aryans civilizing the various "tribal" populations and drawing them into an Indian nation written back into the "classical" past.

Second, by being extremely economical with the truth, British historians could speak of a Hindu India at a time when no person on the subcontinent would have recognized herself or himself as such. The great popular movement against Vedic religion, which came to be called Buddhism, could simply be marginalized in this scheme, though many of the ordinary people and some of the elite of the ancient Gangetic plain regarded themselves as followers of Gautama Buddha's *Dharmapada,* rather than of Vedic religious norms.[114]

Third, nonsubcontinental Muslims, no less and no more conquerors and/or settlers than the Aryans, could be persistently portrayed as interlopers into this preexisting space of Hinduism. Their foreignness was ineradicable, unlike that of the ancient Aryans. Ironically, the vast majority of India's Muslims were local converts to Islam. South Asian Islam became imbricated in the European polemic that considered Islam as alien to European (and Aryan) civilization, despite substantial evidence of cultural interaction in Muslim Spain and its contribution to cultural renewal in Europe, not to mention the numerous conversions in the Balkan regions of the Ottoman Empire. Muslims became victims of a wide-ranging cultural anti-Semitism in the late nineteenth century (European anti-Semitism was not exclusively directed against Jews). Thus, as Muslim influence on European cultures could be marginalized, if not written out, so, too, the rich Indo-Islamic culture that had developed during the "medieval" centuries could be written as if it were an overlay on something essentially Hindu. Like the British Orientalists, subsequent Hindu nationalist historians separated an "authentic" (Hindu) India from Muslim accretions.

Fourth, all traces of maritime influences on subcontinental cultures (maritime syncretisms, for want of a better term) were either wiped clean or rendered into marginal, that is, coastal phenomena. Thus trade between East Africa, the Arabian peninsula, and the west coast of the South Asian subcontinent figures hardly at all in standard textbook accounts of Indian history. The settlements of Arab traders, Siddis from East Africa, and the use of sailors from this region by the Moghul rulers to organize their Indian Ocean trading activities receive passing mention at best. The Siddis, for instance, are not a single group of people, but represent various classes of people — for example, merchants, sailors, and soldiers, who formed an integral part of the western Indian economy and polity from the time of Akbar onward. The only memory that remains of them in the subcontinent, apart from the odd Moghul miniature showing someone of recognizably African features, is the anthropological category of the Siddis as a "scheduled tribe."[115] The schedule into which they have been fitted constitutes a postcolonial offspring of colonial census making, which divided the Indian population into castes and tribes. The Siddis are a people without history to be studied by anthropologists who still insist on measuring skulls and bones. This represents, in some ways, one of the more enduring legacies of colonial racism.

Fifth, one should note the asymmetry in the classificatory scheme of "Indian history." The Hindu and Muslim periods are followed not by the Christian period but by the British period. The British were the bearers of Enlightenment; they came as the representatives of a scientific temper to a subcontinent that reputedly lacked it. Thus they could portray themselves as the people who discovered Indian history for Indians and who would rid India of its oppressive weight of superstition and misrule. By a remarkable alchemy, British colonizers could portray themselves not as conquerors or imperialists but as emancipators.

But even as most, though not all, nationalists challenged that particular British self-representation, they accepted the general perspective of the Aryan model of history. Certain strands within Indian nationalism contained from the beginning the seeds of both anti-Muslim and anti-Western sentiments. What they seem not to have contained — during the colonial period or now, for that matter — is a desire to take apart the construct of ancient India as originally constituted by romantics and Orientalists, that is, the impulse to deconstruct the notion of ancient India as the eastern home of the Aryan diaspora and Indian history as the unfolding of the Aryan genius. A recent textbook intended for use in high school and pre-university classes, notes: "The history of India is regarded as the history of the Aryans in India. Their occupation of India is the most interesting as well as the most momentous event in Indian history."[116] Other texts reject the theory of Aryan occupation, preferring to see them as autochthonous without, however, modifying their world-historical significance.

Indian Nationalism and the Extended Afterlife of the Aryan Model of History and the Oriental Renaissance

The Oriental Renaissance has had a considerable impact in India, the country whose ancient philosophy and poetry inspired it in the first place. While it would exceed the scope of this essay to trace the full impact of the Oriental Renaissance, and its reworking in India itself, it is worth noting that both its universalist and ethnic-particularist sides have had full play. Some thinkers adopted the reasonably generous notion that every "high culture," at least, would have something to contribute to the emergence of a new world civilization. On the other side, Hindu upper-caste north Indians mobilized the concept of the Aryan (race or people) — always a prominent part of the Oriental Renaissance — to claim parity with their European colonizers while denying that same parity to others on the subcontinent itself. This exclusivity became, in due course, a potent instrument in the hands of Hindu revivalists and Hindu nationalists. At one end, the Oriental Renaissance could be selectively mobilized for vapid fantasies about the past and future golden age of India; at the other, it could, equally selectively, become part of a sinister ideology of race war and ethnic cleansing. Either way, it is noteworthy that much of the political spectrum of Indian nationalist thought has had great difficulty thinking outside the terms of the Oriental Renaissance and the Aryan model of history that framed it.

Writers like Nehru, who belonged to the first group, see a long process of "cultural synthesis and fusion" taking place between the "incoming" Aryans and the indigenous Dravidians, not to mention other "races."[117] Nehru rejects the notion of a cataclysmic encounter between the Aryans and Dravidians, and he sees the decline of the Indus Valley civilization (which he thought of as Dravidian) as the result of natural forces, most notably the periodic flooding of the river Indus.[118] He views the continued development of Indian history as the outcome of the arrival of "many other races": "In the ages that followed there came many other races: Iranians, Greeks, Parthians, Bactrians, Scythians, Huns, Turkis or Turks (before Islam), early Christians, Jews, Zoroastrians; they came, made a difference, and were absorbed. India was, according to Dodwell, 'infinitely absorbent like the ocean.' "[119] It is immediately obvious that race had no great metaphysical significance for Nehru, and he was quite able to grant Muslim settlers from central and southwest Asia insider status once they had made a permanent home on the subcontinent. Yet his writing also recapitulates some of the most hackneyed ideas of the Oriental Renaissance. He quotes Max Müller to the effect that the Rigveda was "the first word spoken by the Aryan man,"[120] and in his more extended "speculations" on primitive poetry and the intuitive genius revealed by the Vedic hymns, he says:

> [The Vedic hymns are] a poetic testament of a people's collective reaction to the wonder and awe of existence. A people of vigorous and unsophisticated imagination awakened at the very dawn of civilization to a sense of inexhaustible mystery that is implicit in life. . . . The faith of a race

unburdened with intellectual brooding on the conflicting diversity of the objective universe, though now and again illumined by intuitive experience as: "Truth is one: [though] the wise call it by various names."[121]

Some of the universalist claims of German romanticism occur in both Nehru and Tagore. Tagore, however, extended one of the crucial themes of the Oriental Renaissance in Germany. Whereas for the latter the "discovery of India" was simply the prelude to the reawakening of Germany, for Tagore "the awakening of India is a part of the awakening of the world."[122]

Of course, this kind of thinking was entirely conventional by the late nineteenth century, rephrasing and extending the ideas of the Oriental Renaissance even as those ideas were dying out in Europe itself. In an 1877 speech in Calcutta, Keshab Chandra Sen (1840–85), for example, after ritually noting the providential nature of British rule in India, observed:

> All Europe seems to be turning her attention in these days to Indian antiquities, to gather the priceless treasures buried in the literature of Vedism and Buddhism. Thus, while we learn modern science from England, England learns ancient wisdom from India. . . . in the advent of the English nation in India we see a reunion of parted cousins, *the descendants of two different families of the ancient Aryan race.*[123]

Indian spiritualism also became a refrain in Vivekananda's (1863–1902) work: "This is the ideal before us, and every one must be ready for it — the conquest of the whole world by India — nothing less than that, and we must all get ready for it. . . . Let foreigners come and flood the land with their armies, never mind. Up, India and conquer the world with your spirituality."[124]

Dayananda Saraswati (1824–83), founder of the Arya Samaj, developed a militant variant of a world-conquering Hindu spirituality, suitably armed with ideas of Aryan migration and settlement. He believed that the Aryans of the Vedic age were the chosen people to whom a "formless God [had] revealed perfect knowledge of the Veda."[125] Armed with this revelation, they had descended from Tibet to Aryavarta, a virgin territory stretching from the Indus to the Brahmaputra and from the Himalayas to the Vindhyas becoming "sovereign lords of the earth" before degenerating into superstition and idolatry.[126] For Dayananda, revivalism would take the form of a return to the original revelation, discarding all the superstitious excrescence of the ages, all of which would undoubtedly make the inhabitants of Aryavarta once again sovereign lords of humankind.[127] While

Dayananda's ideas may have mostly concerned religious reform and the refurbishing of the "original monotheism" for the purposes of a revitalized Aryan community in India, the concepts of the Oriental Renaissance were finding their way into the development of a framework for nationalism. Aurobindo Ghose (1872–1950), in a speech to the Society for the Protection of Religion, after his release from prison in 1908, put forth an argument that would become familiar in militant Hindu nationalist circles: "But what is the Hindu religion? What is this religion which we call Sanatan, eternal? It is the Hindu religion only because the Hindu nation has kept it . . . because in this sacred and ancient land it was given as a charge to the Aryan race to preserve through the ages. . . . That which we call the Hindu religion is really the eternal religion."[128] However, as Ghose further maintained, this eternal (and universal) religion was also the deepest expression of Indian nationalism:

> Nationalism is not a politics but a religion, a creed, a faith. . . . I say no longer that nationalism is a creed, a religion, a faith; I say it is the Sanatan Dharma which for us is nationalism. This Hindu nation was born with the Sanatan Dharma, with it it moves and with it it grows. When the Sanatan Dharma declines, then the nation declines, and if the Sanatan Dharma were capable of perishing, with the Sanatan Dharma it would perish.[129]

Over time, just as the original Oriental Renaissance in Europe tended to subsume universalist themes to ethnic-particularist and racist ones, so, too, in India, Vedic or Hindu spiritualism came to be captured by, and serve, political currents hostile to Muslims and others regarded as alien to Aryavarta. No doubt, historical circumstances conspired to produce this result: for example, the virulent propaganda of missionaries and reforming colonizers toward polytheism and what they considered zoolatry; rival reform movements of Muslims and Hindus; and the indubitable, if still inchoate, understanding of the need to find new bases for reimagining community in the face of modernization out of which nationalism was born. But Aryan race theories contributed to the development of strong anti-Muslim sentiments within Hindu revivalism and, in due course, Hindu nationalism. Such theories, as noted in the previous section, struck deep roots in India and contained within them a pronounced tendency to primordialize and naturalize Vedic and, by descent, Hindu religion and its practitioners to the Indian subcontinent, while inscribing Islam and its practitioners in particular with the permanent mark of alienness. Dayananda, for instance, had no use for the Hinduism of his day, but he also thought that contemporary Hindus could return to the pure font of revelation and wisdom in the Vedic texts, a path closed to the practitioners of Islam and Christianity. In an imagined debate between a representative of Vedic faith and representative thinkers of the other religions, he makes especially scathing remarks about the inadequacies of Islamic theology.[130]

Strictures against the Muslim presence and Muslim influence acquired a protonationalist form in Bankimchandra Chatterjee's (1838–94) *Anandamath*. The politicized *sanyasis* (ascetics) in their rebellion against the Muslim rulers of Bengal announce their political credo by noting: "In every country the bond that binds a sovereign to his subject is the protection that he gives; but our Mussulman king — how does he protect us? Our religion is gone; so is our caste, our honour and the sacredness of our family even! Our lives even now are to be sacrificed. Unless we drive these tipsy longbeards away, a Hindu can no longer hope to save his religion."[131] Lest one imagine this as simply a coded way of referring to the British, the final chapter of *Anandamath* spells out clearly the necessary, if limited, role of the British in ultimately giving the Hindus the best crack at realizing the full potentiality of their unique spirituality: "True religion consists not in the worship of 33 crores of gods; that is a vulgar, debased religion which has obscured that which is true. True Hinduism consists in knowledge not in action. Knowledge is of two kinds, physical and spiritual. Spiritual knowledge is the essence of Hinduism."[132] However, physical knowledge, it seems, was the province of the West and so "we must learn it from the foreigners," in this case the British, who must be made to rule in order to discharge their responsibility to impart physical knowledge to the people of Indian. Once that was done, "they will be able to comprehend the nature of the spiritual. There will then be no obstacle to the true Faith. True religion will then shine forth again of itself. Until that happens, and until Hindus are wise and virtuous and strong, the English power will remain unbroken."[133] In the mid-nineteenth century, Pictet had articulated the idea of an Aryan universalism that would bring "religious illumination and universal progress,"[134] but early Indian nationalists adopted it with a different end in view — regional or national cultural renaissance. It is not clear what place Muslims would occupy in this revivified polity and culture, but Bankimchandra's equation of the "Mother Country" with the "Mother Goddess" in his "Bande Mataram" [Hail to the mother] — inserted into *Anandamath* in

1882 and later adopted by the Indian National Congress as its anthem — justifiably made many Muslims uneasy.[135]

However, it is in the articulation and development of Hindu nationalism that the Aryan model of history and an indigenized version of the Oriental Renaissance have had their most significant political impact. Balwantrao Gangadhar Tilak (1856–1920), one of the progenitors of Hindu nationalism, transformed vague, sentimental notions of Hindu cultural and political revival into militant activism, combining in equal measure (anti-Muslim) communalism and anticolonialism, underpinning both with "research" into the Vedic texts and his exposition of the Bhagavad Gita. Tilak's research was politically motivated in that he wanted to establish not only the antiquity of the Vedas — "the oldest book that we now possess and . . . generally admitted that for the study of man, or if you like, Aryan humanity, there is nothing in the world equal in importance with it"[136] — but also their centrality to a revived Hindu nation. As a product ultimately of the age of science and racialism, Tilak maintained that the study of such important texts as the Rigveda could not be entrusted to purely literary methods, and so he drew on disciplines like astronomy (in *The Orion*) and geology (in *The Arctic Home in the Vedas*) to make his case. In so far as Tilak added at all to the Aryan model of history, it was to elongate, with the help of modern astronomical charts, the antiquity of the sacred texts by several thousand years, from the second to at least the seventh millennium B.C.E., and to place the original home of the Aryan race in the Arctic circle, using geological data.[137] In the conclusion to his commentary on the Bhagavad Gita, he revealed the continuing hold of the Oriental Renaissance: "The single Gita religion, which preaches that the whole of one's life should be turned into a sacrifice (*yajna*), contains the *essence of the whole Vedic religion*. . . . When this beneficial religion lost following in this country, it reached its present fallen state."[138] Oddly enough, Tilak, otherwise at great pains to develop a historical rather than a purely theological reading of Vedic texts, is extremely vague as to when this decline or degeneration began. But one may conclude — from his political activity on behalf of the Cow Preservation Societies (Gorakshaka Mandali) in the late 1880s and 1890s and his sponsorship of the Ganapathi festival that took place shortly after Muharram (hitherto observed by Hindus and Muslims alike in Maharashtra), not to mention the militant tone and provocation of Muslim sensibilities promoted by the public festivities associated with both[139] — that Tilak implicated Muslim rule in the process of decline.

National revival would need, therefore, a return to fundamentals. In 1900 Tilak had expressed the view that "the common factor in Indian society is the feeling of Hindutva. . . . We say that the Hindus of the Punjab, Bengal, Maharashtra, Telengana and Dravida are one, and the reason for this is only Hindu dharma."[140] He spoke of a Hindu nation and violently polemicized in his Marathi journal, *Kesari* [the lion], against reform-minded Hindus, calling them "not Hindus . . . but mere renegades and worse enemies than people of other religions."[141] His political concerns were quite modern: to mobilize antiquity to the task of modern nation-state building. Research into the Vedic texts had the purpose of establishing both the virtues of the Aryan race and the Aryan religion, as well as of weaving a thread of cultural (and religious) continuity between the Aryans of furthest antiquity and present-day Hindus. Only the latter, however, could be steered away from the kinds of cultural mongrelization that had occurred in the centuries of foreign domination, including prominently, of course, the centuries of Muslim rule in the subcontinent. The "vitality and superiority of the Aryan races," as revealed primarily in their religious texts, would be the key to a Hindu renaissance — Muslims and members of other religions would have no vital role in a future Hindu nation. In plotting this course, Tilak turned against the "integral humanism"[142] that informed, if all too briefly, the more idealistic side of the Oriental Renaissance, preferring a cultural and religious fundamentalism that some, like Nehru, would have considered ethnocentric and divisive. As to the boundaries of the nation-state itself, Tilak, after some initial tendency to a provincialist view that limited it to the Marathi-speaking areas, fell back on the borders of British India, a clear indication of Hindu nationalism's parasitic nature in regard to secular processes of history.

There is a direct lineage connecting Tilak with V. D. Savarkar (1883–1966) — the founder of the Hindutva movement and seven-time president of the Hindu Mahasabha — K. B. Hedgewar, and M. S. Golwalkar — the latter both leaders of the Rashtriya Swayamsevak Sangh (RSS). The Hindu Mahasabha, the RSS, and similar organizations in north India — and later the Jana Sangh, founded in 1951 as the first political front of the RSS — have developed a far greater organizational cohesiveness than anything Tilak achieved in his lifetime. Nonetheless, the essentials of a Hindu nationalist program were all anticipated in Tilak's thought:[143] a racialized reading of history; the conflation of Hindu culture, religion, and the Indian nation; the unique position of India among the nations of the world; the mobilization of

Brahmanical values in the creation of a right-wing version of the national-popular;[144] this-worldly asceticism; the paradoxical commitment to an anti-modern modernity; not to mention virulent anti-Muslim and antisecular polemics.

Vinayak Damodar Savarkar, whose slogan during World War II was, "Hinduize all politics and militarize Hindudom," had earlier set out his ideas in *Hindutva,* first published in 1923, with the benefit a modified Aryan model of history. Savarkar, like Tilak, accepted the conventional belief that the Aryans originated outside India, migrating from a northern home to settle in today's Punjab, calling themselves Hindu (or Sindhu) for the first time, before spreading out to the rest of the subcontinent and taking their civilization with them. Savarkar, however, introduced a novel twist to the stock model, arguing that a common race evolved in India through the miscegenation of Aryans and non-Aryans. However, such mingling of Aryan and non-Aryan, which in standard race theories signified the degeneration of Aryan civilization in India, became in Savarkar's hands a sign of strength, of the rootedness of Hindu civilization in the soil of India. As Savarkar put it: "No country in the world, with the exception of China, is peopled by a race so homogeneous, yet so ancient and so strong both numerically and vitally. . . . Mohammedans are no race nor are Christians. They are a religious unit, yet neither a racial nor a national one. But we Hindus, if possible, are *all three put together* and live under our ancient and common roof."[145] Hindus are unique in that their holy land and their fatherland coincide. Others are not so fortunate: "Look at the Moham-medans. Mecca is a sterner reality than Delhi or Agra. Some of them do not make any secret of being bound to sacrifice all India if that be to the glory of Islam."[146] What is more, Hindus live, and have lived for aeons, in a land uniquely blessed, stretching from the Indus (Sindhu) to the sea (Sindhu), which "girdles the southern peninsula — so that this one word Sindhu points out almost all the frontiers of the land at a single stroke," a land so "well-knit, so well demarcated" that no other country in the world is "so perfectly designed by the fingers of nature as a geographical unit."[147] A Hindu is, as the frontispiece of *Hindutva* reminds us, "a person who regards this land of Bharatvarsha, from the Indus to the Seas as his Father-land as well as his Holy-land, that is the cradle of his religion."[148] The imagery of blood and soil — the foundation of the organic national community — could not have been more clearly evoked. Not surprisingly, for Savarkar, this segue into romanticism provides but a way of asserting that the heroic wanderers, the

Vedic Aryans, chose this particular land to settle in and develop a precocious "sense of nationality." What Savarkar proposes is nothing less than the coevolution of the land and the race: the race meets its destiny in a particular land; the land, in turn, is immensely enriched by the creative labor of the race. Writers like Ernst Curtius (in his work on Greece) had indeed anticipated this "ecological racism," for want of a better term, but Savarkar vastly amplified its potential into a highly exclusivist political doctrine and bequeathed to Hindu nationalism one of its more distinctive tenets.[149]

In this framework, the "conflict of life and death began" when Mohammad of Ghazni crossed the Indus; "nothing makes Self conscious of itself so much as a conflict with non-self."[150] This conflict, and the honing of a Hindu identity that it supposedly gave rise to will, in Savarkar's chilling words, have their day of reckoning: "Thirty crores of people, with India for the basis of their operation, for their Fatherland and Holyland, with such a history behind them can dictate terms to the whole world. *A day will come when mankind will have to face the force.*"[151] Savarkar closes his book by reminding his readers that "the actual essentials of Hindutva are . . . also the essentials of nationality. If we would, we could build on this foundation of Hindutva, a future greater than what any other people on earth can dream of, *greater even than our own past.*" He ends on a quintessentially social-Darwinist note: "For let our people remember that great combinations are the order of the day. The leagues of nations, the alliances of powers, Pan-Islamism, Pan-Slavism, Pan-Ethiopism. . . . All little beings are seeking to get themselves incorporated into greater wholes, so as to be *better fitted for the struggle for power and existence.*"[152]

Savarkar's *Hindutva* set the tone for the popularization of Hindu nationalism. Much of his thinking has survived and even become canonical among Hindu nationalists. Madhav Sadashiv Golwalkar, for instance, who published in 1939 a book entitled, *We, or, Our Nationhood Defined*, recapitulates many of Savarkar's ideas, though his Aryans originate in India and spread elsewhere, an idea that goes back to Friedrich Schlegel.[153] The autochthonous, as opposed to exotic, origin of the Aryans holds the advantage that it effectively counters the notion of Aryans as invaders or the product of miscegenation. Like Savarkar, Golwalkar brings into intimate fusion race, culture, and territory (the basis of the eternal nation), but writing in the late 1930s, he could draw on an even more mystical set of ideas about the race spirit (*Volksgeist*): "Our Race-spirit is a child of our Religion and so with us Culture is but a product of our all-comprehensive

Religion, a part of its body and not distinguishable from it."[154] Like Savarkar before him, who rejected the idea of a nation-state based on a civic-universal "social contract" in favor an ethno-racial concept of a nation of blood and language, Golwalkar characterized a nation as "a hereditary society of common spirit, feeling, and race bound together especially by a language and customs in a common civilization," and derided as "amazing" a theory that the nation was composed of "all those who, for one reason or another happen to live at the time in the country."[155] In line with "the fears of many political scientists regarding the wisdom of heaping together in one state elements conflicting with the national life,"[156] Golwalkar evoked a jealous and exclusivist race spirit—India for the Hindus, the descendants of the Aryans. His definition of modern-day Hindus echoed Savarkar's: "All Hindus claim to have in their veins the blood of the mighty race incorporated with and descended from the Vedic fathers."[157] He brought to Hindu nationalism an unprecedented level of brutal intolerance of Muslims and other "foreign" minorities: "The foreign races in Hindustan must either adopt the Hindu culture and language, must learn to respect and hold in reverence Hindu religion, must entertain no idea but those of glorification of the Hindu race and culture, i.e., of the Hindu nation." Failing this, they would have to forfeit all rights, claim nothing, "not even citizen's rights." Golwalkar urged his readers to deal "as old nations ought to and do deal, with the foreign races, who have chosen to live in our country."[158]

Inevitably, Hindu nationalists showed public support for European fascism, drawing as they both did on a common fund of romantic racialism. In October 1938, following the Munich Agreement, Savarkar approved the Nazi occupation of the Sudetenland, a predominantly German-speaking province in then-Czechoslovakia, on the grounds that its inhabitants shared with Germans "common blood and language." In 1938 and 1939, both the *Hindu Outlook* and the *Mahratta,* an English-language journal founded by Tilak in 1881, wrote editorials praising Franco, Mussolini and Hitler.[159] In addition, Golwalkar cemented the paradoxical idea of an ultranationalist right-wing internationalism in his book: "To keep up the purity of the Race and its culture, Germany shocked the world by her purging the country of the Semitic races—the Jews. . . . Germany has also shown how well-nigh impossible it is for Races and cultures going to the root, to be assimilated into one united whole, *a good lesson for us in Hindustan to learn and profit by.*"[160]

None of this should imply that Hindu nationalism — or its academic preceptors — operated over time with an entirely consistent and rigid definition of race, race spirit, nation, or even culture. Golwalkar, like Savarkar, tended to shift his emphasis between different combinations of a triad of forces (race, nation, and culture). Biological exclusivism occupied a relatively small portion of their thought. Involved as they were in an ongoing project, their emphasis shifted between ethnic homogeneity and cultural unity, when it did not resort to straight-out blood-and-soil rhetoric. Thus their racism not only expressed a sense of upper-caste domination within a hierarchical setup, but a primordial unity that the passage of time and diffusion across space had eroded and which it was necessary to restore as part of the reawakening of the Hindu nation.[161] Race itself is a highly mobile concept, and it is banal to detect a "traditional Indian xenology" at play in the works of Hindu nationalism that distinguishes it from European (biological) racism.[162] When not drawing on anthropology and biology, racism can incorporate a sense of exclusivity drawing on culture and customs in common. Crucially, it must establish that observable differences in culture, customs, and the like have some primordial element not easily transformed by mere human effort. And it must also include an exercise of power or hegemony by some element in that society over others perceived as essentially different. In this sense, many of the ideas of the Aryan model of history and the Oriental Renaissance contributed significant disciplinary and discursive resources to a continuum of forces in India even at the end of the twentieth century — from ethnic chauvinism to ethnocultural racism, all the way to the blood-and-soil aspirations of the Far Right.

The development of the Aryan model was, in fact, an attempt to write world history with race as a central motif. In Europe, the Aryan model developed out of cults of Christian Europe and the North in the late eighteenth and early nineteenth centuries, an alternative universalism to the radical vision of revolutionary humanism. Nationalism and protofascist ideology in the late nineteenth century further sustained it. In India, as this essay has shown, similar congeries of cultural and political forces — strongly reinforced by notions derived from the romantic Oriental Renaissance — not only fed into nationalism but contributed to the powerful crystallization of a far-right political philosophy and practice today that is, in all but name, fascist.

Indian Hindu nationalists have responded to theories of racial degeneration (of the invading/migrating Aryans) by positing the Aryans as the autochthonous inhabitants of the subcontinent, not as invaders, migrants, or settlers. This view originated, as noted, with Friedrich Schlegel, was incorporated by Aurobindo Ghose into the Indian militant nationalist lexicon, and has now become particularly popular with the political rise of the Hindutva forces. The Bharatiya Itihasa Sankalana Yojana (Authentic History of India Plan) has devoted itself to destroying the "myth" that the "Aryans came from outside and invaded India."[163] For this group, with strong ties to militant right-wing organizations like the RSS, the Vedas and the Upanishads are "our history books."[164] The blurring of the distinction between religious texts and history books, one of the staples of the Hindu Right, draws its leitmotif from nineteenth-century Orientalism.

If the Aryans have autochthonous roots, then the deterioration of Indic civilization could be attributed not so much to racial decline through miscegenation with aboriginal populations as to the invasion of the subcontinent by outsiders. Much as Hitler identified the Jews as the constant outside threat to Aryan civilization in Germany, Hindu nationalists have identified Muslims as the perennial menace to India's Aryan civilization and the future of the nation. School textbooks, mainly in north Indian states that were and/or are under Bharatiya Janata Party rule today, put forth this view in their most stark and uncompromising forms.[165] The slogans of the New Right depend for their success on the incorporation of a certain kind of Aryanist mythography into the curriculum; over time, it has the potential to become the common sense of the "educated" person and, therefore, beyond the reach of critical thought.[166]

The liberal response to Hindu nationalist historiography posits a composite or syncretic Indo-Islamic culture. This constitutes a superficial response because many of the deeper notions that underpin the right-wing discourse remain unquestioned: for example, the foundational status of Hinduism; the north-south (Aryan-Dravidian) divide; India as a fundamentally Aryan civilization overlaid with the contributions of many "races" (as Nehru might have put it); varna as precursor of race; caste as a synonym for racial hierarchy. Rhetorical gestures aside, the common grounds shared by these quite different political positions testify to the continuing power of the Aryan model of history and the Oriental Renaissance in India, even after the racist and romantic myths of their heyday have been deeply modified if not completely set aside in Europe, where the horrors of the Holocaust forced a reconsideration of the model. The failure to develop *through systematic research* an alternative curriculum by historians in other ways radically opposed to the agendas of the Hindu nationalists is noteworthy. Curricula and textbooks that explore the subcontinent's connections with neighboring lands (whether Africa or Asia east of the subcontinent) and deflate the notion of the Aryan arrival and/or dispersal on the subcontinent as the ultimate process of Indic civilization's development and diffusion have yet to be written. This suggests that the enduring hold of philological obscurantism and racial myths have become so imbricated within the ideologies of Indian nationalism that dismantling one without disassembling the other is perhaps no longer possible.

Notes

Parts 2 and 3 of this chapter draw on my earlier essay, "Racism and the Writing of History," *South Asia Bulletin* 9.2 (1989): 32–56. I thank Sucheta Mazumdar, Mohamad Tavakoli-Targhi, and Roland Lardinois for their comments, thoughts, and help with references. I alone am responsible for all remaining errors.

1. Jean-Pierre Vernant, foreword to Maurice Olender, *The Languages of Paradise: Race, Religion, and Philology in the Nineteenth Century,* trans. Arthur Goldhammer (Cambridge: Harvard University Press, 1992), ix–x.

2. This phrase—*biography of a people*—is used by Martin Bernal, *Black Athena: The Afroasiatic Roots of Classical Civilization* (New Brunswick, N.J.: Rutgers University Press, 1987), 217. For a parallel discussion of literature as the biography of the people, see Vasudha Dalmia, *The Nationalization of Hindu Traditions: Bharatendu Harischandra and Nineteenth-Century Banaras* (Delhi: Oxford University Press, 1999), 271. Thinking of history as the biography of a people suggests that it simply recovers and records the nation's "organic development" over time. But it is the burden of this essay and the concluding chapter of this volume to demonstrate that, in fact, nationalist history creates the global categories and narratives within which memory can be created and forgetting takes place.

3. Edmund Leach, "Aryan Invasions over Four Millennia," in Emiko Ohnuki-Tierney, ed., *Culture through Time: Anthropological Approaches* (Stanford, Calif.: Stanford University Press, 1990), 242–43.

4. The precise location of this original homeland still seems to be in dispute. See J. P. Mallory, *In Search of Indo-Europeans, Language, Archaeology, Myth* (London: Thames and Hudson, 1989).

5. Ulrich Wehlen, who flourished under the Nazis, expressed this opinion of Barthold Niebuhr; the second quote is from a letter written by Niebuhr to his father. Both are quoted in Bernal, *Black Athena,* 304 and 305 respectively.

6. This notion of the Volk was put forward by the German philosopher Herder in 1774 in *Also a Philosophy of History,* quoted in Bernal, *Black Athena,* 305. Robert Norton ("The Tyranny of Germany over Greece? Bernal, Herder, and the German Appropriation of

Greece," in Mary R. Lefkowitz and Guy MacLean Rogers, eds., *Black Athena Revisited* [Chapel Hill: University of North Carolina Press, 1996], 403–10) is right to point out that Herder was not a supporter of imperialism and not particularly a racist either. However, this does not mean that Herder's variety of romanticism could not be appropriated, under suitable conditions, to a racialist historiography. Romanticism was one among many streams that watered and fertilized the Aryan model of history, and it was the primary source of the Oriental Renaissance.

7. Percy Bysshe Shelley, *Hellas* (London: C. & J. Ollier, 1822), quoted in Bernal, *Black Athena,* 290.

8. Bernal, *Black Athena,* 290–91.

9. J. Arthur de Gobineau, *Essai sur l'inégalité des races humaines* (Paris: Belfond, 1967), 477–78. All translations, unless otherwise noted, are mine. The paradox of the Aryan model, not to mention the Oriental Renaissance, was that an unbounded and unbalanced admiration for the "classical" periods of Greek and Indian history could coexist with an equally unbounded and unbalanced contempt for the present denizens of both places. A great deal of narcissism about contemporary European civilization accompanied these sentiments. On narcissism, Michael Adas, *Machines as the Measure of Men: Science, Technology, and Ideologies of Western Dominance* (Ithaca, N.Y.: Cornell University Press, 1989).

10. Bernal, *Black Athena,* 441.

11. M. Cowan, *An Anthology of Writings of Wilhelm von Humboldt: Humanist without Portfolio* (Detroit: Wayne State University Press, 1963), 79.

12. *The History of the Greek Tribes and Cities* (1820–24) and *Introduction to a Scientific System of Mythology* (1825) were seminal works in distancing Greece from the eastern Mediterranean world. For an interesting recent attempt to periodize ancient Greek development outside the Aryan model, see Mario Liverani, "The Bathwater and the Baby," in Lefkowitz and Rogers, *Black Athena Revisited,* 425–27.

13. Bernal, *Black Athena,* 314, comments that a demand for "distinct proof" as opposed to competitive plausibility is "absurd" in a field as nebulous as Greek mythology, a point further reinforced in Martin Bernal, *Black Athena Writes Back,* ed. David Chioni Moore (Durham: Duke University Press, 2001).

14. This notion, once almost a dogma in Indian historiography, has come in for a great deal of criticism. See, for example, Thomas R. Trautmann, *Aryans and British India* (Berkeley: University of California Press, 1997), 206–11.

15. Georg Curtius, *Principles of Greek Etymology,* trans. Augustus S. Wilkins and Edwin B. England, 5th ed. (London: John Murray, 1886), 22.

16. John Edwin Sandys, *A History of Classical Scholarship,* 3 vols. (Cambridge: Cambridge University Press, 1903–8), 3:207, quoted in Bernal, *Black Athena,* 332. Bernal's point is that, in doing so, linguists like Curtius simply lost sight of alternative etymologies which would have pointed to Egyptian and Levantine roots for Greek words. Bernal himself has been heavily criticized for doing so, accused of "pre-paradigmatic lack of methodology of earlier antiquarians" (Liverani, "The Bathwater and the Baby," 424).

17. Bernal, *Black Athena*, 292–94.

18. Ernst Curtius, *History of Greece*, trans. Adolphus William Ward, 5 vols. (New York: Scribner's, 1886), 1:32.

19. Ibid., 1:34.

20. For a full discussion of the "broad" and "extreme" Aryan model, see Bernal, *Black Athena*, chapters 7 and 8. My discussion of these models of history is not to endorse Bernal's view of the colonization of Greece by Egyptians or Phoenicians but rather to point to the dogmatic denial that these civilizations could have had any but the most superficial impact on Greek life and culture in antiquity.

21. Ibid., 196–97.

22. Jean-Philippe Lauer, *Observations sur les pyramides* (Cairo: Institut Français d'Archéologie Orientale, 1960), 1–3.

23. Ibid., 10.

24. G. Maspero, *Etudes de mythologie et d'archéologie égyptiennes* (Paris: Leroux, 1893–1916), 277.

25. E. A. W. Budge, *The Gods of the Egyptians: Or, Studies in Egyptian Mythology*, 2 vols. (London: Methuen, 1904), 1:143.

26. See, for example, Michael Grant, *The Ancient Mediterranean* (1969; New York: Meridian, 1988).

27. Maspero, *Etudes de mythologie*, 277.

28. Ernest Renan, *Etudes d'histoire religieuse* (Paris: 1857), 359.

29. This, of course, continues and emphasizes one general theme in Bernal, namely, that the writing of history is deeply, and inescapably, connected with contemporary political events and that historians in particular, and academics in general, tend to shroud their prejudices and biases in the respectable search for origins and roots. See, especially, Bernal, *Black Athena*, 337.

30. John Weiss, *Ideology of Death: Why the Holocaust Happened in Germany* (Chicago: Dee, 1996), chapters 7 and 12 in particular.

31. Ibid., 97–111.

32. Emile Burnouf, *The Science of Religion*, trans. J. Liebe (1872; London , 1888), 190–91.

33. S. A. Cook, "The Semites," *The Cambridge Ancient History*, 1st ed. (Cambridge: Cambridge University Press, 1928–39), 1:181-237, quoted in Bernal, *Black Athena*, 389.

34. J. Arthur de Gobineau, *Oeuvres* (Paris: Pléiades, 1983), 372.

35. Bernal, *Black Athena*, 358.

36. A. Holm, *History of Greece* (London: Macmillan, 1894), quoted in Bernal, *Black Athena*, 364.

37. J. B. Bury, *A History of Greece to the Death of Alexander the Great* (London: Macmillan, 1902), 77. Emphasis added.

38. Robert Knox, *The Races of Men: A Philosophical Enquiry into the Influence of Race over the Destinies of Nations* (London: Renshaw, 1862), 194.

39. Quoted in Bernal, *Black Athena*, 363–64.

40. Renan, *Etudes,* quoted in Bernal, *Black Athena,* 345. Hannah Arendt suggests that Renan's works — *General History of the Semitic Languages* (1847) and *Histoire générale et systeme comparé des langues semitiques* (1863) — first opposed "Semites" and "Aryans" as the decisive *division du genre humain* (Hannah Arendt, "Race Thinking before Racism," quoted in Ivan Hannaford, *Race: The History of an Idea in the West,* Baltimore: Johns Hopkins University Press, 1996), 253.

41. Olender, *Languages of Paradise,* 54–55.

42. V. Gordon Childe, *The Aryans: A Study of Indo-European Origins* (New York: Knopf, 1926), 4.

43. Ernest Renan, *Oeuvres complètes,* ed. Henriette Psichari, 10 vols. (Paris: 1947–61), 2:332. Emphasis added.

44. Ibid., 5:1142. Emphasis added.

45. Guy Bunnens, *L'expansion phénicienne en méditerranée: Essai d'interprétation fondé sur une analyse des traditions littéraires* (Brussels: Institut historique Belge de Rome, 1979), 6–7.

46. The recent volume by Lefkowitz and Rogers, *Black Athena Revisited,* tries to undermine Bernal's thesis of an Aryan model of history for European antiquity by citing his methodological inadequacies and exceptions to the broad picture of European chauvinism, narcissism, and racism. Some of the points are well taken, particularly the ones made by Edith Hall ("When Is a Myth Not a Myth?") regarding the dangers of substituting one myth (the ancient model) for another (the Aryan model) and by Mario Liverani regarding the indubitable methodological breakthroughs made by the classicists. However, can Lefkowitz and Rogers deny that nineteenth-century European historiography of European antiquity conformed broadly to a model of Aryan (race) diaspora and diffusion from an original homeland — variously located in the Caucasus, southeastern Europe, or other similar locations — linking those migrations and settlements of the Aryan race with the civilizing process par excellence, not to mention the future greatness of western and northern Europe? Were the methodological breakthroughs in linguistics, philology, and history not often used for invidious political ends? Did those who resisted the racism, narcissism, and imperialism develop an alternative historical model of ancient Greek civilization, such as the kind suggested by Liverani in the same volume? Can it also be mere forgetfulness that classicists of the post–World War II period did not make systematic corrections to nineteenth-century historiography until Bernal prodded them?

47. E. J. Hobsbawm, *The Age of Capital, 1848–1875* (New York: Vintage, 1996), 296.

48. Renan, *Oeuvres complètes,* 6:32. This will be particularly important later in this essay when discussing views of race developed in India in the period between the two world wars. These drew on this older philological tradition while, at the same time, radical European tendencies moved toward a more purely biological concept.

49. Raymond Schwab, *The Oriental Renaissance: Europe's Rediscovery of India and the East, 1680–1880,* trans. Gene Patterson-Black and Victor Reinking (New York: Columbia University Press, 1984). The French original appeared in *La renaissance orientale* (Paris: Editions Payot, 1950), 1–3.

50. Ibid., 1, 3.

51. For a trenchant attempt to deflate the heroic stature of Abraham Hyacinthe Anquetil-Duperron and William Jones, see Mohamad Tavakoli-Targhi, "Orientalism's Genesis Amnesia," in this volume.

52. Schwab, *Oriental Renaissance,* 4.

53. Ibid., 121.

54. Franz Bopp, *A Comparative Grammar of the Sanskrit, Zend, Greek, Latin, Lithuanian, Gothic, German, and Slavonic Languages,* trans. Lieutenant Eastwick, 3 vols. (London: Madden and Malcolm, 1845–53); Bopp, *Grammaire comparée des langues indo-européennes,* 5 vols. (Paris: Imprimerie impériale, 1866–74); Eugène Burnouf, *Le lotus de la bonne loi,* ed. Theodore Pavie (Paris: 1852).

55. Schwab, *Oriental Renaissance,* 121.

56. Abel Bergaigne, *Les dieux souverains de la religion védique* (Paris: Viewig, 1877); Auguste Barth, *Les religions de l'Inde* (Paris: Fischbacher, 1879). Both are quoted in Schwab, *Oriental Renaissance,* 121.

57. Schwab, *Oriental Renaissance,* 121.

58. Ibid., 9.

59. Léon Poliakov, *Aryan Myth,* 327. Schlegel, Poliakov points out, was not anti-Semitic. He favored the complete emancipation of the Jews.

60. Schlegel, *Über die Sprache und die Weisheit der Indier* (1808), quoted in Schwab, *Oriental Renaissance,* 13.

61. Ibid.

62. Quoted in ibid.

63. However, Forster himself thought of his translation as a program of collecting and propagating the art of "lesser developed peoples as a means of restoring the European taste." Thomas P. Saine, *Georg Forster* (New York: Twayne, 1972), 91, quoted in Robert Palter, "Eighteenth-Century Historiography in *Black Athena*," in Lefkowitz and Rogers, *Black Athena Revisited,* 381.

64. Quoted in Schwab, *Oriental Renaissance,* 59.

65. Ibid., 217.

66. Karl Hillebrand, "De la philologie en Allemagne dans la première moitié du siècle: L'école historique," *Revue moderne* 33 (1865): 239–68.

67. Quoted in ibid., 262.

68. bid., 216, 274.

69. Edmond Vermeil, *L'Allemagne: Essai d'explication* (Paris: Gallimard, 1940), 134.

70. Olender, *Languages of Paradise,* 95.

71. Ibid., 138–39.

72. Ibid., 139.

73. Quoted in Sheldon Pollock, "Deep Orientalism?" in Carol A. Breckenridge and Peter van der Veer, *Orientalism and the Postcolonial Predicament: Perspectives on South Asia* (Philadelphia: University of Pennsylvania Press, 1993), 86.

74. Schwab, *Oriental Renaissance,* 403, 477.

75. Quoted in ibid., 324 (emphasis added).

76. Ibid., 431.

77. Quoted in ibid., 432.

78. Ibid., 433

79. Ibid., 275.

80. Renan, *Etudes,* 175.

81. *Sacountala: Drame en sept actes mêlés de prose et de ver,* trans. Abel Bergaigne and Paul Lehugeur (Paris: Librairie de bibliophiles, 1884), preface.

82. Nathaniel Brassey Halhed, *A Code of Gentoo Laws: Or, Ordinations of the Pundits, from a Persian Translation, Made from the Original, Written in the Shanscrit Language* (London: n.p., 1776).

83. Schwab, *Oriental Renaissance,* 192, 193.

84. I don't wish to imply an overly neat division but, by and large, the former notion was popular among German romantics and some of their French counterparts, for example, Jules Michelet, and has made a reappearance among present-day proponents of Hindutva. The latter view had currency among British historians and their "secular" Indian counterparts, both during the colonial period and today. Neither position disturbs the essential outlines of a model of history built around global Aryan diaspora and diffusion.

85. Vincent Arthur Smith, *The Oxford History of India,* 3d ed. (1919; Oxford: Clarendon, 1958), 2.

86. Ibid., 32 (emphasis added).

87. Ibid., 2 (emphasis added).

88. Ibid. The parallel with the picture of the Phoenicians drawn by J. B. Bury should be apparent.

89. Ibid., 68 n. 1. It is not clear why a Malabar Brahman would enter the hut of such low-ranked castes as the Kuricchans.

90. Ibid., 2.

91. W. H. Moreland and A. C. Chatterjee, *A Short History of India,* 3d ed. (London: Longmans, Green, 1953), 12.

92. Ibid.

93. Renan, *Oeuvres complètes,* 6:34–35.

94. Moreland and Chatterjee, *Short History of India,* 12.

95. As Lanz von Liebenfels declared in 1908: "Only the man who is wedded to the soil, the peasant, is truly a man. . . . The Aryan race will prosper only in the culture of the countryside; the city is its grave." Quoted in Weiss, *Ideology of Death,* 109.

96. See, for example, J. M. Blaut's criticism of this perduring notion (*The Colonizer's Model of the World: Geographical Diffusion and Eurocentric History* [New York: Guilford, 1993], 129–35). He cites numerous sources: Michael Mann, *The Sources of Social Power,* vol. 1, *A History of Power from the Beginning to A.D. 1760* (Cambridge: Cambridge University Press, 1986); Patricia Crone, *Pre-Industrial Societies* (Oxford: Blackwell, 1989); E. L. Jones, *The European Miracle: Environments, Economies, and Geopolitics in the History of Europe and Asia* (Cambridge: Cambridge University Press, 1981);

Alan Macfarlane, *Marriage and Love in England: Modes of Reproduction, 1300–1840* (Oxford: Blackwell, 1986).

97. Moreland and Chatterjee, *Short History of India,* 12.

98. Ibid., 14.

99. A. L. Basham, *The Wonder That Was India: A Survey of the Culture of the Indian Sub-continent before the Coming of the Muslims* (New York: Grove, 1959).

100. Ibid., 35.

101. Ibid., 25.

102. A. L. Basham, "Aryan and Non-Aryan in South Asia," in Madhav M. Deshpande and Peter Edwin Hook, eds., *Aryan and Non-Aryan in India* (Ann Arbor: Center for South and Southeast Asian Studies, University of Michigan, 1979), 5; emphasis added.

103. Robert Eric Mortimer Wheeler, *Civilizations of the Indus Valley and Beyond* (London: Thames and Hudson, 1966).

104. Ibid., 136.

105. Devadatta Ramakrishna Bhandarkar, *Lectures on the Ancient History of India in the Period from 650 to 325 B.C.* (Calcutta: University of Calcutta Press, 1919), 15–20.

106. Ibid., 24–25. Again the parallels with the dominant forms of Indo-European linguistics developed in nineteenth-century Europe should be clear.

107. Ibid., 39.

108. Radhakumud Mookerji, *The Fundamental Unity of India* (New York: Longmans, Green and Co., 1914), 17.

109. Ibid., 18; emphasis added. This shows the extent to which romantic clichés animated nationalist historiography. Mookerji was an active member of the Hindu Mahasabha, later switching to Congress and being nominated to the Rajya Sabha.

110. A. C. Das, *Rigvedic India* (Calcutta: University of Calcutta Press, 1921), 132.

111. P. L. Bhargava, *India in the Vedic Age: A History of Aryan Expansion in India* (Lucknow: Upper India Publishing House, 1956), 1.

112. Ibid., 56.

113. V. T. Rajashekar, "The Black Untouchables of India: Reclaiming Our Cultural Heritage"; Runoko Rashidi, "Dalits: The Black Untouchables of India," in Ivan Van Sertima and Runoko Rashidi, eds., *African Presence in Early Asia* (New Brunswick, N.J.: Transaction, 1988), 236–43 and 244–46, respectively.

114. Mookerji expressed the common sense of Aryanist historiography when he described Buddhism and Jainism as no more than "offshoots or sects of Hinduism," citing Vincent Smith to buttress his position. Mookerji, *Fundamental Unity of India,* 44.

115. See, for example, K. S. Singh, *The Scheduled Tribes* (Delhi: Oxford University Press, 1994). The Siddis "are believed to be of African origin, and to have been brought to India by the Portuguese towards the end of the seventeenth century, presumably as slaves" (1077). The cursory historical material presented by Singh draws on R. E. Enthoven, *The Tribes and Castes of Bombay* (Bombay: Government Printing Office, 1922).

116. D. N. Kundra, *New Text Book History of India,* quoted in Avril Powell, "Perceptions of the South Asian Past: Ideology, Nationalism, and School History Textbooks," in

Nigel Crook, ed., *The Transmission of Knowledge in South Asia: Essays on Education, Religion, History, and Politics* (Delhi: Oxford University Press, 1996), 202.

117. Jawaharlal Nehru, *The Discovery of India,* ed. Robert I. Crane (Garden City, N.Y.: Anchor, 1960), 39.

118. Ibid., 38. This was, it turns out, a much more realistic view than Kosambi's notion of a cataclysmic race war (Damodar Dharmanand Kosambi, *An Introduction to the Study of Indian History* [Bombay: Popular Book Depot, 1956]).

119. Ibid.,39.

120. Ibid., 40.

121. Ibid., 43.

122. Rabindranath Tagore, "The Call of Truth," *Modern Review* 30.4 (1921): 432.

123. Keshub Chunder Sen, "Philosophy and Madness in Religion," in *Keshub Chunder Sen's Lectures in India* (London: Cassell, 1901), 322–26 (emphasis added).

124. Swami Vivekananda, *The Complete Works of the Swami Vivekananda,* 9 vols. (Calcutta: Advaita Ashrama, 1964–97), 3:276.

125. Dayananda Saraswati, *The Light of Truth: English Translation of Swami Dayananda's Satyartha Prakasha,* trans. Ganga Prasad Upadhyaya (Allahabad: Kala, 1960), 248.

126. Ibid.

127. Modern Hinduism was regarded by the leaders of the Arya Samaj as a degenerate form of the Vedic religion, and indeed members of that organization were asked to identify themselves to the census takers as "Aryas," not Hindus, to signify their distance from not only idolaters but from other reform movements that Dayananda disliked. See Saraswati, *Light of Truth,* 548–49; and Christophe Jaffrelot, *The Hindu Nationalist Movement in India* (New York: Columbia University Press, 1996), 17. Shortly after the 1911 Census, the Arya Samajists reversed their self-designation, declaring themselves Hindus instead of Aryas, moved, it seems, by practical considerations of dealing with the colonial regime (Christophe Jaffrelot, "The Genesis and Development of Hindu Nationalism in the Punjab: From the Arya Samaj to the Hindu Sabha, 1875–1910," *Indo-British Review* 21.1 [1989]: 3–40).

128. Aurobindo Ghose, *Speeches* (Calcutta: Arya, 1948), 76–77.

129. Ibid., 79–80.

130. Har Bilas Sarda, *Life of Dayananda Saraswati: World Teacher* (Ajmer: 1946), 170–72.

131. Bankimchandra Chatterjee, *The Abbey of Bliss: A Translation of Bankim Chandra Chatterjee's Anandamath,* trans. Nares Chandra Sen-Gupta (Calcutta: Neogi, 1906), 36–37.

132. Stephen Hay, ed., *Sources of Indian Tradition* (New York: Columbia University Press, 1988), 2:138, quoting T. W. Clark, trans., *Anandamath,* pt. 4, ch. 8.

133. Ibid.

134. Pictet, *Les origines indo-euopéennes,* 3:537.

135. Sugata Bose and Ayesha Jalal, *Modern South Asia: History, Culture, Political Economy* (New York: Routledge, 1998), 121.

136. Bal Gangadhar Tilak, *The Orion: Or, Researches into the Antiquity of the Vedas* (1893; Poona: Tilak, 1955), 1.

137. Tilak, *Orion*, 211, 220; and Bal Gangadhar Tilak, *The Arctic Home* (1903; Poona: Tilak, 1956), 386. Tilak, while denouncing Western education, did not hesitate to ransack the classicist and Orientalist archives to make his case. Of course, he could not even have conceptualized his case in global racial terms if it had not been for the power and reach of those archives. He was especially drawn to F. Max Müller, *India: What Can It Teach Us? A Course of Lectures Delivered before the University of Cambridge* (New York: Funk and Wagnalls, 1883).

138. Bal Gangadhar Tilak, *Srimad Bhagavadgita Rahasya,* trans. Bhalchandra Sitaram Sukthankar, 2 vols. (Poona: Tilak, 1935), 2:713.

139. Stanley D. Wolpert, *Tilak and Gokhale: Revolution and Reform in the Making of Modern India* (Berkeley: University of California Press, 1962), 43, 67.

140. Tilak, *Journey to Madras, Ceylon, and Burma,* quoted in Wolpert, *Tilak and Gokhale,* 135.

141. Quoted in Wolpert, *Tilak and Gokhale,* 61. This was in the context of the heated debates over the Age of Consent Bill about the minimum legal age at which a girl could be married. Hindu nationalism has always been directed as much at the "enemies" within as without, a sign of its double paranoia.

142. Schwab, *Oriental Renaissance,* 4.

143. Bruce Graham, too, places the roots of Hindu nationalism in the late nineteenth century (B. D. Graham, *Hindu Nationalism and Indian Politics: The Origins and Development of the Bharatiya Jana Singh* [Cambridge: Cambridge University Press, 1990], 44). Gyanendra Pandey, "Which of Us Are Hindus?" in Pandey, ed., *Hindus and Others: The Question of Identity in India Today* (New Delhi: Viking, 1993), and Christophe Jaffrelot, *The Hindu Nationalist Movement in India,* 25, consider the 1920s the starting point of Hindu nationalism.

144. Gramsci coined the term and meant something entirely different by it than the Hindu nationalists, but the molecular diffusion of a new humanism, the attempt by the bourgeoisie to become the national class, and the valorization of civil society have important parallels with Gramsci's concept (David Forgacs, "National-Popular: Genealogy of a Concept," in *Formations of Nation and People* [New York: Routledge and Kegan Paul, 1984], 83–98).

145. Vinayak Damodar Savarkar, *Hindutva: Who is a Hindu?,* 5th ed. (Bombay: Veer Savarkar Prakashan, 1969), 135.

146. Ibid.

147. Ibid., 32, 82.

148. Ibid., frontispiece.

149. Ibid., 5. Savarkar's idea has become canonical; see *The Manifesto of the All-India Bharatiya Jana Sangh* (New Delhi: 1951), 3: "Bharat Varsha . . . is and has been through the ages a living organic whole." One may trace here the influence on Indian thinkers of Johann Gottfried Herder via Johann Kaspar Bluntschli. See Jaffrelot, *The Hindu Na-*

tionalist Movement in India, 53–54, though he does not make the connection back to Herder.

150. Savarkar, *Hindutva,* 42–43.

151. Ibid., 141 (emphasis added).

152. Ibid., 137–38 (emphasis added).

153. M. S. Golwalkar, *We, or, Our Nationhood Defined* (Nagpur: Bharat Prakashan, 1939).

154. Ibid., 22.

155. Golwalkar, *We,* 19, quoting J. K. Bluntschli, and 59, respectively.

156. Ibid., 38.

157. Savarkar, *Hindutva,* 84–85, a definition no less fanciful than those in use in Europe that purported to find in the Dorians the descendants of primeval Nordic peoples or in the speakers of the "Indo-European family" one ancestral tribe that diffused in different directions but nonetheless maintained a prediasporic memory in its myths.

158. Golwalkar, *We,* 47–48.

159. Savarkar's piece appeared in the *Hindu Outlook,* October 12, 1938; the editorials published were in the *Hindu Outlook,* November 2 and November 30, 1938, and in *Mahratta,* November 6, 1939. All are quoted in Jaffrelot, *The Hindu Nationalist Movement in India,* 51–52 n. 174.

160. Golwalkar, *We,* 35 (emphasis added).

161. It should be remembered that racist thought is simultaneously communitarian and hierarchical.

162. Unfortunately, Jaffrelot makes too much of this distinction. The very notion of a "traditional" Indian xenology is a modern construction that makes sense only in a global comparative framework. In Europe, biological racism constituted only a small part of the spectrum of racist thought. See Victor Kiernan, *The Lords of Humankind: Black Man, Yellow Man, White Man in an Age of Empire* (Boston: Little, Brown, 1969) on the transfer of class into race stereotypes in the course of the nineteenth century; Theodore W. Allen, *The Invention of the White Race* (London: Verso, 1994) on the role of history and politics in influencing racial typecasting; and, most importantly, George L. Mosse on the preponderance of "racial mysticism" over strictly biological notions even in the interwar years: "The perimeters of racial thought are as elusive and slippery as the ideology as a whole"; and "perhaps racism was . . . so effective just because it was so banal and eclectic." (*Towards the Final Solution: A History of European Racism* [Madison: University of Wisconsin Press, 1985], 235, 236).

163. Bharatiya Itihasa Sankalana Yojana, "Scientists Tracing India's History through Saraswati," *India West,* October 30, 1998. The "All-India Organizing Secretary" of this group, Haribhau Chintaman Vaze, is a chemist and a member of the RSS. He is one of more than one hundred researchers attempting to reinterpret Indian history by tracing the course of the river Saraswati, now said to be buried several miles below the surface of the Rajasthan desert. See, also, Shrikant G. Talageri, *The Aryan Invasion Theory: A Reappraisal* (New Delhi: Aditya Prakashan, 1993).

164. Bharatiya Itihasa Sankalana Yojana, "Scientists Tracing India's History through Saraswati."

165. Navnita Chadha Behera, "End of History," *HIMAL: South Asia* 9 (1996): 41–42; Gyanendra Pandey, "The Civilized and the Barbarian: The 'New' Politics of the Late Twentieth Century India and the World," in Pandey, *Hindus and Others*, 1–23.

166. Tanika Sarkar, "Educating the Children of the Hindu Rashtra: Notes on RSS Schools," *South Asia Bulletin* 14.2 (1994): 10–15.

Andrew E. Barnes

Aryanizing Projects,

African "Collaborators,"

and Colonial Transcripts

■ This essay examines the writings of European colonizers in Nigeria over a period of approximately fifty years (1900–1950) in relation to the search for indigenous groups who would collaborate in various ways with colonial social, political, and economic projects. I examine the writings of a specific set of Europeans, in this instance colonials, not so much for what they reveal about the differences Europeans postulated between themselves and the African peoples they sought to subordinate, but for what these writings reveal about the affinities some Europeans posited between themselves and the Africans whose collaboration they sought. The search for collaborators encompassed more than merely transporting a racialist discourse developed both in Europe and India into what would seem distinctly unsuitable territory, namely Africa. It also meant the unfolding of a polemic between missionaries and administrators whose varied perspectives on the colonial project, and the particular Africans who could best be relied on to further it, evince the universalizing power of the racialist ideas then hegemonic in the European academic world. The debate also attests to the flexible uses to which these ideas could be put. The essay further argues that European writers "on the ground," in this case colonial northern Nigeria, described Africans differently from European writers in the metropole, without, however, discarding the categories generated at "home." The latter may have exploited every opportunity to see the African as the Other.

The former, concerned with identifying and promoting African collabora-tors, tended to exempt specific groups from such characterizations, usually by granting an affinity with Europeans which made those groups "excep-tions" to the rule about Africans. In the process, a fascinating three-way "interchange" of ideas opened up between the Europeans on the ground, European metropolitan interlocutors, and potential African collaborators. This interchange was never explicit, but it is arguably crucial to the de-velopment of the colonial discourse, not to mention anthropology and notions of African modernity. Writings on European racism in Africa fre-quently miss this dimension.

Orientalism as Colonial Knowledge:
The Application of the Aryan Model in Nigeria

The affinities colonial writers granted to some Africans owed a substantial debt to British ideas about the peoples and cultures of the Indian subconti-nent. This point is worth mentioning here at the beginning for it helps locate the discussion below within the broad scholarly debates concerning the nature of European racism and colonialism and also points to these debates' global dimension. British writing on northern Nigeria made use of Orientalist discourse in two related ways. First, Orientalist constructions served for British writers as a palette of characteristics for the portrayal of African peoples and institutions. Racial stereotypes and cultural maxims developed to explain the course of Indian history, now saw secondary duty in narratives relating the history of northern Nigeria. The region was pic-tured as part of Britain's Muslim, that is, its "Eastern" empire, the assump-tion being that Britons and other Europeans had arrived in an area already in the throes of colonization by peoples moving in from the northeastern edge of the Sudan. At issue in the various narratives was not the inherent inferiority or barbarism of the aboriginal "Bantu" (read Dravidian) popu-lation. Rather, the point of contention was whether the racial virtues asso-ciated with the "invaders from the East" were Aryan (read Hindu) or Semit-ic (read Muslim) in origin, Aryan clearly signaling the higher affinity.[1] Christian missionaries, reacting to the limits on their proselytizing that the positive embrace of Orientalism by government officials dictated, re-sponded in turn by subjecting indigenous political and cultural institutions to critiques that drew on the ideas of leading nineteenth-century "Indo-phobes" such as Charles Grant and James Mill.[2]

Secondly, colonial writers made use of the Orientalist discourse through what David Ludden has labeled "colonial knowledge,"[3] in this case a positivistic conventional wisdom about the unavoidably negative outcomes of various strategies of colonial development. This surfaced most obviously in the insistence of colonial administrators that the profusion of "bush" schools was creating a "babu" class in Nigeria. Less obvious, but just as pernicious, was the case made by missionaries that the government's policy of indirect rule was institutionalizing a Brahmin-like priestly caste in Nigeria.

Making the case that an African people were actually "Easterners," constituted one way to present this group as an exception and thus worthy of being considered as potential collaborators. As appropriated by colonial writing on northern Nigeria, Orientalism marked a starting point for the European explanation of cultural contact with local peoples. Arguments for exceptionalism represented the chief intellectual strategy used to justify such contact. As such, a study of the formulation and application of this type of argument can reveal a great deal about European aspirations regarding interracial collaboration, and it ultimately gives insight about how much Europeans felt such aspirations were met.

Scholars specializing in the study of race relations, that is, those most conscious of how racist intellectual constructions have applied in specific contexts, have often taken note of arguments for exceptions, but have dismissed them as simply serving the further promotion of racism. St. Clair Drake, for example, points out how even in the heyday of scientific racism, sociological literature admitted the existence of "exceptional" people of color who disproved the generalizations made about those of African ancestry.[4] Kenneth King, discussing the reception of Booker T. Washington's educational ideas in Britain, makes mention of Sir Harry Johnston's seemingly paradoxical evaluation of "Negro colleges" in his *The Negro in the New World*. At once castigating them for their failure to produce much needed supplies of "intelligent field hands," he conceded that those schools did well enough training the "few geniuses" among people of African descent.[5] As these examples suggest, the acknowledgment of African-heritage exceptions to the stereotypes has occurred most commonly in rhetorical formulations that reinforce exactly those stereotypes. The prevalence of arguments of exceptionalism as props to broader arguments for racial difference perhaps serves as the best explanation for the scholarly blind spot with regard to the use of these arguments as vehicles for racial affinity across the colonial divide.

Yet such arguments did occur, and there are at least two reasons for distinguishing them from their more prevalent kin. First, as suggested above, is the role they played in the intellectual rationales used by European colonials to build relations with colonized peoples. Arguments for exceptionalism often lay at the heart of development schemes. They allowed colonials to "have their cake and eat it too," that is, to maintain racist stereotypes in general, while simultaneously championing the cause of a specific subgroup. One difference between the Europeans who went to the colonies and those who stayed home is that the former felt some confidence about their ability to negotiate with indigenous peoples. Some perceived affinity, or shared trait with those peoples usually marked the source of this confidence. The majority of the indigenous population, of course, did not exhibit this shared characteristic. Indeed, its very rarity justified its cultivation. Neither did this shared trait grant any sort of equality between the colonizer and the colonized, though it did provide a foundation on which equality might evolve over time.[6] Most important, the shared trait needed to have sufficient magnitude to become the starting point for future interracial collaboration. Thus, for administrators in northern Nigeria, the assumption that, like themselves, the Muslim emirs hailed from "ruling races," in fact in some instances were "Aryans," supported their hopes for the latter's willing cooperation in "indirect rule." The missionaries, for their part, were equally certain that an Augustinian elect existed within the African population who, once having heard the call of "the Word," would step forward to join the missionaries in Christianizing the continent.

The fact that colonials placed so much faith in the potential of some shared trait to bridge the chasms separating them from indigenous peoples suggests the second reason for studying colonial thinking on the subject of exceptionalism. This thinking provides insight on the guises colonized people assumed in order to negotiate with colonials. Colonial declarations about certain similarities between the two groups gave Africans an idea of how to behave when around certain kinds of colonials. The articulated expectations of colonials, as distinct from their articulated frustrations, were rarely based on experience of actual interaction with indigenous peoples. Rather these expectations usually emerged out of the search for a set of behaviors that, in a European setting, supposedly reflected a specific mind-set. For example, missionaries looked for the disdain for indigenous cultural institutions that they associated with righteousness, while administrators sought out the distaste for intergroup social interaction, which they took as a sign of natural breeding. It did not take the chosen Africans long to pick up on such cues and to turn them to their own advantage.

Several factors make the corpus of colonial writing on northern Nigeria an excellent source for the study of colonial depictions of African collaborators. Foremost among them is the discourse's intensity and its level of sophistication. Because they saw the future of a prized colony at stake, perhaps nowhere else in Africa did colonials exhibit as much ardent advocacy of their protégés' capacities, and equally important, as much vehement denunciation of the capacities of the protégés of the opposing set of colonials and missionaries.

Significantly, the discourse turned on the characterization not of the "untouched" indigene, but of the African already "coated" with what was identified as "civilization." Colonials agreed that the assault of the modern world had doomed local so-called traditional societies. There also existed broad consensus with the notion that climate and the like mitigated against a more than supervisory role for Europeans in bringing local societies into the twentieth century, and that Africans trained by Europeans would have to perform the bulk of the task. The confrontation arose over which group of Africans would undertake it.

On one side stood colonial administrators who favored indirect rule through existing political institutions. These administrators celebrated the natural ruling abilities of local, predominantly Muslim elites, while condemning, as a form of pestilence, African Christian converts who migrated into the region.[7] On the other side stood Christian missionaries who pushed for the introduction of Western values and institutions through the vehicle of Christian conversion. Missionaries looked on African converts as proof of the level of civility an African could achieve once given a chance. For them, Muslim emirs represented slave raiders who continued to hold the rest of the region's inhabitants in a backward thralldom.[8]

Guiding the war of words between the administrators and missionaries was a political battle over the entry of Christian missions into Muslim-controlled territories. From the beginning the colony missions were denied such entry. Administrators characterized the political situation as too unstable to permit Christian proselytizing. Missionaries never conceded this argument. They remained convinced that behind this stance hid a determination to keep Christianity out of the region. Thwarted in Nigeria, missionaries turned to a lobbying effort at the Colonial Office in London, a step that appeared to bear fruit in 1927, when the new Governor-General of

Nigeria, Graeme Thomson, agreed to permit limited Christian access to Muslim territories.[9] During the rest of the colonial era, administrators continued to devise strategies to limit the proselytizing of missionaries in the Muslim territories, rendering the missions' 1927 victory more apparent than real.[10]

Even before Thomson's decision, the battle over Christian proselytization, and implicit in it the battle over African collaborators, had been outrun by events. By the 1920s, Africans determined the cultural exchange between themselves and Europeans. For Muslim elites, faced with the program of political acculturation implicit in the policy of "indirect rule," this mostly involved successful resistance to administrative initiatives.[11] More significant in terms of creating new cultural dynamics in the region was the arrival of large numbers of Christians from Nigeria's Southern Province and the development of southern Christian enclaves. Attracted by the opportunities that the railroad's extension from the coast to major regional cities created, and by the discovery of tin on the Jos (Bauchi) plateau, ever increasing numbers of Christian southerners made the trek northward beginning around 1910. Once there, they began to challenge the authority of both the Europeans and the Muslim elite.[12] They also provided the local inhabitants with an introduction to Western civilization different from that envisioned by either group of colonials.[13]

Colonial writing recognized an African capacity to frustrate European initiatives; it did not recognize an African ability to take the initiative away from the Europeans. Thus the discourse among colonials never took direct cognizance of the fact that Africans had seized control of the cultural agenda. Undesired African responses to European actions were collectively discussed under the rubric of "lying." The work of James C. Scott has already called attention to the relationship between charges of lying by politically dominant groups and acts of resistance by politically subordinated ones. British writing on northern Nigeria suggests that Scott's point can be taken further, toward a more nuanced appreciation of the role of subordinated elites in manipulating what Scott calls the "public transcript" to their own advantage. Scott's work assumes a relatively high level of political naïvité on the part of subjected groups. Yet the Muslim and Christian elites who competed for influence over affairs in colonial northern Nigerian were anything but politically naive. Habituated to dominating others themselves, individual members of both groups became increasingly more adept over the years at inserting themselves into the political spaces between the African underclasses and the European overlords. A key ingredient in the success of those who did gain the right to play intermediaries was an ability to turn European cultural projections to their own advantage. As colonial writers complained, Africans quite easily and quickly figured out what Europeans wanted to see and hear, and they then masked their true ambitions within these disguises. The colonial writers assured their readers that any "old hand" could figure out such ruses. But the question that motivated most of their texts was not whether an African could be caught in a lie, but whether he or she could be convinced voluntarily to tell a European the truth, the latter act signaling the desired basis for future collaboration. Later generations of colonial-era writers remained convinced of the existence of true collaborators. They often presented these affirmations in the context of an explanatory justification of acts of lying.

Aryans, Semites, and Bantu

Administrators took the field second in northern Nigeria, but they immediately assumed command of their contest with missionaries. The Church Mission Society (CMS) had sent out an expedition with the goal of converting the caliph in Sokoto even before the official outbreak of hostilities between the British and the Fulani emirs. The expedition of the "Hausa Party" of 1900 proved an embarrassing failure, the missionaries getting no further than Kano, and only just escaping from that city with their lives.[14] This failure partially allowed the colonial regime, which came into existence that same year, to insist that Muslim lands were unsafe and thus should remain closed to unprotected Christian evangelists. As pressure from the missions to open the emirates increased, administrators progressively, and revealingly, defended the position that in accepting the allegiance of the emirs, Sir Frederick Lugard — conqueror and first High Commissioner of the North — had given his word of honor never to compromise the integrity of Islam in their territories. The emirs had continued to honor their pledges of allegiance, the argument went. How then could His Majesty's government repay such loyalty with an affront such as the one signaled by permitting Christian missionaries to proselytize in the emirs' territories? The idea of keeping the emirates free of Christian missions as a question of British honor did not prove particularly persuasive for any group other than the administrators. And its sway with the latter mostly reflected their conviction that what they were about in the region was preserving aristocratic civilization.[15]

It is pointless to try to distinguish the administrators' enthusiasm for Islam from their fascination and identification with the elites they found in place on arrival. It was not Islam as such, but the aristocratic society they saw Islam as promoting that they sought to nurture. Here, on the semiarid margins of the world's greatest desert, administrators saw an opportunity to (re)create a perfect aristocracy, one free of the corrupting influences of, to use Lugard's term, "traders."[16] For them, the Fulani, the Kanuri, and the other Muslim ruling elites of the Sudan were, like the administrators' Norman ancestors (and the various elites of northern India), "warrior races," bred to rule. Unfamiliar with the ways of the West, these elites needed protection, especially from the predations of Christian southerners, until they learned the ways of a world dominated by the so-called traders.[17]

These sentiments help explain the two related principles on which administrators built their case for the exceptional qualities of the Muslim elite as collaborators. First was an unwavering commitment to the emirs as superior to all alternatives. As late as 1936, a recently arrived governor, Sir Bernard Bourdillon (1935–43), warned northern administrators that "I dislike the habit of hoisting an Emir onto a pedestal and leaving him there."[18] Both Robert Heussler and Henrika Kuklick have argued that behind this commitment was an empathy for "ruling races," which constituted an aspect of the institutional mentality of the Colonial Service.[19] Sir Ralph Furse, who controlled appointments to the Colonial Service from before World War I to the years following World War II, was convinced of the existence of such a thing as "natural-born rulers," and that these were the kind of men who should serve as the proconsuls of the British Empire. He reserved the prize postings to northern Nigeria for the men who to his mind best realized his values.

Ruling races became ruling races because something in their blood gave them the power of command. This principle held true even if the performance of the contemporary scion of some line left something to be desired. Ancestry was the primary reason why the Fulani and the Kanuri were considered exceptions to the generally held belief that Africans had no capacity of governing themselves. Indirect rule might not work with other ethnic groups, but it could with these two because something in their genetic makeup gave them the ability to govern. Habits of rule and ancestry surfaced as constants in the arguments put forward by administrators. Over the years, these arguments continued to build on Orientalist constructs but, reflecting changing intellectual sensibilities, became progressively more positivistic. Four examples provide a sense of the progression.

The first comes from Flora Shaw, Lugard's wife, and, at the time, the London *Times'* star foreign correspondent. Lugard had conquered the Sokoto caliphate, the empire that made up most of the territory of the province, without authorization from London. In defense of his actions Shaw wrote *A Tropical Dependency: An Outline of the Ancient History of the Western Soudan, with an Account of the Modern Settlement of Northern Nigeria* (1905). Here she explained the history of the Sudanic belt as the history of superior races forcing inferior ones to the region's margins. In general, the superior races could be identified as coming from the desert, where they had been "modified by intercourse with the white pressure from the north." They in turn forced out the inferior races, whom she associated with the "diminutive men," "the dwarfs," discovered by Stanley in the "impenetrable regions of barbarism and equatorial Africa."[20] Thus, even before the Fulani appeared and conquered the "finer" black races of the western Sudan, the latter had already conquered and marginalized their inferiors:

> In the later history . . . of every one of the superior black kingdoms which established themselves upon the borders of the desert from Kordofan to the Atlantic, there is to be found at some point in the description the information that to the south of this country lies the country of the "Lemlems," or it may be the "Yem-yems," or the "Dem-dems," or the "Rem-rems" or the "Gnem-gnems," and after the double name comes invariably the same explanation, "who eat men."[21]

In light of the latter debate about the racial origins of the Fulani, it is worth commenting that Shaw made it clear that the above mentioned "white pressure" was Aryan in nature. After going through several possible explanations for the origins of the Fulani, she comes to the "theory which seems most generally received and most logically supported." This theory was that "the origin of the Fulani people must be sought in India." She then relates the gloss of a "M. de Lauture" on the myth that the Fulani sprang from, "a marriage of a Hindu, who entered the Soudan by way of Egypt, with the female of a chameleon." M. de Lauture took the legend to mean that the Fulani were the "outcome of a union of Hindu stock with different tribes of the Soudan, in this way accounting for the great diversity of their characteristics."[22]

According to Shaw, the rise of the Fulani had resulted from their embrace of Islam. Yet once in power, they had gone into decline, the slave trade proving too great a drug for even this devout people to withstand: "Under Dan Fodio and Bello the conquering armies of the Fulani were enjoined to spread the true faith and to convert the pagans to Islam. At a later period it was found more profitable to leave the pagans in a condition in which it was lawful to make slaves and to exact tribute, and Fulani wars degenerated into little more than slave-raiding expeditions."[23] The Fulani became so corrupt that they began to raid and sell their own peasantry into slavery.[24]

Shaw was writing too soon after the event to have any proof that British intervention had set the Fulani on the right path. She implies, though, that not much beyond an inhibition of a self-destructive instinct toward slaving was needed to set the Fulani on a trajectory toward British-style parliamentarianism. After noting the resemblance between the "feudal system" of the Fulani and that of "the northern nations in Europe in the early portion of the Middle Ages," she goes on to find proof of the Fulani "desire for self-government" in the "constitution of Bida" by which the emirate of Nupe was governed. Here the emir was advised by a "council of princes" not unlike the English House of Lords, as well as a "council of notables, corresponding in some degree to our own House of Commons."[25]

C. L. Temple, who arrived with Lugard and then went on to serve as Acting Governor and then Lieutenant-Governor of the North (1911–17), provides the second example. Temple took a less romantic, and more eugenic, tack than Shaw. In *Native Races and Their Rulers* (1917), Temple characterized "ruling races" by their capacity for self-control and subject races by their lack of it, beginning what he called a "sociological and ethnological" map of Nigeria by celebrating the Fulani's "stiff upper lip":

> We have in the Emirate of Sokoto a good example of the effects of Islam at their best. The tenets of this creed appear to have appealed especially to the naturally haughty, reserved, and serious character of the Filane, a Semitic race allied to the Arabs and Jews, and at Sokoto and its neighbourhood we find in large numbers Muslims who carry out in the strictest manner the spirit as well as the letter of the Koran and the Commentaries. ... No act of religious fanaticism has yet occurred among the people, on

the contrary they have been particularly law-abiding and have shown real loyalty to the Government on more than one occasion.[26]

Temple goes on to illustrate how the admixture of Negro blood alters the local disposition in the direction of a lack of discipline: "Leaving Sokoto and preceding South, say to Kano, the characteristics alter, there is more intermixture with Negro blood, they are less austere, their bodies are less attenuated, they look much happier, what they lose in refinement they gain in vivacity and the picturesque."[27] Once past Kano, "there is more rude savage display and less courtly dignity, and the people get less reserved and more open in their speech. This is sometimes taken as indicating a bolder, franker habit of mind. But . . . what is really indicated is a more rudimentary mode of life, thought, and greater absence of self-control."[28]

Beyond Muslim lands, in the mountainous region just north of the Niger-Benue Rivers, the indigenes, devoid of "Semitic blood" approach "rather toward that of the negro, but as yet, they are not by any means pure negroes, but rather negroid." Temple speculated that probably the home of the Bantu race was to be found just to the north of the Benue on the Bauchi Plateau and opined that "for the most part they are extremely, almost absolutely, primitive."[29] One measure of self-control being clothing, Temple goes on to observe of the "hill pagan" of the Jos (Bauchi) Plateau:

> His body smeared with red clay, his hair matted and stiffened with grease . . . nothing at all resembling clothes on his body, unless it be a goatskin hung over his buttocks giving him the appearance of a tail; his highly developed muscles forming a series of rippling convex curves all over his burly frame, a good specimen of the natives of these parts fills in reality the frame of the ideal savage of the imagination.[30]

On the other side of the Niger-Benue resided the "denizens of the forest belt . . . the real aborigines . . . negroes of the most primitive description." Finally, further south near the coast, contact is made with Christianized Africans, the bête noire of colonial administrators. On the "actual coast," trade with Europeans, bringing with it opportunities for acquiring cloth and ornaments and contact with the missionaries, "[has] raised these people very greatly in the material side, and among them are to be found some who have advanced intellectually also, though not I fear . . . on lines which will lead them very far."[31]

The third example moves beyond eugenics to anthropology. Sir Richmond Palmer was another of the men who arrived with Lugard. During the 1920s, as Lieutenant Governor of northern Nigeria, Palmer fought a ferocious but losing battle against administrators in Lagos, the colonial capital, who wanted to further integrate the government of the northern and southern provinces and so reduce the priority given in the north to the spread of Islam. During his almost thirty years in northern Nigeria, Palmer compiled a treasure trove of myths and legends about the region's past. After leaving, he arranged to have them published. In his introductions to these compilations, Palmer explains the motivation behind his actions. Like Temple, Palmer identifies the Fulani as being of Semitic descent, describing them as the "half-breed" result of the union of Phoenician fathers and Berber mothers.[32] Like Shaw, however, Palmer was convinced of the Aryan pedigree of one local elite, in this case the Kanuri, who ruled the kingdom of Kanem-Bornu. Distinct from both his predecessors, Palmer sought to prove his case scientifically, through linguistic analysis. As he argues in the introduction to his *The Bornu, Sahara, and Sudan* (1936), there existed linguistic proof that the rulers of Kanem-Bornu originated in Iran:

> The name Bornu is a general term for an eastern group of Iranian Barbars who came into Africa via the Horn of Africa and the Red Sea before the Christian era, then gradually spread west to the Atlantic. It was . . . as Egyptian or Greek plurals of these races' own word denoting their warrior caste, that *Barbarata* and *Barburoi*, reduplicated forms of *bar*, an Indo-European word for 'male,' best known in the Latin form *vir*, came to mean "barbarian." Such people names as Barna (bar), Balau (bal) . . . are all compounds of *bar* (*vir*). The Bello of Adel (Adulis) were "nobles," and the Bulwas of Kanem were equally (a) "nobles," (b) "white men."[33]

To explain the obvious blackness of the white men about whom he was writing, Palmer also had recourse to science, in this instance a theory of climatic adaptation:

> The Sudan zone is . . . preeminently the zone of "mingled peoples," of miscegenation and absorption of lighter skinned northern races by the dominant and darker races more adapted physically to climate and environment. This latter process is rapid. In three or four generations the type of the lighter-skinned ancestor disappears. Fantastic as it may seem to the casual observer who judges from physical appearance, there is

often no good reason to doubt the substantial truth of a Sudanese notable's statement that he is descended from a Syrian Ummayid or an Abbasid Caliph of Baghdad.[34]

Palmer's determination to save the north from southern encroachment was tied to his perception of the Sudan as a vast natural attic storing the cultures of the ancient Near East: "The Sudan . . . has preserved—though often doubtless in an attenuated or distorted form—much that once belonged to the ancient world: for it contains the living cultural residuum of very much that was characteristic of Babylon or Nineveh, Ophir, Tarshish or Punt, Egypt or Carthage."[35] The racial characteristics of these cultures' carriers having "rapidly become recessive," their Indo-European origins would not easily be recognized. Thus

> the casual traveller seeing in a compound of some remote African village a pile of sand and on the top of it two earthen platters on one of which is painted a rude cross, would not surmise that the pile of sand was a pyramid or Brahmin "fire-altar," and that the painted cross was the equivalent of the small golden spirit of Prajapati, the "world-spirit," by means of which the pious Brahman still wafts the soul of the devotee to heaven.
>
> Nor perhaps would it be suspected that the name of the petty market broker of the Hausas who battens on both seller and buyer, and thus makes his living by "facing both ways"—the market broker called Dan Baranda—is of similar origin to that of Zeus Labarandeus, the Greek deity of ancient Crete. Both names come from the sacred doubleheaded axe which by the Hausa is called Barandami.[36]

Palmer believed in the anthropological theory that all civilization had its beginning in the ancient Middle East and diffused outward from that point, becoming progressively more diluted as new peoples assimilated it. Implicit in this theory is a dichotomy between superior groups, who carry civilization, and inferior ones, who receive civilization.[37] As the above excerpts make clear, for Palmer, all the carriers of civilization were at least initially Aryan. Palmer's various studies and compilations of West African history all confirm the same conclusion, that for centuries African "negroes" had been receiving whatever civilization they could claim from peoples coming "from the North or East, more especially the East."[38]

The fourth example demonstrates how the illusion of scientific fact allowed the case for Muslim elite exceptionalism to be incorporated into ethnographic studies. The investigations of C. K. Meek, the first "anthropological officer" appointed by the government for the region, purported to move beyond race as a causal explanation of cultural behavior. As Meek insisted in his *The Northern Tribes of Nigeria* (1925), "the definition of a tribe must rest, in the main, on a linguistic basis."[39] The peoples of the Western Sudan were too racially mixed, he argued, to provide scientific analysis from that perspective. Thus "the most satisfactory classification we can at present offer is that based on language."[40] Keeping in mind Shaw's earlier depiction of the history of the Sudanic belt as a story of mixed races (i.e., those "modified by white pressure from the desert") forcing out less mixed races (i.e., Bantu), before being forced out themselves by Aryans, one can appreciate that Meek was following form in describing the history of northern Nigeria as a region where tribal groups of mixed descent were conquered by tribes of less mixed descent before being conquered in turn by peoples of pure descent. What was new with him was the notion that descent should be calculated from the presence or absence of a written language. As his study of the Jukun, published in 1931, explained, the group constituted a "Hamitic or half-Hamitic" race, these terms signifying a people whose language retained the ideational content if not the grammatical form of the written language of ancient Egypt. The Jukun had carved out a kingdom for themselves among "Bantu" speakers, primitives who had never had a written language. The Jukun in turn were forced into obscurity by the Fulani, a group of Hamites who had to a "remarkable" extent retained their "proto-Egyptian" appearance, which went along with their role as the scholars and historians of Islam in the western Sudan.[41]

Administrators identified the sense of empowerment converts mistakenly perceived in Christianity as the source of most of Nigeria's social ills. The "delusions of grandeur" supposedly prompted in Nigeria's emerging "babu" class are nowhere more effectively described than in the African novels of Joyce Cary, most spectacularly in his *Mister Johnson*.[42] But Cary, who spent two tours as an assistant district officer in northern Nigeria, was only cashing in on the conventional wisdom shared among generations of northern Nigerian administrators. For example, District Officer J. F. J. Fitzpatrick (who trained Cary), in a report from rural Kabba Province dated 1920, complained that once they established a beachhead in a village, Christians terrorised the village head-men: they refused to obey the lawful orders of the properly constituted Native Authority. I have personally visited every place in the Division where a Xtian community is in being. In almost every case, 90% at least, the chief and elders complain bitterly that all the small boys and young men are turning Xtian, and that directly they do this, they scorn the orders alike of their parents and of the chief. The "teacher" becomes their leader and protector. They cast off all obedience, duty, deference, respect, responsibility to their own people, and threaten them with the "teacher." The "teacher" often dresses like a clerk and talks English — and no more need be said on that head.[43]

Former district officer Walter Crocker, in his *Nigeria: A Critique of British Colonial Administration* (1936), observed that

the boys in the South who go to schools and learn to speak pidgin English and to read and write (after a fashion) regard themselves as above the life and work of the village: they go off and swell the number of that growing class of parasites which will soon form one of the major problems in the country. They are already a problem. Every town already has its little colony of the Southern literates, the local crime centre.[44]

Note the association of education — provided overwhelmingly by mission schools — with crime, laziness, and general disrespect for authority. To administrators, Christian education was the equivalent of a modern narcotic, spreading social chaos in its wake, while the Westernized African became a combination of the Orientalist construct of the babu and, it would appear, the equally Orientalist construct of the thug (*thag*).[45] However, in Africa the criminal is pictured as one alienated from the traditional gods, as opposed to the "original" thugs who were devoted to the goddess Kali. As Governor-General Hugh Clifford explained in the context of justifying a reform of the Education Ordinance, which granted the government the authority to suppress unlicensed "bush schools" run by African converts:

Partially educated Africans . . . are more or less completely cut adrift from their fellows and their tribal and family obligations, which were of old enforced by unshakable belief in local spiritualistic and animistic superstitions. . . . they derive from the "so-called" education which has been imparted to them nothing save a notable deterioration of character and a rejection of the responsibilities and duties proper to their natural state as members of a family and tribe.[46]

Despite their alarmist qualities, administrative depictions of Christian converts are easily recognized as inversions of administrative depictions of Muslim elites. Just as the Muslims were knights, so the converts were knaves. Administrators acknowledged contact with Christianity as an empowering experience. But the only Africans seeking such empowerment were villains, in part because, as more than one administrator asserted, the Europeans who allowed them such contact were themselves "men of straw."[47] The social consequences of Christianization were not nearly as dire as the administrators had forecast, as later generations of the same group themselves admitted.[48] And more than a bit of irony lies in the fact that most of the clerks who typed out the reports containing these foreboding evaluations were Christians.[49] But the commitment to the preservation of aristocratic civilization, which they must have evinced to obtain their positions, forced administrators to see the clerks sitting on the other side of their office doors as part of a growing calamity.

Mothers against Salvation

In southern Nigeria, a forceful lobby in support of African Christians playing a major role in bringing "civilization" to other Africans was in place several decades before the British colonized the northern province.[50] Missionaries to the north did not need to add much to the existing case for the value of Christian converts as collaborators. Playing Whigs to the administrators' Tories, Indophobes to the administrators' Indophiles, they contentedly equated Christianity with modernism and insisted that those Africans most exposed to modernism, that is, converts, would best serve to introduce other Africans to the modern world. The problem for missionaries to the north was a paucity of conversions, even in the areas in which they were permitted. Administrators trumpeted this lack of success as proof of a local absence of interest in Christian evangelization. For administrators, Christianity intellectually went over the heads of local folks. As Lugard observed in his *The Dual Mandate in Tropical Africa,* Christianity's "more abstruse tenets . . . its recognition of brotherhood with the slave, the captive and the criminal, do not altogether appeal to the temperament of the negro."[51] Missionaries were thus wasting their time trying to convey a message to Africans to which the latter were oblivious.

Missionaries bought more of the administrators' rationale than they would ever admit. And this best explains why arguments for Christian evangelism in northern Nigeria took as their premise the idea that some of God's elect were "out there" and that the missionary's task was to identify them and aid in their conversion. Just as administrators insisted on the existence of "natural-born rulers," missionaries in effect insisted on the existence of "natural-born Christians," the latter wandering around in the darkness waiting for the light. Since administrators questioned the Africans' grasp of the Christian concept of compassion, missionaries made a special effort to illustrate acts of Christian charity performed by Africans as a sign of their fitness for conversion.

There were three types of Christian missions operating in colonial northern Nigeria: Protestant evangelical, Anglican (CMS), and Catholic. The term *conversion* meant something different to each mission, and in their writings, missionaries from the respective groups came to emphasize different types of "proof" that there were exceptional Africans just waiting for conversion. All the missions, however, followed similar strategies in making their cases for the exception that proved that northern Nigeria was ready for Christian evangelization. In all three instances, African (Islamic) culture was presented as maternal and old, while Christian faith was depicted as virile and young, and in all three, the testament of conversion came in the form of young men's repudiation of motherly demands.

The Protestant evangelicals who made up the Sudan United Mission (SUM) and the Sudan Interior Mission (SIM), the largest Protestant missions, saw conversion as an instantaneous transformation, and they believed contact with "the word of God" as sufficient to bring it about. Evangelical missions focused (as much as the government permitted) on itinerant preaching through interpreters, in this way seeking maximum exposure to the gospel. Their writings celebrated the power of this approach for identifying God's chosen even among Africans living in the "darkest" of conditions. In his autobiography, Roland Bingham, founder of the SIM, provides an example. After categorizing the Tangale as a people "lower than any we had ever seen," Bingham proceeds to describe their degradation:

> Men, women and children were living in nakedness. From the time they come into the world naked, until they went out of the world naked, they never possessed a piece of cloth as large as one's hand. . . . There was more than rumour in the story of their fierceness and cannibalism. They marked with a stone the place where they buried the skulls of the victims they had killed and eaten, and there were plenty of such stones around.[52]

This depiction, though, served only as a prelude to Bingham's most thrilling story of conversion. Within a year of receiving missionaries in their midst, Bingham narrates, several young Tangale men had converted. Then Satan began his counterattack, leading two old "witches" (mothers), who were used to doing all the "cruel devilish work that went with their profession," to have all the young girls in the village declare they would never marry any Christian young man. Being "gripped by the Gospel," however, the young men had the moral strength to shout back that they would "never marry heathen women." Soon not only did the young women choose to convert but the old witches followed them. After this breakthrough, the entire village turned to Christianity.[53]

Bingham's autobiography also provides a measure of African charity. At Egbe, during a Bible conference at an unknown date, the "native converts" gave an offering of "twenty-five hundred dollars," a sum made more incredible by the fact that the wage for a "hard day's labour" was only "twenty-four cents," with women earning only half this amount. Later that same day, a missionary appealed before the same congregation for funds to print translations of the Bible in several local vernaculars, with the result that another "one hundred fifty" dollars were pledged and delivered within a month.[54] Even more spectacular were the Tangale, who, within a generation of receiving the Word, not only contributed to the mission's general fund but also sent out their own missionaries.[55]

Anglican missionaries saw conversion as an intellectual embrace of true faith. They focused their mission on the conversion of what they saw as intellectually predisposed peoples, that is, Muslims. Church Mission Society missionaries treated the Fulani as an "Eastern" race of "robbers and oppressors" and agreed with administrators that the Fulani's Muslim beliefs were genuine. The Hausa, the people conquered by the Fulani, however, were regarded as a yeoman race of "able builders, weavers and blacksmiths" who had only adopted Islam to placate their foreign conquerors.[56] The key to the conversion of the Hausa, then, was to break the back of Fulani intimidation. As the first issue of the journal edited by the Sudan Party—the CMS group that set out in 1890 to convert the Hausa—explained, the task ahead simply required interposing Europeans between Hausa and Fulani:

> Though the military skill of the fierce Fulani conquerors has reduced the Hausa to the position of a subject people, yet they are probably the best

race in Africa. Every traveller who has met with them has written of them with enthusiasm, and their capacity for good seems great. In intelligence they seem in no way inferior to the Europeans, and though brave enough when occasion requires, they seem peaceably disposed, their requirement and courtesy of manner being attractive. Unlike the Fulani they seem to have no ferocious fanaticism, and the tenets of Islam are followed in a very lax manner, and almost entirely discarded when they are away from the surveillance of their conquerors.[57]

Confronted with the reality of Hausa religious fidelity, CMS missionaries fell back on the conviction that the truth would attract those perceptive enough to appreciate it. The story of the first Anglican convert from Islam offered ample evidence for this conviction. As narrated by Dr. Walter Miller in *Audu: A Hausa Boy (A True Story)* (1904), Audu had set out on the hajj with his father, but was left stranded on the way when his father died. Christian missionaries took him in, had him visit England for a spell, and then sent him on to Mecca. Audu returned to Nigeria a Muslim, but, after a tearful encounter with his mother, narrated with Victorian embellishment by Miller, he chose Christ over Muhammad.[58]

Roman Catholic missionaries understood the task before them differently. Catholicism recognizes a distinction in status between lay person and priest, a distinction that corresponds to the level of faith. The measure of conversion for Roman Catholic missionaries was an expressed desire to join the priesthood. In those early years, no northern local is known to have made such a request. Still, one missionary found evidence to believe in the future likelihood of such a development. In the published lectures describing his trip to the Society of African Missions (SMA) outposts in West Africa, Monsignor Chabert, superior general of the order in 1926, related the story of one young convert in Kano. "Small," "homely," with few natural gifts, the fourteen-year-old still possessed above-average intelligence and an "ardent" soul. He knew how to read and taught himself the catechism. Put to a rigorous test on the latter, he passed with flying colors. Proud of his success, he asked to be baptized. The missionary asked if he had the permission of his parents. "My father is dead," the boy responded. "Would your mother consent to you becoming a Christian?" came the next question. "No." Then suddenly, after an agonizing silence, the boy won his baptism with a statement of faith strikingly similar to that expressed by Miller's

Audu: "My eternal salvation is a personal concern which only involves me. I love and respect my mother, but if she refuses the truth, she can not go to heaven. Me, I want to go there."[59]

Later, as the priests took their leave of Kano, the new convert came to see them off. His hands, arms, and shoulders were covered with the welts of a recent beating. The priests asked him what happened. Since the Catholic mission had yet to open a school in Kano, the convert had been attending a school run by the "African Church," one of the nativist sects, which Chabert described as a "new indigenous Protestant sect which permits blacks . . . up to seven wives." When asked to stand and offer prayer in class, the convert had refused, insisting that his credo made no mention of the African Church, which was neither Catholic, nor apostolic, nor Roman. At that point, the teacher beat him.[60]

Having proven the depths of both his faith and hope, the young convert next gave evidence of his *caritas*. As Chabert continued, "a young black, our hero," stricken with small pox, took refuge in the bush outside the city with a young companion similarly afflicted. The companion had also sought baptism, yet had not displayed sufficient knowledge of the catechism to merit the sacrament. Death closing in on the companion, the young convert, now characterized as "our young apostle," took it on himself to complete the former's religious instruction and then to baptize him.[61]

Monsignor Chabert's romantic tale, while useful as an example of how the Catholic mission was represented back in Europe, does not give a full sense of local Catholic missionary sensibilities. More reflective are the comments of Father André Schal, who filed the annual reports sent back to Europe through the late 1920s into the 1930s. Schal lacked Chabert's conviction that among the local population natural "apostles" awaited their discovery. His exceptional Africans were converts from the south. As Schal pointed out in his 1927 report, three-fourths of the indigenous population was Muslim and off-limits to Christian missions. As for the one-fourth open to proselytization, they were, after centuries of hiding in the mountains to escape Muslim slave raids, naked or hide-wearing "cannibals." As evidence, he passed on reports, gathered from administrators, of one tribe that ate its own family's corpses — "Fathers and mothers eating the fruit of their own insides [*entrailles*] after death has ravished them" — and of others that exchanged corpses for consumption as commodities, either from tribe to tribe, or village to village.[62]

Therefore Schal saw the future of the Catholic mission in the north as tied to the development of a laity composed of emigrant southerners. Schal pictured these as imperfect but still honest working-class people. As he noted in his 1931 report:

> As already stated, we work mostly with people from the South (Yorubas and Ibos) coming to the North to find employment, . . . They are generally reliable. Once they become Catholics they continue to come regularly to Church and a good many are sincere and loyal Christians to the ends of their lives. Some, amongst them — here as elsewhere — fall back into certain pagan practices especially as regards marriage. Numerous are the couples one encounters being only united by a simple promise instead of the Sacrament: but even amongst these, rare are the cases of a complete drawback, as even when leading a loose life they are always frequenting the Church and attending the services regularly.[63]

In their case against Christianity, administrators condemned what they identified as a social class of African converts. In their case against Islam, (Protestant) missionaries condemned what they identified as an Oriental way of life. The letterhead of the SUM, crafted around the turn of the century when the mission society came into existence, contains an emblem of a crescent moon and a cross, with a logo that poses the question, "Christ or Mohammed?" Implicit in this choice was another between West and East. Missionary rhetoric sought to explicate the dichotomy. Thus, as seen above, it equated the Oriental (Muslim) way of life with slavery. It also identified it with moral degeneration. As Karl Kumm, founder of the SUM explained in his *The Sudan: A Short Compendium of Facts and Figures about the Land of Darkness*: "Wherever Mohammedism has gone, lying and stealing and sexual diseases have spread, until certain pagan places which were clean fifteen years ago, have become syphilitic cesspools."[64]

Lastly, Islam, or at least the office of emir, was made synonymous with a species of Oriental despotism, with the depiction of its parasitical qualities traceable back to Charles Grant and with sacerdotal characteristics that went back to James Mill.[65] What is noteworthy here is the search back beyond a critique of Islam for a set of negative characteristics to neutralize the colonial administration's argument for the potential utility of the emir's office as a building block for colonial rule. As Walter Miller observed in one of the barrage of letters he wrote (which eventually forced the government to remove the Emir of Zaria in 1920):

They [the Fulani] are unprogressive, obscurantist tyrants, whose only idea is to squeeze and oppress their people. Diseased, corrupt, backward, gross and irreligious, they are an object of hatred to the far more progressive, pious, religious (but never intolerant) and industrious Hausa and Pagan. The indefatigable work of a body of Government servants who have lived out here has been largely thwarted and spoilt by this little oligarchy of miscreants.[66]

The decision of the Protestant missions to put their case against the government in the hands of the "wise ecclesiastical statesman" J. H. Oldham of the International Council of Missions, toned down the invective.[67] Under Oldham's tutelage, the missions' attack came to center on emphasizing Islam's antimodern nature. In the "Memorandum on Missionary Work in Northern Nigeria," jointly presented by the missionary societies to the new Governor-General Sir Graeme Thomson in 1927, one of the arguments made was that the British administration, "by the mere fact of its existence," had introduced ideas that "must inevitably and increasingly lead to changes in the existing order of things."[68] African societies cried out for some "spiritual" way to respond to these changes. As for the possibility that Islam might provide that spirituality, the missionaries called on the authority of the Islamicist Snouck Hurgronje to make the point that "Mohammedan law" was in "flagrant contradiction with the exigencies of the times" and that there was nothing in the history of Islam to suggest "the least sign of any hope of reform."[69]

But *modern* remained for the missionaries a synonym for *Western,* as a complaint from H. G. Farrant, a SUM missionary, to Oldham notes: "Not only are Christian Missions robbed of the opportunity of bringing Moslems into the region of Western thought, but many thousands of pagans who have no leaning to the East have been forced by isolation into the Islamic system and have become part of the world force which by instinct is antagonistic to the domination of the West."[70] The irony here is that from the beginning, administrators had tried to deflect missionary attention away from Muslim territories and toward the "thousands of pagans" in need of an introduction to Western thought. The crusading spirit among missionaries was seemingly too strong to allow them to become preoccupied with building the medical dispensaries and schools that the traditionalist communities asked for and that the government offered to subsidize. Only after the replacement of the French Catholic by an Irish Catholic mission in the 1930s triggered a scramble for converts, did the Protestant missions concentrate some of their energies on providing these long requested services.

The Anatomy of Lying

By the 1920s, few colonials were voicing the expectations of earlier generations, a fact that reflected the lack of headway made at cultural contact by either administrators or missionaries. Later colonial writings in fact reveal both a burning sense of frustration over being continually "duped" by Africans and an almost desperate insistence that no Europeans worth their salt could be manipulated by such simplistic stratagems. Still, though chastened, Europeans remained optimistic that they could find exceptional Africans to work with them. The apologia written by colonials in defense of African protégés provide the most striking examples of this optimism. With "lying" as the catchall designation for any act on the part of an African that went against European will, these writings tended to justify the protégés' "lying ways."

James C. Scott's study *Domination and the Arts of Resistance* places this phenomenon in a broader context. Scott argues the existence of a "public transcript," that is, an explicit, historical interaction between the dominating and the dominated. While politically dominant groups, like the colonials, control the public transcript, this control is subject to ongoing resistance from the dominated.[71] In doing their best to contain public discussion of African reactions to their rule under the negative rubric of lying, colonials behaved as conquering groups normally do. Likewise, in dissimulating, posturing, and otherwise adopting disguises that served to delude Europeans, Africans did what conquered groups do.[72]

The argument can be taken further than Scott proposes. As the battle between administrators and missionaries demonstrates, there is no necessary consensus within the dominant group over the public transcript. Also, Scott's one-dimensional view of the political sophistication of dominated peoples constitutes an important lacuna in his theory. Scott's work does not come to grips with interactions between colonizers and preexisting or emergent indigenous elites, dominated people cognizant of the public transcript from both perspectives. Northern Nigeria had not one but two such groups. And their examples suggest that manipulation of the public transcript from the middle, by groups who succeed in interposing themselves between the dominating and the dominated, is more significant than Scott appreciates. Last, but perhaps most important, Scott presumes such a degree of hegemonic control of the public transcript by the dominant group as to preclude anything other than a defensive reaction from the dominated. But such a level of control did not exist in every instance. At the heart of the colonial concern with African lying was an awareness of how Africans used disguises, disguises drawn from the public transcript, to further their own agendas. In sum, subordinated peoples can do more than defend themselves from the public transcript. They can exploit it for their own causes.

Whether such exploitation constitutes an example of collaboration or resistance depends on the eye of the beholder. For example, in a memorandum directed to the Colonial Office in 1915, Hans Vischer, Director of Education for the Northern Province, requested that when his education officers return home on leave, the Colonial Office pays for them to attend courses in "moral instruction" at either Oxford or Cambridge. Vischer felt that if education officers folded moral instruction into the curricula of northern schools correctly, the student might possibly progress to the point that "he would not . . . look at 'Morality' merely as a coat to be worn in the presence of Europeans." With this last point in mind, there is another way of reading Vischer's comment. Vischer, a naturalized Swiss, first appeared in northern Nigeria as a CMS missionary. After a few years he left the mission for government service, convinced that Islam, not Christianity, provided the true path forward for the African. It seems likely that when he made his comment about "morality as a coat," he had in mind the 1904 pamphlet by his former colleague Walter Miller about the conversion of Audu, the young Hausa man mentioned earlier. What still catches the eye is the cover of the pamphlet, which displays two photographs. The upper left photograph represents a younger Audu, seated, dressed in Hausa gown and hat, the very image of a young Oriental despot. The lower right picture shows an older, anglicized Audu, stalwartly standing before the camera in a Western-style tunic and trousers, with an uncovered, surprisingly full head of hair parted down the middle. As the changes of clothes and posture convey, Audu's conversion had been simultaneously from Islam to Christianity and from Oriental to Occidental. Vischer would have known Audu, would have known that for many years he remained Miller's right-hand man. But one of the truisms in the polemic between administrators and missionaries was that conversions to the other side could only be poses, "coats" donned in the presence of Europeans. Vischer had to question the sincerity of Audu's convictions if he did not want to concede that there was something to efforts, like Miller's, to westernize the African.

During his days as an assistant district officer, Joyce Cary once wrote back to his wife: "But no black man on God's earth is reliable. Let those blasted 'my brother the poor black' put that in his [*sic*] pipe. No black man is morally, or mentally, or even physically reliable. Not one can you trust. . . . I don't know about your Indian and Aryan generally. . . . But your black, your Negroid and his near relations is a broken reed."[73] Similarly, after a trying day bargaining with African ferrymen along the Benue River, the SUM missionary J. Lowery Maxwell wrote in his diary: "You don't know how sickening it is to live among lying, to walk about in a stifling cloud of lies, lies, lies, cunning and duplicity, falsehood and crookedness, apparently . . . so needless and cowardly sometimes, at others so annoying and aggravating, but so persistent . . . until you begin bitterly to say . . . we can trust nothing with a black skin on it."[74]

The racism animating these private exclamations of frustration with the African Other can be contrasted with the rationalism at work in public discussions of frustration with African collaborators. In his *Native Races and Their Rulers*, Temple frankly admitted that the Fulani had used the authority granted them by the British government to advance their own interests relative to that of both local populations and the British government itself. He recognized the lies they told to achieve these advances as a form of art, perfected for reasons of state.[75] According to him, any administrator worth his salt quickly developed proficiency in a sister art form, one he labeled the "anatomy of lies and lying," which required not just figuring out the lie but also the motivation behind it.[76] Concerning a Fulani skillful enough to successfully dupe an administrator, the latter should "immediately note that he has had to do with a village head of exceptional diplomatic and administrative powers. Such a man he will know is capable of filling positions of responsibility and trust."[77]

Temple took pains to distinguish this type of lying from the ordinary sort of duplicity. Administrators made a distinction between two kinds of Fulani: "town" Fulani, who in the course of ruling had come to interbreed with the indigenous "negro" population in a form of miscegenation, and "cattle" Fulani, who in the course of maintaining their pastoral ways had kept themselves racially pure. According to Temple, cattle Fulani, "[did] not practice the art of lying, they refrain[ed] from telling the truth, simply."[78] On the other hand, the art of lying, as practiced by the town Fulani, "lies in so mixing up absolute falsehood with truths, half truths, appropriate inaccuracies, and exaggerations, as to reduce the mind of the recipient to such a condition of bewilderment and bemusement as to render it incapable, for at least some time, of any action at all outside itself."[79] As Temple concluded: "Between the most crude processes as practised by the Cattle-Filane in abstaining from the truth altogether, and the art of lying as presented by the well-informed Filane, village or district head, there is all the difference that exist between a geometric pattern for a wall paper traced with rule and a compass and the delicate delineation of sunlight on mountain mist and sea by Turner."[80]

Walter Miller, a member of the original Hausa expedition of 1900 and patron of Audu, found himself, toward the end of his almost half-century-long residence among the Hausa, making an effort to correct his own instinct to "draw the Hausa racial face and leave out the warts."[81] Large numbers of Hausa never did convert to Anglicanism. Maintaining the fiction that the Hausa remained Muslim out of fear of the Fulani, Miller sought to explain in his *Yesterday and To-Morrow in Nigeria* (1938) why his protégés lacked the stuff to break the Fulani's Norman-like yoke. He concluded that Hausa culture short-circuited the development of the altruism from which both Christian charity and patriotism sprang. Hausa boys got married too young, he argued, the perception of other males as rivals emerging at a time when in England boys were just learning to perceive other males as friends. As a result, "The strong attachment or even deep affection which often exists between two boys or men in England, persisting from school-days on till college life is almost unthinkable among Hausa Moslems."[82] Lacking the experience of even this rudimentary form of self-transcendence, Hausa men found it impossible to think in larger terms than self:

> This serious lack of friendship between boys and men with each other
> . . . has largely been responsible for a real lack of power of combination
> in the Hausa people. . . . All that we associate with school, athletics,
> university and club life is not known or only beginning to be known.
> Such terms as "playing the game," "noblesse oblige," "the team spirit,"
> or "working for the good of the community rather than of the individual" could not be translated into the language, and would convey little
> meaning, anyhow. From this has resulted little love of country, village,
> or town in the way that Western nations think of that emotion.[83]

Miller went further in his critique of the Hausa personality. He condemned the Hausa for their love of empty pomp; for their lack of sufficient "intensity of character to 'live dangerously'"; for their conviction that "love of self is best." He acknowledged that there had always been a large criminal class in Hausa land and that "burglary is quite monotonous in its frequency."[84] As among the Fulani, among the Hausa, "all kinds of deceit and mental dishonesty are almost universal," though the Hausa, "lack[ed] the artistic ability of the Eastern to convert his mental curves into fine art."[85]

But the true cause of Miller's frustrations surfaces in the source he identifies for these "petty vices," an all-inclusive traditionalism, with its two laws or principles: "What has been inherited—whether good or bad—must be conserved and guarded without investigation or criticism"; and "Evils, not previously considered or recognized as such, should not be avoided, but endured without seeking a remedy."[86] Miller could not let go of more than forty years of insisting on the virtues of the Hausa as collaborators, however. After acknowledging that they preferred their own culture to that of Britain, Miller fell back on the idea of Fulani oppression to explain the Hausa's disinclination to adopt Western ways:

> It is hard for us to realize what the petrifying and demoralizing influence of centuries of insecurity of life from tyrants can mean; nor what it can induce of meanness in the character of a people. We have never had grinning at us the cruel stocks and the rhinoceros whip; the filthy prison, to go into which was to die; the old wells with men's bones in them, where human beings are thrown and left to rot at the whim of an Amir. . . . When the ignorant critic complains to-day of all the failures in the Hausa character, he should reflect that these vices, though only too clearly present, are often the result of fear and the over-mastering urge to avoid detection and unjust punishment.[87]

Like Temple's counterintuitive optimism that a Fulani smart enough to get away with lying was just the sort of man the government wanted in a position of authority, Miller's ultimate inability to admit Hausa indifference reveals the degree to which advocacy dictated the colonial perception of the situation. Of course their views reflected the paternalistic sentimentalism colonials were expected to maintain for "their people." But we must appreciate the substance of this sentimentalism. Temple and Miller were both defending their protégés from categorization as the Other.

The irrational lengths to which they willingly took these defenses should be recognized as an aspect of the colonial mentality. Here one must keep in mind the poses colonials themselves maintained before readers back in the metropole. To the extent to which colonies had some perceived value for communities of readers in England, that value was a function of the colonies' potential as venues for the validation of some social verity apparently discarded in the metropole itself. Thus for readers sympathetic to Britain's effort to conquer and maintain an empire, among the truths successful collaboration with Muslims would demonstrate would be the existence of ruling races and the value of leaving them to rule, instead of casting them aside as had happened to Britain's own aristocracy. The Christians who subsidized missionary endeavors wanted to read in missionary newsletters that the virtuous Christian world that once existed in Britain could be and had been established in Africa. If it could be established in the land of darkness, they hoped, it could be reestablished in Britain itself. For these audiences, the affinities colonials postulated between themselves and collaborators represented a necessary precondition to the colonial enterprise's social relevancy in the metropole. As such, advocates for a particular group of collaborators had just cause to present themselves as prospectors, seeking aid from those audiences for the development of the rich vein of gold they had discovered. The sought-after affinities surfaced in collaborators in impure form, as did social rectitude in the Fulani for Temple or evangelicalism in the Tangale for Bingham. The task before colonials, then, was to refine away these impurities, or as Miller explained it, to "indicate" the "spiritual and moral massage" that might remove the Hausa's warts and thus "produce a really noble result."[88] It was their inability to discern the nature of this spiritual and moral massage, not the continued presence of the warts, that colonials identified as the source of their frustrations. Continued faith that such a "massage" could be discovered, however, tested their own individual mettle, both for themselves and for their audiences back home.

As Miller's comment suggests, no hard-and-fast boundary existed between chemistry and alchemy in the minds of colonials. Likewise their audiences did not hold them to any exacting standards. Exactly because colonials situated the pursuit of collaborators in the context of the search for pathways back to worlds seen as lost in the metropole, expectations of success, on all parts remained low. After all, if Europeans collectively could not see the error in throwing away the world now lost, how fair was it to expect Africans collectively to perceive the potential of the world collaboration held in store for them? It was for this reason that, despite African resistance, indifference, or opportunism, colonials in northern Nigeria remained convinced that exceptional Africans would perceive and accept the superiority of European ways. Faith in a greater gleaning in the future was pervasive, and it emerged in the colonial's consciousness at moments of greatest despair. After conveying his bitterness about his boat trip on the Benue, the SUM missionary Maxwell consoled himself with the thought that "Thank God that even out here He has put His truth in some lives at least and we can see it beginning to work. Thank God that He granted to some of us to see that men are not utterly unreliable, but His light has, to some extent, lightened this darkness that was otherwise intolerable. The night is dark, but there are stars."[89]

Conclusion

It makes sense briefly to reflect on the import of this study for the various scholarly debates mentioned. In regard to the scholarship on the African as Other, the criticism here aligns with that aimed at the work of Edward Said and his students: in looking only at what metropolitan writers have to say, they ignore the dialogues that occurred between Europeans and indigenous peoples.[90] When dealing with metropolitan writers, it is perhaps best to look at their portrayals as aimed at that portion of the European audience *not interested* in experiencing contact with indigenous people. The portion of the European audience *interested* in making contact wanted to read from those who similarly believed that such contact would bear fruitful results.

As for the appropriation of Orientalist discourse by colonials writing on northern Nigeria, I have suggested that it occurred selectively and was compensatory in application. When in doubt, or when lacking an Africanist paradigm on which to build some argument — as when, for example, assessing the future impact of a government policy — colonials had recourse to an Orientalist paradigm. In this sense, Orientalism can be posed as an anterior and ultimately overlapping empiricism to anthropology. Anterior because, eventually, most of the questions earlier generations of writers sought to answer through recourse to Orientalist "knowledge," later generations sought to answer through anthropological investigations. Overlapping, because those anthropological investigations took Orientalist constructs as their starting points.

As argued here, there existed a real African interest in and curiosity about Western civilization. It is valid, then, to raise the question why the schemes developed by colonials failed to recruit more collaborators. One answer, probably the historically most significant one, is that those schemes did not offer sufficient access to have many takers. One can conclude this response from two facts: that during the early years of the colonial era colonialists sought to be as parsimonious as possible in allowing Africans contact with Europe; and because during the later years of that era, when colonialists ceased to try to control African access, the rate of appropriation of European norms increased. Another possible answer, one prompted by the above discussion, is that colonialist schemes failed to attract African collaborators because every one of these schemes, from mission station to government school, proceeded from a utopian vision not of Africa and Africans but of Europe and Europeans. Affinity implied to colonials a capacity to empathize, and what colonials most sought to discover in collaborators was a shared sense of what was wrong with the (European) world. Unlike European empires carved out in earlier centuries, those conquered in the nineteenth century had to offer at least the pretence of something for the people back home. There was, of course, the promise of economic prosperity. But alongside that, and to this point underappreciated, were hopes that new soldiers could be found for the struggle to return to some European golden age. The schemes put forward by Europeans could positively recognize Africans only to the extent to which Africans fit preexisting paradigms of social and cultural behavior extracted from collective European ideas of virtue. Thus the frontispiece of one of Miller's many memoirs presents a group photograph, with him in the center, of a collection of young African men impeccably attired in the various suits of the British gentleman. A photograph in one of Palmer's collections of Sudan stories features a Muslim official astride a horse, looking down at the world with an unmistakably aristocratic mien. Both of these images promoted the universality of an idea with only limited resonance in Britain itself: Miller's, that the upper classes should be composed of those who did well at (Christian) schools; Palmer's, that habits of rule are instinctive. They were published to reassure British audiences not that Africans were successfully taking to Western-style education or political training, but that those Africans who did successfully complete school or training looked at the world from the same perspective as did their instructors.

The idea that utopian visions drove colonials is not new, but the implications of these visions for notions of collaboration remain unexplored.[91] If the argument just made has any value, one of those implications might be that the colonialist search for affinity was hopelessly befuddled by an inability to distinguish between a collaborator's potential to cooperate and his or her potential to empathize. If we can accept Joyce Cary's novels as offering some indications of the dialectic between colonials and potential collaborators as it occurred in northern Nigeria, it was in moments of such befuddlement that racism intruded into the equation. Here, perceptions of the capacity to empathize then served as a rough guide to a potential collaborator's value, which is to say that only those Africans thought to understand genuine Europeanness were thought worthwhile collaborators. All others were dismissed as "just" Africans: the character Mr. Johnson's tragedy lay in the fact that he could not convince a colonial that he shared his pain. Racism suggested that African exceptions from the rule ultimately reinforced the rule; after all, racism constituted the medium in which both affinity and distance were measured, even in seeking collaborators. The best that any colonial could say about any African was that he or she could be like a European. Such a statement did not celebrate anything positive about Africanness. What it did was buttress the European's worldview.

Notes

ABBREVIATIONS

AHA: Arewa House Archives, Kaduna, Nigeria
CO: Colonial Office
NAK: National Archives, Keduna, Nigeria
PRO: Public Record Office, London, Great Britain
SMAC: Society of African Missions Archives, Cork, Ireland
SNP: Secretariat Northern Province

1. On British constructions of race in India, see Thomas R. Metcalf, *"Ideologies of the Raj* (Cambridge: Cambridge University Press, 1994), 66–112; Thomas R. Trautmann, *Aryans and British India* (Berkeley: University of California Press, 1997), 190–216.
2. Trautmann, *Aryans and British India,* 99–130.
3. David Ludden, "Orientalist Empiricism: Transformations of Colonial Knowledge," in Carol A. Breckenridge and Peter van der Veer, eds., *Orientalism and the Postcolonial Predicament: Perspectives on South Asia* (Philadelphia: University of Pennsylvania Press 1993), 250–78.
4. St. Clair Drake, *Black Folks Here and There: An Essay in History and Anthropology,* 2

vols. (Los Angeles: Center for Afro-American Studies, University of California, 1987), 1:23–30.

5. Kenneth James King, *Pan-Africanism and Education: A Study of Race, Philanthropy, and Education in the Southern States of America and East Africa* (Oxford: Clarendon, 1971), 49.

6. Johannes Fabian, *Time and the Other: How Anthropology Makes Its Object* (New York: Columbia University Press, 1983).

7. For administrative ideas on the development of northern Nigeria, see Robert Heussler, *The British in Northern Nigeria* (London: Oxford University Press, 1968); I. F. Nicolson, *The Administration of Nigeria, 1900–1960: Men, Methods, and Myths* (Oxford: Clarendon, 1969), pp. 124–79; J. A. Ballard, " 'Pagan Administration' and Political Development in Northern Nigeria," *Savanna* 1.1 (1972): 1–14.

8. For missionary ideas concerning the development of northern Nigeria, see E. A. Ayandele, "The Missionary Factor in Northern Nigeria, 1870–1918," in O. U. Kalu, ed., *The History of Christianity in West Africa* (London: Longman, 1980), 133–58; E. P. T. Crampton, *Christianity in Northern Nigeria* (London: Chapman, 1979), 35–78; Jan Harm Boer, *Missionary Messengers of Liberation in a Colonial Context: A Case Study of the Sudan United Mission* (Amsterdam: Rodopi, 1979), 111–217.

9. On the battle between administrators and missionaries, see Andrew E. Barnes, " 'Evangelization Where It Is Not Wanted': Colonial Administrators and Missionaries in Northern Nigeria during the First Third of the Twentieth Century," *Journal of Religion in Africa* 25.4 (1995): 412–41.

10. C. N. Ubah, "Christian Missionary Penetration of the Nigerian Emirates, with Special Reference to the Medical Missions Approach," *Muslim World* 77.1 (1987): 16–27.

11. Heussler, *The British in Northern Nigeria*, 170–91.

12. Elizabeth Isichei, *A History of Nigeria* (London: Longman 1983), 432–38; Bill Freund, *Capital and Labour in the Nigerian Tin Mines* (London: Longman, 1981); Crampton, *Christianity in Northern Nigeria*, 137–44; Heussler, *The British in Northern Nigeria*, 122–23.

13. Crampton, *Christianity in Northern Nigeria*, 138–39; Andrew E. Barnes, "Catholic Evangelizing in One Colonial Mission: The Institutional Evolution of Jos Prefecture, Nigeria, 1907–1954," *Catholic Historical Review* 84.2 (1999): 242–64.

14. Ayandele, "The Missionary Factor in Northern Nigeria," 137–42; Crampton, *Christianity in Northern Nigeria*, 37–40.

15. For arguments based on Lugard's alleged promise, see in particular the responses sent in by administrators to the query whether the restrictions on Christian proselytizing in the North were "contrary to the principles of religious toleration." These responses are contained in AHA 15246. For some discussion of the responses in this file, see Barnes, "Evangelization Where It Is Not Wanted," 429–32. For the debate over whether indeed Lugard made such a promise, see Ayandele, "The Missionary Factor in Northern Nigeria," 145–49; Crampton, *Christianity in Northern Nigeria*, 45–49; C. N. Ubah, "Problems of Christian Missionaries in Muslim Emirates of Nigeria," *Journal of African Studies* 3.3 (1976): 351–71.

16. Nicolson, *Administration of Nigeria,* 132–35.

17. Ibid., 143–46; Henrika Kuklick, *The Savage Within: The Social History of British Anthropology, 1885–1945* (Cambridge: Cambridge University Press, 1991), 242–78.

18. Memorandum Regarding Social Relations with Moslem Chiefs and Their Women Folk, 1936, CO 583/213/30252, PRO.

19. Robert Heussler, *Yesterday's Rulers: The Making of the British Colonial Service* (Syracuse: Syracuse University Press, 1963), and Henrika Kuklick, *The Imperial Bureaucrat: The Colonial Administrative Service in the Gold Coast, 1920–1939* (Stanford, Calif.: Hoover Institution Press, 1979), 19–42.

20. Flora Louisa Shaw, *A Tropical Dependency: An Outline of the Ancient History of the Western Soudan, with an Account of the Modern Settlement of Northern Nigeria* (London: Nisbet, 1905), 20. See also Helen Callaway and Dorothy O. Helly, "Crusader for Empire: Flora Shaw/Lady Lugard," in Nupur Chaudhuri and Margaret Strobel, eds., *Western Women and Imperialism: Complicity and Resistance* (Bloomington: Indiana University Press, 1992), 79–97.

21. Shaw, *A Tropical Dependency,* 20–21.

22. Ibid., 378.

23. Ibid., 401.

24. Ibid., 404.

25. Ibid., 406.

26. Charles Lindsey Temple, *Native Races and Their Rulers: Sketches and Studies of Official Life and Administrative Problems in Nigeria* (1918; London: Cass, 1968), 4.

27. Ibid.

28. Ibid., 5.

29. Ibid., 7.

30. Ibid.

31. Ibid., 8.

32. J. R. Wilson-Haffenden, *The Red Men of Nigeria: An Account of a Lengthy Residence among the Fulani, or "Red Men," and Other Pagan Tribes of Central Nigeria, with a Description of Their Headhunting, Pastoral, and Other Customs, Habits, and Religion.* (1930; London: Cass, 1967), 93–94.

33. Herbert Richmond Palmer, *The Bornu, Sahara, and Sudan* (London: J. Murray, 1936), viii.

34. Ibid., 2.

35. Ibid.

36. Ibid.

37. Kuklick, *The Savage Within,* 119–81.

38. Palmer, *The Bornu, Sahara, and Sudan,* 2.

39. C. K. Meek, *The Northern Tribes of Nigeria: An Ethnographical Account of the*

Northern Provinces of Nigeria together with a Report on the 1921 Decennial Census, 2 vols. (London: Oxford University Press, 1925), 1:xv.

40. Ibid., 1:31.

41. See C. K. Meek, *A Sudanese Kingdom; An Ethnographical Study of the Jukun-Speaking Peoples of Nigeria* (London: Paul, Trench, Trubner, 1931); Palmer, introduction to his *The Bornu, Sahara, and Sudan;* and Meek, *The Northern Tribes of Nigeria,* vol. 1, chap. 1.

42. Joyce Cary published four novels based on his experiences in northern Nigeria: *Aissa Saved* (1931); *An American Visitor* (1932); *An African Witch* (1936); and *Mister Johnson* (1939). These novels remain an underutilized source for the study of British colonialism in northern Nigeria. For literary discussion of the novels' historical value, see M. M. Mahood, *Joyce Cary's Africa* (Boston: Houghton Mifflin, 1965); Michael J. C. Echeruo, *Joyce Cary and the Novel of Africa* (New York: Africana, 1973); and Malcolm Foster, *Joyce Cary: A Biography* (Boston: Houghton Mifflin, 1968).

43. NAK SNP 17 16413. For a discussion of Fitzpatrick's report and the contents of this file, see Barnes, "Evangelization Where It Is Not Wanted," 417–22. On Fitzpatrick and Cary, see Mahood, *Joyce Cary's Africa,* 12–17.

44. Walter R. Crocker, *Nigeria: A Critique of British Colonial Administration* (London: Allen and Unwin, 1936), 128.

45. On the British construction of the Indian babu, see Metcalf, *Ideologies of the Raj,* 105–6, 166–67; Lewis D. Wurgaft, *The Imperial Imagination: Magic and Myth in Kipling's India* (Middletown, Conn.: Wesleyan University Press, 1983), 28–31, 141–44. On the construction of the thug, see Metcalf, *Ideologies of the Raj,* 41–42, 123–25; Patrick Brantlinger, *Rule of Darkness: British Literature and Imperialism, 1830–1914* (Ithaca, N.Y.: Cornell University Press, 1988).

46. Sir Hugh Clifford, Memorandum on the Subject of Primary Education in the Southern Provinces of Nigeria, CO 583/138, PRO. The memorandum and the file that contains it are from 1925. See also A. Baba Fafunwa, *History of Education in Nigeria* (London: Allen and Unwin, 1974), 124–34; Albert Ozigi and Lawrence Ocho, *Education in Northern Nigeria* (London: Allen and Unwin, 1981), 14–56.

47. Barnes, "Evangelization Where It Is Not Wanted," 428–32.

48. Ibid., 432–36.

49. On the life of African clerks in northern Nigeria, see Michael Mason, "The History of Mr. Johnson: Progress and Protest in Northern Nigeria," *Canadian Journal of African Studies* 27.2 (1993): 196–217.

50. See the various works of E. A. Ayandele, most especially *Holy Johnson: Pioneer of African Nationalism, 1836–1917* (London: Humanities Press, 1970).

51. Frederick John Dealtry Lugard, *The Dual Mandate in British Tropical Africa* (Edinburgh: Blackwood, 1923), 78.

52. Roland K. Bingham, "Seven Sevens of Years and a Jubilee: The Story of the Sudan Interior Mission," in Joel A. Carpenter, ed., *Missionary Innovation and Expansion* (1943; New York: Garland, 1988), 55.

53. Ibid., 58–61.

54. Ibid., 42–43.

55. Ibid., 55, 60–61.

56. Ayandele, "The Missionary Factor in Northern Nigeria," 143.

57. E. A. Ayandele, *The Missionary Impact on Modern Nigeria, 1842–1914: A Political and Social Analysis* (London: Longmans, 1966), 123.

58. Walter Miller, *Audu: A Hausa Boy (A True Story)* (London: Church Missionary Society, 1904).

59. J.-M. Chabert, *La société des missions africaines de Lyon en Afrique: L'islam chez les sauvages et les cannibales de la Nigerie du nord* (Lyon: Impr. des Missions Africaines, 1926), 27–29. All translations, unless otherwise noted, are by the author.

60. Ibid., 27–28.

61. Ibid., 29.

62. SMAC, Prefecture of Northern Nigeria, Annual Report to Propaganda Fide 1927.

63. SMAC, Prefecture of Northern Nigeria, Annual Report to Propaganda Fide 1931.

64. Quoted in Boer, *Missionary Messengers of Liberation,* 128.

65. Trautmann, *Aryans and British India,* 101–9; James Stuart Mill, *The History of British India* (Chicago: University of Chicago Press, 1975), especially 40–56, 137–89.

66. AHA 16212.

67. Crampton, *Christianity in Northern Nigeria,* 62.

68. AHA 5533.

69. Ibid.

70. Quoted in Boer, *Missionary Messengers of Liberation,* 304.

71. James C. Scott, *Domination and the Arts of Resistance: Hidden Transcripts* (New Haven, Conn.: Yale University Press, 1990), 1–16.

72. Ibid., 88–89.

73. Joyce Cary, letter of September 24, 1917, reprinted in Foster, *Joyce Cary,* 149.

74. Quoted in Boer, *Missionary Messengers of Liberation,* 147.

75. Temple, *Native Races and Their Rulers,* 103–21.

76. Ibid., 106.

77. Ibid., 107.

78. Ibid., 111.

79. Ibid., 113.

80. Ibid.

81. Walter Miller, *Yesterday and To-Morrow in Nigeria* (London: Student Christian Movement Press, 1938), 86.

82. Ibid., 77.

83. Ibid., 86–87.

84. Ibid., 77–81.

85. Ibid., 83.

86. Ibid., 97.

87. Ibid., 95–96.

88. Ibid., 77.

89. Quoted in Boer, *Missionary Messengers of Liberation,* 147.

90. See, for example, the essays in Breckenridge and van der Veer, *Orientalism and the Postcolonial Predicament*; and Eugene F. Irschick, *Dialogue and History: Constructing South India, 1795–1895* (Berkeley: University of California Press, 1994).

91. On colonial efforts to recreate lost worlds, see Ian Linden (with Jane Linden), *Catholics, Peasants, and Chewa Resistance in Nyasaland, 1889–1939* (Berkeley: University of California Press, 1974).

Mohamad Tavakoli-Targhi

Orientalism's Genesis Amnesia

■ Orientalism as an area of academic inquiry of Asia came to be grounded on a "genesis amnesia"[1] that systematically obliterated the dialogic conditions of its emergence and the production of its linguistic and textual tools. The "Orient" thus evolved into an object of analysis and gaze while Oriental Studies as a European institution of learning anathematized the Asian pedagogues of its practitioners. Embedded in an active process of forgetting, histories of Oriental Studies have attributed to the "pioneers" of the field the heroic task of entering "this virgin territory," breaking into "the walled languages of Asia," unlocking "innumerable unsuspected scriptures," and making "many linguistic discoveries."[2] In this rewriting of history, Orientalism appropriated as its own the agency and creativity of its Other, which it now proceeded to construct and objectify.

The subsequent sedimentation and institutionalization of Orientalism further authorized the history of its Other. Ironically, in recent years the study of Orientalism as a field of critical inquiry has further contributed to the underdevelopment of its earlier history. A few exemplary statements by Bernard Lewis, a renowned Orientalist scholar, and Edward Said, a leading critic of Orientalism, display the unequal development of Orientalism and its nemesis. In direct contrast to "the Oriental renaissance" and "Europe's rediscovery of India and the East," Bernard Lewis asserts that "there was a complete lack of interest and curiosity among Muslim scholars about what went on beyond the Muslim frontiers in Europe."[3] By the end of the eighteenth century, Lewis observes, there was a "total lack of any such literature in Persian or with the exception of Moroccan embassy reports in Arabic." The more advanced Ottoman writings on Europe "had not yet amounted to anything very substantial."[4] Evaluating the "Muslim scholarship about the West," he postulates that "the awakening of Muslim interest in the West came much later, and was the result of an overwhelming Western presence."[5] Lewis suggests that Asians lacked the curiosity of Europeans in the study of languages and religions:

> Europeans at one time or another have studied virtually all the languages and all the histories of Asia. Asia did not study Europe. They did not even study each other, unless the way for such study was prepared by either conquest or conversion or both. The kind of intellectual curiosity that leads to the study of a language, the decipherment of ancient texts, without any such preparation or motivation is still peculiar to western Europe, and to the inheritors and emulators of the European scholarly tradition in countries such as the United States and Japan.[6]

While critical of such historically inaccurate accounts, Edward Said's pioneering work was also grounded on the assumption that Orientalism "had no corresponding equivalent in the Orient."[7] Viewing Orientalism as a "one way exchange,"[8] Said argues that it would be unlikely "to imagine a field symmetrical to it called Occidentalism."[9] Likewise, Said observes that "the number of travelers from the Islamic East to Europe between 1800 and 1900 is minuscule when compared with the number in the other direction."[10]

These representative observations made by eminent scholars are based on the binary assumption of "Oriental silence" and "Western writing"[11] and are products of Orientalism's genesis amnesia. The assumed silence and lack of scientific curiosity among "Orientals" constituted a strategic choice for authorizing the "disciplinization" of Orientalism and for legitimating its claim to objective knowledge. Without these assumptions, the perspectival nature of Orientalist knowledge, finally skillfully elucidated by Edward Said,[12] would have become obvious from the outset. This essay marks an attempt to retrieve the dialogic conditions of the emergence of modern Orientalism. It is a preliminary exercise in retracing the contributions of "Persianate" scholars to the education of so-called pioneering Orientalists.[13] In retracing the dialogic relations between European and Persianate scholars, I hope to recover an unexplored history of Indian and Iranian modernism, a common history suppressed by the nationalist historiographies of India and Iran.

Perspectival Knowledge

Recounting a situation experienced by most eighteenth- and nineteenth-century Occidental and Oriental travelers, Mirza I'tisam al-Din, who journeyed to England in 1766–69, recounted: "The young and old gazed at my countenance and shape and I stared at their beauty and face. I journeyed for a spectacle and became a spectacle myself."[14] Some seventy years later, another Persian traveler, Prince Riza Quli Mirza, is reported to have turned abruptly to his translator and urged, "Let us just sit down here on this bench, and look at these people passing before us." Acutely aware that he was himself a spectacle, the prince added, "Wherever I sit they will be sure to come fast enough. I am as great a *tamasha* (spectacle) myself as anything here."[15] Commenting on this incident, his translator, James Baillie Fraser (1783–1856), recalled, "And, sure enough, he was right. No sooner had we seated ourselves than the crowd began to gather round, passing and repassing us in a manner that enabled us to see much more than we should have done had we been walking about; and my friend, now in a state of greater comfort, made free and amusing remarks."[16] Like Persian voyagers, Europeans also experienced the interlocking of gazes during their journeys to the "exotic Orient." On a tour to the outskirts of Julfa in Isfahan on November 29, 1824, R. C. Money remarked: "In these busy and hurried scenes life is much the same all over the world, whether in London or Paris, Pekin or Ispahan. Only here a Feringee [European] creates a great stir. All run to look and stare; and I am induced sometimes to think that some malicious spirit had turned me into a curiosity, and that I am not what I am."[17]

Seeing themselves being seen, that is, achieving the consciousness of themselves as at once spectators and spectacles, grounded all eighteenth- and nineteenth-century Oriental and Occidental voyageurs' narrative emplotment of alterity. The traveling spectators appeared to the natives as traveling spectacles; voy(ag)eurs seeking to discover exotic lands were looked on by the locals as exotic aliens.

Asians and Europeans reciprocally shared the anxiety and the desire to represent and narrate alterity. The formation of modern European dis-

courses on the Orient were contemporaneous with the Persianate explorations of Europe (*Farang/Farangistan*). Orientals gazed and returned the
gaze, and in the process of "cultural looking," they, like their Occidental
counterparts, exoticized and eroticized the *Farangi*-Other.[18] In the interplay of looks between Asians and Europeans, there was no steady position
of spectatorship, no objective observer, and no "aperspectival" position. As
understood by Asaad Khayat, the Lebanese companion of three Iranian
princes who traveled to England in 1836, visitors and natives did not see
things "with the same eyes." In his estimation, all narratives of alterity were
perspectival and validated the cultural perspective of the reporter:

> Some who are acquainted with the scenes through which their Royal
> Highnesses passed, and were in company with them at the time, will
> perhaps be astonished that they themselves saw not the same things
> which they described. To this it is but candid to reply, that their Royal
> Highnesses could not see with the same eyes as Englishmen, and being in
> a strange land, their language must seem to be quite *de traverse,* while yet
> it expresses the impressions which were made upon their own minds.[19]

There were recurrent attempts to label as "uncivilized" those who did not
see things "with the same eyes." Yet Persianate travelers narrated the spectacle of Europe, and European onlookers reported the spectacle of the
exotic Persians in their midst. The field of vision and the making of meaning
were perspectival, contestatory, and theatrical.

Thus Oriental and Occidental travelers each saw themselves being seen
and narrated the locals who narrated them. This conjunction of knowing
subjects from different cultures, who gazed simultaneously at the other and
exhibited the self, foregrounded the transformation of modern national
identities. In these ambivalent encounters, the narrator-spectacles often
fetishized the spectators and reduced them to visible signs of otherness.[20]
Through a process of projection and introjection, the visible features of the
other became a locus for self-reflection and reconstruction for both Oriental and Occidental narrators. In this conjoined process the other served as a
vantage point for cultural mimicry and mockery.

As divergent strategies of identification and disidentification, mimicry
and mockery were anchored in the contesting local, regional, and global networks of power and knowledge. In the nineteenth-century Iranian political
discourse, for example, identification with Europe served as an oppositional
strategy for the disarticulation of the dominant Islamicate discourse and the

construction of a new pattern of self-identity grounded on pre-Islamic history and culture.[21] Mimesis constituted not a mindless imitation but a strategy for creative reconstruction of Iranian history and identity.[22] By mocking Europe, Islamists sought to preserve dominant power relations and to subvert the oppositional strategy of secularization and de-Islamization. Thus mockery did not constitute a reactionary and traditionalist rejection of Europe. By mocking Europe, Islamists rather recoded Perso-Islamic history and culture in opposition to Europe. Both the secularist Europhilia and the Islamist Europhobia constituted Europe as a point of reference, but both actively engaged in the creative construction of alternative modernities.

Persianate accounts of Europe, like Orientalist narratives, based their authority on self-experience and eyewitness accounts of alterity. Exotic Others were observed and witnessed either at home or abroad. Montesquieu's *Lettres persanes* [Persian letters], for instance, was partly motivated by the visit of an Iranian envoy to France in 1714. Similarly, traveling Europeans ignited the imagination of the multitudes who viewed the exotic Farangis passing through their homeland. Among those surveying the Farangis were the Indian and Iranian state-appointed *mehmandars* (guest-keepers) assigned to the distinguished foreign visitors.[23] James Morier (1780–1849), who traveled through India and Iran in 1810–12, described the mehmandar as "an officer of indispensable necessity in a country where there are no public inns, and little safety on the roads, for strangers." According to Morier, the mehmandar "acts at once as commissary, guard, and guide; and also very much in the same capacity as Tissaphernes, who in conducting the ten thousand Greeks through Persia, besides providing markets for them, was also a watch upon them, and a reporter to the king of all their actions."[24] Traveling in Iran between 1627 and 1629, Sir Thomas Herbert (1606–82) was assigned to Khwajah 'Abd al-Riza, whom he identified as a harbinger.[25] Sir John Malcolm, traveling to Iran in 1809, identified one of his mehmandars as Mahomed Sheriff Khan Burgashattee who had shown him "a journal he had written for the information of the court by whom he was deputed, in order to enable them to judge, by the aid of his observations, what kind of a person and nation they had to deal with." Sheriff Khan, whom Malcolm described as "a keen observer,"[26] characterized his British guests as "very restless persons." Commenting on his relationship with the British envoy, Sheriff Khan remarked, "My office is very fatiguing, for the Elchee [ambassador], though a good-natured man, has no love of quiet, and it is my duty to be delighted with all that he does, and to attend him on all occasions."[27] The mehmandars, who as early as the sixteenth century closely observed the visiting Europeans, can be viewed as important authorities for the dissemination of knowledge about Europe and Europeans.[28]

A Genealogy of Origins

In modulated histories of Orientalism, the intellectual contributions of Abraham-Hyacinthe Anquetil-Duperron (1731–1805), Sir William Jones (1746–94), and other pioneering Orientalists are grounded exclusively in a European intellectual context. This historiographical selection played a strategic role in constituting "the West" as the site of progress and innovation and "the Orient" as the locus of backwardness and tradition. The fully differentiated East and West are the historical products of these paradigmatic selections, which have been deeply embedded in the historiographical methods of the interlocutors of Europe's Other in the past two hundred years.

But in the field's formative phase, Orientalist efforts were a product of cultural and intellectual hybridization. Its development into "a style of thought based upon an ontological and epistemological distinction between 'the Orient' and (most of the time) 'the Occident' "[29] marked a later development. The transformation of Orientalist inquiry into a discourse of Western domination was ultimately connected to colonization and the obliteration of all traces of "Oriental" agency, voice, writing, and creativity. I wish to offer an account of the conjoined process of the silencing of "the Orientals" and the authorizing of Western writers. More particularly, I will elucidate the Persianate scholarly and textual culture that authorized Anquetil-Duperron and William Jones as "pioneers."

ANQUETIL-DUPERRON
Viewed by Max Müller as "the discoverer of Zend-Avesta,"[30] Anquetil-Duperron was in essence "a disciple of Indian Sages."[31] During his residence in India between 1755 and 1761,[32] Zoroastrian scholars Dastur Darab bin Suhrab, also known as Ustad Kumana Dada-Daru of Surat (1698–1772), Dastur Kavus bin Faraydun (d. 1778), and one Manuchihrji Seth (dates not known) trained Anquetil-Duperron to read and decipher texts by Pahlavi.[33] The study of Avestan and Pahlavi texts had constituted

an important component of the Parsi intellectual life in India well before Anquetil-Duperron translated and published his Zend-Avesta (1771). Although according to Raymond Schwab, Anquetil-Duperron for "the first time . . . succeeded in breaking into one of the walled languages of Asia,"[34] the breakthroughs in comparative religion and linguistics, constituting the high marks of "the Oriental Renaissance"[35] in Europe, in reality built on the intellectual achievements of Moghul India.

Aspiring to create a harmonious multiconfessional society, Emperor Akbar (r. 1556–1605) sponsored debates among scholars of different religions and encouraged the translation of Sanskrit, Turkish, and Arabic texts into Persian.[36] Persian translations of Sanskrit texts included *Ramayana, Mahabharata,* Bhagavad Gita, *Nalopakhyana, Bhagavat-purana, Harvamsa, Atharva-veda,* and *Jug-bashasht,* among many others.[37] In the introduction to the Persian translation of *Mahabharata,* Abu al-Fazl 'Alami (1551–1602) describes Akbar's motivation for sponsoring these translations:

> Having observed the fanatical hatred between the Hindus and the Muslims and being convinced that it arose only from mutual ignorance, that enlightened monarch wished to dispel the same by rendering the books of the former accessible to the latter. He selected, in the first instance the *Mahabharata* as the most comprehensive and that which enjoyed the highest authority, and ordered it to be translated by competent and impartial men of both nations.[38]

These efforts helped to make Persian the lingua franca of India. Furthermore, Akbar encouraged the expansion of the lexical repository of Persian by commissioning the compilation of a dictionary "containing all of the old Persian words and phrases" that had become obsolete "since the time that Arabs gained domination over the Persian land [bilad-i 'Ajam]."[39] To facilitate the learning of Persian by Sanskrit pundits who were increasingly employed in translation projects, Vihârî Srî Krishna dâsa Misra wrote a book on Persian grammar in Sanskrit, *Parasi-prakasa* (1717), dedicated to Emperor Akbar.[40] In addition, Mirza Jan Ibn Fakhr al-Din Muhammad wrote his *Tuhfat al-Hind,* an original study of Sanskrit and Indian prosody, poetics, and music.[41] On the request of the lexicographer Mir Jamal al-Din Inju (d. ca. 1626), commissioned to compile a comprehensive Persian dictionary, Akbar invited Dastur Ardshir Nawshirvan of Kirman to the court in 1597 to assist Inju with the compilation of the Zand and Pazand components of *Farhang-i Jahangiri.*[42] This dictionary functioned as an essential tool for Saraj al-Din Khan Arzu who was to ascertain the affinity of Persian and Sanskrit quite a few decades before William Jones.

Orientalists did not invent the compiling and collating of Avestan and Pahlavi manuscripts as methods. A religious controversy among the Parsis of India in the early eighteenth century motivated the development of textual criticism.[43] In response to this controversy, Dastur Jamasb Vilayati was invited from Kirman for advice. He visited Surat in 1720, brought a collection of manuscripts, and offered Avestan and Pahlavi lessons to young dasturs Darab Kumana of Surat, Jamasp Asa of Navsari, and Dastur Kamdin of Broach.[44] Among the ranks of Dastur Jamasb's students were the "Indian sages" who later educated Anquetil-Duperron. Dastur Darab, Dastur Kavus, and other Parsi scholars who taught him Pahlavi language and manuscript collation made possible the translation and publication of the Zend-Avesta by Anquetil-Duperron.[45]

Neither was comparative religion exclusively a product of European intellectual curiosity. Prince Dara Shikuh's (1615–59) interests in the comparative understanding of Hinduism and Islam prompted him to seek assistance from the pundits of Benares for a Persian translation of the Upanishads. Completed in 1657 as *Sirr-i Akbar* [The great secret] or *Sirr-i Asrar,* this text was retranslated into English by Nathaniel Halhed (1751–1830) and into French and Latin by Anquetil-Duperron. It was published in 1801–2.[46] François Bernier, who rendered "India familiar and desirable to educated society in the seventeenth century" in Europe, had served as a physician and translator for Danishmand Khan Shafi'a Yazdi (d. 1670), a Persian-Indian courtier and scholar.[47] This enabled Bernier to interact with Hindu pundits:

> My Aqah [master], Danechmend-khan, partly from my solicitation and partly to gratify his own curiosity, took into his service one of the most celebrated Pendets in all the Indies, who had formerly belonged to the household of Dara, the eldest son of the King Chah-Jehan [r. 1628–58]; and not only was this man my constant companion during a period of three years, but also introduced me to the society of other learned Pendets, whom he attracted to the house.[48]

The cultural and intellectual environment in India provided an important context for the Oriental Renaissance in Europe. In its early phase, modern Oriental studies did not constitute a discourse of domination but a reciprocal relation between European and Indian scholars. But with European hegemony and the rise of a heroic model of science in the eighteenth century, the contribution of non-European scholars was increasingly marginalized and deemed nonobjective. Most histories of Orientalism from Raymond Schwab to Edward Said fail to take into account the intellectual participation of native scholars in the formation of Oriental Studies. By not accounting for the contributions of indigenous scholars in "his discovery" of the Zend-Avesta, Anquetil-Duperron secured himself the image as the Columbus of Oriental Studies.

WILLIAM JONES

Sir William Jones, viewed as the founder of British Oriental Studies and as "one of leading figures in the history of modern linguistics,"[49] also relied on the intellectual labor of numerous Persianate scholars. He was in contact with an extensive network of intellectuals, whom he labeled "my private establishment of readers and writers."[50] This network included several men who were contemporaries, such as Tafazzul Husayn Khan Kashmiri,[51] Mir Muhammad Husayn Isfahani,[52] Bahman Yazdi,[53] Mir 'Abd al-Latif Shuhtari,[54] 'Ali Ibrahim Khan Bahadur,[55] Muhammad Ghaus,[56] Ghulam Husayn Khan,[57] Yusuf Amin, Mulla Firuz, Mahtab Rai, Haji Abdullah, Sabur Tiwari, Siraj al-Haqq, and Muhammad Kazim.[58] In addition, Jones relied on the assistance of many "pandits," including Radhakant Sarman.[59] In one letter, Jones specified that "my pendits must be nik-khu, zaban-dan, bid-khwan, Farsi-gu [well-tempered, linguist, Vedantist/Sanskrit-reader, and Persophone]."[60]

Jones's connection to Persianate scholars predated his 1783 arrival in India. Mirza I'tisam al-Din, an Indian who, as we have seen, traveled to England between 1766 and 1769, reported that during his journey to Europe he helped translate the introductory section of the Persian dictionary *Farhang-i Jahangiri*, which was later available to Jones when he composed his academic best-seller, *A Grammar of the Persian Language* (1771). I'tisam al-Din recounted:

> Formerly, on ship-board, Captain S[winton] read with me the whole of the Kuleelaah and Dumnah [*Kalilah va Dimnah*], and had translated the twelve rules of the Furhung Jehangeree [*Farhang-i Fahangiri*], which comprise the grammar of the Persian language. Mr. Jones having seen that translation, with the approbation of Captain S[winton], compiled his Grammar, and having printed it, sold it and made a good deal of money by it. This Grammar is a very celebrated one.[61]

While at Oxford, I'tisam al-Din met Jones and "went to the libraries" with him.[62] In the preface to *A Grammar of the Persian Language,* Jones acknowledged the assistance of an unidentified "foreign nobleman," whom the editor of his collected works later identified as Baron Charles Reviczki (1737–93).[63] Jones acknowledged: "I take a singular pleasure in confessing that I am indebted to a foreign nobleman for the little knowledge which I have happened to acquire of the Persian language; and that my zeal for the poetry and philology of the Asiaticks [*sic*] was owing to his conversation, and to the agreeable correspondence with which he still honours me."[64] In light of I'tisam al-Din's remarks in his travelogue, one may doubt the editor's assertion that Jones had intended to thank Reviczki whom he had met in 1768.[65] By leaving the "foreign nobleman" unidentified, Jones may have sought to use this ambiguity to account for different individuals who assisted him with his Persian, including his "Syrian teacher," who turns out to have been none other than Mirza I'tisam al-Din.[66] Significantly, Jones in the preface to *A Grammar of the Persian Language* distinguishes his own work from that of others: "I have carefully compared my work with every composition of the same nature that has fallen into my hands; and though on so general a subject I must have made several observations which are common to all, yet I flatter that my own remarks, the disposition of the whole book, and the passages quoted in it, will sufficiently distinguish it as an original production."[67] Demonstration of the extent of Jones's originality exceeds the scope of this study.[68] But it should be noted that the text bore a Persian title, *Kitab-i Shikaristan dar Nahv-y Zaban-i Parsi tasnif-i Yunis-i Oxfordi,* where Jones or "Yunis-i Oxfordi" (Yunis of Oxford) is identified as the *compiler* of the work and not the author.

Publication of Jones's Persian grammar coincided with that of Anquetil-Duperron's Zend-Avesta. Jones, who had claimed in the preface to be working on "a history of the Persian language from the time of Xenophon to our days,"[69] seemed unaware of the Avestan and Pahlavi languages from which Anquetil-Duperron had translated his work. To protect his own reputation, Jones attacked the authenticity of Anquetil-Duperron's source texts.[70] Relying on the authority of John Chardin (1643–1713), Jones argued that the "old Persian is a language entirely lost; in which no books are extant."[71] He argued that the translations of "the rosy-cheeked Frenchman," ascribed to Zoroaster, were in fact "the gibberish of those swarthy vagabonds, whom we often see brooding over a miserable fire under the hedges."[72] John Richardson (1741–1811), a leading Persian lexicographer and the compiler of *A Dictionary of English, Persian, and Arabic,* joined Jones in his attack against Anquetil-Duperron, arguing that the two languages of Zend and Pahlavi were mere fabrications. Having evaluated the work of Anquetil-Duperron, Richardson, like Jones, concluded: "Upon the whole, M. Anquetil has made no discovery which can stamp his publication with the least authority. He brings evidence of no antiquity; and we are only disgusted with the frivolous superstition and never-ending ceremonies of the modern Worshippers of Fire."[73] Richardson maintained the inauthenticity of Zend and Pahlavi from numerous Arabic words found in both.[74]

Jones, who had grown more erudite and informed by 1789, revisited the controversy with Anquetil-Duperron in his "The Sixth Discourse: On the Persians." His observation that "Zend was at least a dialect of the Sanscrit"[75] earned him recognition as "the creator of comparative grammar."[76] In Max Müller's estimation, however, "this conclusion that Zend is a Sanskrit dialect, was incorrect, the connection assumed being too close; but it was a great thing that the near relationship of the two languages should have been brought to light."[77] While Jones continues to be lionized for his remarks concerning the affinity of languages,[78] the Persian-Indian scholars and texts that informed Jones's work remain unknown.

A few decades prior to Jones, the Persian lexicographer and linguist Saraj al-Din Khan Arzu (ca. 1689–1756) wrote a comprehensive study of Persian language discerning its affinity with Sanskrit in *Muthmir.*[79] Textual evidence indicates that Jones might have been familiar with this work and so might have used it in writing the famous lecture that gained him recognition for all posterity. In his study of phonetic and semantic similarities and differences of Persian, Arabic, and Sanskrit and the interconnected processes of Arabization (*ta'rib*), Hindization (*tahnid*), and Persianization (*tafris*) in Iran and India, Arzu was fully aware of the originality of his own insight on the affinity of Sanskrit and Persian. He wrote, "Amongst so many Persian and Hindi [Sanskrit] lexicographers and researchers of this science [*fann*], no one except faqir Arzu has discerned the affinity [*tavafuq*] of Hindi and Persian languages." Arzu was amazed that lexicographers such as 'Abd al-Rashid Tattavi (d. ca. 1658), the compiler of *Farhang-i Rashidi* (1653) who had lived in India, had failed to observe "so much affinity between these two languages."[80] The exact date of the completion of Arzu's *Muthmir* has not been ascertained, but it is clear he had used the technical term *tavafuq al-lisanayn* — the affinity/correspondence of languages—in his *Chiraq-i Hidayat* (1747), a dictionary of rare Persian and Persianized concepts and phrases.[81] In this dictionary, he offered examples of words common to both Persian and Hindi (Sanskrit).[82] The work must have been written prior to 1756, the year Arzu died. Arzu's works on the affinity of Sanskrit and Persian certainly predated the 1767 paper by Father Coeurdoux who had inquired into the affinity of Sanskrit and Latin.[83]

Based on a set of Zand and Pazand terms (*Lughat-i Zand va Pazand*), technically known as *huzvarish*,[84] appearing in an appendix to *Farhang-i Jahangiri*, Arzu also conjectured the "affinity of Pahlavi and Arabic languages" (*tavafuq-i lisanayn-i Pahlavi va 'Arabi*).[85] What Arzu failed to recognize was that Pahlavi occasionally used Aramaic words as ideograms for conveying their Persian equivalents. These words were written in Aramaic, but were meant to be read as Persian equivalents. Jones similarly repeated Arzu's mistake a few decades, asserting that "the Zend bore a strong resemblance to Sanscrit, and Pahlavi to Arabick [*sic*]."[86] More consistently historical in his thinking, Arzu argued that the change from Pahlavi to Dari and contemporary Persian resulted from diachronic linguistic changes. He likewise attributed the differences between the Zoroastrian texts in Avesta, Zand, and Pazand to a historical transformation of the Persian language.[87]

The intensified conflict between the Persian poets of Indian and Iranian descent motivated Arzu's study of Persian's transformation. His essays, *Dad-i Sukhan, Siraj-i Munir,* and *Tanbih al-Ghafilin,* all focused on these tensions. In search of courtly patronage in India, Iranians sought to advance their lot by questioning the linguistic competence of the poets of Indian descent. For example, Shayda Fatihpuri (d. 1632), whose poem Arzu analyzed in his *Dad-i Sukhan,* complained that Iranians dismissed him because of his Indian lineage.[88] Unlike his Iranian nemeses, Shayda argued that "being Indian or Iranian cannot become an evidence of excellence"[89] Abu al-Barakat Munir Lahuri (d. 1644), another poet whose work Arzu evaluated in his *Siraj-i Munir* and *Dad-i Sukhan,* had also responded to the same ethnic-professional tension that inspired Shayda to criticize the work of Iranian Malik al-Shu'ara (King of Poets) Muhammad Jan Qudsi (d. 1646). Like Shayda, Munir Lahuri complained that Iranian lineage (*nasab-i Iran*) — in addition to old age (*piri*), wealth (*tavangari*), and fame (*buland avazigi*) — was unfairly viewed as a criterion for the recognition of one's mastery of language. He observed, "If a Persian makes one hundred mistakes in Persian, his language will not be questioned. But if an Indian, like an Indian blade [*tiq-i Hindi*], reveals the original essence [of Persian], no one will applaud him."[90] He complained that despite his achievements in Persian, "if the infidel I [Munir Lahuri] tell the truth and reveal that the land of India is my place of descent [*nizhadgah-i man-i kafar*], these villains of the earth will equate me with the dark soil."[91] Munir Lahuri elaborated his views in his *Karnamah,* an outstanding text challenging the Iranian poets' self-congratulatory definition of linguistic competence.

These productive tensions also inspired Arzu to undertake a pioneering historical study of the Persian language and the processes of lexical Arabization, Persianization, and Hindization. His discernment of the affinity of Persian and Sanskrit bolstered his argument that Indians held the authority to resignify Persian words and phrases and use Hindi concepts in their writings. Pursuing this historically informed path, Arzu's students initiated a process of vernacularization and the cultivation of literary Urdu, *Urdu-yi mu'alla.*[92] It was for this reason that Muhammad Husayn Azad (ca. 1834–1910) argued that Arzu "has done for Urdu what Aristotle did for logic. As long as all logicians are called the descendants of Aristotle, all Urdu scholars will also be called the descendants of Khan-e Arzu."[93] In other words, vernacularization resulted from poetic and literary conflict between Indian and Iranian poets and was well under way prior to the British colonization of India.

Like Arzu's, Jones's speculation concerning the historical relation of Sanskrit, Persian, and Arabic was informed by the historical imagination of *Dabistan-i Mazahib,* which Mir Muhammad Husayn Isfahani had introduced to him.[94] *Dabistan* and other Dasatiri texts provided a mythohistorical narrative inaugurated by the pre-Adamite Mahabad, who was supposed to have initiated the great cycle of human existence well before Adam. Compiled, composed, or "translated" by Zar Kayvan (1529–1614) and his disciples, these texts fashioned a new historical framework that challenged the hegemonic biblical/Islamic imagination in which human history begins with the creation of Adam.[95] This protonationalist historical imagination provided Jones with necessary "evidence" for establishing the origins of languages and nations. Writing about his "discovery" of *Dabistan,* Jones explained: "A fortunate discovery, for which I was first indebted to Mir Muhammed Husain, one of the most intelligent Muslims in India, has at once dissipated the cloud and cast a gleam of light on the primeval history of Iran and the human race, of which I had long despaired, and which could hardly have dawned from any other quarter."[96] The historical narrative of *Dabistan,* by extending the history of Iran to the pre-Adamite eras of Abadiyan, Jayan, Sha'iyan, and Yasa'yan, offered a new origin for languages and races:

> If we can rely on this evidence, which to me appears unexceptionable, the Iranian monarchy must have been the oldest in the world; but it remains dubious, to which of the three stocks, Hindu, Arabian, or Tartar the first King of Iran belonged, or whether they sprang from a fourth race distinct from any of the others; and these are questions, which we shall be able, I imagine, to answer precisely, when we have carefully inquired into the languages and letters, religion and philosophy, and incidentally into the arts and science, of the ancient Persians.[97]

Based on the historical imagination of *Dabistan* and *Dasatir,* Jones argued that Kayumars, a progenitor of humankind in Zoroastrian cosmology, "was most probably of a different race from Mahabadians, who preceded him." By assuming a racial difference between Kayumars and Mahabad, responding to the dispute with Anquetil-Duperron, Jones was as "firmly convinced, that the doctrines of the Zend were distinct from those of the Véda, as I [Jones] am that the religion of the Brahmans, with whom we converse every day, prevailed in Persia before the accession of Cayumers [Kayumars], whom the Parsis, from respect to his memory, consider as the first of men." Speculating further on the basis of *Dabistan,* Jones conjectured "that the language of the first Persian empire was the mother of the Sanscrit, and consequently of the Zend, and Parsi, as well as of Greek, Latin, and Gothick; that the language of Assyrians was the parent of Chaldaick and Pahlavi, and that the primary Tartarian language also had been current in the same empire; although, as Tartars had no books or even letters, we cannot with certainty trace their unpolished and variable idioms."[98] The historical narrative of *Dabistan,* in other words, enabled Jones to imagine both linguistic and racial diversification of human societies.

In his important lecture "On the Persians," which earned him a permanent place in the history of comparative linguistics, Jones solicited recognition for his originality:

> In the new and important remarks, which I am going to offer, on the ancient *languages* and *characters* of *Iran,* I am sensible, that you must give me credit for many assertions, which on this occasion it is important to prove for I should ill deserve your indulgent attention, if I were to

abuse it by repeating a dry list of detached words, and presenting you with a vocabulary instead of a dissertation.[99]

Describing his reliance on evidence, Jones noted:

> Since I have habituated myself to form opinions of men and things from *evidence*, which is the only solid basis of *civil*, as *experiment* is of *natural*, knowledge, and since I have maturely considered the question which I mean to discuss, you will not, I am persuaded suspect my testimony, or think that I go too far, when I assure you, that I will assert nothing positively, which I am not able satisfactorily to demonstrate.[100]

Yet Jones followed these introductory remarks with an explanation of the affinity of Persian and Sanskrit without offering any examples: "I can assure you with confidence, that hundreds of Parsi [Persian] nouns are pure Sanscrit, with no other change than such as may be observed in numerous *bhashas*, or vernacular dialects, of India; that very many Persian imperatives are the roots of Sanscrit verbs."[101] Jones asserted that "in pure Persian I find no trace of any Arabian tongue, except what proceeded from the known intercourse between Persians and Arabs, especially in the time of Bahram."[102] With the assistance of Bahman Yazdi, Jones articulated the thesis that established his reputation:

> I often conversed on them with my friend Bahman, and both of us were convinced after full consideration, that the *Zend* bore a strong resemblance to *Sanscrit*, and the *Pahlavi* to *Arabick*. He had at my request translated into *Pahlavi* the fine inscription, exhibited in the *Gulistan*, on the diadem of Cyrus; and I had the patience to read the list of words from *Pazand* in the appendix to the *Farhangi Jehangiri*: this examination gave me perfect conviction, that the Pahlavi was a dialect of the Chaldaick; and of this curious fact I will exhibit short proof.[103]

Jones supported his thesis about Pahlavi by noting: "By the nature of the Chaldean tongue most words ended in the first long vowel like *shemia*, heaven; and that very word, unaltered in a single letter, we find in the Pazand, together with *lailia*, night, *meya*, water, *nira*, fire, *matra*, rain, and a multitude of others, all Arabick or Hebrew with Chaldean termination."[104] Curiously enough, these identical words appear first in a list of over forty terms analyzed by Arzu under the heading "On lexical affinity" (*dar tavafuq-i alfaz*).[105]

Could it be that Jones had access to Arzu's *Muthmir* when he drafted his lecture "On the Persians" and delivered it on February 19, 1789? If so, his contribution to the inauguration of comparative linguistics needs to be reevaluated and the role of scholars such as Arzu and Bahman Yazdi, and of texts such as *Muthmir* and *Dabistan,* demands reexamination. Clearly, European Orientalists such as Anquetil-Duperron and William Jones had entered into the fields of Oriental languages, religions, and history as novices. Their intellectual contribution was closely connected to the network of native scholars with whom they interacted. In its postcolonial phase, histories of Orientalism cannot remain silent about the participation of the intellectual laborers who educated the initiators of the Oriental Renaissance.

Many other scholars of India and Iran have vanished into obscurity, and their contributions to the formation of Oriental Studies and comparative linguistics have gone equally unnoticed. Mirza Salih Shirazi served as a guide for the delegation led by Sir Gore Ouseley (1770–1844),[106] the British Ambassador Extraordinary and Plenipotentiary, who visited Iran between 1811 and 1812. He accompanied and kept records of this delegation's journey, a group that included leading Orientalists such as William Ouseley (1767–1842), William Price, and James Morier.[107] Price wrote: "While we were at Shiraz, I became acquainted with Mirza Saulih, well known for his Literary acquirements: he entered our train and remained with the Embassy a considerable time, during which, I prevailed upon him to compose a set of dialogues in his native tongue, the pure dialect of Shiraz." These were subsequently published in Price's *A Grammar of the Three Principal Oriental Languages.*[108] In his *Travels* thirteen years earlier, William Ouseley had cited an "extract from some familiar Dialogues, written at my request by a man of letters at Shiriz." The extract offered by Ouseley was the opening of Mirza Salih's *Persian Dialogues.*[109] Both Ouseley and Price insisted that the *Dialogues* were written at their request. These competing claims may account for the preservation of the name of Mirza Salih as the author. In the introduction to the *Persian Dialogues,* Price humbly noted, "having myself no motive but that of contributing to the funds of Oriental literature, and of rendering the attainment of the Persian language to students; I have given the Dialogues verbatim, with an english [*sic*] translation as literal as possible."[110] Mirza Salih also assisted Price in the research for his dissertation.[111] William Ouseley credited Mirza Salih for providing him with a "concise description and highly economiastick [*sic*]" narrative on historical and archaeological sites used in his *Travels in*

Various Countries of the East, More Particularly Persia.[112] Having relied on Mirza Salih's contribution, Ouseley viewed part of the work as "the result of our joint research."[113]

Conclusion

The obliteration of the intellectual contributions of Persianate scholars to the formation of Orientalism coincided with the late-eighteenth-century emergence of authorship as a principle of textual attribution and creditation. The increased significance of authorship is attributed to the Romantic revolution and its "destruction of rhetoric." According to John Bender and David Wellbury, "One major Romantic innovation was the full articulation of the concept of 'author' as the productive origin of the text, as the subjective source that, in bringing its unique position to expression, constitutes a 'work' ineluctably its own."[114] With the increased cultural significance of innovation (*inventio*), European interlocutors constituted themselves as the repositories of originality and assigned non-European scholars the function of "native informants." It was precisely at this historical conjuncture that contemporary works by non-European scholars began to be devalued and depicted as *traditio* (tradition). This rhetorical strategy authorized the marginalization of Persianate scholarship at a time when the existing systems of scholarly patronage began disintegrating. Without institutional and material resources authorizing the Persianate scholars, Orientalists were able to appropriate their intellectual products. Like the process of commodification, the institutionalization of Orientalism made it possible to forget the agency and creativity of Persianate intellectual laborers.

Nationalist historiographies in India and Iran sustained this genesis amnesia. Modern Indian historians posit the Persianate literary culture as the domain of "medieval" history and remain reluctant to reconsider a periodization that would redefine the Anglo-centered understanding of Indian modernity. The ethnocentric view of Iranian historians who depict the Indian-Persian textual heritage as "degenerate" and unworthy of scholarly consideration, reinforces these ideas. The resistance to considering the continuation of Persianate textual culture into the modern period also exposes the limits of subaltern and postcolonial Indian historiography. The colonial encounter is privileged over all other histories, and a project engaged in recuperating silenced voices becomes complicit in perpetuating certain types of historical amnesia.

Notes

Research for this essay was made possible in part by a fellowship from the American Institute of Indian Studies (1992–93) and a summer grant from Illinois State University (1995). The Centre for Historical Studies of Jawaharlal Nehru University and the Khuda Bakhsh Oriental Public Library (Patna, India) provided exceptional opportunities for research. Earlier versions of this essay were presented at a symposium titled "Questions of Modernity," Departments of Middle Eastern Studies and Anthropology, New York University, April 19–20, 1996, and at "South Asian Islam and the Greater Muslim World," Rockefeller Humanitites Institute, Chapel Hill, North Carolina, May 23–26, 1996. I received invaluable comments from Lila Abu-Lughod, Muzaffar Alam, Talal Asad, Alison Bailey, Shiva Balaghi, Mansour Bonakdarian, Abid Reza Bedar, Charlotte Brown, Partha Chatterjee, Jorge Canizares, Carl Ernst, Dipesh Chakrabarty, Michael Gilsanon, Khalid Fahmy, Sandria Freitag, Vasant Kaiwar, Zachary Lockman, Sucheta Mazumdar, Barbara Metcalf, Pardis Minuchehr, Farzaneh Milani, Timothy Mitchell, Harbans Mukhia, C. M. Naim, Afsaneh Najmabadi, Gyan Prakash, Stefania Pandolfo, and Win Chin Ouyang. Needless to say, I alone am responsible for the errors in this article. All translations, unless otherwise noted, are mine.

1. On "genesis amnesia," see Pierre Bourdieu, *Outline of a Theory of Practice,* trans. Richard Nice (Cambridge: Cambridge University Press, 1977), 79.

2. All quotes are from Raymond Schwab, *The Oriental Renaissance: Europe's Rediscovery of India and the East, 1680–1880,* trans. Gene Patterson-Black and Victor Reinking (New York: Columbia University Press, 1984), 8, 7, 5, 33.

3. Bernard Lewis, *The Muslim Discovery of Europe* (New York: Norton, 1982), 142.

4. Ibid., 168.

5. Lewis maintains: "It is not until the 1820s that for the first time we find in Egypt translations of Western books." Ibid., 170.

6. Bernard Lewis, *Islam and the West* (New York: Oxford University Press, 1993), 123–24.

7. Edward W. Said, *Orientalism* (New York: Vintage, 1979), 204.

8. Ibid., 160.

9. Ibid., 50. Criticizing Said's Foucauldian analysis of power/knowledge, Bernard Lewis writes: "The 'knowledge is power' argument is no doubt emotionally satisfying, to some extent even intellectually satisfying, and it serves a double purpose: on the one hand, to condemn the Orientalism of the West; on the other, to make a virtue of the absence of any corresponding Occidentalism in the East" (*Islam and the West,* 125). Oddly enough, both Said and Lewis agree on the absence of Occidentalism. On Occidentalism or "Reverse Orientalism," see Mehrzad Boroujerdi, "Westoxication and Orientalism in Reverse," *Iran Nameh* 8.3 (1990): 375–90; Mohamad Tavakoli-Targhi, "The Persian Gaze and Women of the Occident," *South Asia Bulletin* 11.1–2 (1991): 21–31; Tavakoli-Targhi, "Imagining Western Women: Occidentalism and Euro-Eroticism," *Radical America* 24.3 (1993): 73–87.

10. Said, *Orientalism,* 204.

11. Defining "The Scope of Orientalism," Said explains: "I called such a relation between Western writing (and its consequences) and Oriental silence the result of and the sign of the West's great cultural strength, its will to power over the Orient." Ibid., 94.

12. According to Said, "Orientalism is a style of thought based upon the ontological and epistemological distinction made between 'the Orient' and (most of the time) 'the Occident.' . . . Taking the late eighteenth century as a very roughly defined starting point Orientalism can be discussed and analyzed as the corporate institution for dealing with the Orient . . . by making statements about it, authorizing views of it, describing it, teaching it, settling it, ruling over it: in short, Orientalism as a Western style of dominating, restructuring, and having authority over the Orient." Ibid., 2–3.

13. I am grateful to Carl Ernst for suggesting the term *Persianate* instead of *Persophone.*

14. Munshi I'tisam al-Din, "Shigirf namah-'i vilayat," 58a, O.C.13663, British Museum.

15. James Baillie Fraser, *Narrative of the Residence of the Persian Princes in London, in 1835 and 1836* (London: Bentley, 1838), 83.

16. Ibid.

17. R. C. Money, *Journal of a Tour in Persia during the Years 1824 and 1825* (London: Teape, 1928), 110–11.

18. On "cultural looking," see Sara Suleri, *The Rhetoric of English India* (Chicago: University of Chicago Press, 1992), 18–19.

19. Najaf Khoolee Meerza, *Journal of a Residence in England, and of a Journey from and to Syria of their Highness Reeza Koolee Meerza, Najaf Koolee Meerza, and Taymoor Meerza, of Persia. To Which Are Prefixed Some Particulars Respecting Modern Persia, and the Death of the Late Shah,* trans. Assaad Y. Kayat, 2 vols. (London: Tyler, 1839), 1:xiii–xiv.

20. On the ideological construction of otherness, see Homi Bhabha, "The Other Question . . . ," *Screen* 24.6 (1983): 18–36.

21. Mohamad Tavakoli-Targhi, "Refashioning Iran: Language and Culture during the Constitutional Revolution," *Iranian Studies* 23.1–4 (1992): 77–101.

22. My definition of mimicry parallels that of Luce Irigaray for whom mimicry is a strategy in which women intentionally perform the feminine posture assigned to them in a phallocentric discourse. See *This Sex Which Is Not One,* trans. Catherine Porter (Ithaca, N.Y.: Cornell University Press, 1985), 76.

23. On mehmandar during the Safavid period, see Jean Chardin, *Voyages de chevalier Chardin en Perse, et autres lieux de l'orient,* ed. L. Langlés (Paris: Normant Imprimeur Libraire, 1811), 5:372; Engelbert Kaempfer, *Amonitatum exoticarum politico-physico-medicarum fasciculi V* (Lemgoviate: Meyer, 1712), 82; Nichola Sanson, *Voyage ou relation de l'état présent du royaume de Perse: Avec une dissertation curieuse sur les moeurs, religion et gouvernement de cet état* (Paris: Cramoisi, 1695), 38.

24. James Justinian Morier, *A Second Journey through Persia, Armenia, and Asia Minor, to Constantinople, between the Years 1810 and 1816 with a Journal of the Voyage by the Brazils and Bombay to the Persian Gulf* (London: Longman, Hurst, Rees, Orme, and Brown, 1818), 46. Morier's reference to Tissaphernes was based on Xenophon's *Anabasis.*

25. Thomas Herbert, *Travels in Persia, 1627–1629,* ed. William Foster (1634; New York: Books for Libraries, 1972), 62.

26. John Malcolm, *Sketches of Persia from the Journals of a Traveller in the East* (Philadelphia: Carey, Lea, and Carey, 1828), 52–53. Fath'ali Khan Nuri, Nayib-i Ishik Aqasi was the head mehmandar for Sir John Malcolm. See 'Adb al-Razzaq Maftun Dunbuli, *Ma'a–ir-i Sultaniyah* (1825; Tehran: Ibn Sina, 1972), 64; Hasan Husayni Fasa'i, *Farsnamah-'i Nasiri,* ed. Mansur Rastigar Fasa'i (Tehran: Amir Kabir, 1988), 1:678; Malcolm, *Sketches of Persia,* 53.

27. Malcolm, *Sketches of Persia,* 52.

28. The future publication of reports written by *mehmandars* and so-called newswriters (*akhbarnawis*) on European visitors to India and Iran would shed more light on the nature of early encounters between Asians and Europeans. On the office of akhbarnawis, see Michael Fisher, "The Office of Akhbar Nawis: The Transition from Mughal to British Forms," *Modern Asian Studies* 27.1 (1993) 45–82. On intelligence gathering, see C. A. Bayly, "Knowing the Country: Empire and Information in India," *Modern Asian Studies* 27.1 (1993): 3–43.

29. Said, *Orientalism,* 2.

30. Max Müller, "Preface to the Sacred Books of the East," in *The Upanishads,* trans. Müller (1879; Delhi: Motilal Banarsidass, 1965), xvii.

31. Schwab, *Oriental Renaissance,* 158

32. For an account of Anquetil-Duperron's residence in India, see Jivanji Jamshedji Modi, "Anquetil Du Perron of Paris — India as Seen by Him (1755–60)," in *Anquetil Du Perron and Dastur Darab* (Bombay: Times of India, 1916), 1–69.

33. In conventional accounts of this relationship, Anquetil-Duperron is often lionized while his educators are demeaned. For instance, Martin Haug, explaining Anquetil-Duperron's journey to western India to purchase manuscripts of all the sacred books of the Zoroastrian religion, recounted: "The Parsi priests, being full of distrust toward him, were not willing to sell him valuable manuscripts, and far less to teach him the language of their sacred books. Finally, the only means of obtaining the object wished for was money. He bribed one of the most learned Dasturs, Dastur Darab, at Surat, to procure him manuscripts, and to instruct him in the Avesta and Pahlavi languages. But to ascertain that he was not deceived by the Dastur, he opened an intercourse with some other priests (Kaus and Manjerj), and was very well satisfied at finding that the manuscripts he purchased first were genuine. When he thought himself proficient enough in the Avesta and Pahlavi, he set about making a French translation of the whole Zend-Avesta" (*The Parsis: Essays on Their Sacred Language, Writings, and Religion* [1878; New Delhi: Cosmo, 1978], 17–18). For a critical analysis of Anquetil-Duperron's exaggerations and self-glorification, see Modi, *Anquetil Du Perron and Dastur Darab,* 70–141.

34. Schwab, *Oriental Renaissance,* 7.

35. According to Schwab, "An Oriental Renaissance — a second Renaissance, in contrast to the first: the expression and the theme are familiar to the Romantic writers, for whom the term is interchangeable with Indic Renaissance. What the expression refers to is the revival of an atmosphere in the nineteenth century brought about by the arrival of Sanskrit texts in Europe, which produced an effect equal to that produced in the fifteenth century by the arrival of Greek manuscripts and Byzantine commentators after the fall of Constantinople" (ibid., 11).

36. Abu al-Fazl 'Alami, the historian of Akbar's reign, reported: "Philologists are constantly engaged in translating Hindi, Greek, Arabic, and Persian books into other languages. Thus a part of *Ziich-i Jadid-i Mirza'i* . . . was translated under the superintendence of Amir Fathu'llah Shirazi . . . , and also the Kishnjoshi, the Gangadhar, the Mohesh Mahanad, from Hindi (Sanscrit) into Persian, according to the interpretation of the author of this book. The Mahabharata, from Hindi into Persian, under the superintendence of Naqib Khan, Mawlana 'Abdu'l-Qadir of Radaon, and Shaykh Sultan of Thanesar. . . . His Majesty calls this ancient history Razmnamah, the book of Wars. The same learned men translated also into Persian the Ramayana, likewise a book of ancient Hindustan. . . . Haji Ibrahim of Sarhind translated into Persian the Atharban which, according to the Hindus, is one of the four divine books. The Lilawati, which is one of the most excellent works written by Indian mathematicians on arithmetic, lost its Hindu veil, and received a Persian garb from the hand of my elder brother, Shaykh 'Abdu'l-Fayz-i Fayzi." Among other works translated into Persian, Abu al-Fazl mentioned the *Tajak*, *Memoir of Babir* (from Turkish), *The History of Kashmir* (from Kashmiri), *Mu'jam al-Buldan* (from Arabic), *Haribas* (from Sanskrit), *Nal Daman* (from Sanskrit), and the New Testament." Abu al-Fazl 'Alami, *The A-in-i Akbari,* trans. H. Blochman, ed. D. C. Phillott (Delhi: Low Price, 1989), 1:110–112.

37. For Persian translations of Sanskrit works, see Fathullah Mujtabai, "Persian Hindu Writings: Their Scope and Relevance," in *Aspects of Hindu Muslim Cultural Relations* (New Delhi: National Book Bureau, 1978); see also Shriram Sharma, *A Descriptive Bibliography of Sanskrit Works in Persian* (Hyderabad: Abul Kalam Azad Oriental Research Institute, 1982); N. S. Shukla, "Persian Translations of Sanskrit Works," *Indological Studies* 3 (1974): 175–91.

38. Quoted in Mujtabai, *Aspects of Hindu Muslim Cultural Relations,* 66.

39. Quoted from a statement by Emperor Akbar appearing in Mir Jamal al-Din Husayn Inju Shirazi, *Farhang-i Jahangiri,* ed. Rahim 'Afifi (Mashhad: Danishgah-i Mashhad, 1351 A.H./1972), 4. The full text of Akbar's statement as translated by Modi follows: "Since the time the Arabs had the hand of authority in the country of Persia, the Persian language having been mixed with Arabic words, most of the Parsi and Dari and Pahlavi words have become obsolete, nay, have disappeared altogether. So the explanation of the books, which have been written in Old Persian languages, and the meaning of poems, which poets of old times have adorned with ornaments of poetry, have remained concealed and hidden. . . . Therefore, before this time, I had ordered some of the members of the court . . . to prepare a book containing all the old Persian words and phrases. . . . It is necessary that in this noble branch of learning, you should prepare a book of good fame and sublime name, so that in consequence of its always being united with my good fortune, its effect may remain permanently on the pages of time for day and night"

(Jivanji Jamshedji Modi, "Notes on Anquetile Du Perron (1755–61) on King Akbar and Dastur Meherji Rana," in B. P. Ambashthya, ed., *Contributions on Akbar and the Parsees* [Patna: Janaki Prakashan, 1976], 6).

40. V. S. Ghate, "Persian Grammar in Sanskrit," *The Indian Antiquary* (1912): 4–7.

41. Mirza Khan ibn Fakhr al-Din Muhammad, *Tuhfat al-Hind,* ed. Nur al-Hasan Ansari (Tehran: Bunyad-i Farhang-i Iran, 1975).

42. Dastur Ardshir Nawshirvan was invited on the recommendation of the Zoroastrian Dastur Meherji Rana. On this point, see Jivanji Jamshedji Modi, "The Parsees at the Court of Akbar and Dastur Meherji Rana," in Ambashthya, *Contributions on Akbar and the Parsees,* 1–177; Mary Boyce, *Zoroastrians: Their Religious Beliefs and Practices* (London: Routledge and Kegan Paul, 1979), 183. For a list of "Zand and Pazand" terminologies compiled in cooperation with Ardshir Nawshirvan, see Mir Jamal al-Din Husayn Inju Shirazi, *Farhang-i Jahangiri,* 3:553–700.

43. Boyce, *Zoroastrians,* 188–95.

44. Abraham Hyacinthe Anquetil-Duperron, *Zend-Avesta* (New York: Garland, 1984), 1:326; Boyce, *Zoroastrians,* 189; Haug, *The Parsis,* 57; Modi, *Anquetil Du Perron and Dastur Darab,* 37.

45. On the eve of Anquetil-Duperron's departure for Europe, Darab and Kavus sued him for his failure to pay for the purchased manuscripts and tutorial charges. Details in Modi, *Anquetil Du Perron and Dastur Darab,* 55, 95.

46. For the Persian translation, see Muhammad Dara Shikuh bin Shahjahan, *Sirr-i Akbar-Sirr al-Asrar,* ed. Tara Chand and Muhammad Riza Jalali Na'ini (Tehran: Taban, 1961). For a description of this translation, see Mahesh Prasad, "The Unpublished Translation of the Upanishads by Prince Dara Shikoh," in Darab Peshotan Sanjana et al., eds., *Dr. Modi Memorial Volume: Papers on Indo-Iranian and Other Subjects* (Bombay: Fort Printing Press, 1930), 622–38. Halhed's translation remains unpublished. On his contribution, see Rosane Rocher, *Orientalism, Poetry, and the Millennium: The Checkered Life of Nathaniel Brassey Halhed, 1751–1830* (Delhi: Motilal Banarsidass, 1983); Wilhelm Halbfass, *India and Europe: An Essay in Understanding* (New York: State University of New York Press, 1988), 64. Abraham Hyacinthe Anquetil-Duperron, trans., *Oupnek'hat: id est, Secretum tegendum* (Argentorati: Levrault, 1801–2).

47. On Danishmand Khan, see Ahmad Gulchin Ma'ani, *Karvan-i Hind: Dar ahval va asar-i sha'iran-i 'asr-i Safavi kah bah Hindustan raftahand* (Mashhad: Intisharat-i Astan-i Quds-i Razavi, 1369), 526.

48. François Bernier, *Travels in the Moghul Empire* (Delhi: Chand, 1968), 323–24.

49. From the publisher's note reprint edition of William Jones, *A Grammar of the Persian Language* (Menston: Scholar Press, 1969), v.

50. William Jones, *The Letters of Sir William Jones,* ed. Garland Cannon (Oxford: Clarendon, 1970), 2:798.

51. In a letter to William Steuart (September 13, 1789), Jones wrote: "Give my best compliments to Major Palmer & tell him that his friend Tafazzul Husain Khan is doing wonders in English & Mathematicks. He is reading Newton with Borrow, & means to translate the *Principia* into Arabick" (ibid., 838–40). On Tafazzul Husayn Khan, see Mir 'Abd al-Latif Shushtari, *Tuhfat al-'Alam va Zil al-Tuhfah*, ed. S. Muvvahid (Tehran: Tahuri, 1984), 363–7; Rahman 'Ali, *Tazkirah-'i 'Ulama-yi Hind* (Lucknow: Matba'-i Munshi Niwal Kishur, 1914), 36–37.

52. William Jones, "The Sixth Discourse: On the Persians, Delivered 19 February 1789," in Anna Maria Shipley-Jones, ed., *The Works of Sir William Jones*, 6 vols. (London: G. G. and J. Robinson and R. H. Evens, 1799), 77–78; Jones, "A Conversation with Abram, an Abyssinian concerning the City of Gwender and the Source of the Nile," in Shipley-Jones, *Works*, 1:517.

53. For Bahman's cooperation with Jones, see "The Sixth Discourse," 80, 81, 82, 84, 89. In a letter to Sir John Macpherson (May 6, 1786), Jones wrote, "I read with pleasure, while at breakfast, Mr. Forster's lively little tract, and having finished my daily task of Persian reading with a learned Parsi of Yazd, who accompanied me hither" (*Letters*, 697). In another letter to John Shore (August 16, 1787), Jones wrote, "If Bahman should return to Persia, I can afford to give him one hundred rupees a month. . . . I will cheerfully join you in any mode of clearing the honest man, that can be suggested; and would assist him merely for his own sake, as I have more Brahmanical teachers than I can find time to hear" (*Letters*, 763).

54. For instance, Shushtari, *Tuhfat al-'Alam*, 370, noted that Jones had written a commentary on Muhammad 'Ali Hazin and asked him "to note the deficiencies and excess."

55. According to Garland Cannon, Ibrahim Khan "[a] fine scholar of Persian . . . had been appointed Chief Magistrate of Benares in 1781. Twice offered the office of Naib Nazim, involving revenue collection, he declined because of Council dissensions and his own wish for independence" (Jones, *Letters*, 659). 'Ali Ibrahim Khan provided Jones with a copy of *Tuhfat al-Hind*, which he used in writing "On the Musical Modes of the Hindus," in *Works*, 1:413–43. See Nur al-Hasan Ansari, "Muqaddimah-i musahhah," in Muhammad, *Tuhfat al-Hind*, 41.

56. In a letter to Charles Wilkins (September 17, 1785), Jones wrote, "In the meantime, pray tell Mohammed Ghauth, that, if he will call on Mr. Chambers, he will receive some money, and that I will pay him his wages regularly when I come myself. I wish him to set about the Inscription from Gaia, which you so wonderfully decyphered" (*Letters*, 682).

57. Author of *Siyar al-muta'akhirin*, published as *A Translation of the Seir Mutagherin* (1789; Lahore: Sheikh Mubarakali, 1975).

58. In a letter to "the first Marquis of Cornwallis, Governor-General of Bengal in Council" (April 13, 1788), Jones recommended hiring four "Hindu and Muselman lawyers, whose assistance will be necessary in compiling a Digest of their respective laws." And he continued: "I have made very diligent inquiries for persons eminently qualified to engage in the work; and I beg leave to recommend four, whom, partly from my own personal knowledge of them, and partly from the information of those, in whose judgment I have perfect confidence, I believe to be Men of integrity and learning . . . 1. as the Pandit of this province, Radhacant Sarman, a Brahmen of distinguished abilities, and highly revered by the Hindus in Bengal for his erudition and virtue; 2. as the Pandit of Bahar, Sabur Tiwari,

who formerly attended the council at Patna, and is universally esteemed in the province as a lawyer of accurate and extensive knowledge; 3. as the Maulavi for the doctrines of the Sunnis Muhammed Kasim, who has applied himself from the earliest youth to the study of jurisprudence, and has acquired very just fame for his proficiency in it; 4. for the doctrine of the Shiâhs, where the two sects differ . . . Siraj'lhakk, who is an excellent scholar, well versed in law and many branches of philosophy." In additions to these four, Jones recommended, "As writers of Sanscrit and Arabick, I cannot recommend . . . two men better qualified, than Mahtab Raï and Haji Abdullah; the first, a native of the Decan, and the second, born at Medina, but educated at Mecca: both write beautifully and distinctly, and both are completely skilled in several languages, which they undertake to copy" (*Letters*, 801–2).

59. In a letter to John Shore dated August 16, 1787, Jones wrote, "I am assisting the court by studying Arabic and Sanscrit, and have now rendered it an impossibility for the Mohammedan or Hindu lawyers to impose upon us with erroneous opinions. . . . This brings to my mind your honest pundit, Rhadacaunt, who refused, I hear, the office of pundit to the court, and told Mr. Hastings that he would not accept of it, if the salary were doubled" (*Letters*, 762).

60. Jones to Charles Wilkins, September 17, 1785 (*Letters*, 683).

61. Mirza Itesa Modeen, *Shigurf Namah i Velaët; or, Excellent Intelligence Concerning Europe: Being the Travels of Mirza Itesa Modeen, in Great Britain and France,* trans. James Edward Alexander (London: Parbury, Allen, 1827), 65–66.

62. Mirza I'tisam al-Din reported, "Whilst here I visited Mr. Jones; this gentleman is now in the court of Calcutta. Captain S. and Mr. Jones taking me along with them, went to the libraries, where I saw numerous books in Persian and Arabic. Amongst these there were three papers written in Persian and Turkish characters, which a certain Mulekool Joosea had sent to the king of England. At that time there was nobody in England who could read Persian (fluently); for this reason the purport and meaning of these papers were not properly understood, and in every place there was the mark of doubt. They shewed them to me, and I read them with facility. They likewise, in order to examine me and try my abilities, put different books in my hand, and according to my capacity I explained their meaning and sense" (*Shigurf Namah,* 64–65).

63. Jones, *Works,* I: fn.129.

64. Jones, *Grammar,* xvi–xvii.

65. According to Arberry, "Early in 1768 Jones made the acquaintance of Count Reviczki, at that time resident in London, and was delighted to hail him as a fellow-admirer of Persian poetry." See A. J. Arberry, "The Founder: William Jones," in *Oriental Essays: Portraits of Seven Scholars* (London: Allen and Unwin, 1960), 50. For Jones's correspondences with Reviczki, see his *Letters,* #2 (1768), #3 (April 1768), #4 (1768), #9 (Nov. 1768), #28 (1770), #30 (May 1770), #32 (1770), #46 (1771), #58 (1771), and #101 (1775). See also Garland Hampton Cannon, *Oriental Jones: A Biography of Sir William Jones, 1746–1794* (New York: Asia Publishing House, 1964), 14–15.

66. Cannon, *Oriental Jones,* 10–13.

67. Jones, *Grammar,* xiv.

68. On the limitation of Jones's knowledge of Persian, see Garland Hampton Cannon, "Sir William Jones's Persian Linguistics," *Oriental Society* 78 (1958): 262–73.

69. Jones, *Grammar,* xv.

70. William Jones, *Lettre à Monsieur A*** du P***, dans laquelle est compris l'examen de sa traduction des livres attribués à Zoroastre* (London: Chez P. Elmsly, 1771). For a summary of this controversy, see Arthur D. Waley, "Anquetil Duperron and Sir William Jones," *History Today* 2 (1952): 23–33; Haug, *The Parsis,* 18–23; F. Max Müller, introduction to *The Zend-Avesta,* trans. James Darmesteter and Lawrence H. Mills (1880; Westport, Conn.: Greenwood Press, 1972), xiv–xxv; Edward G. Brown, *A Literary History of Persia: From the Earliest Times until Firdawsi* (New York: Scribner's, 1902), 44–59; Cannon, *Oriental Jones,* 14–15.

71. Jones, "The History of the Persian Language," in *Works,* 2:306.

72. Jones continued, "It is sufficient for us to have exposed his follies, detected his imposture, and retold his invectives, without insulting a fallen adversary, or attempting, like the Hero in Dryden's Ode, to *slay the slain*" (ibid., 2:307).

73. John Richardson, "A Dissertation on the Languages, Literature, and Manners of Eastern Nations," in *Dictionary, Persian, Arabic, and English* (London: Cox, 1829), vb.

74. Commenting on Anquetil-Duperron's *Zend-Avesta,* Richardson observed: "No Arabic was introduced into the Persian idiom earlier than the seventh century of the Christian era. . . . the harsh texture of his Zand seems opposite to the genius of Persian pronunciation; being apparently incompatible with their organ of speech. . . . It appears not to bear the most distinct resemblance to the modern dialect of Persia: a circumstance which all observation declares to be impossible, had it ever existed as an ancient Persian idiom" (ibid., ivb–vb).

75. Jones, "The Sixth Discourse," 83.

76. F. Max Müller, *The Sacred Languages of the East Translated by Various Oriental Scholars* (Delhi: Motilal Banarsidass, 1965), xx. Hans Aarsleff also views Jones as the founder of modern philology (*The Study of Language in England, 1780–1860* [Minneapolis: University of Minnesota Press, 1983], 124).

77. Müller, *The Sacred Languages of the East,* 4:xx–xxi.

78. Texts on the history of linguistics often open with entries on William Jones. For instance, Thomas A. Sebeok, *Portraits of Linguists: A Biographical Source for the History of Western Linguistics, 1746–1963* (Bloomington: Indiana University Press, 1966). The first three articles in this volume are devoted to Jones.

79. Saraj al-Din Khan Arzu, *Muthmir,* ed. Rehana Khatoon (Karachi: The Institute of Central and West Asian Studies, 1991). Khatoon notes in the introduction: "Khan-i Arzu is also the first scholar in both the East and the West who introduced the theory of similarities of two languages [*tavafuq-i lisanayn*], meaning that Sanskrit and Persian are sister languages. His ideas in this regard are contained in his monumental work . . . the *Muthmir.* The work has not yet been thoroughly studied and made a subject of serious assessment. . . . And this has prompted me to undertake and prepare a critical edition" (43).

80. Ibid., 221.

81. Arzu offered a detained definition of *tavafuq al-lisanayn* under the concept of *ang*. See his *Chiraq-i Hidayat* (published with Ghiyas al-Din Rampuri's *Ghiyas al-Lughat*), ed. Mansur Sirvat (Tehran: Amir Kabir, 1984), 1017–18. The editor of this edition, without any explanation, has eliminated Arzu's introduction to *Chiraq-i Hidayat*.

82. Ibid., 1050, 1061, 1068, 1091, 1119, 1020–1021, 1214.

83. According to Julia Kristeva, Father Coeurdoux had written a paper entitled "Question Proposed to Abbot Barthélémy and the Other Members of the Academy of Belles-Lettres and Inscriptions: How Is It That in the Sanskrit Language There Are a Large Number of Words That This Language Has in Common with Latin and Greek, but Especially with Latin?" (Kristeva, *Language, the Unknown: an Initiation into Linguistics*, trans. Anne M. Menke [New York: Columbia University Press, 1989], 196).

In 1773 Lord Monboddo (James Burnet), elaborating on the affinity of Sanskrit and Greek, wrote: " I will begin with the Greek, the language the most perfect that . . . is known; though, from what we hear of the Indian Sanscrit language, we have reason to think that it is likewise a language of wonderful art . . . that, in some respects . . . resembles very much the Greek, particularly in the verbs, of which the Sanscrit has a class that are conjugated in the same manner as the verbs in Greek." In a footnote, he added: "This curious fact is averred by a gentleman from India, whom I know, Mr. Brassey, who has written a grammar of the Bengallese language, which he says is a dialect of the Sanscrit, as well as the other languages spoken in India" (Burnet, *Of the Origin and Progress of Languages* [1773; Menston: Scholar Press Limited, 1967], 6:25).

84. According to Muhammad Javad Mashkur, "In Pahlavi writing there is a certain number of pure Semitic words . . . mostly Aramaic. . . . These Semitic words were probably never numerous, and not more than four hundred of them are to be found in the Pahlavi writings now extant. The language with this kind of admixture and complication, however, was not spoken as it was written. This Semitic element is called Huzvaresh. The Semitic words were used in writing only as representatives of Persian words that were spoken; for example, when the writer of a text wrote the Semitic word 'lahma' (bread) it was read 'nan' . . . its Iranian equivalent" (preface to *Farhang-i Huzvarish ha-yi Pahlavi* [Tehran: Bunyad-i Farhang-i Iran, 1967], 303).

85. Arzu, *Muthmir,* 195.

86. Jones, "The Sixth Discourse," 81.

87. Arzu, *Muthmir,* 13, 20.

88. "Iraniyan mara bah Hini nizhad budan bah miqdari nanahand." Quoted in Akram's "Pish guftar" in Siraj al-Din 'Ali Khan Arzu, *Dad-i Sukhan,* ed. Akram (Rawalpindi: Iran Pakistan Institute of Persian Studies, 1974), xxxiv.

89. Akram, "Pish guftar," xxxiv.

90. Abu al-Barakat Munir Lahuri, *Karnamah,* ed. Sayyid Muhammad Akram (Islamabad: Iran Pakistan Institute of Persian Studies, 1977), 26.

91. Ibid., 27.

92. Students and disciples of Arzu included Tik Chand Bahar, Rai Rayan Anand Ram

Mukhlis, Bindraban Das Khushgu, Mir Taqi Mir, Mirza Muhammad Rafi' Sauda, Najm al-Din Shah Mubarak Abru, Sharaf al-Din Mazmun, and Mustafa Khan Yakrang.

93. Muhammad Husayn Azad, *Ab-i Hayat* (1907; Lucknow: Uttar Pradesh Urdu Akademi, 1982), 121, quoted in Muhammad Sadiq, *A History of Urdu Literature* (Delhi: Oxford University Press, 1984), 91. Earlier, Qudartullah Qadiri remarked, "Just as all theologians are the lineal descendants of Abu Hanifa, similarly it would be quite appropriate to consider all Hindi [Urdu] poets as his [Arzu's] descendants"; quoted in Sadiq, *A History of Urdu Literature,* 91.

94. In a letter to John Shore (June 24, 1787), Jones wrote: "The Dabistan also I have read through twice with great attention.... Mr. R. Johnston thinks he has a young friend who will translate the Dabistan, and the greatest part of it would be very interesting to a curious reader, but some of it cannot be translated. It contains more recondite learning, more entertaining history, more beautiful specimens of poetry, more ingenuity and wit, more indecency and blasphemy, than I ever saw collected in a single volume.... On the whole, it is the most amusing and instructive book I every read in Persian" (*Letters,* 739).

95. See Mohamad Tavakoli-Targhi, "Contested Memories: Narrative Structures and Allegorical Meanings of Iran's Pre-Islamic History," *Iranian Studies* 29.1–2 (1996): 149–75.

96. Jones, "The Sixth Discourse," 77–78.

97. Ibid., 78.

98. Ibid., 88, 90, 92.

99. Ibid., 79. The significance of such an assertion had been brought to Jones's attention by Lord Monboddo who in a letter dated June 20, 1789, wrote, "If you can discover the central country from which all those nations, which you have named, have derived their affinity in language, manners and arts, which you observe, it will be a most wonderful discovery in the history of man" (quoted in Jones, *Letters,* 818 n. 2).

100. Jones, "The Sixth Discourse," 79.

101. Ibid., 80.

102. Ibid.

103. Ibid., 81.

104. Ibid.

105. Arzu, *Muthmir,* 175–79; the word list appears on 176–77.

106. Denis Wright, *The English amongst the Persians: During the Qajar Period, 1787–1921* (London: Heinemann, 1977), 12–17.

107. For a fraction of Mirza Salih's report, see Mirza Salih Shirazi, "Safar Namah-'i Isfahan, Kashan, Qum, Tihran," in *Majmu'ah-'i Safar namah-hayi Mirza-alih Shirazi* (Tehran: Nashr-i Tarikh-i Iran, 1364 A.H./1985), 5–36. The official mehmandar of this delegation was Mirza Zaki Mustawfi-i Divan-i A'la. See Dunbuli, *Ma'a–ir-i Sultaniyah,* 247.

108. William Price, *A Grammar of the Three Principal Oriental Languages, Hindoostani, Persian, and Arabic on a Plan Entirely New, and Perfectly Easy; to Which Is Added, a Set of Persian Dialogues Composed for the Author, by Mirza Mohammed Saulih, of Shiraz*

(London: Kingsbury, Parbury, and Allen, 1823), vi. The text of Mirza Salih's *Persian Dialogues* appear on 142–88, followed by a French translation, "Dialogues persans et français," 190–238.

109. The extract in Ouseley's *Travels in Various Countries of the East* (London: Rodwell and Martin, 1819–23), 1:xvii, is identical to the opening of Mirza Salih's text as printed in Price, *A Grammar,* 142–43.

110. Price, *A Grammar,* vii. In a note Price remarked: "Since that period Mirza Saulih came to England with Col. Darsy, in order to learn the English Language, returned to Persia in 1819, and lately arrived on a special Mission from the King of Persia to his Majesty George the Fourth. On my presenting him with a copy of his own dialogues, he expressed himself much pleased, and promised to compose a new set" (vi).

111. William Price, *Journal of the British Embassy to Persia; Embellished with Numerious Views Taken in India and Persia; Also, a Dissertation upon the Antiquities of Persepolis,* 2 vols. (London: Thorpe, 1932).

112. Ouseley, *Travels in Various Countries,* 3:363.

113. Ibid., 2:16.

114. John Binder and David Wellbery, eds., *The End of Rhetoric: History, Theory, and Practice* (Stanford, Calif.: Stanford University Press, 1990), 16.

A. R. Venkatachalapathy

Coining Words: Language and
Politics in Late Colonial Tamilnadu

Forming words with Sanskrit roots will certainly ruin the beauty and growth of the Tamil language and disfigure it; and is sure to inflame communal hatred.—E. M. Subramania Pillai, memorandum to government of Madras, September 5, 1941

Though a common terminology may be possible in Northern India where Hindustani and Sanskrit have mingled together very much and local languages have been greatly modified by them, such a terminology would be unsuited to the Tamil area where Tamils have preserved the purity of their language. Words coined must have Tamil roots and suffixes to make them intelligible to the Tamils.— Committee of Educationists, memorandum to the government of Madras, August 22, 1941

Some months ago, there raged in the academic world, a controversy regarding the coining of technical terms. While some said that there should be no bar on borrowing terms from other languages to express new scientific disciplines, others argued that only pure Tamil terms should be used. . . . [This] has raged since the beginnings of the Tamil language. But, in earlier days, . . . there were no acrimonious polemics; there was nobody to say "Our language is ruined by the admixture of other languages."—S. Vaiyapuri Pillai, *Sorkalai Virundu,* Madras, 1956 (originally published in *Dinamani,* May 10, 1947)

■ Drawing on Raymond Williams's formulation from his classic *Keywords* that "important social and historical processes occur *within* language,"[1] this essay will seek to explore the cultural politics surrounding the coining of technical and scientific terms for pedagogic purposes in late colonial Tamilnadu. But while Williams takes up a cluster of words, I will focus on the conscious struggle between two broadly defined ideological schools to establish their own set of principles.

In studying the debates surrounding the coining of technical terms in late colonial Tamilnadu, and delineating the counterhegemonic efforts of Tamil scholars to displace Sanskrit and other "foreign" languages in this arena (such as English), I will try to demonstrate how the latter lead to a general consensus by the 1940s about the existence of a common Tamil past that was rich and independent (especially of Sanskrit). This understanding directly resulted in demands that the development of the Tamil language on modern lines be free of all foreign influence. These processes took place in the context of the non-Brahmin movement, which gave political voice to such aspirations. The question, then, concerned not just the coining of words but also the fundamental definition of Tamil identity.

To understand these developments, we need to look into certain processes that obtained in colonial India and Tamilnadu. We now have enough studies showing how the Orientalist moment in India — from the late eighteenth to the mid-nineteenth centuries — produced knowledge about the country and its antique past. The paradigmatic works in this tradition — from William Jones to Max Müller — constructed an Indian past that neatly skirted Islamic India and explained it away as a "dark age" succeeding a glorious (Vedic) antiquity. The Sanskrit language was seen as the fount of all things Indian. The newly emergent discipline of comparative philology traced the roots of Sanskrit to a common Indo-Aryan/European family of languages. This construction was, of course, complicit in the metropolitan political project of exercising power over the colony by the production of a specific kind of knowledge about it.

There is another side to this Sanskrit-centered construction of knowledge — the challenge posed to it in the south of India, especially Tamilnadu. There, drawing on similar intellectual tools, an alternative understanding of the Indian/Tamil past was propounded. In this regard, Bishop Robert Caldwell's *A Comparative Grammar of the Dravidian Family of Languages* (1856) is considered the defining work — and the defining moment.[2] In this influential work, which played an authoritative role among a range of Tamil intellectuals engaged in the debate under discussion here, Caldwell argued that Tamil—along with Telugu, Kannada, Malayalam, and Tulu—belonged to a different linguistic family than other Indian languages that drew from Sanskrit. He held that, through the passage of time, Sanskrit had exerted a baneful influence on these languages by the admixture of its vocabulary. Caldwell contended that, especially in the case of Tamil, this "tainting" could easily be done away with and that Tamil could function without further reliance on Sanskrit. I would like to refer to this body of knowledge as *counter-Orientalism.*

A few decades after Caldwell's philological work, the Tamil literary canon underwent a dramatic change by the so-called rediscovery of a corpus of literature from the turn of the Christian era. Termed *Sangam literature,* these texts were meticulously retrieved, edited, and published by a group of scholar-editors—especially C. W. Damodaram Pillai (1832–1901) and U. V. Swaminatha Iyer (1855–1942)—in the late nineteenth and early twentieth centuries. Intellectuals seized these texts, which portrayed a society in transition from a tribal to a sedentary agricultural social formation, to portray an alternative Tamil history. This literature, glorifying love and war, was seen to embody the real genius of the Tamil people. The Tamil past so imagined envisioned an ancient and egalitarian society, free of caste and institutionalized religion, where only valor and munificence were valued. This imagining counterposed the Vedic/Aryan understanding of India's past, which was characterized by religion and ascriptive differences based on birth. It linked the downfall of the glorious Tamil society to the advent of Aryans/Brahmins/Sanskrit, concepts it used almost synonymously.

The knowledge produced by the counter-Orientalist moment fed into notions about the glory of Tamil and the antipathy toward Brahmins and Sanskrit in colonial Tamil society. In a context where Brahmins and upper-caste non-Brahmins were pitched against each other not only in civil society but also in the struggle for political power, the battle came to be waged on different planes. This essay deals with one such struggle. Through a mapping of the debates surrounding appropriate scientific terminology, we can see the articulation of notions of purity and the independent functioning of language, and we can investigate how such views came to be entrenched in Tamil society.

The gradual expansion of education under the colonial aegis made the need to produce standard textbooks based on commonly understood terminology in indigenous languages keenly felt. Early Tamil textbooks man-

ifested an excessive reliance on English terms, many of them little more
than awkward transliterations into Tamil. Not surprisingly, the nationalist
intellectuals were the first to react to this situation. Along with a friend, C.
Rajagopalachari, a prominent Congress leader in Tamilnadu, in 1917 created the *Journal of the Tamil Scientific Terms Society.* Predictably enough,
the "Tamil" technical terms coined in the journal were almost exclusively
drawn from Sanskrit. Subramania Bharati, the great modern Tamil nationalist poet, in his review of the journal, opposed its publication in English,[3] but was in broad agreement with its aim of drawing technical terms
from Sanskrit:

> The "Nagari Pracharini Sabha" of Varanasi is producing a huge glossary
> by translating European technical terms into simple Sanskrit. Our ver-
> nacular languages may, to the best possible and desirable extent, draw
> from these terms. All European languages, likewise, draw from Greek
> and Latin. If we do the same [adopting from Sanskrit] there will be
> uniform terminology in our vernaculars.[4]

Bharati's views constitute a typical nationalist perspective, shared by a
wide range of Brahmin intellectuals. Fed on a staple diet of Orientalist
scholarship, the newly emerging English-educated Brahmin intellectuals
sought to reestablish the inferiorization of Tamil vis-à-vis Sanskrit.[5] In the
specific context of Tamilnadu, the activities of the Theosophical Society
reinforced this attitude. V. Krishnaswamy Iyer, a prominent Congress
leader of the pre-Swadeshi era, claimed that "Sanskrit is the parent of all
Indian literature including Tamil; for much that is claimed in Tamil as
original is indebted to conceptions which are entirely to be found in the
field of Sanskrit."[6] And P. S. Sivaswamy Iyer saw Sanskrit "as the language
which enshrines the highest ideas of Indo-Aryan."[7] As its flip side, this
glorification of Sanskrit resulted in the demotion of Tamil. Nambi Arooran
has shown how, at the University of Madras, Tamil was marginalized as a
"vernacular" language, while Sanskrit was accorded the status of a classical
language.[8] M. S. S. Pandian has argued that the hegemonic position of the
Brahmin in civil society had its roots in the privileging of Sanskrit and the
accompanying contempt for Tamil.[9] Given the contemporary perspective
on Sanskrit and Tamil, and the nationalist compulsion to imagine a united
and homogeneous Indian nation, Sanskrit was "naturally" stressed as the
root (both etymologically and figuratively) of all new word coinage.

The mainstream construction of an Indian/Tamil past did not go unchallenged. By the late nineteenth century, a group of non-Brahmin Tamil scholars from the elite Vellalar caste — P. Sundaram Pillai, V. Kanakasabhai Pillai, and J. M. Nallaswami Pillai among them — drawing on the philological works of Robert Caldwell, Miron Winslow, and G. U. Pope, counterposed their own construction of history. It effectively displaced Sanskrit and Brahmins with Tamil and Vellalars, conjuring up a vision of a glorious and independent Tamil past. As M. Srinivasa Aiyangar commented in 1914: "Within the last fifteen years a new school of Tamil scholars has come into being. . . . Their object has been to disown and to disprove any trace of indebtedness to the Aryans, to exalt the civilization of the ancient Tamils, to distort in the name of historical research current traditions and literature, and to pooh-pooh the views of former scholars, which support Brahmanization of the Tamil race."[10] If we discount an opponent's prejudice from this assessment, a more pithy summary of the Vellalar scholars' work cannot be made.

Thus it should come as no surprise that this very group of scholars came to contest word coinage based on Sanskrit roots. By 1920, P. N. Appuswamy, the editor of *Tamilar Nesan* (which contributed no small amount to Tamil technical terminology) had identified three lines of thought on the issue: "Some stress that technical terms should be based on pure Tamil root-words. Some are of the view that they may be drawn from the fraternal language, Sanskrit. While yet others say, why waste our efforts, let us adopt in toto the English terms used all over the world. It is time we decided this [issue]."[11] But the problem was not be settled so easily. It took decades to resolve the question, and well over a decade passed before it was even seriously, if acrimoniously, debated.

The first round of the debate started around the organization of the Tamil Anbar Mahanadu (The Tamil Enthusiasts' Conference) in Madras in December 1933. From the beginning, controversy plagued the conference. It was generally perceived that the conference was the handiwork of Brahmin scholars to push through their own program of Tamil development. The monthly *Bharati* queried why some of the major non-Brahmin Tamil scholars — such as Maraimalai Adigal, Somasundara Bharati, Pandithamani Kathiresan Chettiar, V. O. Chidambaram Pillai, K. Subramania Pillai, Umamaheswaran Pillai, Satchidanandam Pillai, and N. M. Venkatasami Nattar — had received no invitation to the conference. It also stressed that issues of caste, religion, and politics should remain outside of common issues like language and literature.[12] If this was the criticism voiced by nonpartisan intellectuals, the Self-Respect Movement, which under Periyar E. V. Ramasamy constituted the vanguard of the non-Brahmin movement, launched more open and vehement attacks. An editorial in the *Kudi Arasu*, titled "Purohita Atchiyin Pithalattangal" [The skullduggery of priestly rule], expressed the view that the conference was little more than a conspiracy by the "priestly class" to ensure their control over the Tamil language.[13]

The Tamil Enthusiasts' Conference opened with much fanfare on December 23, 1933, at Pachaiyappa's College, Madras. Leading nationalist and literary personalities like V. S. Srinivasa Sastri, S. Satyamurty, Varadarajulu Naidu, Thiru Vi, Kaliyanasundara Mudaliar, Kumaraswamy Raja, T. K. Chidambaranatha Mudaliar, "Sangu" Subramaniam, Va. Ra. (V. Ramaswamy Iyengar), R. Krishnamurty ("Kalki"), Ambujam Ammal, Sister Balammmal, Kodainayaki Ammal, and others participated. Messages sent by Mahatma Gandhi, C. P. Ramaswamy Iyer, and P. S. Sivaswamy Iyer were read out.[14]

The doyen of Tamil scholars, U. V. Swaminatha Iyer, presided over the conference. Inter alia, he referred to the question of coining Tamil technical terms and expressed the opinion that no attempt should be made to replace already existing vocabulary (even if they were of non-Tamil origin). In his view, the terms needed to be simple and easy to understand; it mattered little whether they were of pure Tamil origin or not. But then he introduced the caveat that the borrowed terms should remain in keeping with Tamil phonological conventions.[15] Swaminatha Iyer's views did not satisfy Sanskrit diehards who felt his opinions were not clear-cut enough and had tried to accommodate the ideas of the pure-Tamil champions.[16] The hard-hitting speech of Raja Sir Annamalai Chettiar,[17] attacking "pedants" who insisted on coining pure Tamil terms at the expense of simplicity and easy comprehensibility, more accurately reflected the general tenor of the conference.[18]

Some activists of the Self-Respect Movement seem to have raised questions and caused commotion during the conference.[19] However, many of the resolutions passed emphasized the need for education in Tamil, announced the preparation of an encyclopedia in Tamil, and assigned classical status to Tamil in the universities.[20] But two resolutions, one urging the use of terms already in currency when suitable Tamil terms could not be coined, and another recommending the pruning of the Tamil alphabet of some supposedly redundant letters and the incorporation of new ones to spell foreign sounds, stirred up a hornet's nest. Within a fortnight of the

Tamil Enthusiasts' Conference, a group of Vellalar Tamil scholars led by
M. V. Nellaiyappa Pillai and E. M. Subramania Pillai gathered at the Vasantha Mandapam, Tirunelveli, to condemn these resolutions. They urged
the culling of suitable terms from the ancient Tamil classics and the coining
of new ones from Tamil root words.[21] Interestingly, even when this meeting
adopted the other, noncontroversial resolutions passed at the Tamil Enthusiasts' Conference, they placed the Sanskrit words in the original resolutions in parentheses, substituting them with Tamil equivalents.[22] The meeting also resolved to hold a Tamil provincial conference some months
later.

The proposed conference stimulated much debate, with various views
being expressed about the coining of Tamil technical terms.[23] In fact, the
secretary of the conference, E. M. Subramania Pillai,[24] and the moving
spirit behind the whole venture, had to issue a statement clarifying the
organizers' position:

> Various views are being expressed by some people about the Madras
> Presidency Tamil Conference to be held shortly in Tirunelveli. Some
> members of the Tamil Enthusiasts' Conference held last December in
> Madras say this is a rival conference. The Self-respect group dubs this as
> a Vellalar conference.[25] . . . We have for a long time thought of ways to
> develop the Tamil language. . . . In the public meeting held on 7 January
> 1934 the name "Madras Presidency Tamil Conference" was accepted
> unanimously after much deliberation. We invite all Tamil people and
> enthusiasts irrespective of caste and religion to take part in the con-
> ference. There is space for even divergent political parties. Therefore
> there will be no resolutions regarding caste, religion or politics. The aim
> of the organizers of this conference is to maintain the purity of Tamil.
> Only resolutions which put forth the development of Tamil and ensure
> unity and love, without detriment to its purity and richness will be taken
> up.[26]

The conference, out of which was born the Chennai Magana Tamilar
Sangam (Madras Presidency Tamil Sangam) to coin technical Tamil terminology, was finally held in June 1934.[27] Beginning in 1934, Tamil Sangam
organized a series of seminars for the specific purpose of coining terms.[28]
The journal *Tamil Thai* was also published in pursuance of this objective.
Special committees were formed for disciplines like mathematics, physics,
chemistry, botany, zoology, physiology, geography, and agriculture.[29] In

1938 the Sangam published a volume called *Kalaichorkal* [Technical terms] out of the efforts of these committees and conferences.

By this time, a wide range of intellectuals and Tamil scholars, never identified with either the non-Brahmin movement or the Vellalar Tamil scholars, found themselves drawn toward the Sangam's endeavors. For instance, the widely respected Swami Vipulanandar (of the Ramakrishna mission, Batticoloa) presided over the 1936 conference.[30] The various committees consisted of scholars like Vipulanandar, S. G. Manavala Ramanujam, V. P. Subramania Mudaliar, A. Sreenivasaraghavan, K. P. Santosham, Sami Velayutham Pillai, R. P. Sethu Pillai, and Arul Thangaiah. T. P. Meenakshisundaram Pillai (a much respected scholar and nationalist) and T. N. Seshachalam Iyer, editor of the literary journal *Kalanilayam,* also participated in the conferences.[31] The committees also included a number of Brahmins (as could be surmised from their caste surnames).[32] This broad spectrum of scholars from diverse groups and factions shows how the cause originally espoused by Vellalar scholars only had begun to gain acceptance in a wider scholarly community.[33] The champions of Tamil had won the first round when *Kalaichorkal* received a foreword from C. Rajagopalachari (Rajaji), who appreciated the work in broad terms. In addition, the government of Madras subsequently recommended the volume be distributed to all secondary schools at government expense.[34]

But this victory, if indeed it can be counted as one, was marked by ambivalence. Spurred by the initial success, E. M. Subramania Pillai wrote to Rajaji, then the premier of Madras Presidency, asking the government to adopt the terms prepared by the Sangam in all schools after the vocabulary had undergone some further revision in light of suggestions made by actual teachers.[35] While Rajaji categorically opposed the adoption of English terms, he believed that "it is wrong to create confusion in the task of compiling ancient technical terms and coining new terms by aligning with the Pure Tamil movement. One should not bear an unreasonable hatred for Sanskrit words that tend to mix [with Tamil] naturally."[36] He therefore did not underwrite E. M. Subramania Pillai's endeavors to the full extent. His comment in the government order was: "Perhaps we may keep aloof for the time being."[37] Such governmental ambivalence ultimately led to the next round of conflict.

In June 1940, the government of Madras, having "recognized the importance of providing for a more extended use of the mother tongue in teaching non-language subjects in high schools" and the necessity for suitable textbooks for this purpose, felt the need for "a proper and commonly accepted vocabulary of scientific and technical terms." In pursuance of this objective, it appointed a committee headed by V. S. Srinivasa Sastri to settle the "general principles on which a uniform system of standardized technical and scientific terms" could be introduced, and further proposed subcommittees for each language after such general principles were laid down.[38] The main terms of reference were: (1) the extent to which equivalents of foreign technical terms in south Indian languages then in use were acceptable for educational purposes; (2) the desirability of retaining the use of English terms when there were no accepted equivalents in the south Indian languages; and (3) whether, as an alternative, it was necessary to draw up new and standardized lists of equivalents of certain foreign technical terms for all the south Indian languages.[39] The Madras Presidency Tamil Sangam received with shock the news of the constitution of that committee. The association's secretary, E. M. Subramania Pillai immediately shot off a letter to the government:

> It is . . . surprising to find that the Government . . . should now think it desirable to form a new committee with very poor representation of Tamilians and no representation of the Tamil Sangam that has laboured so much in the field till now. . . . The Tamilians . . . view the constitution of the Committee and the terms of reference with considerable distrust and alarm and feel that their language and culture that has withstood the onslaughts of several centuries and can even now shine independent of foreign help should have come to be thus smothered . . . in the guise of uniform scientific terminology.[40]

Subramania Pillai called for the withdrawal of the terms of reference, the dissolution of the committee, and the constitution of separate language committees for work along the lines suggested by the Sangam. He also threatened to "agitate both in the platform and through the press" if his demands were not met.[41] The fears of Subramania Pillai and the Madras Presidency Tamil Sangam were not unfounded. The government committee's chairman, V. S. Srinivasa Sastri, had definite views on the subject of coining technical terms. By his own admission, he was far from proficient in Tamil and had a clear bias toward Sanskrit. As he wrote to the secretary of the Education Department: "Uniformity of phraseology is . . . a desideratum . . . [but we] cannot wait for the ideal system of nomenclature which shall [have] at the same time the approval of the purist who stands up for the niceties of linguistic correctitude and that of the chauvinist who abhors borrowing from foreign sources."[42]

Apart from these prejudices, which dubbed the perspective of the pro-Tamil scholars as chauvinist, Srinivasa Sastri also showed undue interest in the choice of the committee. He insisted on two teachers each from colleges and high schools and one representative each from the Madurai and Karanthai Tamil Sangams, deliberately excluding the Madras Presidency Tamil Sangam. Lastly, he strongly recommended the inclusion of S. Vaiyapuri Pillai, a scholar generally perceived as anti-Tamil.[43]

The Madras Presidency Tamil Sangam issued a series of pamphlets condemning the government's move. These explained the necessity of coining technical terms only in Tamil and refuted the arguments of those who stood for loanwords.[44] Another pamphlet "exposed" the definite Sanskrit leanings of at least six committee members and deplored the failure to appoint even a single pro-Tamil scholar to the committee. It went on to suggest a dozen widely respected Tamil scholars who were better qualified for the task than members of the existing committee.[45] It argued that frequent changes in terminology would only end up creating confusion and demonstrated, by listing earlier Sanskrit-based word coinage, that these were awkward and unsuitable for Tamil.[46] Other Tamil scholars expressed similar views.[47]

Unmindful of these protests, the Sastri Committee went about its business quickly and submitted its recommendations within three months of its constitution. The Madras Presidency Tamil Sangam complained that it felt "strange that the Technical Terms Committee [had] . . . concluded its labours in so short a time and in haste, considering the importance of the work entrusted to it."[48] A government official jotted the following note on the file: "As was done with previous representations from the Sangam, the present representation may also . . . be ignored."[49]

The Sastri Committee's report confirmed the pro-Tamil scholars' worst fears. It made the following recommendations:

(i) The equivalents of foreign technical terms in the south Indian languages now in use in the lower secondary classes have mostly established themselves and are acceptable;

(ii) it is necessary to draw up a standardized list of technical terms, common to all south Indian languages, for conceptual or abstract names and ideas;

(iii) the remaining technical terms . . . will be bodily taken from English and transliterated into the south Indian scripts accompanied wherever necessary, by the original words in English script enclosed within brackets.[50]

These recommendations were met with a further series of pamphlets and articles in scholarly journals and periodicals, wherein the pro-Tamil scholars emphasized Tamil's membership in an entirely different language family, non-Sanskrit in origin, namely, the Dravidian. They also maintained that new terminology could be coined on the basis of Tamil root words. They rallied the evidence for this purpose from the philological works of Max Müller, Robert Caldwell, and Suniti Kumar Chatterjee.[51]

The memorandum sent by the Madras Presidency Tamil Sangam, dated November 25, 1940, contains the most elaborate, cogent, and lucid case for the pro-Tamil position.[52] *The Modern Review* described it as "very informative and well-argued."[53] First, the memorandum claimed that the "Committee of Experts" was quite unrepresentative, packed with men having "a special and definite leaning towards English and Sanskrit terms"; that it was insufficient, as just fifteen men could not seal the fate of so many languages; and that it was quite incompetent since the members had "precious little" knowledge of Tamil and Dravidian philology. Second, the memorandum noted that the terms of reference were narrow (limited to educational purposes), ambiguous (as the phrase "all the south Indian languages" could mean the languages taken individually or together), and faulty. Finally, the memorandum argued that the recommendations themselves were quite arbitrary since they gave no reason for choosing Sanskrit roots in some cases and English terms in others. It further described the recommendations as inconsistent, for while Arabic and Persian roots were recommended for Urdu, Dravidian was not similarly recommended for the Dravidian languages. Moreover, the memorandum's writers considered the committee's suggestions unscientific: while direct borrowing was preferable to indirect borrowing through a dead language (Sanskrit), the former remained unsuitable and injurious as the mechanical transliteration of English terms would sound hideous in the middle of a Tamil sentence; it could not be written or spelt in the native languages properly; it would undergo changes in pronunciation which would make the terms unrecognizable and even ridiculous; and it would constitute a dead weight in the language, quite incapable of generating further derivatives, especially verb forms. It followed that the recommendations hampered the spread of scientific knowledge among the masses. Finally, the pro-Tamil scholars found the recommendations shortsighted and impractical, as Indian languages would soon displace English as the medium of instruction and since every attempt at uniformity in various languages was only doomed to failure.[54]

A further committee headed by T. S. Nataraja Pillai, A. Muthia Pillai, and Arul Thangiah submitted a similar memorandum to the government.[55] These memoranda were followed by a massive meeting held at Gokhale Hall, Madras, on August 31, 1941. Sir Mohammed Usman, vice chancellor of the University of Madras, presided over the meeting. As the *Free Press Journal* noted, "Leaders belonging to all shades of political opinion and communities," such as S. Muthiah Mudaliar, T. S. Tirumurty Iyer, Arul Thangiah, T. P. Meenakshisundaram Pillai, and Kunjitham Guruswami, addressed the meeting.[56] Speakers condemned the recommendations of the Sastri Committee and underscored the danger of adopting foreign words, which they believed would spell disaster for Tamil. Resolutions stating that common scientific terminology applicable to the whole of India, which comprised a variety of languages and cultures, was impracticable and unnecessary, and that suitable Tamil equivalents for scientific terms could be found in almost all cases, were passed unanimously. S. Muthiah Mudaliar warned that the government would face an upheaval of the magnitude of the anti-Hindi agitation in 1937–39, which had brought the Congress ministry to a standstill.[57] In the *Sunday Observer* Balasubramania Mudaliar held out a similar threat. T. P. Meenakshisundaram Pillai expressed the hope that Rajaji would have fully supported the cause had he not been imprisoned. He added that interpolated Sanskrit and English words were only "millstones around the neck."[58]

Despite the all-around support that the cause of coining technical terms in Tamil had won, a mood of despondency permeated the pro-Tamil camp with the government's increasing stubbornness. E. M. Subramania Pillai's personal communication from that time reveals this mood: "The government has succumbed to the conspiracy of the Sanskrit Brahmins. . . . Our resolutions have not been heeded. Perhaps, if we meet the government in person and explain to it the conspiracy of Sanskrit Brahmins there might be a change [in its attitude]."[59] He was no less unhappy with non-Brahmin leaders. In an earlier letter to V. Subbaiah Pillai, dated November 20, 1934, he had written:

Brahmins have roped in some of us to destroy our non-Brahmin association, and have even met with three-fourths success. This is due to the
selfishness of our leaders. The non-Brahmin ministry runs the government. But the minister has scaled down the salary of vernacular language teachers, much to the detriment of the mother tongues. . . . Unless
our leaders mend their ways, realize the truth and work for the com-
monweal, can the conspiracy of our enemies be foiled?[60]

Despite such disillusionment, the discussion continued with Tamil
scholars representing a wide spectrum.[61] And the debate spared no one. At
the Provincial Tamil Music Conference and Tamil Pandits' Conference held
in Tiruchi in December 1941 under the presidency of K. Ponniah Pillai,
professor of music at the University of Madras, and S. Somasundara
Bharati, the noted scholar and professor of Tamil at Annamalai University,
participants passed a resolution condemning "very strongly the action of
U. V. Swaminatha Iyer in misrepresenting pure Sanskrit phrases as Tamil
idiom, in spite of holding all the highest titles in Tamil and amassing enormous wealth through Tamil from Tamilians, and [urging] him to admit his
error."[62] Another resolution called for the immediate dissolution of the
Sastri Committee.

In yet another controversy, A. Ramaswamy Gounder, principal of Salem
College and the only dissenting member of the Sastri Committee, took issue
with comments on Sundaram Pillai made by Vaiyapuri Pillai in an article
attacking "sectarian" perspectives in regard to the coining of technical
terms, which called for the adoption of Sanskrit terms following Sundaram
Pillai's example.[63] The appeal to Sundaram Pillai's authority is ironic since
he was generally perceived as the doyen of the Tamil "renaissance" in the
late nineteenth century. (His invocation to "Mother Tamil" was adopted as
the Tamil anthem after the Dravida Munnetra Kazhagam took over as the
state government in Tamilnadu in the 1960s). Ramaswamy Gounder exposed the partisanship behind this argument and declared it as part of a
larger diabolical plan of the Brahmins and their collaborators to destroy
Tamil. He quoted from Sundaram Pillai's writings to show that not only
had he fully subscribed to the theory of the Dravidian family of languages
but that he had also condemned Sanskrit as a dead language.[64] Ramaswamy Gounder went on to reproduce a personal exchange of words with
Vaiyapuri Pillai during the course of a Technical Terms Committee meeting
and detailed his pro-Sanskrit views.[65]

Periyar E. V. Ramasamy, single-handedly responsible for the radicalization of the non-Brahmin movement from the late 1920s onward, also entered this debate. While emphasizing the need for simplicity and easy comprehensibility when coining technical terms, he condemned the terms coined by the Technical Terms Committee and praised the efforts of the Madras Presidency Tamil Sangam whose preferable word choices he attributed to the association's real love for Tamil. He concluded: "We can borrow words from any language which is in keeping with our dignity and self-respect, and which will instill a sense of independence and rid us of our present debasement. It does not matter with which language we are associated. But we should never have any truck with Sanskrit."[66] The struggle, then, pertained not only to certain aspects of language, but was closely tied to the forging of a new identity based largely on language. Periyar, as was his wont, had once again pithily and forcefully highlighted the crucial issues at stake.

In 1946, the Congress formed an interim government in Madras. This turning point of sorts led to the final round of the controversy, crowning the efforts of the pro-Tamil school with success. Under the interim ministry, T. S. Avinasilingam Chettiar took over the education portfolio of the Madras government. Though a Congressman, he was generally perceived as pro-Tamil, and his ministership raised the hopes of Tamil scholars. The Madras Presidency Tamil Sangam released pamphlets putting forward its case. In a pamphlet titled "Namathu Sangamum Tamil Magana Congressum"[67] [Our sangam and the Tamilnadu Congress], E. M. Subramania Pillai recapitulated the various efforts of the Sangam and the cooperation extended to it by the earlier Congress ministry. He pleaded for the coining of technical terms only in good Tamil, and that the mother tongue should be the medium of instruction in all schools and colleges.

Avinasilingam Chettiar showed much enthusiasm and reacted positively. He went about the task of overhauling the standardization of the Technical and Scientific Terms Committee, which had more or less become defunct after the demise of its chairman V. S. Srinivasa Sastri in April 1946. On his own initiative, Avinasilingam Chettiar appointed T. S. Thirumurty Iyer (who had participated in many of the meetings organized to condemn the Sastri Committee's recommendations) as the chairman of the committee. Avinasilingam Chettiar further suggested the following members for the Tamil subcommittee: Swami Vipulanandar, R. P. Sethu Pillai, Vaiyapuri Pillai, G. Subramania Pillai, and A. Chidambaranathan Chettiar.[68] Except for Vaiyapuri Pillai, the others, though representing diverse political camps and factions, were all part of the emerging hegemonic formation in the world of Tamil scholarship. But, in a sense, the government sanction only affirmed the fait accompli of pro-Tamil influence. The committee had by then submitted its draft report, which stands testimony to the victory of the Tamil scholars. The Tamil subcommittee openly acknowledged its indebtedness to the *Kalaichorkal* published by the Madras Presidency Tamil Sangam, claiming to have drawn many fruitful suggestions for the formation of new words from it. Then it added: "The sub-committee felt that a strict and literal conformity with the recommendations of the Technical Terms [Sastri] Committee was inexpedient, as the adoption of a very large number of English words and words of Sanskrit origin would run counter to the current tendency of Tamil scholarship."[69]

The subcommittee also added two additional terminological categories, overriding the earlier recommendations: (1) adopting Tamil words that had already been in common use in high school classes; and (2) making straight translations from English into Tamil of the terms for qualities, processes, and the like. Finally, the Tamil subcommittee claimed "that the lists now offered by the sub-committee represent a just and reasonable balance between the purely academic and educational ideals of the Technical Terms Committee and the insistent claims of linguistic patriotism."[70] What had once been dubbed chauvinism was now validated, if only indirectly, as patriotism.

The controversy around the coining of technical terms constitutes one example of how larger political issues regarding power, representation, and identity were fought out in and through issues of language. As part of a larger process of identity formation amongst the Tamils, Brahmin hegemony in a range of cultural fields was being contested. The rediscovery of the ancient Tamil classics and the formulation of a theory of the Dravidian family of languages in the second half of the nineteenth century provided the intellectual ammunition for this challenge and the creation of a new Tamil identity. Earlier histories of the Tamil-Sanskrit contestation were recast and reinterpreted in a new light.

Pro-Tamil scholars believed Sanskrit had done great harm to the natural growth of the Tamil language, suppressed it, and relegated it to an inferior status. Further, the foreign "contamination" of Tamil was also seen to have divorced the language from the people. To redeem the self-image of both the Tamil language and the Tamil people, nationalist scholars regarded it as essential to counter the high status accorded Sanskrit. The counterhege-monic efforts of Tamil scholars started late in the nineteenth century. With the progressive study of the Tamil classics, involving meticulous research and much reinterpretation, a more egalitarian conception of the Tamil past and, by implication, a more democratic Tamil present were being forged. A growing number of Tamil scholars across a wide spectrum was to share this new view of the Tamil past and present. This had little to do directly with the organized non-Brahmin movement, nor was it restricted to the Vellalar scholars, who had done much initially to formulate the Dravidian ideology for the genesis of the non-Brahmin movement. Ultimately, the emerging consensus regarding the Tamil past and the nature of the Tamil language did not even spare scholars of the stature of U. V. Swaminatha Iyer (who had done more than anyone else for the rediscovery of the Tamil classics) and Vaiyapuri Pillai of criticism.

In 1946, when the Chennai Tamil Arignar Kazhagam recommended T. P. Meenakshisundaram Pillai, A. Ramaswamy Gounder, Devaneya Pavanar, R. P. Sethu Pillai, Sami Velayudam Pillai, M. S. Sabesa Iyer, A. Chidambaranathan Chettiar, and others for appointment to the Techni-cal Terms Committee, sectarian boundaries had clearly been transcended. The Tamil subcommittee's acceptance of the principles behind the coining of technical terms adopted by the Madras Presidency Tamil Sangam sig-naled the final victory for the pro-Tamil camp. The controversy also brings to the forefront the problematic relationship between the world of Tamil scholars/scholarship and the non-Brahmin/Dravidian movement. Else-where I have argued against a one-to-one reduction of the Vellalar/Saivite elite to the non-Brahmin movement.[71] Much deeper cultural undercurrents fed into the Dravidian movement and gave it intellectual succor while si-multaneously drawing political support for its cause. The Dravidian move-ment is best interpreted as an overtly political manifestation of more deep-seated contradictions in Tamil society, which sharpened early in this cen-tury against the background of colonial rule.

Notes

This essay forms part of a joint project on the social history of the Dravidian movement with M. S. S. Pandian and S. Anandhi. An expanded version of this article, in Tamil, has recently been published in A. R. Venkatachalapathy, *Andha kalathil kappi illai mutha-lana aivu katturaigal* (Nagercoil: Kalachuvadu, 2000). I thank Pandian for his rigorous reading of earlier drafts. For additional comments I am grateful to K. N. Panikkar, S. Anandhi, A. S. Paneerselvan, V. R. Muraleedharan, and D. Veeraraghavan. However, I would like to stress my responsibility for the views expressed in this essay.

1. Raymond Williams, *Keywords: A Vocabulary of Culture and Society* (London: Fontana, 1983), 22. Original emphasis.

2. A recent work by Thomas Trautmann in my view plausibly seeks to push this moment to the 1820s when Francis Whyte Ellis, a scholar-administrator, formulated similar views based on a study of the Telugu language. Trautmann, "Hullabaloo about Telugu," *South Asia Research* 19.1 (1999): 53–70.

3. *Bharati katturaigal,* vol. 3, *Kalaigal* (Madras: Bharati Prachuralayam, n.d.), 110. These articles by Subramania Bharati were originally written in the nationalist Tamil daily *Swadesamitran* during 1916–19. Translations from the Tamil are mine, unless otherwise noted.

4. Ibid., 110. For an argument in favor of retaining English terms, see A. V. Subramania Iyer, *Tharkala Tamil ilakkiyam* (Madras: Makkal Veliyeedu, 1985), 56–58.

5. See M. S. S. Pandian, "Notes on the Transformation of 'Dravidian' Ideology, Tamil Nadu, c. 1900–1940," *Social Scientist* 252–53 (1994): 84–104.

6. *Indian Review,* January 1911 and April 1910. Quoted in ibid., 3.

7. *New India,* November 19, 1914. Quoted in ibid.

8. K. Nambi Arooran, *Tamil Renaissance and Dravidian Nationalism, 1905–1944* (Madurai: Koodal, 1980).

9. Pandian, "Notes on the Transformation," 86–87.

10. M. Srinivasa Aiyangar, *Tamil Studies: Essays on the History of the Tamil People, Language, Religion, and Literature* (Madras: Guardian Press, 1914), 46.

11. P. N. Appuswamy, "Arivu Nool Mozhigal," *Tamilar Nesan* 4.6 (Routhri, Purattasi [Tamil calendar], September 1920).

12. "Asiriya Kurripugal," *Bharati* 5.6 (September–October 1933).

13. *Kudi Arasu,* September 12, 1937.

14. See the report of the proceedings in *Manikkodi,* December 24, 1933.

15. The text of U. V. Swaminatha Iyer's inaugural address was published in *Manikkodi,* December 24, 1933.

16. See the article by "Oru Anbar" (An enthusiast), *Manikkodi,* December 31, 1933.

17. Annamalai Chettiar, however, later in his life patronized the pro-Tamil scholars through his Annamalai University, which was conceived as a university for Tamil. In the early 1940s he was the moving spirit behind the Tamil Isai (music) movement.

18. For the text of Annamalai Chettiar's speech, see *Manikkodi,* December 24, 1933. "Oru Anbar" welcomed this speech and described it as "clear-cut." Ibid., December 31, 1933.

19. Ibid.

20. For the text of the resolutions, see *Manikkodi,* December 24, 1933.

21. *Kumaran,* January 25, 1934.

22. For example, *moli* instead of *bashai* (language), *muthanmai* instead of *pirathanyam* (primacy), *manadu* instead of *mahanadu* (conference). That these alternatives are in usage even today in Tamilnadu proclaims the success of the counterhegemonic project of the pro-Tamil scholars.

23. See, for instance, the editorial in *Kumaran,* March 15, 1934.

24. For details of his life and work, see the biography by his son, E. S. Muthusamy, *Tamil perumpulavar Ee. Mu. Subramania Pillai* (Madras: Pari Nilayam, 1984), which also contains an account of his contribution to the project of coining technical terms in Tamil and the controversies surrounding it (46–66).

25. For the ambivalent and tension-ridden relationship between the Vellalar/Saivite elite and the Dravidian movement, see A. R. Venkatachalapathy, "The Dravidian Movement and the Saivites, 1927–1944," *Economic and Political Weekly* 30.14 (2002): 761–68. (For an extended Tamil version, see my *Dravida iyakkamum vellalarum* [Madras: South Vision, 1994]).

26. *Kumaran,* May 10, 1934. For similar views about the need to maintain the purity of Tamil in the context of the approaching conference, see the article by one V. P. S., ibid., May 31, 1934.

27. For criticism about the conference, especially the views of the Tamil scholar K. Subramania Pillai, see the article by Va. Ra., who was part of the earlier Tamil Enthusiasts' Conference, *Manikkodi,* June 17, 1934. This article is reproduced in Va. Ra., *Mazhaiyum puyalum* (Madras: Navayuga Prachuralayam, 1951), 47–52.

28. See the report/history of the Madras Presidency Tamil Sangam published in 1946. Many of the pamphlets, memorials, memoranda, and press clippings referred to in this essay are to be found in a separate file in the Saiva Siddhanta Works Publishing Society's Archives in the Maraimalai Adigal Library, Chennai (henceforth referred to as Kalaichollakkam Papers). I am grateful to Thiru R. Muthukumarasamy for access to these papers.

29. See E. M. Subramania Pillai's memorandum to the governor of Madras, dated June 26, 1940, which provides a full list of the committee members. Government of Madras Government Orders (GO) 1319, Education and Public Health (Edn. & PH), July 17, 1940, Tamilnadu Archives, Madras.

30. See "Kalaichollakka Manattu Thalaimaiyurai," *Siddhantam* 9.10 (October 1936), for the text of Swami Vipulanandar's speech. Also *Navasakti,* October 2, 1936.

31. *Navasakti,* August 21, 1936.

32. GO 1319, Edn. & PH, July 17, 1940.

33. After the anti-Hindi agitation (1937–39), when numerous public meetings were conducted and countless propaganda materials printed, ideas about the purity, glory, and independence of Tamil language and culture percolated to the lower strata of society and gradually became a part of the Tamil public imaginary. The exploration of this theme, however, goes beyond the scope of this paper.

34. GO 2164, Edn. & PH, September 12, 1938.

35. GO 1051, Edn. & PH, June 8, 1940.

36. For Rajaji's views on this subject, see his *Katturaigal* (Karaikkudi: Pudumai Pathippagam, 1944), 19.

37. Rajaji's note, March 5, 1939, GO 1051, Edn. & PH, June 8, 1940; also GO 2638, Edn. & PH, November 15, 1938.

38. This committee was known variously as the Sastri Committee, the Technical Terms Committee, or the Technical and Scientific Terms Committee.

39. GO 1051, Edn. & PH, June 8, 1940.

40. GO 1319, Edn. & PH, July 17, 1940.

41. Ibid.

42. GO 1051, Edn. & PH, June 8, 1940.

43. Ibid.

44. See, for instance, the "Tamil arignar kazhaga arikkai" [Association of Tamil Scholars pamphlet], no. 1, Kalaichollakkam Papers.

45. Ibid.

46. Ibid., no. 3.

47. See, for instance, "Kalaichollakkam," *Tamil Pozhil* 16.3 (Aani, Vikrama [Tamil calendar], June 1940).

48. GO 1319, Edn. & PH, July 17, 1940.

49. Ibid.

50. GO 1818, Edn. & PH, September 18, 1940.

51. See "Tamil arignar kazhaga arikkai," nos. 5–8; N. M. Venkatasami Nattar, "Tamilil Kalai chorkal," *Sentamil Selvi,* August 1941, 249–50; and G. Devaneyan [Pavanar], "Kalaichollaka Nerimuraigal," ibid., 251–52.

52. See GO 1319, Edn. & PH, July 17, 1940.

53. *Modern Review,* February 1941.

54. Ibid.

55. Ibid.

56. Clipping dated September 1, 1941. Also clippings from *Hindu,* September 1, 1941; *Indian Express,* September 1, 1941; *Bharata Devi,* September 1941, all in Kalaichollakkam Papers. Also see report in *Sentamil Selvi,* August 1941.

57. For an account of the agitation, see Arooran, *Tamil Renaissance.* Venkatachalapathy, *Dravida,* provides an interpretive account of the role of Tamil scholars and Vellalars in the agitation.

58. T. M. Meenakshisundaram Pillai's report in *Sentamil Selvi,* August 1941, 253.

59. Letter to V. Subbaiah Pillai, February 13, 1941, E. M. Subramania Pillai Papers, Maraimalai Adigal Library, Chennai.

60. Letter to V. Subbaiah Pillai, November 20, 1934, ibid.

61. See, for instance, resolutions passed in the Ninth Madras Presidency Tamils' Conference, Tirunelveli, in March 1943, reprinted in *Kumaran,* April 8, 1943; for resolutions of the tenth conference, held in Madras in December 1943, see *Tamil Pozhil* 19.10 (January 1944): 211–12.

62. U. V. Swaminatha Iyer papers housed in the U. V. Swaminatha Iyer Library, Madras.

63. Originally published in *Vasantham,* November 1943, reproduced in S. Vaiyapuri Pillai, *Tamil chudarmanigal* (Madras: Tamil Putha Kalayam, 1949).

64. A. Ramaswamy Gounder, "Kalaichollakkam," *Tamil Pozhil* 19.9 (December 1943): 169–72 and *Tamil Pozhil* 19.11 (February 1944): 223–26.

65. *Tamil Pozhil* 19.11 (February 1944).

66. Ve. Anaimuthu, ed, *Periyar Ee. Ve. Ra. chinthanaigal,* vol. 2 (Tiruchi: Sinthanaiyalar Kazhagam, 1974), 922–23. For similar views, see *Viduthalai,* October 11, 1946, quoted in Muthusamy, *Tamil perumpulavar,* 63–64.

67. Kalaichollakkam Papers, n.d.

68. GO 1222, Edn. & PH, June 20, 1946.

69. Ibid.

70. Ibid.

71. Venkatachalapathy, *Dravida.*

Michael O. West

An Anticolonial International? Indians, India, and Africans in British Central Africa

> If the country was to be maintained as a white man's country they would have to put restrictions on Asiatics and more especially a limitation as regards their being granted trading licences in this country. Otherwise it would only be a question of time when the white man would have to go under to the Asiatic.—Colonel Heyman, Debates in the Legislative Council, Southern Rhodesia, 1914

> Europeans want to be separated from Coloureds, Indians and Africans. Coloureds and Indians consider it an insult to be separated from Europeans but do not mind being separated from Africans. Everything would be alright if they were included in the European group and the Africans left out. The Africans say, "Oh, no! . . . In fact we can make things tough for . . . [coloureds and Indians], particularly the Indians who are a race of shopkeepers and dependent on us."—Stanlake Samkange, *Concord* (Salisbury), 1956

■ Direct and indirect links between the Indian subcontinent and Africa, particularly coastal East Africa, go back many centuries. Well before the era of European overseas expansion, the two regions were constituent parts of a kind of Indian Ocean political economy involving the transfer of goods, people, and various aspects of material and nonmaterial culture.[1] However, this earlier commerce produced no recognizable Indian community on the African mainland. Thus the presence today of populations of

South Asian descent in the countries of eastern, southern, and central Africa is largely a consequence of European (primarily British) imperialism, which introduced hundreds of thousands of people from the Indian subcontinent to fulfill numerous functions in the colonial economy, from agricultural labor to trading.

The story of the more numerically significant Indian communities on the African mainland, particularly in South Africa and Kenya, has been often told, usually from the viewpoint of the economically and socially dominant merchant classes.[2] By contrast, historians and social scientists have virtually ignored the admittedly smaller groups of Indians in what was formerly known as British Central Africa[3] — Nyasaland (Malawi), Northern Rhodesia (Zambia), and Southern Rhodesia (Zimbabwe).[4] When scholars have bothered to acknowledge their presence, the Indians of central Africa have generally been portrayed as existing in a bifurcated world: fully integrated into the economic life of the society, but living in cultural and social isolation from their non-Indian neighbors.[5] This is, of course, a picture all too familiar to students of the Indian diaspora elsewhere in Africa as well as other parts of the world.[6]

The present essay offers an exploration into the post–World War II history of the British central African territories. From a political standpoint, the establishment in 1953, over strong African and milder Indian objection, of the Federation of Rhodesia and Nyasaland — an event destined to exert a powerful influence on the character and direction of the anticolonial struggles over the course of the following decade — proved the most important event of the postwar era. The individuals most readily associated with African nationalism in the region — Hastings Banda (Malawi), Kenneth Kaunda (Zambia), and Joshua Nkomo (Zimbabwe) — made their reputations largely by serving as spokesmen for political movements whose raison d'être was opposition to what Banda, with characteristic dourness, dubbed "the stupid so-called Federation."

By far, the most pressing issue facing the federation's founding fathers, whether in the colonial periphery or the imperial metropole, was the "native problem," meaning, in this particular case, how to contain and diffuse African opposition to the proposed scheme. But behind the so-called native problem or question loomed another colonial dilemma, less visible and explosive, but still old and thorny: the Indian or "Asiatic" problem.[7] In the Federation of Rhodesia and Nyasaland, as in all African colonies with a significant (or sometimes insignificant) South Asian or South Asian–

descended population, the Indian problem centered primarily on immigration, an issue historically related to trading and other forms of economic competition. Thus grew around the immigration of Indians to Africa a crude and elaborate propaganda, proclaiming that Indians specifically, and the "Asiatic" way of life generally, posed an imminent threat to the entire structure of white supremacy—economically, socially, and politically. And nowhere were the traducers of Indians more numerous and vociferous than in those colonial territories, such as British Central Africa, where white settlers held political dominance or influence.

It comes as no surprise, therefore, that the Federation of Rhodesia and Nyasaland would set out blatantly to erect an iron curtain against Indian immigration. What is more, at the insistence of Southern Rhodesia, by far the most important component of the triterritorial state, longtime Indian residents of the federation were prohibited from moving freely between the territories lest those north of the Zambezi River, especially in Nyasaland, migrate to Southern Rhodesia.

Several consequences followed from this assault on Indian rights. To begin with, for the first time in the history of their settlement there, Indians in central Africa began to organize politically on a transterritorial basis. The government of India, pursuing a policy initiated by its colonial predecessor, intervened on behalf of Indian diaspora communities in Africa, especially where their rights were being trampled most seriously, namely in South Africa and in the federation. Independent India, by its very existence, also served as an inspiration to Africans in central Africa; and many of them, from budding nationalists to knowledge-hungry students, spent time on the subcontinent. Moreover, Indian government representatives assigned to the federation, where they (along with Pakistani diplomats) became the objects of intense racial discrimination, helped to stimulate African national consciousness. Lastly, the emergence within the federation of a generation of South Asian–descended intellectuals, some of them educated in India, paved the way for Indian participation, albeit on a rather limited scale, in various movements for colonial freedom in central Africa.

Indians and the Foundations of White Settler Colonialism

The idea of uniting the British central African territories politically, especially the two Rhodesias, went back to the early days of colonial rule. As creations of the same chartered company—the British South Africa Company (BSAC) — the Rhodesias, especially Southern Rhodesia, were considered "white man's" countries from the outset; that is to say, places ideally suited for the settlement of "Europeans," as the whites generally called themselves, irrespective of place of origin or birth. Operationally this meant, in the world of late-nineteenth and early-twentieth-century settler colonialism, a regime based on naked and unmitigated coercion: land enclosure, cattle confiscation, forced cultivation, forced labor, and forced taxation. In the opinion of the Rhodesian settlers, the majority of whom initially came by way of what would later become the Union of South Africa, where anti-Indian sentiments and laws were already firmly established, a white man's country also meant closing the door to Indian immigration.

In Nyasaland, by comparison, no such opposition to Indian immigration existed. Indeed, the first British colonial administrator there encouraged Indian immigration, going so far as to call for the "Indianization" of the colony. This approach, which contrasted so sharply to the one adopted by Southern Rhodesia, resulted from the fact that unlike the Rhodesias, Nyasaland had comparatively few white settlers and was never considered a white man's country. But, for the very reason it did not become a white man's country — namely, the virtual absence of the mineral and natural resources that actually existed or were thought to exist in the Rhodesias — the idea of Nyasaland as a beacon of light proved singularly unattractive to Indian immigrants. Despite its open-door policy, up to the time of World War II, Nyasaland's Indian population was smaller than that of Southern Rhodesia where, Indophobia aside, greater economic opportunities existed.[8]

Yet even in Southern Rhodesia that most acute of colonial problems, "labor shortage," initially clashed with the desire to keep Indians out. In fact, Indians had been associated with the BSAC colonial enterprise in the Rhodesias from its early stages and served the company loyally, helping it, for example, suppress rebellions by Africans in Southern Rhodesia in the 1890s. Under these circumstances the white settlers, while in no way welcoming them, apparently grudgingly tolerated the Indians, who appear to have numbered in the several hundreds at the turn of the century. But most white settlers — and more especially the "small" whites, that is, wage workers, smaller traders, and farmers — drew a sharp distinction between individual Indian immigrants, who like themselves had come from or by way of South Africa, and indentured Asian laborers. To these whites, the kind of organized immigration implied by indentured Asian labor seemed entirely incompatible with the notion of a white man's country; and condoning it would have been tantamount to class suicide.

The stage was thus set for a confrontation when, in the late 1890s, the mine owners and big landholders, backed by the BSAC administration, itself the biggest investor in the colony, attempted to bring Indian and/or Chinese workers into Southern Rhodesia. Seen from the viewpoint of mining and agrarian capital, this constituted a perfectly logical solution to the labor problem, one with ample precedents in the British empire, and certainly in British-ruled Africa: the use of Indian indentured labor in the sugar plantations of Natal since 1860, and more recently in railway construction in East Africa; or the use of Chinese strikebreakers in the South African gold mines at the conclusion of the South African (Anglo-Boer) War of 1899–1902.[9]

For the small Rhodesian whites, however, the proposal to introduce Asian labor into the colony amounted to nothing less than a political casus belli. Almost all white settlers agreed that Southern Rhodesia ought to remain a white man's country, but no consensus existed as to exactly what this meant. The Asian labor scheme presently brought the matter to a head. White settlers joined the battle to help determine the precise form of white supremacy in Southern Rhodesia; namely, whether the "big" whites would rule supreme or whether they would have to share power with the "smaller" members of their race.

Seizing the initiative, the opponents of Asian immigration formed "anti-banyan" societies and embarked on a vicious campaign involving both physical violence and verbal abuse. Among other actions, they attacked Indian trading establishments and drove the owners out of town; denounced those whites who supported Asian immigration as traitors to their race; and pressed home the point that Asian workers would corrupt the gullible "natives" both morally and politically. Intensifying their propaganda offensive, the anti-banyan forces sketched in lurid details what they foresaw as the inevitable consequences of coolie labor, whether of the Indian or "John Chinaman" variety. The "Asiatic hordes," they predicted, would turn Southern Rhodesia into a hopelessly degenerate society, awash in immorality, filth, miscegenation, diseases, and drugs; in short, the very antithesis of a white man's country.[10] Nor were these activities entirely ineffectual. The British government, acting partly in response to the opposition within the colony, eventually disapproved the Asian labor scheme.[11]

This decision had important implications for the social composition of the Indian population in Southern Rhodesia and central Africa as a whole. In South Africa (and East Africa to a lesser extent), the vast majority of Indians have always been workers and peasants, despite the political and social dominance historically exercised by the commercial strata. By contrast, the failure of the Asian labor scheme in Southern Rhodesia ensured that there, as elsewhere in British Central Africa, the "typical" Indian would indeed engage in the fabled trade of white settler propaganda, though this did not become a reality until the 1930s.[12] In any case, the working-class white coalition had succeeded in holding off the dreaded Asian onslaught. Their next objective would be to make this victory permanent by legally prohibiting Indian immigration.

Claiming that Southern Rhodesia had become a "dumping ground" for Asians, the opponents of Indian immigration moved decisively in 1908 and successfully shepherded through the legislative council — made up of "unofficial" members elected from among the settlers and "official" ones appointed by the BSAC — an "Asiatics Ordinance." The ordinance empowered the administration to restrict "Asiatic," meaning in fact Indian, immigration into the colony and to compel those Indians already there to obtain "certificates of registration," effectively extending to them the "pass system" used to control Africans.

Mobilizing quickly, members of the local Indian community responded by drawing up a petition of protest, which they promptly fired off to the British authorities. The ordinance, they argued, would reduce them to the level of "natives." Even more galling, they, as "British Indians," would be subjected to the added indignity of having "any native Constable . . . demand[ing] to see their certificate at any time."[13] The British colonial administration in India, claiming to represent public opinion, which had been "deeply stirred" by this latest attack on the diaspora in Africa, also inveighed against the ordinance. After careful deliberation, the imperial power disallowed it.[14]

Politically, the opponents of Indian immigration had overreached, but they learned a valuable lesson in the process. Never again would they attempt explicitly and openly to pass anti-Indian legislation, that is, legislation with the word "Asiatic" in its title and directed solely against individuals so designated. Instead, they would resort to subtler, though equally effective, means of barring Indian immigrants, notably administrative control.

The ability of the Southern Rhodesian settlers to control Indian immigration administratively increased dramatically in 1923 with the advent of self-government. The white settlers, whose ranks by now included elements that began to coalesce into a "national bourgeoisie,"[15] had long smarted under the rule of the BSAC administration, which they considered the political arm of "foreign" capital. As the BSAC mandate to rule drew to an end, the issue of the colony's future was put to a referendum, the choice boiling down to joining South Africa or opting for self-government. Fearing Afrikaner domination, the predominantly British and British-descended settlers chose self-government, which gave them independence in all but name. The only significant constitutional constraint on the new self-governing authority was an imperial reservation of the right to veto legislation adversely affecting Africans, which, in the event, was never done, despite repeated requests from Africans to do so.[16]

The coming of self-government meant that the "Indian problem" could now be dealt with on terms determined more or less exclusively by the settlers, unmediated by imperial or other outside interference, as long as they did not pass "class" legislation. Carefully avoiding this pitfall, the immigration department instead used its administrative authority to prohibit Indian immigrants, with the exception of teachers, religious figures, and women intending to marry established residents. To guard against "illicit" immigration, which even its chief officer admitted did not occur to "any great extent," the department offered to pay Africans to inform on Indians suspected of entering the colony illegally.[17]

Speaking in the legislative council in 1914, Colonel Heyman had argued that unless Indian immigration was cut off, "it would only be a question of time in the majority of towns in this country when the Asiatic trader would practically supplant the European trader." If, he went on, Southern Rhodesia was going to be a white man's country, as he believed it should be, both for the big and small whites, it was up to the administration "to take the necessary steps to ensure that being fulfilled."[18] A decade later, the administration, now answerable entirely to the settlers, had finally taken those steps.

From Amalgamation to Federation

Having turned their backs on union with South Africa, the Southern Rhodesian settlers, their gaze now firmly fixed northward, went in search of a partner with which to effect a political marriage. Indeed, as we have seen, union between the Rhodesias, now referred to as *amalgamation,* had been widely discussed during the BSAC period. With both colonies now freed from company rule, Northern Rhodesia having become a crown colony under the Colonial Office in 1924, the settlers were finally in a position to pursue union on their own terms. In Northern Rhodesia, where by the late 1920s a powerful amalgamationist lobby had emerged among the settlers, the movement toward closer union enjoyed the wholehearted backing of the South African–dominated combine that controlled the colony's rapidly expanding copper mining industry. Initially, amalgamation was envisaged as a purely Rhodesian affair, but Southern Rhodesia's interest in the labor reserves of Nyasaland eventually resulted in the latter's inclusion in the proposed union.[19] No doubt, too, Nyasaland's relatively small white settler community, fearing being left to drown in a sea of Africans, sought to share the political security and economic prosperity that amalgamation with the Rhodesias promised.[20]

Subsequently, the imperial power came under increasing amalgamationist pressure from the settler communities in central Africa. Opting for pressure release through mechanisms under its control, Whitehall, in typical British colonial fashion, appointed a commission to look into the issue. After an exhaustive inquiry, the commission tabled a report opposing amalgamation, largely on the grounds of African opposition and differences in the constitutional development of the three territories. The fact that Southern Rhodesia was a self-governing entity answerable to the Dominion Office while Northern Rhodesia and Nyasaland constituted regular colonies under the "protection" of the Colonial Office was cited as detrimental to the planned project.

The Africans and Indians who gave evidence to the commission, overwhelmingly opposed amalgamation. Citing immigration policy as the issue of greatest interest to them, the Indians of Nyasaland and Northern Rhodesia showed particular concern, "lest any change in the direction of closer co-operation or amalgamation with Southern Rhodesia should adversely affect their own position."[21] A similar fear of Southern Rhodesian domination, in this case the introduction of its more repressive "native" policy into the two northern territories, was the main reason for the virtual unanimous rejection of amalgamation by Africans, both in the Rhodesias and Nyasaland. Africans were open to the idea of greater political unity between the British central African territories, but not one which, they maintained, would buttress the power of Southern Rhodesia and curtail the few political and social rights they had.[22]

Undaunted by the African opposition, which they dismissively attributed to ignorance and a primitive aversion to change, the indignant settlers kept up their agitation for amalgamation. But the war intervened and, as the loyal subjects of his majesty's realm that they were, the settlers dutifully put aside their preoccupation with amalgamation and rallied to the defense of the beleaguered British Empire. No sooner had the war ended, however, amalgamation resurfaced squarely at the top of the settler political agenda once again.

While the dominant settler opinion in all three central African territories favored amalgamation, its most important boosters resided in Southern Rhodesia. In addition to pursuing a long-term political ambition, the Southern Rhodesians had powerful economic motives for aspiring to amalgamation in the postwar years. Wartime-induced industrial development could only be sustained by expanding and creating new markets in the north. Industrial expansion, in turn, depended to a large extent on Southern Rhodesian access to the foreign currency earned from the sale of Northern Rhodesian copper and from preferential access (in relation to South Africa) to Nyasaland's labor pool. The northern settlers, for their part, stood to gain greater political security and to benefit from the increased prosperity that amalgamation was said to hold in store.

Similarly, the imperial power, which had been less than enthusiastic about amalgamation prior to the war, now warmed to the idea for economic and political reasons. An economically buoyant central Africa would at once provide expanded markets for British industries and relieve the imperial treasury of all burdens of colonial administration in the region, principally in relation to Nyasaland. By the late 1940s, the British also had powerful strategic reasons for supporting amalgamation. Ever since the end of the South African War, British policy in southern Africa had keenly sought to keep Afrikaner nationalism in check. The election in 1948 of the National Party, with its apartheid manifesto and its anti-British rhetoric, was seen as a failure of the policy of containment. An amalgamated central Africa, prosperous and pro-British, would prove a bulwark against possible Afrikaner expansionism.[23]

With these goals in mind, imperial and settler representatives entered into negotiations. After protracted talks, during which the British insisted on some concessions to "native opinion," the settlers purportedly agreed to give up their demand for "amalgamation" and to settle instead for "federation." Partly a play on words, which allowed the Labour government to claim that it had not sold out the colonial people,[24] federation was described as a loose political arrangement that gave greater autonomy to the individual territories, whereas amalgamation would have involved a more centralized unitary state.

Opponents remained unimpressed by this legalistic distinction, and they continued to reject a central African union under white settler domination, whatever its name. Yet by 1952 it had become clear that the settlers and the British government were determined to bypass African (and Indian) opposition and press ahead with the proposed federation. Outraged by the disregard of their sentiments, African movements running the gamut from political organizations to trade unions and religious associations redoubled their efforts and intensified the campaign against federation. The scope and depth of political mobilization among Africans in all three territories was without precedent in the history of British colonialism in central Africa.[25]

Everywhere meetings were called and resolutions passed denouncing federation as a descent into a more complete subjugation, a sinister exercise in Southern Rhodesian subimperialism. Representations were made and delegations sent to interview any official who might possibly be in a position to sway official opinion. Quite uncharacteristically, even the opinion pages of the white-controlled African-oriented press began to reflect popular sentiments. There was talk of noncooperation and civil disobedience, even a generalized uprising, should federation be forcefully imposed on the Africans. On the imperial front, delegations, dispatched to London on funds provided by workers and peasants, lobbied the government, the media, and the anticolonial societies telling all who would listen of the horrors federation held in store for the subject population.[26]

Meanwhile, as the broad outlines of federation began to take shape, the realization gradually dawned that it was not just Southern Rhodesia's "native" policy that would be exported to the northern territories. As the Indians who had given evidence to the 1939 commission had predicted, its rigid control of Indian immigration would also become federal policy. "The position of the Indians in the Federation," the Southern Rhodesia Indian Conference now protested, "will be more or less similar to their fellowbrethren in the Union of South Africa," where apartheid was then under ardent construction.[27]

It was in these circumstances that Indians throughout the region began to organize politically, both on a territorial and a federal level. The initiative for the formation of an Indian political movement embracing all three territories appears, not accidentally, to have come from Nyasaland. The Indians of Nyasaland, with its comparatively liberal Indian policy, felt they had the most to lose from federation. Their fears were not confined merely to immigration or trading policies. Indians employed in lower-level positions in the Nyasaland colonial bureaucracy—jobs definitely off-limits in Southern Rhodesia—also worried about being "eliminated and replaced by Europeans."[28] Thus it was a Nyasalander, Sattar Sacranie, who became president of the Central Africa Asian Conference on its formation in 1952.

The Central Africa Asian Conference signaled the first attempt at Indian political organization in central Africa as a whole. Long divided along religious, caste, class, and other lines, and hemmed in by immigration barriers and social conventions, Indians in this part of Africa had no tradition of political mobilization across colonially imposed territorial boundaries. Indeed, other than organizing petitions and sending delegations to call on officials in times of crisis, they had no such tradition within the individual territories. Heretofore, Indians in the Rhodesias and Nyasaland maintained their most important transterritorial ties with the Indian subcontinent and the larger Indian communities in East Africa and South Africa, communities where family members often lived and from which they recruited teachers, religious leaders, and spouses.

In the early 1950s, the Indian population of the three territories stood at around 12,000 in a total population of perhaps 6 million, including nearly 200,000 whites, over 70 percent of these in Southern Rhodesia. About 5,000 Indians lived in Nyasaland, 4,500 in Southern Rhodesia, and 2,500 in Northern Rhodesia. In all three territories, the greater part of the Indian population consisted of traders or members of trading families, largely Gujarati in origin. From a religious standpoint, most Indians in the Rhodesias were Hindu, but there was also a significant Muslim element. In Southern Rhodesia, where Christian missionary societies worked among the Indians, there was a small number of Christians as well. By contrast, a majority of Nyasaland's Indians were Muslim, Hindus making up a minority. Clear divisions along generational, caste (though in a modified form), and class lines also existed.[29]

Such, in brief, was the social composition of the communities that the Central Africa Asian Conference set out to organize politically, so that Indians in central Africa could speak with "one voice" on federation. In accordance with long-standing Indian opinion, the conference, at its inaugural meeting in 1952, came out against federation, at least until Indian rights could be constitutionally guaranteed. The following year, at what was billed as its "first annual meeting," held barely a week before the new state's official proclamation, it passed a resolution "deploring" the imposition of federation "against the wishes of the majority of the populations in the three territories." However, since federation had "become a reality it is the duty of the members of the Asian community to cooperate with and strive for the success of the Federal scheme." This meant, in the opinion of the conference, abolition of the color bar in the public and private spheres, an upgrading of Indian educational facilities, and, very importantly, an immigration policy "based on the merits of the immigrants and not on their race, colour or creed." The trader-dominated conference also called for "complete freedom of inter-territorial movement within the Federal state" for all citizens.[30]

This, however, proved wishful thinking. More so than "native" policy, which under the federal arrangement remained officially a territorial issue, Southern Rhodesia's anti-Indian policy, especially in the sphere of immigration, would become the model for the federal government. Any disagreement within Southern Rhodesian settler society did not extend to Indian policy. Even the Capricorn Africa Society, generally on the liberal extreme of the settler political spectrum, rejected Indian immigration which, along with African nationalism and Afrikaner republicanism, it cited as its chief enemies.[31] While conceding that Indians already resident in the federation should be given equal citizenship status, the society took the view that, for the good of the Africans, Indian immigration "must be effectively controlled." Otherwise, the result would be "a tug-of-war between Eastern and Western values with the African as victim."[32]

But the tug-of-war took place not so much between so-called Eastern and Western values as between politicians in Southern Rhodesia who felt the need to prove to the white electorate that they were not soft on "natives," and certainly not on Indians. Unlike in the other two territories, where the white-dominated legislative councils merely ratified it, federation was put to a referendum in Southern Rhodesia. Inevitably, the Indian question was interjected into the campaign. Taking to the stump, partisans of the apartheid-oriented, xenophobic Far Right opposed federation outright, claiming that it would dilute the whiteness of Southern Rhodesia and thereby open the door to eventual African political domination and Indian imperialism.

In response, Godfrey Huggins—chief architect of federation, prime minister of Southern Rhodesia since 1933, and a man who perhaps had done more than any single individual to make it a white man's country — assured white voters that Indians would have no visible role in the new state. In particular, Huggins promised, no Indians would participate in the federal parliament, which would have a total of thirty-five seats, six of them reserved for Africans.[33] In making this commitment, Huggins at once put his right wing on the defensive and increased his stature among the almost lily-white electorate, which handily ratified federation. But, unwittingly, the federal prime minister in waiting simultaneously put himself at odds with an evolving British foreign policy objective.

After 1947, the government of India, flush with the aura of independence, embarked on an activist foreign policy. As far as Africa was concerned, this translated into providing scholarships for students to attend Indian universities, giving diplomatic support to the emerging nationalist movements, and championing the cause of the Indian diaspora on the continent, especially in South Africa and central Africa.

Alarmed by these activities, which they considered a threat to their African empire, British officials looked for a way to undermine India's African policy.[34] The evolving Federation of Rhodesia and Nyasaland, they thought, would make an ideal test case. Under the planned strategy, the federal government would be encouraged to remove the barriers to Asian immigration and generally to improve the lot of the Indian population. This plan of action, British officials reasoned, would encourage the Indians of central Africa to "look to us rather than to Nehru." And what better way to get them to do so than to have an Indian member sitting in the federal parliament in Salisbury (now Harare), Southern Rhodesia? In the Rhodesias, especially Southern Rhodesia, with their overwhelmingly white and anti-Asian electorates, there was virtually no possibility of an Indian being elected to parliament. However, in Nyasaland, where alone among the three federal territories, Indians outnumbered whites (by an estimated 5,000 to 4,000), this was a distinct possibility. Accordingly, the governor of Nyasaland was directed to frame the electoral regulations so as to make "probable" the election of at least one Indian among the colony's four at-large MPs.[35]

In devising this strategy, the British were unaware of Huggins's campaign pledge and, perhaps, of the intense character of the racism and Indophobian Southern Rhodesia. But the governor of Nyasaland, better briefed in this regard than his superiors in London, declared himself unable to carry out their instructions. The presence of an Indian in the federal parliament, he wrote back in the language of diplomatic restraint, "would have a very unfortunate effect on the [Southern] Rhodesians. My advisors are unanimous on this point."[36] Huggins was more blunt. The election of an Indian, he told the visiting British secretary of state for Commonwealth relations, would cause a "riot" in Southern Rhodesia.[37]

Frightened by the Southern Rhodesian reaction, the imperial authorities hastily abandoned their plans for an Indian member of the federal parliament. Far from working for the election of an Indian, they now worked against it. With their active connivance, the Nyasaland colonial administration intentionally gerrymandered the electoral system to ensure that an Indian would not be elected. Using (English) literacy and property qualifications, the governor concocted a system "which would give the Indian community a voice in the elections, but which would in effect, though not specifically, exclude the possibility of an Indian being elected."[38] The British would have to find some other trump card with which to counter Nehru.

Even as they conspired to keep Indians out of parliament, and before the federation officially came into existence in September 1953, the authorities were actively at work on another anti-Indian project — federalizing Southern Rhodesia's immigration policy. Indeed, the Immigration Bill was among the first pieces of legislation the new parliament considered. The minister who introduced the bill admitted that while it did not refer specifically to Indians, federal immigration policy, patterned on the old Southern Rhodesian model, would seek to exclude Indian immigrants, with the usual exception of teachers, ministers of religion, and intended spouses of individuals already living in the federation. Instead, the minister went on, "European immigration must be encouraged and British patterns of life maintained in contradistinction to Asian cultures and standards."[39]

The British authorities attempted to play their part in maintaining "British patterns of life" in the federation, evidently giving up the idea of encouraging the Indians of central Africa to look to them rather than to Nehru. Further, to guard against a perceived Afrikaner demographic threat, British representatives in Salisbury scrambled to "ensure that as many immigrants come to the Federation from the United Kingdom as . . . from the Union [of South Africa]."[40] In this way, concrete expression could be given to previous informal understandings, for in the talks leading to federation, high-level British and central African officials had huddled to discuss ways "to control the influx of Asians and Afrikaners" into the proposed state.[41]

As far as the Southern Rhodesian settlers were concerned, it was not enough to control the influx of new Indian immigrants into the federation; they also demanded control of the movement of Indians between the federal territories. Specifically, they wanted effective influx control measures against the Indians of Nyasaland who, they imagined, were just waiting to stream south across the Zambezi. The federal government, newly sensitized to international (read Indian government) reaction, proposed to handle the issue of interterritorial movement quietly and administratively in the time-honored Southern Rhodesian fashion. However, this was not sufficient guarantee for the Southern Rhodesians, who insisted on greater legal protection against "Asian penetration" from within the federation. Eventually the Southern Rhodesian territorial legislature bypassed the federal government and enacted its own law, empowering the authorities there to prohibit entrance to entire categories of "undesirable" migrants. The legislation, as usual, did not mention Indians. But it did not have to; its principal targets were never in doubt.[42]

Indian and Pakistani Diplomats in the Federation

One reason for the federal government's greater image consciousness relative to the legal status of citizens of Indian descent was the fact that Indian and Pakistani diplomats assigned to the federation monitored its actions. In Salisbury, which doubled as both the federal and the Southern Rhodesian capital, these Asian diplomats, who held the ranks of consular officials and trade representatives since the federation was not a fully independent state, were subjected to the full force of Southern Rhodesian Indophobic angst. Like their local ethnic compatriots, they encountered discrimination in all areas of public and private life, their diplomatic status providing them little immunity. Even the municipality of Salisbury singled them out for separate and unequal treatment.

Indian and Pakistani diplomats first came face to face with Rhodesian racism in trying to obtain accommodation. In the white suburbs,[43] where many of the houses had restrictive covenants forbidding their sale to Asians,[44] they met with complete rejection. Besides these restrictive agreements, a legal sleight of hand carried out with the full complicity of the municipality, the Rhodesian settlers gave a myriad of reasons for keeping Asians out, including plummeting property values, the "social stigma" attached to selling out to the other, and the notion that "if you let in one Asian irrespective of whether he is a diplomat or not many more will follow."[45] Denied the comforts and aesthetic pleasures of suburbia, the urbane Indian and Pakistani diplomats were reduced to bunking down in the local "Indian quarters" among traders and craftsmen whom they regarded as unsophisticated and rude and with whom they had little in common save ethnicity and religion.

Embarrassed by the negative publicity and under pressure to find accommodation for the Asian officials commensurate with their diplomatic status, the federal government attempted to purchase homes with the intention of reselling them to the Indians and Pakistanis. But word of its intentions got around quickly, and suddenly, from the most highbrow to the lowliest suburb, there were no more houses for sale. Ultimately, government officials resorted to subterfuge and high-handed tactics. They simply purchased houses without informing the sellers of who the occupants would be and proceeded to "install" the Asian diplomats in them without "warning" the neighbors.[46]

Huggins, the federal prime minister, who had done so much to help construct the racist practices and attitudes that now haunted him as he attempted to gain international respectability and lure foreign investors to the federation, could forcibly acquire houses for the Asian diplomats. He could even put his foot down and compel the admission of the six-year-old son of a Pakistani diplomat to a previously all-white government school, over strong opposition in the community, in his own party caucus and, indeed, in his very cabinet. He was, however, powerless to protect the diplomats from the forces of racism in the more private sectors of society.

Among other slights and indignities, the Indian and Pakistani representatives were routinely denied admission to hotels and restaurants, forced to sit in the balconies of movie theaters, and obliged to obtain special permits in order to purchase alcohol.[47] Attending an official event sponsored by the municipality of Salisbury, where the officials were notorious for their racist policies even by Southern Rhodesian standards, the Asian diplomats were ushered in the balcony section "reserved for Asian and coloured persons" while white members of the diplomatic corps sat in the council chamber.[48] The Asian dignitaries also faced exclusion from settler "club life." When embarrassed European and U.S. diplomats intervened to secure them access to the dining room at the Salisbury Club, the settler elite's favorite lunch spot in the capital, they were told "not even to mention the matter."[49]

Indians and Africans: The First Phase

The white settlers of central Africa stand out for the bluster and bravado with which they defended their racially determined position at the top of the social pyramid that they built, but they were not the only ones who sought to defend the notion of racial privilege. The emergence of a social order in which race constituted the single most important determinant of class, had a ripple effect, creating a situation in which racist complexes polluted all and sundry. More particularly, the attitudes of the dominant group trickled down and found fertile ground among the other "racial" categories, not least those that had been assigned an intermediary status, namely Indians and "coloureds," that is, racially mixed individuals.[50] Thus began the construction by Indians and coloureds of an ideological defense of their own social standing, a project which had at its foundation the adoption and recreation of dominant white prejudices and stereotypes about Africans. In time, the material benefits that became associated with being Indian or coloured, benefits denied the African majority, would greatly facilitate this task.

Nor could Africans, the ultimate objects of what amounted to a disinformation campaign, escape the consequences of the racialization of all social thought and action. But here, much more so than among the other "races," these consequences varied according to class. Members of the African petty bourgeoisie, who generally had more frequent and sustained interactions with non-Africans than black workers and peasants, were more sensitive to as well as more likely to be directly affected by overt anti-African prejudice and discrimination. By the same token, petty-bourgeois Africans, especially the aspiring capitalists among them, often deployed white-constructed segregationist rhetoric against Indians in general and Indian traders in particular. "The truth is," lamented Samkange, a leading Southern Rhodesian African intellectual, "we are all suffering from apartheid mania."[51]

While most Indians occupied themselves in the retail sector of the economy, catering largely (though not exclusively) to the African market, non–self-employed Indians and coloureds received preferential access to skilled and clerical jobs that whites could not or would not do. Similarly, Indians and coloureds, while remaining very much the poor cousins of the whites in this respect, generally had access to better housing, schooling, and other social amenities than Africans. Unlike the Africans, who came under a separate legal regime and whose daily existence was governed by repressive "native affairs" departments, matters pertaining to Indians and coloureds, as to whites, fell within the purview of the "general" affairs of state. Many Indians, however, resented being paired in this way with coloureds,[52] though the small size of both groups ruled out the kind of clear-cut, privilege-descending four-tier social order that emerged in South Africa.

Indians entering central Africa from the earliest days of colonization would have learned quickly that there was little to gain, and everything to lose, by association with Africans. Indeed, coming as they mostly did, from other white settler territories in South Africa and East Africa, the Indians of central Africa likely arrived with preconceived ideas of the psychological and material benefits (though the latter would generally come later) of social distance from Africans.[53] Furthermore, some scholars have suggested that the caste system, with its ingrained pigmentocracy, predisposed Indian immigrants to Africa (and the Caribbean) to equate blackness with pollution.[54]

In any event, as we have seen, one of the principal reasons advanced by the Southern Rhodesian Indian community for opposing the Asiatic Ordinance of 1908 was that it would put them on par with Africans, to say nothing of leaving them vulnerable to being stopped and possibly arrested by African members of the police force. Africans complained bitterly about such attitudes and practices on the part of Indians generally and in their capacity as employers, shopkeepers, and eating-house keepers specifically. As late as 1955 Jasper Savanhu, an African federal MP from Southern Rhodesia, was denied service at an Indian-run restaurant for Indians and coloureds in Salisbury, the proprietor explaining that his other clients would object to a black person's presence.[55]

Africans often gave the Indians as good as they got. Bulawayo, Southern Rhodesia's second city, emerged as a major site of interaction between the two groups in central Africa, a result of the authorities' concerted campaign to drive Indians out of the countryside, principally by refusing to grant or renew their trading licenses. A native commissioner's comments in 1906 reflects this policy well:

> There are four trading Stations in this district, owned by Indians and Afghans. The Govt. very wisely refused to renew their licences this year, for as long as these Asiatics are carrying on business here, it will be impossible for any European traders to settle and make a living in these parts. This is one of the largest grain-producing districts in Rhodesia, and it is only right that the Asiatics — most of whom have made fortunes

here, and who are not British Subjects — should be made to stand aside for Europeans.[56]

Eventually, most Indian traders in the rural areas of Southern Rhodesia forcibly relocated to the urban centers, a relatively large concentration gathering in Bulawayo.[57] Once in Bulawayo, many Indians, unable to find housing elsewhere, moved into the African township and went into business, mostly as traders and eating-house keepers. By the 1920s, as the African petty bourgeoisie announced its emergence by forming political movements, Indian traders in the Bulawayo township, as in other parts of the colony, became one of its many targets.[58]

In this regard the lead was taken by the Industrial and Commercial Workers Union of Africa (ICU), officially the Rhodesian wing of a South African movement by the same name, but in fact quite independent of the latter. While styling itself "proletarian," the Rhodesian ICU, like its putative parent body, took up much more than labor issues, acting as a militant tribune of the African petty bourgeoisie. Chief among its demands was the expulsion of Indian traders from the township to make room for aspiring African capitalists.[59] The appointment of committees in 1930 to look into the living conditions of Africans residing in designated urban centers gave ICU activists and fellow travelers a forum to express themselves. Responding with alacrity, they accused the (mostly male) Indian traders, who were also involved in the "motor lorry" business, of involvement in prostitution by transporting "loose" women to the surrounding mines, cheating their customers, and "interfering" with African women in the township. The problem could only be solved, they insisted, by removing the Indians from the township which, after all, had been established for the benefit of the Africans under the segregationist system.[60]

In its campaign to drive Indians out of the Bulawayo township, the ICU found support in the city council and sections of Bulawayo's Indian community. As part of the fine-tuning of segregation, the municipality attempted over several years to induce Indian residents and traders to leave the township, mainly by offering to buy them out.[61] But some Indians, finding the compensation package too low, continued to reside and do business in the township well into the 1940s.

The British Indian Association, evidently representing the more economically stable members of the community, also demanded that Indians be prohibited from living or trading in the African township. The association considered it "a disgrace to the Indian Community that Indian children should be reared and trained amongst Natives"; that there was a "danger of undue familiarity between Indian males and Native women"; and that Indians in the township might become "careless of their standard of living and . . . inclined to make no effort to improve the conditions under which they live."[62] The association — speaking mainly for the better capitalized traders — probably had more mundane reasons for wanting all Indians out of the Bulawayo African township. Its members, who had moved their residences and businesses out of the township, or who were never located there in the first place, likely resented the competitive advantage enjoyed by the smaller Indian traders in an area officially designated for Africans.

Indians, India, and the Epochal Struggle for Central Africa

From the political point of view, this legacy of antagonism between Indians and Africans resulted in the failure to coordinate their mutual opposition to amalgamation and federation. There is no indication, for example, that Indians were ever invited to join the various African umbrella movements that coordinated antifederation activities within and between the individual territories, or that they sought to do so. It was left to the government of India, whose chief representative in Salisbury helped to foster interterritorial cooperation among Africans — for instance by bringing Joshua Nkomo and Kenneth Kaunda together for the first time[63] — to make the connection between African and Indian opposition to federation.[64]

As the Federation of Rhodesia and Nyasaland failed to deliver on its promised "racial partnership," that is, removing the barriers that impeded the aspirations of the black petty bourgeoisie, Africans increasingly turned to anticolonial nationalism as the solution to their problems. Here, too, India would play a role in helping to mould African nationalist consciousness and otherwise assist the nationalists and their movements in concrete ways.

In the first instance, the Indian government's anticolonial rhetoric served as an inspiration to African nationalists; and a trip to India, especially before the independence of Kwame Nkrumah's Ghana in 1957, became something of a political rite of passage for many an African nationalist. Kaunda, whose crowded political schedule had forced him to decline a scholarship to Delhi University, made the pilgrimage to India in 1958. He was known to move about with Gandhian tracts and other political propaganda from India, materials given him by a friend of Indian descent when he entered politics in the early 1950s as an organizing secretary for the Northern Rhodesia African National Congress. Kaunda consistently peppered his speeches with "lessons" learned from the Indian struggle for independence and, by his own account, led the movement for Zambian freedom by seeking "to combine Gandhi's policy of non-violence with Nkrumah's positive action."[65]

African nationalists in Southern Rhodesia also rhapsodized about the spell of India. Nkomo, who preceded Kaunda there, was only slightly less impressed by what he saw. Once vice president of Zimbabwe and one of the most enduring figures in modern African politics, Nkomo recalled that Gandhi's movement "was an inspiration to us, showing that independence need not remain a dream."[66] Nathan Shamuyarira, former foreign minister of Zimbabwe, went further, virtually crediting India with sowing the seeds of mature African nationalism in Southern Rhodesia. According to this account, which perhaps not surprisingly has Shamuyarira himself at the center of the drama, the formation of the City Youth League, the chief forerunner to Nkomo's Southern Rhodesian African National Congress, was inspired by a pamphlet on self-determination obtained from the Indian diplomatic mission in Salisbury. The individual who obtained the pamphlet from the mission, Dunduzu Chisiza, a Nyasalander who worked there, excitedly brought it to Shamuyarira, suggesting that they "form an All-African National Youth League."[67] The actual circumstances under which the Youth League emerged were, of course, rather more complicated than this rendition suggests.[68] Still, the affecting political presence of Nirmal Singh, India's top diplomat in Salisbury during this period, and his easy relationship with African activists, is widely acknowledged.[69]

Furthermore, by providing scholarships to African students, the Indian government helped to increase the pool of educated cadres who everywhere formed the core of the nationalist leadership. Some of the most militant nationalists in central Africa, such as Munukayumbwa Sipalo, who went on to become secretary general of Kaunda's Zambia African National Congress and a fellow detainee or "prison graduate," received their education in India.[70] In the late 1950s, India offered six scholarships annually to Africans from Nyasaland alone, though certain individuals in central Africa looked askance at degrees from Indian universities,[71] much like the British-educated elite in colonial West Africa derided those who had gone to school in the United States, including such legendary nationalist figures as Nigeria's Nnamdi Azikiwe and Nkrumah.[72]

India's anticolonial stance made a similarly deep imprint on an emerging group of Indian-descended intellectuals in central Africa, a number of whom were also educated in India. These individuals, who adopted a militant political posture, were highly critical of the accommodationist politics of their forebears and openly attacked the system of white supremacy. Whereas the older generation humbly petitioned for "concessions" and "privileges," Hasu Patel, himself a leading member of this former group, explained, their more militant successors demanded "rights."[73] Eventually, some of these militants would change over to an African nationalist position.

The formation of the so-called Lotus Group in 1954 in Bulawayo, that pivotal center of Indian life in central Africa, marked a major event in the emergence of the newfangled Indian activists. Organizing around a monthly magazine called *Lotus,* the group also established a political association, the Bulawayo Asian Civil Rights League, later changed to the Bulawayo Civil Rights League. The Indian activists carried on a lively debate among themselves both in their own magazine and in the alternative white liberal press that opened its pages to them (and to the African literati). The debate revolved mostly around what Hasu Patel called the "Indian dilemma," its causes, consequences, and solution.[74] In Southern Rhodesia, where they were most prominent, many of these Indian activists had converted to African nationalism by 1960. Patel, writing at the time, noted:

> The younger generation, though still in a minority, are fast increasing their influence. They have completely identified themselves with the cause of "Nationalism" (not out of convenience but out of conviction) in their rejection of "Partnership" (under which they consider that they and the other non-Whites are the underdogs), in their rejection of the Federation as at present constituted (seen as a means whereby the minority position will be entrenched), and in their work towards a "transfer of power."[75]

The willingness of a small though socially significant group of Indians to work for the "transfer of power" to what would essentially be African hands was a signal development in the racial politics of colonial central Africa, where, unlike in eastern Africa (especially Kenya) and South Africa, there was no earlier tradition of political cooperation between Indians and Africans.[76] There had, however, been earlier instances of political interface and sporadic contacts over the years between the two groups. For example, a representative of the British Indian Association attended the inaugural meeting of the elite-oriented (Southern) Rhodesia Bantu Voters Association in 1923, while the Nyasaland Chiefs Conference and the Nyasaland African National Congress sent messages of goodwill to be read at the Central Africa Asian Conference meeting in 1953.[77] Kaunda, as noted above, had been supplied with tracts and pamphlets by an Indian friend at the beginning of his political career, and Nkomo was known to have close connections to certain members of the Indian community in Bulawayo.[78] However, these interactions were based more on courtesy and personal friendships and hardly amounted to a tradition of cooperation founded on mutual political objectives.

Indians more actively engaged in the realm of social welfare, supporting various African-initiated self-help and improvement schemes. The two most important examples in the post–World War II era were the Bulawayo-based African Physically Defective Society (now renamed the Jairos Jiri Association, after its founder) and Samkange's Nyatsime College, a technical school modeled on the U.S. Tuskegee Institute (now Tuskegee University),[79] both of which received financial contributions from members of the Indian community.[80] Yet for Charlton Ngcebetsha — himself a leading African promoter of Indo-African concord in Bulawayo and prominent if sometimes critical Nkomo ally — the "good feelings" generated by Indian philanthropy were largely "confined to certain personalities on either side of the racial divide."[81]

The new generation of younger Indian activists set out consciously to breach this racial divide. Their forthright stand against white supremacy and promotion of dialogue with Africans did not go unnoticed by the old-line Indian leaders, who also began to talk of an alliance of all "dark skinned people in the Federation."[82] But by this time the younger activists had moved beyond such nebulous assertions to concrete demonstrations of solidarity with Africans. For many of these Indian activists, the declaration in 1959 of states of emergency by the authorities in the Rhodesias and Nyasaland, acting in concert with the federal government, became a defining moment. Concomitantly, the African National Congresses in all three territories were banned and hundreds of their leaders and supporters detained.

While few, if any, Indians appear to have been caught in the dragnet of nationalist militants, the open repression of the African opposition did much to undermine the confidence of the Indian activists (as well as of white and African moderates) in the federation's putative policy of racial partnership. Officially, the banning of the congresses was explained as a preemptive strike to avert planned chaos and violence, but knowledgeable observers had no difficulty seeing through this smoke screen. Writing to nationalist sympathizers in Britain, an unidentified Indian from Southern Rhodesia, undoubtedly a member of the new activist group, was emphatic on this point: "Personally, my association with the congressites has not on a single occasion made me feel that intimidation or assassinations were planned. These I am afraid are ugly rumours that have arisen to justify the Emergency."[83] The resulting disillusionment with official duplicity played no small part in pushing many of these earnest young Indians, a number of whom were known to engage in a certain amount of moral crusading,[84] into the African nationalist camp.

Meanwhile, in the wake of the emergency, new movements surfaced to replace the banned congresses — or, to be more precise, to resurrect the congresses under different names. By this point, late 1959 going into 1960, it had become evident that the forces of African nationalism would not succumb to repression and that any attempt by the British government and the settlers to renew the federation's ten-year mandate when it expired in 1963 would likely face violent resistance. Furthermore, at the request of the settler regime, which wanted to move toward territorial independence if federation failed, Southern Rhodesia's constitution was also coming up for review. In that event, Africans there demanded black majority rule, which most whites certainly were not prepared to concede. Against the backdrop of this deepening political polarization, the "minorities," coloureds and Indians, the latter especially, were called on or felt compelled to make a choice.

In Northern Rhodesia, Kaunda, now the undisputed nationalist leader, courted coloureds and Indians, evidently with some success.[85] However, in Nyasaland, with its larger Indian population, the situation proved rather more complicated. Strapped for operating funds in this poorest of the three federal territories, some African nationalists there reputedly turned to Indian merchants — seen as better capitalized than their African counterparts on the one hand and more politically vulnerable than white business people on the other — making financial exactions.[86] More seriously, in 1958, Hastings Banda had clashed with Sattar Sacranie, the longtime éminence grise of the Nyasaland Indian community and one-time president of the now defunct Central Africa Asian Conference.

Sacranie, attempting to politically entrench racial privilege, proposed that the Nyasaland legislative council be reconstituted to give equal representation to whites, Indians, and Africans. In response, Banda angrily pointed out that Africans outnumbered Indians by a ratio of two hundred to one and strongly advised the "Asians to keep out of Nyasaland politics for their health's sake."[87] Many Indians appear to have taken his advice, especially as Nyasaland moved inexorably toward independence on the dissolution of the federation in 1963, to be followed by Northern Rhodesia the next year.

The influence of Indians on the rise of African nationalism in central Africa, it turned out, would be greatest in Southern Rhodesia, where the young Indian radicals were concentrated. There the white settlers, who held a much more powerful position than their counterparts in the north, drew a line in the sand against African nationalism. Eventually, the nationalists were forced to resort to armed struggle to gain independence, and then only in 1980, over a decade and a half after the nonviolent birth of Malawi and Zambia. In the initial phase of the resulting struggle, the Rhodesian regime and the nationalists both competed for the hearts and minds of Indians.

The National Democratic Party, which superseded the banned Southern Rhodesian Congress in 1960, actively courted Indian support. In an unprecedented move, and one no doubt made with an eye toward the party's bottom line, an Indian activist, D. K. Naik, was appointed financial secretary of its Bulawayo branch. Naik barnstormed the area around Bulawayo, warning Indians that they "could not be excused if they did not align themselves" with the wind of change blowing across central Africa.[88] Whether out of convenience or conviction, many Indians responded to the nationalist overtures.

Maurice Nyagumbo, a hotheaded nationalist known for his disdain of do-nothing intellectuals, recalled addressing "a big gathering" of Indian sympathizers at Naik's house in Bulawayo. Later, campaigning in the city of Gwelo (now Gweru), Nyagumbo attended a function where he "had the impression that the whole Asian population of Gwelo was gathered there for the occasion."[89] Indian financial support proved especially crucial to the nationalists on various occasions.[90] Some Indians, however, put more than their money on the line. Nkomo, who like most of the top nationalist leadership suffered detention and rustication, noted that at one detention camp, "there were people of Indian descent and coloured citizens . . . , fellow-members of our party and colleagues in our cause."[91]

At the same time, the government also began actively to solicit the backing of the so-called minorities, Indians and coloureds alike, in its war against the rising tide of African nationalism. Samkange, always the astute observer of Southern Rhodesian racial politics, commented:

> Ever since . . . African Nationalism took a more militant form, there have been signs that the Government is trying to woo Indians and coloureds so that they remain on the white man's side. They have in the past succeeded to divorce these communities from Africans by according them a higher status than Africans. Now, apparently some Indians are beginning to want to identify themselves with the African struggle and in Northern Rhodesia the Coloured Community have disbanded their organisation and thrown in their lot with Kenneth Kaunda's United National Independence Party [the successor to the Zambia Congress]. It is unlikely that there will be a similar move in Southern Rhodesia as far as the Coloured Community is concerned. The Indian Community will tend to be divided into the younger group supporting the National Democratic Party; while the older people continue to support the Government.[92]

Endeavoring to increase the ranks of "the older people" who supported them, the authorities made a series of highly visible and politically symbolic moves. Within weeks of the banning of the congress, the Southern Rhodesian legislative assembly appointed a select committee to look into the issue of socioeconomic "disabilities" among coloureds, also called "Eurafricans," and Indians.

The chairman of the committee, who also moved the motion for its creation, did not seek to mask its essential political nature. He and other legislators who spoke in support of the motion expressed particular fondness for coloureds, whose socioeconomic base and racial identity owed more to state patronage than was the case with Indians. Unlike the Indians, who were said fanatically to preserve their outlandish "Eastern" ways, the coloureds, as "cousins" of the whites (though many coloureds, those of Indo-African heritage, had no "white" blood), were seen as ideal candidates for "assimilation" into the racially dominant culture. In the wake of the emergency, the chairman pointed out:

> The Government had detained for political offences a number of African people. It has also found it necessary to detain one European. Sir, it has

not been found necessary to include or to mention any question of the banning of a Eurafrican or Coloured National Congress. [HON. MEMBERS: Hear, hear.] The reason is quite obvious, there is no such congress; and again, there is no such congress because these people are loyal and are not concerned in any way to subvert and disrupt our normal daily lives and constituted authority. So far as I am aware, whereas a European has been detained and numbers of Africans have been detained no Eurafrican or Coloured or Asian has been detained.[93]

Another legislator supported the appointment of the committee because he wanted to impress the British government with the "liberality of our approach" to race during the upcoming constitutional review. Specifically, he sought to demonstrate that Southern Rhodesia could deal with its racial "minority problem" in a just and peaceful way, avoiding the kind of violence that accompanied the then recent resistance to the implementation of the U.S. Supreme Court ruling to desegregate the public school system in Little Rock, Arkansas, and the race riots in Notting Hill, England.[94]

As far as Indians were concerned, the most important outcome of the newfound zeal to improve the position of minorities was the repeal of the section of the 1954 law restricting the movement of Asians into Southern Rhodesia from the other two territories. Seeking at once to score political points with the Indians without alienating their white electoral base, government officials explained this gesture as quite harmless since the dreaded inundation of Indians from Nyasaland had not occurred and was not likely to occur. The official opposition, however, which continued to argue the existence of such an Indian demographic threat from the north, strenuously disputed this view.[95]

However, the new political phase soon came to a screeching halt in 1962 when the white electorate entrusted the opposition, reconstituted as the Rhodesian Front, with the task of ruling. After banning a succession of African nationalist movements over a three-year period the front, under its new leader Ian Smith, effectively outlawed African nationalism itself, arresting virtually all of its leading figures or forcing them into exile. Independence from Britain was declared unilaterally, and the never ending process of making Rhodesia (the Southern having been dropped with the independence of Northern Rhodesia) a white man's country began all over again.

Smith promised that the new Rhodesian *Reich* would hold out against African nationalism for a thousand years. The nationalists, determined to prove him wrong, took to the bush to wage guerrilla war. As this brutal and deadly political drama unfolded, that is, as Rhodesia was compelled by force of arms to become Zimbabwe, Indians were ushered to the sidelines. The attendant state-sponsored repression put paid to the budding anti-colonial international represented by the joint Indo-African agitation of the previous decade. Individual Indian partisans and collaborators there continued to be. But never again would Indians, as a group, occupy the politically enviable position of being openly cultivated by the two leading antagonists. The high point of the impact of Indians on the politics of British Central Africa had come — and gone. Thus began a new chapter in the history of Indians in central Africa, one that will likely be decisively influenced by the fate of their more numerous compatriots in South Africa, where individuals of South Asian descent have emerged as important players in the postapartheid dispensation.

Notes

1. Roland Oliver and Gervase Matthew, eds., *History of East Africa,* vol. 1 (Oxford: Clarendon, 1963); J. E. G. Sutton, *Early Trade in Eastern Africa* (Nairobi: East African Publishing House, 1973); Basil Davidson, *The Lost Cities of Africa,* rev. ed. (Boston: Little, Brown, 1987).

2. See, for example, Fatima Meer, *Portrait of Indian South Africans* (Durban: Avon House, 1969); Haraprasad Chattopadhyaya, *Indians in Africa: A Socio-Economic Study* (Calcutta: Bookland, 1970); J. S. Mangat, *A History of the Asians in East Africa, c. 1886 to 1945* (Oxford: Clarendon, 1969); Robert G. Gregory, *South Asians in East Africa: An Economic and Social History, 1890–1980* (Boulder, Colo.: Westview, 1993).

3. In the broader scheme of things, the three countries in question are usually considered part of the southern African subcontinent. However, the European colonialists who carved up Africa determined both the territorial and regional lines of demarcation. Thus the British and the French had different definitions of "central Africa," which in each case conveniently coincided with their own colonial possessions.

4. Floyd Dotson and Lillian O. Dotson, *The Indian Minority of Zambia, Rhodesia, and Malawi* (New Haven, Conn.: Yale University Press, 1968). An ethnographic study, this is the only book-length work of its kind that I am aware of.

5. See, for example, Dotson and Dotson, *The Indian Minority*; Richard Gray, *The Two Nations: Aspects of the Development of Race Relations in the Rhodesias and Nyasaland* (London: Oxford University Press, 1960); and L. H. Gann, *A History of Southern Rhodesia: Early Days to 1934* (London: Chatto and Windus, 1965), 319–21.

6. The cultural isolationist view is not without merit; however, it does not tell the full story, and it certainly does not have universal validity. See the following articles in *South*

Asia Bulletin: Gloria Waite, "East Indians and National Politics in the Caribbean," 2.2 (1982): 16–28; Waite, "The Role of Black Consciousness in the South African Liberation Struggle: An Interview with Saths Cooper," 7.1–2 (1987): 112–22; Michael O. West, "Indian Politics in South Africa, 1860 to the Present," 7.1–2 (1987): 97–111; and Allison Drew, "Political Representation and the Indian Question in South African Politics," 12.2 (1992): 57–69.

7. The term the colonialists and South Asians themselves used to refer to immigrants from the Indian subcontinent and their descendants changed over time. Up to the 1940s or so, they were usually called *Asiatic* in official circles, but *Indian* was employed as well. In the postwar period, *Asian* became the official name of choice. Technically, *Asian* or, in the older construction, *Asiatic,* was more appropriate than *Indian,* since there was also a handful of other Asians around, mainly Chinese. But, in fact, the overwhelming majority of Asians were of South Asian origin, and these were the people colonial officials and white settlers in central Africa had in mind when they talked about "Asiatics" or "Asians." On the other hand, up to around 1948, the Asians mostly called themselves *Indians.* They appear to have settled on this designation for two reasons. First, to reject the otherness that the term *Asiatic* denoted, both in their minds and those of the officials and white settlers who used it; second, to emphasize the "Britishness" of the Asians, to call attention to the fact that the vast majority of them were British colonial subjects who, legally speaking, had the same rights as the white settlers, or so they claimed. However, after the decolonization of the British Empire in India and the formation of the Indian and Pakistani nation-states, the term *Asian* increasingly gained currency among the Indians of central Africa, probably to avoid conflicts between Muslims and Hindus, partisans of India and of Pakistan. In this essay I use mostly *Indian,* interspersed with *Asian* and *South Asian.* *Asiatic* is used only between inverted commas.

8. Dotson and Dotson, *The Indian Minority,* 34–49.

9. Peter Richardson, *Chinese Mine Labour in the Transvaal* (London: Macmillan, 1982).

10. The consistent repetition by white workers in different parts of the world of the same racist stereotypes of Asians and Africans deserves systematic historical inquiry. It is suggestive of a commerce in working-class racist ideas across national and continental boundaries, a kind of proletarian racist international at once related to and autonomous of the white hegemonic ruling-class centers of racist construction. These proletarian racist ideas were circulated in literary form (books, pamphlets, newspapers, cartoons, etc.) as well as orally by workers who sold their labor in marketplaces throughout the world, on land and sea. Chief among these workers were, I would suggest, miners, railway men, and sailors. In this connection it is interesting to note that a number of individuals from Australia and the United States — who evidently were quite conversant with the habits and shortcomings of "John Chinaman" from previous encounters with "him" — played a prominent role in the Southern Rhodesian anti-Asian campaign. For an intriguing discussion of the development of white working-class racism in the United States, see David R. Roediger, *The Wages of Whiteness: Race and the Making of the American Working Class* (London: Verso, 1991).

11. E. P. Makambe, "The Asian Labour Solution in Zimbabwe, 1898–1904: Labour Practices and Racial Attitudes in a Colonial Society," *Transafrica Journal of History* 13 (1984): 110–45.

12. B. A. Kosmin, " 'Freedom, Justice, and Commerce': Some Factors Affecting Asian Trading Patterns in Southern Rhodesia, 1897–1942," *Rhodesian History* 6 (1975): 15–32.

13. Petition from Indian Population of Southern Rhodesia, 1908, DO 119/523, 174–77, Public Record Office (PRO), London; Resident Commissioner to High Commissioner, August 11, 1908, ibid., 178. As a "concession" to the Indians, women were exempt from the requirement to carry these certificates.

14. Resident Commissioner to High Commissioner, 11 August 1908; Sec. of State to High Commissioner, 12 December 1908, DO 119/523, 159–63, PRO.

15. The term is Ian Phimister's. See *An Economic and Social History of Zimbabwe, 1890–1948: Capital Accumulation and Class Struggle* (London: Longman, 1988).

16. In theory, the Southern Rhodesian political system was open to African control. Unlike South Africa, which attained juridical independence from Britain in 1910 under a constitution that enshrined a whites- (and initially males-) only electorate, Southern Rhodesia pulled back from the brink of full-scale de jure white supremacy in politics. There, anyone meeting the "color-blind" property and English literacy qualifications could become a voter. However, manipulation of the qualifications plus pervasive racial inequality and discrimination in education, employment, and remuneration guaranteed white supremacy just as effectively in Southern Rhodesia as in South Africa. While almost all whites (including, eventually, white women) qualified for the franchise, no more than a few hundred Africans ever did.

17. Chief Immigration Officer to Police Staff Officer, 9 April 1924, S138/10, National Archives of Zimbabwe (NAZ), Harare; Chief Native Commissioner to Superintendent of Natives, 15 April 1924, ibid.

18. Debates in the Legislative Council, 11 May 1914, col. 253.

19. Alfred John Wills, *An Introduction to the History of Central Africa* (London: Oxford University Press, 1964), 304–46.

20. The Nyasaland settlers, however, must have approached the issue with some trepidation, since amalgamation also carried with it the possibility of an even greater "leakage" of labor southward into the better-capitalized industries of Northern and especially Southern Rhodesia.

21. Rhodesia-Nyasaland Royal Commission Report, Cmd. 5949, 1939, 238–39, His Majesty's Stationary Office, London.

22. Ibid.

23. J. R. T. Wood, *The Welensky Papers: A History of the Federation of Rhodesia and Nyasaland* (Durban: Graham, 1983).

24. See Stephen Howe, *Anticolonialism in British Politics: The Left and the End of Empire, 1918–1964* (Oxford: Clarendon, 1993).

25. By contrast, the rebellions in Southern Rhodesia in the 1890s and the Nyasaland rising of 1915 were much more localized. Even the workers' strikes in Northern Rhodesia in 1935 and in Southern Rhodesia in 1945 and 1948 were more confined and less sustained.

26. Robert I. Rotberg, *The Rise of Nationalism in Central Africa: The Making of Malawi and Zambia, 1873–1964* (Cambridge: Harvard University Press, 1965), 214–52; T. R. M. Creighton, *Southern Rhodesia and the Central African Federation: The Anatomy of a Partnership* (New York: Praeger, 1960).

27. Southern Rhodesia Indian Conference, Federation as it Affects Central African Asians, Mss Afr S1681, ABP 231/4 (12–13), Rhodes House Library (RHL), Oxford.

28. Ibid.

29. Dotson and Dotson, *The Indian Minority.*

30. Central Africa Asian Conference, 26 and 27 August 1953, Mss Brit Emp S365, FCB 99/4, RHL.

31. Ian Hancock, *White Liberals, Moderates, and Radicals in Rhodesia, 1953–1980* (London, Croom Helm, 1984), 30.

32. Capricorn Africa Society, *Capricorn Africa* (London: Newman Neame, 1953), 7.

33. The twenty-nine "general" (which in practice meant white) seats consisted of fourteen from Southern Rhodesia, eight from Northern Rhodesia, and four from Nyasaland. The other three seats were held by "special" (i.e., white) representatives for "African interests," one from each territory. The six seats reserved for African members were distributed equally between the three territories.

34. Indian Govt. Aide Memoire, 16 November 1953, CO 1015/798, PRO; Extract from Secretary of State's Minute, 16 November 1953, ibid.; Indian Government Aide Memoire, 29 March 1954, CO 1015/806, PRO.

35. Barnes to Colby, 29 July 1953, CO 1015/185, PRO.

36. Nyasaland Gov. to Barnes, 30 July 1953, ibid.

37. J. C. Morgan, memo,11 August 1953, ibid.

38. Nyasaland Gov. to Barnes, 30 July 1953; Lyttelton to Swinton, 14 August 1953, ibid. A British official later denied to the Indian government that the elections had been rigged to "discriminate against Asians either as electors or as candidates." Reply to Indian Aide Memoire, 17 March 1954, 1015/806, PRO.

39. U. K. High Commissioner in Federation to U. K. High Commissioner in India, 3 August 1954, 1015/806, PRO.

40. MacLennan to Williams, 23 April 1954, ibid.

41. Wood, *Welensky Papers,* 268.

42. Ibid., 416–17.

43. White, that is, with the exception of the "native" servants who generally lived in the backyards on permanent call.

44. It was not necessary to include Africans in this ban since the idea of a "native" wanting to buy a house in a "white" suburb did not occur to anyone living there.

45. Reed to Fowler, 16 June 1955, CO 1015/1162, PRO.

46. Ibid.; Reed to Coe, 3 September 1955, ibid.

47. Reed to Fowler, 25 June 1955, ibid.; Reed to King, 25 June 1955, ibid. Throughout much of colonial Africa, Africans were prohibited from consuming "European" liquor. In Southern Rhodesia, Indians were allowed to purchase alcohol, but only with a permit. On the European liquor question in the Rhodesias, see Charles Ambler, "Alcohol, Racial Segregation, and Popular Politics in Northern Rhodesia," *Journal of African History* 31.2 (1990): 295–313; Michael O. West, " 'Equal Rights for All Civilized Men': Elite Africans and the Quest for 'European' Liquor in Southern Rhodesia, 1924–1961," *International Review of Social History* 37.3 (1992): 376–97.

48. U. K. High Commissioner in Federation to U. K. High Commissioners in India, Pakistan, and Ceylon, 27 January 1955, CO 1015/1162, PRO.

49. Hoover to Dept. of State, 1 February 1954, 745C. 00/2–154, National Archives (US).

50. It bears emphasizing that "coloured" was a social construction rather than a biological reality. Coloureds were generally concentrated in urban centers. By contrast, many other racially mixed individuals in the countryside were unavailable for racial mobilization to make them "coloured." They lived "in the manner of natives," considered themselves "natives," and were so considered by others.

51. Stanlake Samkange, "Comment," *Concord* (Salisbury), April 1956, 11–12.

52. Floyd Dotson and Lillian O. Dotson, "Indians and Coloureds in Rhodesia and Nyasaland," *Race* 5.1 (1963): 61–75.

53. Indians schooled in the British system would have been exposed to anti-African propaganda even before leaving the subcontinent. While the Indians of central Africa left little in the way of published personal reflections, one visitor from the subcontinent, a Bombay-based intellectual who had formed his impressions of Africa from Henry Stanley's *Darkest Africa,* went to Africa to see "for myself those savage creatures, both human and non-human, in their native African homes and haunts." A good example of this mindset is Ardaser Sorabjee N. Wadia, *The Romance of Rhodesia* (London: Dent, 1947).

54. See, for example, Dotson and Dotson, *Indian Minority*; Waite, "East Indians and National Politics in the Caribbean."

55. "Mr. Savanhu Should Not Complain," *Bantu Mirror* (Bulawayo), June 11, 1955, 13.

56. Gutu-Chilimanzi District, Annual Report for the Period Ended 31 March, 1905, DO 119/770, 22, PRO. The assertion that "most" of the Indians were not British subjects, even if true of this particular district, was incorrect for the colony as a whole.

57. Kosmin, " 'Freedom, Justice, and Commerce,' "15–32.

58. For instance, in the town of Fort Victoria (now Masvingo), where there was also an important Indian presence, another political movement, the Southern Rhodesia Native Association, demanded the removal of Indian traders from the adjacent rural areas to make room for African entrepreneurship. However, the authorities denied that there were any Indian traders in the "reserves," claiming that official policy had been to exclude them. See Mukarthei to Fort Victoria Superintendent of Natives, 30 July 1929, S2584/37, NAZ; Chief Native Commissioner to Secretary to Premier, 23 August 1929, ibid.

59. Superintendent of Natives to Chief Native Commissioner, 12 December 1929, S482/815/39, NAZ; A Cosmopolitan Public Meeting, 30 November 1929, ibid.

60. Notes on Evidence of Enquiry into Bulawayo Location, S235/477, NAZ.

61. 23/3/7R, 6493, NAZ.

62. President and Secretary of British Indian Association to Chairman of Native Affairs Commission, 14 March 1930, S235/440 (244–45), NAZ.

63. Joshua Nkomo, *Nkomo: The Story of My Life* (London: Methuen, 1984), 48–49, 192.

64. Indian Govt. Aide Memoire, 16 November 1953, CO 1015/806, PRO; Indian Government Aide Memoire, 29 March 1954, CO 1015/806, PRO.

65. Kenneth D. Kaunda, *Zambia Shall Be Free: An Autobiography* (London: Heinemann, 1962); Rotberg, *Rise of Nationalism,* 264. The quotation is from Kaunda, *Zambia,* 140.

66. Nkomo, *Nkomo,* 73–74.

67. Nathan M. Shamuyarira, *Crisis in Rhodesia* (London: Deutsch, 1965), 26–27.

68. T. O. Ranger, "African Politics in Twentieth-Century Southern Rhodesia," in Ranger, ed., *Aspects of Central African History* (Evanston, Ill.: Northwestern University Press, 1968), 210–45; Wellington W. Nyangoni, *African Nationalism in Zimbabwe (Rhodesia)* (Washington, D.C.: University Press of America, 1977).

69. Nkomo, *Nkomo,* 47–48; Lawrence Vambe, *From Rhodesia to Zimbabwe* (Pittsburgh: University of Pittsburgh Press, 1976), 259.

70. Rotberg, *Rise of Nationalism in Central Africa,* 291.

71. *Central African Examiner* (Salisbury), 22 November 1958; *Bantu Mirror,* 3 August 1957.

72. Richard D. Ralston, "Political Change in Colonial African Leadership (ca. 1914–ca. 1945): American and Afro-American Influences," *Ufahamu* 4.2 (1973): 78–110.

73. Hasu Patel, "Changing Asian Politics," *Central African Examiner,* 27 August 1960.

74. Hasu Patel, "The Indian Dilemma," *Dissent* (Salisbury), 18 February 1960; Mohammed Kassim, "Reflections on the Indian Dilemma," *Dissent,* 28 April 1960.

75. Patel, "Changing Asian Politics."

76. P. Stigger, "Asians in Rhodesia and Kenya: A Comparative Political History," *Rhodesian History* 1 (1970): 1–8; Kenneth James King, "The Nationalism of Harry Thuku: A Study in the Beginnings of African Politics in Kenya," *Transafrican Journal of History* 1.1 (1971): 39–59; Robert G. Gregory, "Co-operation and Collaboration in Colonial East Africa: The Asians' Political Role, 1890–1964," *African Affairs* 80.319 (1981): 259–73; see also West, "Indian Politics"; and Drew, "Political Representation."

77. The Constitution of the Rhodesia Bantu Voters Association, N3/21/6 (5–9), NAZ; Central African Asian Conference; Minutes of Proceedings, 26 August 1953, Mss Afr S1681, ABP 231/4, 9, RHL.

78. Nkomo, *Nkomo,* 95, 166.

79. In addition to its documented impact on the pan-African world, the Tuskegee model of development, as I have called it elsewhere, was keenly studied by observers in India, both colonial officials and colonized Indians. The papers of Booker T. Washington, the founder of Tuskegee, and his immediate successor, Robert R. Moton, contain correspondence with admirers in India. For a summary of the literature on Tuskegee and Africa, see

Michael O. West, "The Tuskegee Model of Development in Africa: Another Dimension of the African/African-American Connection," *Diplomatic History* 16.3 (1992), 371–87.

80. See, for example, "Nyatsime College: Samkange Addresses Indian Community," *Bantu Mirror,* June 27, 1953, 1; "Indians Contribute to Nyatsime College," *Bantu Mirror,* July 4, 1953, 1.

81. "Indians and Africans," *African Home News* (Bulawayo), December 10, 1953, 4.

82. "Indians Aiming at Co-operation," *Bantu Mirror,* February 2, 1957, 13.

83. Extracts from Letter from an Asian of S. Rhodesia, 3 August 1959, Mss Brit Emp S365, FCB 99/6 (85–87), RHL.

84. Some of them were staunch prohibitionists, and Lotus (like a number of African commentators) strongly attacked the decision to amend the law forbidding Africans from consuming European alcohol, hinting suspiciously that base political motives were behind the decision. The magazine advised its "African friends that there are worthier rights to fight for than to commit suicide." "Lotus Attacks European Liquor," *Bantu Mirror,* June 29, 1957, 2.

85. Kaunda, *Zambia,* 157–60.

86. *Central African Examiner,* November 22, 1958.

87. *Central African Examiner,* November 22 and December 6, 1958 (quotation from November 22).

88. "Naik Urges Asians to Join NDP," *Bantu Mirror,* April 22, 1961, 1; "Naik Forecasts Disaster if Constitution Is Imposed on Majority," *Bantu Mirror,* July 22, 1961, 1; "NDP Only Asian Official for UK," *Bantu Mirror,* September 9, 1961, 9.

89. Maurice Nyagumbo, *With the People: An Autobiography from the Zimbabwe Struggle* (London: Allison and Busby, 1980), 155, 163.

90. Patel, "Changing Asian Politics"; Nyagumbo, *With the People,* 181; Nkomo, *Nkmomo,* 166.

91. Nkomo, *Nkomo,* 134.

92. Stanlake Samkange, *Newsletter,* January 27, 1961, 3–4.

93. Southern Rhodesia, *Debates of the Legislative Assembly* (Salisbury: Government Printer), 18 March 1959, cols. 2550–51; brackets and caps original.

94. Ibid., col. 2555.

95. Ibid., 20 August 1959, cols. 1749–95.

Neville Alexander

The "Moment of Manoeuvre": "Race," Ethnicity,

and Nation in Postapartheid South Africa

■ Whether we like it or not, nation building stands at the top of the political, cultural, and economic agendas in "the new South Africa." One may
consider it irrelevant, outdated, and dangerous (or not), but every major
political tendency in South Africa — at the very least since February 2, 1990,
when F. W. de Klerk, the last president of apartheid South Africa, announced
the release of Nelson Mandela and the unbanning of the liberation movement — has set out to engage in nation building. Men and women of a
leftward orientation who used to deny the relevance and even the existence
of "the national question" find themselves today preaching reconciliation
and national unity, that is, the formation of a new nation on the territory of
the former Union of South Africa. Even more disconcerting is the fact that
many of them have suddenly discovered the "exaggeration" of class issues in
the past, or that they prove "unhelpful" in the building of this new South
Africa.[1] We are, in fact, living through a period brilliantly described by
Partha Chatterjee as "the moment of manoeuvre."[2] It names that historical
moment in which: "the search . . . [is] for an ideological means to unite the
whole people . . . [while] there . . . [is] also a determinate political structure
and process, specific and historically given, within which the task . . . [has] to
be accomplished."[3] Behind all of this lurks the essential delusion that "the
truth of the moral conception of utopia . . . [is] forever safe, no matter what
compromises one . . . [has] to make in the world of practical politics."[4]

The nation is being imagined, invented, created before our very eyes. Indeed, Clio has fortunately afforded us ringside seats, enabling us to observe most concretely the contest between the nation conceived as a community of culture and the nation conceived as a political community.[5] At best, as organic intellectuals, resembling Brechtian rather than Aristotelian theater-goers, we want to be involved in the formation of the new nation. At worst, we resign ourselves to the position of mere critics.

I have said that the nation of South Africa is being invented. But, as is well known, necessity is the mother of invention, and I wish to point briefly to the structural and historical imperatives that to a large extent put a limit to the inventiveness of the founders of the new nation. In this regard, I shall be doing no more than restating my preoccupation with the relationship between economic, political, and cultural structures on the one hand and ideas on the other. Beyond that, I want to explore what I consider the vitally important pedagogical distinction between social engineering and the provision or creation of social options as a nation-building strategy. In this endeavor, I use the compass provided by Balibar and Wallerstein in their conversations about the "ambiguous identities" of race, nation, and class:

> [The] multiple communities to which all belong, whose "values" we hold, towards which we express "loyalties," which define our "social identity," are all, one and all, historical constructs. And, even more importantly, they are historical constructs perpetually undergoing reconstruction. That is not to say they are not solid or meaningful or that we think them ephemeral. Far from it! But these values, loyalties, identities are never primordial and, that being the case, any historical description of their structure or their development through the centuries is necessarily primarily a reflection of present-day ideology.[6]

Indeed, as I hope to demonstrate, the expansion of the realm of freedom, which is or ought to be one of our main concerns, to a large extent depends on human beings in general, and social activists in particular, learning to approach all social phenomena similar to the manner in which quantum theorists understand matter as a duality of wave and particles.

Nonracialism and the Raceless Society

Nonracialism constitutes the founding myth of the new South African nation. This is, to put it mildly, one of the major ironies of the developing situation, since none of the major players — with the exception of the South African Communist Party — has traditionally based its policy on this notion.[7]

The one well-known political movement in South Africa traditionally associated with the idea of nonracialism, the Non-European (now "New") Unity Movement, has proven marginal to recent developments in the country and cannot claim to have had any direct influence on the proliferation of the ideology after approximately 1976. It is simply inaccurate to claim that nonracialism has been "the unbreakable thread" in the liberation movement.[8] Heribert Adam says quite justifiably that "Non-racialism merely holds out the promise that the state will not recognise or tolerate race as a public and legal criterion of exclusion, private racism notwithstanding. *South Africa resembles a multiracial rather than a non-racial society*."[9]

Adam's contributions to the renewed debate on nation building and to our understanding of the relationship between this process and other vectors of social development, such as class interest and ethnic consciousness, are important since he has the knack of phrasing in the language of sociology the intended strategies of particular social agents based on their conceptualization of the terrain of action. He canonizes, as it were, conventional wisdom and provides it with an air of authority. He informs us, for example, that "Coloureds, Indians and English-speaking whites in particular, to a lesser extent, urban Africans, and increasingly Afrikaners too, stress their South African identity before their subgroup."[10] On the basis of various opinion polls, he arrives at the conclusion that "the fundamental cleavages in South African society do not revolve around issues of culture or race and identity, but social equity and increasing intraclass divisions, particularly in black society."[11] Yet he arrives at an optimistic assessment of the situation: unlike other "divided societies," such as the United States of America, Ireland, and Israel, he believes South Africa — despite its explicit racist policies and practices — may end up with a better chance of realizing "relative non-racialism" mainly because of "a different psychological predisposition of the colonised in an industrial settler society."[12]

Problematically, though, Adam's evaluation is based on an intuition arrived at inductively, about the psychology of South Africans. It does not face uncompromisingly the attested historical fact that markers of social difference, given a particular intersection of economic and political trajectories in the history of a society, can be and usually are utilized as the ideological basis for the mobilization of the relevant constituency. In short, he seems to forget for a moment that ethnic, at worst separatist, identities are "both *culturally* . . . 'given' and therefore, at the same time, contingent, subject to structural forces and human manipulation, and historically constituted."[13] Whether or not Adam's optimism is warranted, it has certainly become necessary from the point of view of the establishment, or the ruling class, viewed more narrowly. In the words of the editors of the most recent of the many tomes published in recent years on issues of nationalism and nation building in South Africa:

> The large number of internal conflicts currently occurring in ethnically, culturally, ideologically and historically divided countries worldwide, is bringing home to decision-makers the realization that the key to sociopolitical stability lies in democratic nation-building and a culture of tolerance and reconciliation. Governments that are still nursing the wounds inflicted by many decades of internal conflict, are coming to the conclusion that democratic nation-building is the most effective means of conflict management.[14]

Today, it is clear that even the former pro-apartheid ideologues and other political representatives of the ruling bloc have accepted that as a system of specific racist institutions, apartheid has become dysfunctional to capital accumulation.[15] Consequently, for the capitalist class in South Africa, building a single ("nonracial") nation has become a viable and necessary project, one that most capitalist spokespersons and ideologues had rejected during the last century not only as unnecessary but as undesirable. The fundamental changes in the geopolitical balance of power since 1989 have, of course, expedited the somersault for all these conservative and racist forces.

In the compendium edited by Liebenberg and Rhoodie, Kierin O'Malley scathingly attacks "the fuzzy notion of 'non-racialism'" and draws attention to the philistinism and opportunism of South African intellectuals.[16] He mentions the absurd fact, inter alia, that "[a] number of former Afrikaner nationalists have apparently been able to become African nationalists without so much as a backward glance."[17] Using the specter of German social theorist Theodor Hanf's construct of Jacobin nation-building-as-social-engineering, O'Malley warns against the consequences of ignoring the ethnic factor.[18] Even though his portrayal of actual and putative nation-building projects is a caricature and not derived from any systematic texts — as when he suggests that the present rulers want the eradication of "all extant cultural and ethnic sentiment [and] their replacement by a new unified and culturally uniform 'Nation' "[19] — he offers a valid basic critique of recent radical scholarship in South Africa. He adopts Donald Horowitz's view that a pervasive bias against ascriptive social phenomena holds Western scholarship in thrall and that the hegemony of the neo-Marxist paradigm exacerbates this tendency in South Africa. His article provides a thoroughgoing interrogation of the consistency and bona fides of the newfound nonracial discourse among both Afrikaner and African nationalists. Whereas, in his view, the latter delude themselves in believing that social phenomena like ethnic groups are nonexistent or irrelevant, the former disingenuously chant the mantra of nonracialism in their pursuit of a double agenda involving the permanent retention of a share of power by the minority as a group. His plea is for the recognition of the tenacity of "ethnicity" and for the consideration of this element in any equation guiding the nation-building project.

Ran Greenstein recently launched a similar attack on the neglect of "race," which he calls "the excluded presence."[20] Against the neo-Marxist tendency to dismiss race "as little other than a pernicious way for making invidious distinctions among people in order to facilitate class exploitation and political oppression," Greenstein avers that "race can and frequently does become an affirmative principle underlying individual and collective identities, partially overlapping and partially competing with other foci of identity."[21]

Essentially, his article constitutes a polemic against dogmatic Marxist and other reductionist approaches to the study of ideology and identity. As such, it is without a doubt a timely and most appropriate challenge to the hubris of closed paradigmatic blueprints. Contesting the notion that the dominant ideas of an epoch are the ideas of the dominant class(es), he provides us with a useful reminder of the fact that subaltern groups codetermine the terrain on which ideology takes shape. It does not, in my view, weaken the thrust of Marx's aphorism.

It is necessary to reflect on O'Malley's and Greenstein's allegations regarding radical scholarship in South Africa. They undoubtedly have pointed to the spot where the dog lies buried. Apartheid itself, and the fear of being fingered as an apologist for that system, certainly made most left-inclined academics either deny the ontological status of phenomena such as ethnic groups, races, or the like, or at best eschew these social science themes altogether. However, I believe O'Malley overstates his case. Certainly, as one who, in my capacity as a liberation movement activist (i.e., as an organic intellectual), undermined and questioned the relevance and validity of incipient ethnic and racial formations, I also at all times acknowledged the potential for mobilization on this basis, especially after the apartheid laws were repealed.[22] The social science community of South Africa was afforded a timely and valuable opportunity toward the end of 2000 to return to these questions six years after the first democratic elections when Manuel Castells came on his first visit to South Africa. Many intensely interrogated and effectively rejected his culturalist view of the nation. However, his caveat in respect of the state's limitations to create new and enduring social identities certainly introduced a new strand of research and reflection into the South African debate. In particular, it has forced us to review and analyze more carefully our belief in the feasibility of the transitional liberation project that seeks to create the conditions in which nonracial unity can be realized at the national and at all other levels of society without in any way denying the facts of social contradiction. Similarly, given the real contradictions of South African foreign and domestic policy today, Castells's particular analysis of the "network society" and of the "knowledge economy," which leads him to identify the national state as an agent of the international bourgeoisie (rather than of national capitalists), resonated strongly. The government's oscillation between a continental ("African Renaissance") rhetoric, on the one hand, and the toleration of ethnicist, even divisive, social and racial identities (Mbeki's "rich white" and "poor black" nations), on the other hand, are explicable in terms of the logic of the network society. In spite of some important reservations I have about Castells's analysis, his views on the changing function of the national state undoubtedly are exceptionally relevant to understanding the situation in which many of the ex-colonial elites find themselves.[23]

The recognition that all human beings are involved in a hierarchy of multiple identities provides the dialectical answer to the either-or approach to the question of collective identities in practice. In my own writing, I have consistently used the metaphor of overlapping or intersecting circles at the center of each of which stands the individual. As in a Venn diagram, the space that indicates the "union" of x number of individuals delimits a potential collective identity.[24] In principle, any marker of social difference such as language, religion, or region can describe this space which awaits particular conditions to be filled by the relevant people. Activists who wish to further those interests that stand to gain by the occupation of this space, mobilize those people.

The activity suddenly unleashed by a number of ethnic entrepreneurs around the issue of the "Khoisan identity" offers a very good recent example of this process. I refer to the numerous attempts currently made to resurrect fossilized "ethnic groups" associated with the aboriginal inhabitants of South Africa, those whom the Dutch colonists called the "Hottentots" and the "Bushmen." In most cases, the very people undertaking this "historic" task cannot speak a word of the language that the groups they invariably become the "paramount chiefs" of used to speak in days of yore. The absurdity of handfuls of people being blatantly manipulated by men (and some women) whose only purpose is to jockey themselves into a position that will get them closer to the national trough, reveals as in a caricature the generic process by which cultural nationalists mobilize their constituency. Problematically, the South African government not only tolerates this chicanery but actually appears to be conniving at it in a fit of multicultural "sensitivity."

Be that as it may, the kind of critique expressed by O'Malley does not dig deep enough. It rests its case at the point of reification of the social phenomena whose ontological status he questions. While such reified entities have a phenomenal relevance under certain circumstances, a historical sociology, by definition concerned with change, cannot stop there. If we are not to get trapped in unnecessary Aristotelian dilemmas, we must move in the direction of a thorough exploration of something like David Bohm's *rheomode*.[25] Such an exploration, that is, the search for a new language with which to comprehend the realities we construct and reconstruct, need not imply acceptance of Bohm's "cosmology." We have to consider these constructs as phenomena under certain conditions experienced or lived by people as things or definable entities and under other conditions, for example, at moments of accelerated social change, as a flux or a process, an unstable and stormy movement in which new potential identities beckon like havens of security.

In my view, this approach would represent an attempt to shift the frontiers of sociological inquiry in the direction of understanding the new order's social implications which the advances in the mathematical and physical sciences in the twentieth century have generated. Besides enabling us to transcend the limitations of the Cartesian order of discretely existing things, such a new language should make it possible to combine in a mutually enriching manner the advantages of positivist and Marxist procedures. It would also get us away from the vacuous dogmatism of unchangeable and unchanging paradigms, leading us in the direction of a science of praxis whose purpose and outcome is the generation of hypotheses without any social paralysis.

In the course of such a journey of exploration, it will become necessary to locate this new conceptual framework in relation to postmodernist and chaos theories, since it is not at all my position that contingency is absolute or that indeterminacy reigns supreme. While it is essential that we do not deny the fundamental principle of human options, even if they consist only in the choice between living and dying, we have to insist that for most practical purposes, we can identify and define the parameters within which choices are made, proactively, as in all planning operations, and retrospectively, as in historiography.

Core Culture and Nation Building

From the point of view of analytical method, the most important issue is to avoid reification, to move along the grammatical continuum from substantives toward verbs. Reification problematically tends to consolidate what is, to mask what is becoming, and thus to serve the interests of dominating groups, since it is the ideological universe of such groups that proves decisive in the structuring of reality for all, including subaltern elements. My own research and thinking in this area have gone furthest in connection with the concept of culture and the relationship between unity and diversity in multiethnic, multilingual, or "multicultural" societies.

To begin with, the nation-building project in South Africa today no longer promotes the interests of only antibourgeois, essentially working-class and radical middle-class, strata. The increasing ambivalence of vanguard parties such as the Inkatha Freedom Party shows that the conservative black middle class is not necessarily tied to purely ethnic solutions for their self-aggrandizement. They recognize that the notion of a single nonracial South African nation, if it allows them to maintain their ethnic bases, proves quite compatible with the promotion of their specific agendas. The bourgeoisie, having completed its somersault, is busy hijacking the nation-building project, pretending that it has always been its agenda or that it has undergone genuine conversion. Depending on where along the political-ideological spectrum parties and organizations position themselves, more or less stress is placed on the ethnic, communal, or even racial dimensions of the new nation. The white right wing, representing the voice of many farmers and white workers, sees its salvation in the one or other form of ethnic cleansing, with or without violence. It takes its prototypes from the ethnonationalist movements of central and Eastern Europe and the former Soviet Union. In the South African context, while the white right wing can prove more or less disruptive, it represents a cul-de-sac. In the longer term it is doomed to extinction or mass emigration via a second great trek.

The emerging black stratum of the bourgeoisie tends to project the nation in terms of the black population, either in the sense of those not labeled "white," or in the narrower sense of those who under apartheid and segregation had to carry a pass book. As intimated earlier, the tendency is to allow the "minorities" to splinter as much as they choose to—a strategy that bears comparison with that of the Afrikaner nationalists who, for obvious reasons, fabricated numerous "identities" among black South Africans, whom they ghettoized in the infamous Bantustans. However, the transitional period in South Africa still leaves open many spaces that will eventually be closed down. In spite of many signs that those holding political office are beginning to define the category "African" in a racial manner, the more prominent practice follows a geographical definition, one which includes people of all colors, faiths, and languages.

With identities in a state of flux, it is essential for a radical politics that the verbalization of discourse prevent any premature reifications. Let us take the "Afrikaner" identity as an example. Today, in South Africa, there are probably under half a million individuals (those who voted for the right-wing parties in the last elections) who would unproblematically refer to themselves as Afrikaners. Ten years ago, the number would have been well over 2 million. Afrikaans-speaking white South Africans have incessant debates about their "new" identity. Most of them see themselves, like most other people in the country, as South Africans. However, this category has undergone an organic process of including the entire population within its definitional ambit. Most white South Africans also want to be "Africans," and no longer "Afrikaners," even though that is precisely the original meaning of the word.[26] In order to avoid falling back into the apartheid-colonial discourse, we have to disaggregate the original Afrikaner identity into its parts. Those that fit into the postapartheid patterns can, and should, be retained and promoted within a different paradigm, that is, an African or at least a South African one. Thus, in terms of the nonracial nation-building project, the attribute of "whiteness," while not denied, can no longer serve as a marker of a distinct group identity. On the other hand, being Afrikaans-speaking *is* such a marker, one which, incidentally, is shared by people labeled "white" as well as "black" or "coloured." The fact that Afrikaans-speakers constitute the third-largest linguistic community has certain implications in terms of constitutional rights. It means that if the language is taken as a marker of a group, then the guarantee of linguistic human rights to all individuals ipso facto guarantees those rights to that group without other alleged homogenizing features playing any part in the guarantee. In other words, so-called minority rights — in the South African context — prove inimical to the historic project of the postapartheid state. If applied to all social domains, the de-reification of fossilized identities would become possible for the new South Africa. This marks an essential process, if we want to avoid the perpetuation of the recent past's inequalities. We must reconceptualize "cultures" as cultural practices (in sport, religion, education, literature, music, etc.) and identify and protect in terms of the Bill of Rights arithmetic "minorities." This is the practical result of the verbalization of political and, more generally, of social science discourse in a rapidly changing social formation.

The black working class has all options available. However, only the most democratic and the most radical version of nation building, which simultaneously promotes unity and accommodates diversity, will, in the final analysis, strengthen workers in their class struggle against capital in South Africa. For this reason, all attempts at mobilizing the urban and the rural poor on ethnic, racial, or regional bases represent a gain for capital; there can be no doubt about the possibility for such mobilization in the context of economic depression, unemployment, and scarce resources today. Indeed, it is clear that, increasingly, bourgeois strategies will calculatedly strengthen such ethnic elements to keep workers divided. This is the reason why some South African analysts and journalists have pointed out the dangers inherent in the Commission for the Protection and Promotion of the Rights of Cultural, Religious and Linguistic Communities, legislated into existence in 2001. This commission, representing a concession made by the African National Congress (ANC) leadership to the white right wing in the dying hours of the 1993–94 negotiations in order to avoid genocidal bloodletting, amounts to nothing but the ethnicization of South African politics in a postapartheid, antiracist dispensation. It opens the Pandora's box of ethnic conflict. The commission is set up in terms of sections 185 and 186 of the South African constitution, which give these "communities" certain rights to cultural autonomy. It should, however, be read in conjunction with section 235, which promises, albeit in ambiguous terms, "self-determination" to such communities, possibly on a territorial basis.[27]

There is, of course, nothing mechanical about the success or failure of social policy. While contingency is not absolute, the subjective factor as manifested in political parties and leadership will doubtlessly play a decisive role in the turn of events in the direction of greater or less unity and greater or less intraclass manifestations of diversity. Our research leads us to propose the theorization of objective developments in South African society and the political economy, with a special eye toward the sociocultural integration of all different groups of people. We also encourage extrapolations with a view to promoting the interests of the poor and dispossessed. South Africa's population must simultaneously demonstrate its "oneness" and acknowledge extant differences in a way unobtrusive to the developing national consciousness and national identity. As I noted earlier, there is no question of whether this should or should not happen; it *is* happening. It is important, therefore, that the class interests of workers, for example, are foregrounded in the emerging discourse of nation building, lest workers as a group with common economic interests end up simply enacting the agendas of other classes. In this regard, the inevitable shift in discourse from race to class emerges as a favorable factor for the realization of radical perspectives, a supposition borne out by the current struggles of workers of all shades and colors against the depredations of the structural adjustment program being implemented by the government.

In an aside, let me make reference to a curious debate that has been going on quietly in the back rooms, as it were, of the social science community. Johan Degenaar, emeritus professor of political philosophy at the University of Stellenbosch, has almost single-handedly waged a determined struggle against the propagation of nation-building discourses.[28] Against this, he has posited the notion of "democracy-building." He bases his crusade on the belief in the danger of nationalist terminology since it, in his view, feeds on the myth of a collective personality and does not prepare new citizens for the problems connected with the establishment of a democratic order accommodating individuality and plurality.[29] He considers nation-building discourses to belong to the modernist nineteenth and twentieth centuries and maintains that we need to generate postmodernist discourses in preparation for the twenty-first century.

In my view, Degenaar's is an idiosyncratic crusade, one based on a pedantic and narrow positivist notion of such concepts as "nation," "democracy" and "culture." I do not accept any necessary contradiction between so-called democracy building and nation building.[30] By seeing the two processes as mutually exclusive, Degenaar in fact makes way for the kind of ethnic entrepreneurs I referred to earlier. These people, and others, merrily attempt to entrench minority privileges under the guise of "building democracy." In spite of bourgeois attempts to monopolize the nation-building project, it still represents a progressive political strategy for the urban and rural poor of South Africa. The best clothing for the democratic project, so to speak, provided the seductions of xenophobic policies and practices do not disfigure it. As long as it does not give rise to such an exclusivist ideology, a united South African nation could become a driving force for regional and even continental African integration. Far from being passé, the future of the South African nation has just begun.[31] Recent xenophobic outbursts, even though few and far between, serve as a warning that there is no guarantee of the South African struggles' élan and non-racial ethos actually leading to hoped-for results.

In a peculiar twist of history, I find myself back where I began in the 1960s on the national question in South Africa. At that time,[32] I believed that the bourgeoisie could never realize Olive Schreiner's inspiring vision of a united South African nation constructed out of "our political states and our discordant races."[33] I suggested then that "only what she called 'the labouring people' would one day have the total commitment, the real interest and the historic courage to bring this vision to realisation."[34]

These views clearly require revision for many different reasons, but mainly because of the shift in the geopolitical balance of power. However, the fundamental criterion by which radicals have to decide where they stand on the tightrope between national unity and ethnic fragmentation remains the following question: "Which possible solution is likely to promote the interests of the urban and rural poor, that is, to maximize both 'freedom' and 'equality'?" The tension's resolution is obviously not simply a matter of voluntaristic choice. It is vital, however, not to pose the problem in a false either-or manner. For this reason, we must and can generate new discourses within which the contradictions posed can be addressed and resolved in principle.

In various essays, most recently in one entitled "Core Culture and Core Curriculum in South Africa," I have tried to outline a research agenda for social scientists operating in South Africa.[35] Of course, this project is based on the realization that South Africa is indeed caught in "the moment of manoeuvre" and that its implicit class and other struggles have no pre-destined outcome. An appropriate conceptualization of the field contested may help to promote the most radical possible outcomes.

Essentially, I propose an understanding of South African cultural history as a mainstreaming through the confluence of three or four major tribu-taries (as opposed to the conventional image of separate rivers or streams, one of which dominates and eventually absorbs or assimilates the others). There exists, in my view, a peculiarly South African reason for this notion of a core culture as the result of mainstreaming by confluence. This is the demonstrable fact of a white minority with overwhelming economic and, until recently, military power standing over against a black majority with overwhelming demographic and labor power. This peculiar and clearly transient situation of countervailing force makes it possible for a quite different concept of *mainstream* to emerge. In practice, the idea of main-streaming by confluence can mean many different things, ranging from the obvious mixing of cultural practices (e.g., culinary, musical, linguistic, or religious) to the toleration of parallel traits as equal in value (such as the joining together of the two national anthems of Afrikaner and African nationalists!). More generally, in a world transformed into a global village by colonial conquest, technology, and the "communication revolution," most states tend to be multiethnic. Under modern conditions, inevitably, the different cultural practices, beliefs, and traditions flow together and mingle. Under these circumstances, I would argue, what I call a core culture evolves. It is based on the interaction and interpenetration, or, perhaps, "interfluence" of all the relevant currents. The precise definition of the core at any given moment depends on the changing social formation. The tribu-tary cultures do not, and, in the light of our present-day understanding of the importance of diversity for human survival on the planet, *should not,* disappear. Instead, they continue to swell the common pool, and they themselves change in certain respects. They retain their dynamism and continue to be tolerable as long as they do not subvert the need and conse-quent desire for a degree of commonality.[36]

From the perspective of "democracy-building," this conceptualization has important consequences in that, inter alia, it not only underscores the need for a "culture of tolerance" but beyond that points to the contingency of the individual's cultural baggage. Insofar as it thereby makes people realize that no culture taken as a whole is superior to another and that the re-pugnance of specific cultural traits does not necessarily involve the negation of everything else associated with that "culture," this approach goes beyond a mere toleration. It heads, instead, toward potential emulation since it becomes obvious to one and all that "there, but for the contingent, go I!"

Conclusion

Summing up the insights of recent scholarship, Solway writes that "ethnic identities emerge and transform in the context of power relations, that ethnic identities have both ideological and material realities, cultural as well as structural forms, and that while ethnic identities are clearly related to class positions and relations the two are not simply reflections or masks of each other."[37] As a matter of practical political action, in terms of the discursive innovation I am suggesting here, another movement along a different continuum will have to occur. I refer to the need to move away from the value placed by social science and political practice on ascriptive social categories toward the increasing valorization of categories of self-identification. Such a move is, naturally, fraught with the possibility of chicanery and philistinism, but it would undoubtedly enlarge the realm of freedom. While the nondiscursive matrices in which such a new discourse will operate will, obviously, influence and limit the extent of its formative and transformative effects, the new situation, globally and nationally represents a challenge to social science research workers and political activists alike. South Africa today stands as a social laboratory of utmost importance for the future of Africa and the world.

Notes

This paper was originally presented at the Thirteenth International Congress, International Sociological Association, Bielefeld, Germany, July 22, 1994.

1. See examples in Neville Alexander, "Capitalism and Democracy in South Africa," in Marxist Theory Seminar (UWC), *The Limits of Capitalist Reform in South Africa* (Cape Town: University of the Western Cape, 1993).

2. Partha Chatterjee, *Nationalist Thought and the Colonial World: A Derivative Discourse* (Minneapolis: University of Minnesota Press, 1993), 50–51.

3. Ibid., 85–130.

4. Ibid.

5. See note 22 below.

6. Etienne Balibar and Immanuel Wallerstein, *Race, Nation, Class: Ambiguous Identities* (London: Verso, 1991), 228.

7. No Sizwe, *One Azania, One Nation: The National Question in South Africa* (London: Zed, 1979), 95–131.

8. Julie Frederikse, *The Unbreakable Thread: Non-racialism in South Africa* (Bloomington: Indiana University Press, 1990).

9. Heribert Adam, "Nationalism, Nation-Building, and Non-racialism," in Nic Rhoodie and Ian Liebenberg, eds., *Democratic Nation-Building in South Africa* (Pretoria: Human Sciences Research Council Publishers, 1994), 45; emphasis added.

10. Ibid., 48.

11. Ibid.

12. Ibid., 49.

13. J. Solway, "From Shame to Pride: Politicized Ethnicity in the Kalahari, Botswana," *Canadian Journal of African Studies,* 28.2 (1994): 254–75, emphasis added.

14. Rhoodie and Liebenberg, *Democratic Nation-Building,* 1.

15. Alex Callinicos, ed., *Between Apartheid and Capitalism: Conversations with South African Socialists* (London: Bookmarks, 1992), 117–88.

16. Kierin O'Malley, "A Neglected Dimension of Nation-Building in South Africa: The Ethnic Factor," in Rhoodie and Liebenberg, *Democratic Nation-Building,* 77–88.

17. Ibid., 78.

18. Ibid., 81–82.

19. Ibid.

20. Ran Greenstein, "Racial Formation: Towards a Comparative Study of Collective Identities in South Africa and the United States," *Social Dynamics* 19.2 (1993): 1–29.

21. Ibid., 3.

22. Sizwe, *One Azania,* 173–80; Neville Alexander, *Sow the Wind: Contemporary Speeches* (Johannesburg: Skotaville, 1985), 126–53; Neville Alexander, "Approaches to the National Question in South Africa," *Transformation* 1 (1986): 63–95, especially 84–87; Neville Alexander, *Education and the Struggle for National Liberation in South Africa* (Johannesburg: Skotaville, 1990), 211–26.

23. See Johann Müller, Nico Cloete, and Shireen Badat, eds., *Challenges of Globalisation: South African Debates with Manuel Castells* (Cape Town: Maskew Miller Longman, 2001).

24. Neville Alexander, "Core Culture and Core Curriculum in South Africa," in Sandra Jackson and José Solis, eds., *Beyond Comfort Zones in Multiculturalism: Confronting the Politics of Privilege* (Westport, Conn.: Bergin and Garvey, 1995), 22.

25. David Bohm, *Wholeness and the Implicate Order* (London: Routledge and Kegan Paul, 1980).

26. The word *Afrikaner,* which means "a native of Africa," is a poignant example of how a term can become ideologized and rendered "useless" to the point of extinction when the circumstances underpinning the ideology are radically transformed. Nazi and Stalinist totalitarianisms have spawned many similar examples of such instant linguistic fossilization.

27. For a detailed analysis of this question, see Neville Alexander, "Language and the

National Question," in Gitanjali Maharaj, ed., *Between Unity and Diversity: Essays on Nation-Building in Post-apartheid South Africa* (Cape Town: IDASA, 1999), 17–31.

28. Johan Degenaar, "The Myth of a South African Nation," Occasional Paper 40 (Capetown: IDASA, 1991); Johan Degenaar, "Beware of Nation-Building Discourse," in Rhoodie and Liebenberg, *Democratic Nation-Building.*

29. Degenaar, "Beware of Nation-Building Discourse," 24.

30. Neville Alexander, "Comment on Liebenberg by Neville Alexander," in Rhoodie and Liebenberg, *Democratic Nation-Building.*

31. Ibid., 31.

32. Sizwe, *One Azania,* 29–30.

33. Olive Schreiner, *Thoughts on South Africa* (London: T. Fisher Unwin, 1923), 61–62.

34. Sizwe, *One Azania,* 30.

35. Neville Alexander, "Core Culture," 22.

36. Ibid., 8–9.

37. Solway, "From Shame to Pride," 255.

Minoo Moallem

Cultural Nationalism and Islamic

Fundamentalism: The Case of Iran

I think what we call "the global" is always composed of varieties of articulated particularities. I think the global is the self-presentation of the dominant particular. It is a
way in which the dominant particular localizes and naturalizes itself and associates
with it a variety of other minorities.—Stuart Hall, "Old and New Identities," 1991

We must, however, observe that the *exteriority* of the "native" populations in
colonization, or rather the representation of that state as *racial* exteriority, though it
recuperates and assimilates into its discourse very old images of "difference," is
by no means a given state of affairs. It was in fact produced and reproduced within
the very space constituted by conquest and colonization with its concrete structures of administration, forced labor and sexual oppression, and therefore on the
basis of a certain *interiority.* Otherwise one could not explain the ambivalence of
the dual movement of assimilation and exclusion of the "natives" nor the way in
which the subhuman nature attributed to the colonized comes to determine the
self-image developed within the colonized nations in the period when the world
was being divided up.—Etienne Balibar, "Racism and Nationalism," 1991

■ This essay elaborates a theoretical framework for the understanding of
the mobilization of religion to construct an Islamic ethnicity through a
study of the Islamist revolution in Iran from about 1979 to 1994. While
much has indeed changed since 1994, those were the crucial years in which

old and new forms of globalization were articulated with the sphere of interaction between various social relations of gender, sexuality, class, race, and ethnicity. Using that historic case study as an illustration, this essay attempts to understand the complex interplay of global and local spheres, dominant and dominated ethnicity, and "hegemonic masculinity" and "emphasized femininity" in the construction and reconstruction of ethno-religious social identities.[1]

Western representations characterize Islamic fundamentalism as archaic, backward, militaristic, and barbaric. An image of a unified, static, transcultural movement, peculiar to Muslim countries, imputes to the Muslim fundamentalist an intrinsic resistance to modernity, modernization, and industrialization. In addition, the concept of fundamentalism has been used to create an undifferentiated vision of Islam as a religion and of Muslim communities from the Philippines to Lebanon to Afghanistan. The concept of Islamic fundamentalism in general has been thrown into crisis both because of the diverse and sometimes conflicting positions of various Islamic identity movements as well as the formation of new comparative approaches to fundamentalism, which deal with these movements in a range of cultural and religious traditions.[2]

A homogenizing notion of all Muslims as fundamentalists puts all Islamic movements, from liberal to socialist to conservative, as well as those associated with antipoverty or antiracist grassroots movements, in the same frame of reference. In addition, by considering the multiplicity of fundamentalist groups as a unitary phenomenon, Western discourse packages and labels all Islamic groups as the antimodern Other. As a result, they appear as a "natural" threat to the so-called modern West. This friend/foe logic encompasses the parliamentary fundamentalists in Pakistan, the revolutionary Shi'ites in Iraq, and advocates of an Islamic state in Iran, not to mention Muslim diasporic communities in Europe and the United States.

Such logic undermines historical particularity and difference, and it effaces all the internal divisions and antagonisms that exist between the various fragments of Islamic identity-based movements.[3] This holds true with respect to these groups' struggle over state hegemony. Some of them identify with the state, while others oppose the blurring of boundaries between the state and Islam as a religion. There are also tensions regarding the way that the Islamic *ummat* (community of believers) has become a space for both contesting and affirming a Muslim collective identity rather than providing a comfort zone for the inclusion of all Muslims. The notion of Islamic fundamentalism in the postcolonial era is continuous with previous colonial constructions of a Muslim Other, which works to legitimize unequal relations between different geopolitical locations. The prejudicial view of Muslims as backward and fanatical is complicit with the old colonial discourses and the new global regimes of power and knowledge.

In social science discourse, some contemporary approaches have used fundamentalist Islam as a justification for retaining older sociological traditions with a persistent overemphasis on religious-economic determinism in the Middle East.[4] Notions of triumphant reason in the West, accomplishing its mission by defeating any traces of religious dogmatism, defines these traditions of thought.[5] If old forms of Orientalism imposed a singular, essentialist, and unchanging identity on the entire Orient,[6] new forms of Orientalism attribute an absolute alterity to Islam in denying its ability to join the project of modernity.[7] The shifting nature of Orientalist discourse ensures cultural hegemonic power by mediating the changing conditions of power relations in a postcolonial era.[8] In order to contest such determinism, the present essay seeks to establish a conceptual framework which binds together culture and economy as they interact in the material and symbolic construction of social reality and as they are experienced by social agents in different social relations of race/ethnicity, gender, and class. In order to accomplish this task, first, as an analytical tool, I shall propose a definition of fundamentalism. Second, I shall discuss ethnicity and gender in the context of the global politics of identity, using the Islamic fundamentalist movement in Iran as a case study. Finally, I conclude that what is being called Islamic fundamentalism, far from constituting a timeless reality somewhere "out there," is in fact a historical phenomenon, bounded in time and space. It specifically constitutes a modern phenomenon related to global economic, political, and cultural crises, which are themselves the result of both old and new forms of globalization and the internationalization of power relations. The emergence of an Islamic political subject should be viewed in the modern historical context of a "state of emergency" in a number of Middle Eastern, North African, and South Asian countries and in the Muslim diasporas of Europe and North America.

Global Race Relations: From Economy to Culture

In response to criticism that the term *fundamentalism* in a Muslim context proves misleading, recent scholarship on Muslim identity movements has tried to replace it with alternative concepts such as *Islamism, Islamic militants, Muslim extremism,* and the like.[9] Such semantic substitutions have not successfully overcome the othering of Islam and continue to mark Islam as external to modernity. In this essay, I use *fundamentalism* as an identitarian moment, distinguishing between Islamic theology, with its universalistic impulses, and its "ideologization" in particularistic forms.[10] While many different interpretations of the term exist, I shall use *fundamentalism* to refer to what Wuthnow calls "a totalistic world view, organized around absolute values, representing a counter trend to the process of cultural differentiation." He further characterizes fundamentalism "as an ideological system comprised of relatively few elements that are strongly related to one another."[11] Therefore any change in one of the basic elements constitutive of fundamentalism can produce change and instability in the worldview it represents. Here I should emphasize that this notion of fundamentalism is neither fixed in time or space nor peculiar to religion, but it is intended to be understood as a totalistic moment, whether attributed to, or affirmed by, a particular group.

In order to construct a theoretical framework, I am going to make use of some basic concepts borrowed from feminist scholarship and the sociology of race and ethnic relations. I believe that a theoretical framework that includes race and gender as important components of colonial modernity as well as of the anticolonial and postcolonial process of subject formation in the Middle East, will prove fruitful for an understanding of Islamic movements. It will enable us to make sense of the fundamentalist movement in terms of ethnicity and ethnoreligious identification. It is important to note at the outset that this essay does not posit a primordial, homogeneous, unified, and static notion of ethnicity as rooted in a series of frozen cultural traditions. Rather it describes ethnicity as a form of identity constantly reconstructed, redefined, and renegotiated by social agents in a range of social relations. Specifically, I refer to Islamic ethnicity to talk about what Stuart Hall defines as "the recreation, the reconstruction of imaginary, knowable places in the face of the global post-modern which has, as it were, destroyed the identities of specific places, absorbed them into this post-modern flux of diversity. So one understands the moment when people reach for those groundings, as it were, and the reach for those groundings is what I call ethnicity."[12] I argue that religious discourses have provided a fertile ground for the rediscovery of identity in a global world by relying on the particularistic mobilization of religion for political action.

Having defined Islamic fundamentalism as a form of ethnoreligious identity, I will situate it in relation to another phenomenon, namely, "Westernization," considered as a process of assimilation in which the construction of a dominant ethnicity and the imposition of this construction onto peripheral countries occurs in conjunction with what Wallerstein calls a world economy based on an unequal international division of labor.[13] Economically, this process accords with the expansionist logic of the West, the quest for oil and political control of strategically located "Middle Eastern" countries. It is also in accordance with Western measures to ensure the preservation or establishment of friendly local regimes, and with the steady deterioration of culture and indigenous values of the people in this area. The process of Westernization has, of course, a history, and it cannot be abstracted from three centuries of the colonization of Muslim and Arab countries both directly and indirectly. There, a dominant ethnicity, imposed with the assistance and collaboration of the local elite, influenced the discursive construction of oppositional ethnoreligious and cultural nationalist movements in the Middle East. Many of the movements active in the anticolonial and anti-imperialist moment of the twentieth century were marginalized in the postindependence or postrevolutionary era and became a refuge for the expression of cultural difference and resistance to Western assimilationist forces.

Westernization in this sense represents a dominant ethnicity, transcending diversity and differences even in the West, and constructing a homogeneous and superior "we" opposed to "them." Westernization as the imposition of this dominant ethnicity, far from creating a peaceful world order guided by ascetic and all-inclusive humane rationalism, "has produced not a shining global city but a global Tower of Babel in which the superficial, ignorant comparison of everything with everything else is undermining subtle distinctions between right and wrong, good and evil, worth and worthlessness."[14] The ascendant changing "West" was constructed in a dichotomous and hierarchical relation to "the people without history."[15] If "primitives" were completely denied a history, the "timeless Orient" was placed outside of history. The dichotomous notions of "civilized" and "barbaric" prove essential in the historical construction of colonialist racism, especially in relation to what Ella Shohat identifies as the less questioned notion of the "Eurocentric framing of the 'other 1492.' "[16]

The provincials, the people of the periphery, however, are not mere empty entities, but rooted in indigenous cultures and modes of life, grounded in a particular relation to history and various forms of individual and group identity. Their response to this imposition of a dominant ethnicity has been one not of passive absorption but often one of active and dynamic participation. If some responded in a very expansive way to modernity, finding mutual and reciprocal dialogue with it, many responded to the process in a disguised form of cultural colonization. In this context, challenges to Westernization have been intimately related to the construction of social identities. Exposed to a dominant ethnicity, new discourses and practices intersected, giving rise to what Stuart Hall calls "new identities." Yet the discourses of identity merge with those of a dominated ethnicity, which defines "we-ness" and "otherness." Both categories are constantly being reconstructed, explained, and renegotiated as social identities evolve. In this way, the discourses of ethnicity are always changing, which makes bad news for those on either side claiming closure and purity.

The confrontation between a dominant and a dominated ethnicity evolves through the articulation of such social relations as gender and class, not only at the level of economy and politics but at the level of culture and representation. I consider gender relations here as material and symbolic constructions that transact, influence and are influenced by other social relations. At a symbolic level, the dominant ethnicity of the West incorporated and was itself based on a "hegemonic masculinity" and an "emphasized femininity," all of which guaranteed the subordination, exploitation, and domination of women in its modern forms and traveled along with the colonial administrators, soldiers, settlers, and occidental tourists to "alien lands." The "civilizing mission" attacked existing gender relations in the colonies, and it encouraged instead the Victorian standards of masculinity and femininity, thought of as central to the colonial order.[17] The creation of a racialized global patriarchy shaped an important part of colonial and postcolonial social formations.[18] However, postindependent and postrevolutionary nation-states have relied on what Grewal and Kaplan have called "scattered hegemonies" to legitimize particular notions of normativity and respectability based on the modern constructions of gendered, racialized, and sexualized bodies in a postcolonial era.[19]

From the Construction of a Dominant Ethnicity to the Otherness of Islam

The creation of the world market in the eighteenth and nineteenth centuries is closely related to the notion of so-called dominant ethnicity.[20] The exotic

Other emerged as the object of both hatred and desire. The politics of power infiltrated the various spheres of knowledge, such that a certain kind of historiography, consisting largely of Orientalism and a discourse on otherness, came to display "the world as an exhibition."[21]

In March 1883, Ernest Renan, in his famous paper entitled "Islam and Science," declared: "Anyone even somewhat acquainted with our times clearly sees the present inferiority of the Islamic countries, the decadence of the states governed by Islam, the intellectual insignificance of the races that derive their culture and education from this religion alone." Renan believed that Arabs were neither receptive to, nor capable of, metaphysics and philosophy, which for him remained specialties of the Aryan race, constituting a sort of spatial division of intellectual activity.[22] Al-Afghani, in his response to Renan in the *Journal des débats* makes two important contributions to the debate.[23] Firstly, he refutes Renan's depiction of Muslims as "living in barbarism and ignorance," and secondly he calls on Muslims to overcome the divisions that hold them apart. In other words, he demands a reform of Islam.[24]

The Koranic slogan, "Truly God does not change the situation of people if they do not change it themselves," calls on Muslims to participate in a project of religious revival.[25] Al-Afghani was, in the colonial period, the founder of an Islamic revival movement, but his revivalism had a rather expansive nature and always remained open to discussion and reform. Later on, in the late nineteenth century, with Muhammad Abduh (1849–1905), a prominent Egyptian Islamic modernist, al-Afghani founded an influential periodical, *Urwa al-Wathka* [Indissoluble link], and also established, with the Syrian Muhammad Rashid Rida, an Islamic reform movement called *Salafiyya* ("return to Salaf the ancestor"). It sought to revert to "true Islam" to cleanse it of an outdated scholastic theology and bring it into harmony with modern scientific thought.

The colonial period marks the construction of an Islamic otherness in which gender stereotypification became an essential component. Indeed, the alluring image of veiled Muslim women proved central to Orientalist ideology.[26] The sexist and racist components of Orientalism became fertile ground for the emergence of gendered nationalism, provincialism, and so-called Occidentalism.[27]

Islamic revivalism in this period encouraged the mobilization of the sociopolitical resources of the Islamic religion to the ends of social action.

In this context, the reinvention of tradition required religious discourses to engage with the discourse of colonial modernity. Various historical and social factors functioning at the national, regional, and international levels condition the shift from al-Afghani's brand of revivalism to contemporary Islamic revivalist and fundamentalist movements. I will try to address some of these factors in the case of Iran, but for a broader understanding of the question, a detailed and systematic study of the revivalist movement in each country as well as in specific regions seems both essential and unavoidable.

Iran: From *Tajaddod Talabi* to Sacred Kingship

During the twentieth century, a whole sequence of events at both the local and global levels bred a new form of Islamic revivalism. In Iran, Reza Khan's 1921 coup d'état, supported by the so-called great powers, interrupted the debate on *"tajaddod talabi"* ("wanting modernity"). The formation of a new intelligentsia, either educated in the West or exposed to the major modern debates and discussions elsewhere, enabled a translational and transactional movement of ideas from Europe and authorized new ways of knowing.[28] A tradition of nationalist and masculinist writing emerged in this context.

The debate on tajaddod talabi, some aspects of which were most clearly argued by poets, writers, politicians, and religious reformers, had begun prior to the constitutional revolution (1905–12). One of the main debating points concerned the question of how an Iranian might adopt modernity without at the same time adopting Western cultural domination. Some of the intelligentsia believed in Westernization; others found alternative ways to reconcile indigenous culture and modernity. The responses to modernity ranged from "no" to "yes" to "yes and no." A second debate centered on the rights of women; it was understood that defense of the individual would bring more women into the political sphere. Yet these debates were not given any chance to bear fruit; they were interrupted by the authoritarian imposition of modernization from above, Reza Khan's project of modern nation-state building.[29]

The pattern repeated itself with the direct assistance offered to Mohammed Reza Shah (1941–79) by the CIA, and the closer alliance between him and the Western powers (particularly the United States) after the overthrow of the nationalist government of Mosaddeq in 1953. The coercive and repressive state became an obstacle to the development of a multifarious political culture.[30] Any opposition to the will of the state elite was marginalized and exiled to the netherworld of underground resistance.

Coercive Patriarchy: The Rule of Father in the Mother Homeland

The establishment of a centralized state by Reza Shah was based on two axes: the first involved the construction of a patriotic pseudonationalist ideology predicated on the revival of the pre-Islamic past and on references to a sacred kingship. The monarchy's aim was to weaken religious ideology as well as to achieve authoritarian hegemony of the state over other institutions, especially religious ones.[31] This patriotic nationalism referred extensively to the Orientalist views of Gobineau on the "Aryan race."[32] Indeed, a new terminology was invented to give sense to this new form of nationalism. The territorial term *Iran*, referring to *Aryan*, replaced *Persia*, and Farsi was proclaimed the national language. The motherland *Mam-e-Vatan* was eternally married to and ruled by a father/king who became the procreator of *Irani*, the descendant of Aryans and the nurturer of *Iraniyat*, a particular way of cultural being.

The second axis centers on the construction of a coercive patriarchy. With the centralization of the political system, the king became the sole focus of national loyalty, a position never before enjoyed by such a personage, given the ethnic and religious plurality of Iran. The preservation of filial piety within the family system constituted a value similar to loyalty in its ability to motivate people to obey or conform to the will of a superior authority. This facilitated the process of modernization in an arbitrary way. Thus the state became the sacred father/king, and coercion and violence guaranteed obedience to it. A redefinition of gender roles constituted an important component of this coercive patriarchy. The state effected it by implanting at the cultural level a "hegemonic masculinity" and an "emphasized femininity" as the appropriate gender identities for social agents in a modernized country. The new system of gender identification provided a source of reference for the recently emerged state-related classes (military, bureaucratic, and *comprador* bourgeois). But it also facilitated the entry of women into the public sphere and the gender-divided segments of the market without, thereby putting into question the structural and cultural relations of gender domination. The enforced unveiling of Iranian women, as well as the encouragement of men to dress in a Western fashion during the time of Reza Shah contributed to gendered and racialized notions of this forced modernization.[33]

The authoritarian state was imposed through the construction of a coercive public patriarchy based on obedience and loyalty to it as father and king. However, the nation became a site of contestation since it included only those willing to join the project of Westernization and modernization and marginalized those deviating from it. Moreover, Reza Shah's secularization incorporated a particular notion of clerical Islam (limited to Islamic law and rules of the religion) for better control of the religion's content; both Islamic nationalist movements and Shi'a popular religious practices were outlawed and discredited. The repressive measures of the state restricted civil society, and the imposition of a modern state from above, with its violent insertion into day-to-day life, intensified the gap between a public and a private patriarchy. The state had a contradictory approach to civil society. On the one hand, it prohibited certain discussions, and on the other hand, due to such evasion, it could not affect private life. The public and private spheres became not only sharply separated, but also came to represent different interests within the patriarchal classes. The new state-related patriarchal classes publicized their discourse, while the private patriarchs continued to protect their power in the private sphere, waiting for the day when they could overthrow the usurper state. Indeed, the public sphere was never completely established, and as a result, internal tension, contradiction, and antagonism continued between the public and private spheres.

With the marginalization of the *ulama* ("Muslim clergy") from the power centers and the expansion of the state into areas related to education and the regulation of sexuality, the state became the direct adversary of religion.[34] The new rigidities also had other consequences due to the now enlarged gap between the state-related classes, the comprador bourgeoisie, and the middle/lower middle classes. Rapid urbanization encouraged the migration of hundreds of thousands of poor peasants to urban areas after the land reforms of 1963 and the so-called White Revolution under Mohammed Reza Shah, increasing the numbers of the urban lower middle classes as well as the underclass. This was compounded by the differences between the new upper- and middle-class women present in the public sphere and the middle- and lower middle-class and underclass men. The fall of oil prices in the world market in 1970 heightened the tension between unemployed men and employed women. These divisions caused the gap between the pro-West culture of local elites and the popular culture of the

masses to widen even further. In the case of women, the extension of capitalism and their gradual inclusion in the labor market did not in the long
run bring equality, but instead created the double burden shared by women
in other parts of the world.

As a result of the structural and cultural changes ensuing from rapid
urbanization and industrialization, and the failure of both the nationalist
movement and the left opposition, a new generation of educated young
men and women emerged who tried to overcome their sense of alienation
and powerlessness. Coming from the middle and lower middle classes, this
group of young people employed religious zeal, grounded in popular culture, as a means to make sense of their own culture and the society in which
they had been raised. This generation of college and university students,
composed of men and women discontented with social repression and injustice, was concerned with finding a sense of identity and empowerment. It
played a particular and powerful role in the Islamic revivalist movement
and reworked some of the ideas that emerged in the context of the Iranian
Shi'a nationalism interrupted by the coup d'état of Reza Shah.[35]

Islamic Cultural Nationalism: From Shari'ati to Khomeini

Two ideological versions of Islamic revivalism existed in Iran: one, formulated by Ali Shari'ati, emphasized the construction of a local identity as a
way to de-alienate and politicize the masses; the other, articulated by Motahari, called for the construction of an identity in polar opposition to the
West, demanding a "pure" Islam relying on traditional metaphysics of unquestionable faith.[36] As one of their similarities, both versions partake in a
concept of ethnicity. Both also define themselves in relation to the dominant
ethnicity of the West, and both are communitarian and deploy religion for
purposes of political action. They differ radically, however, in their attitude
toward other ideologies. The former version, proposing a rather expansive
identity, includes elements from other political ideologies such as Third
Worldism and socialism, while the latter, in its defensive stance, depends on
notions of purity and nonmixture. Here I will use fundamentalism to describe the second form of identification.

For many educated, professional young Iranians, the search for an identity emerged in response to the uncontrolled realities of their community
and the difficulties they experienced in relating to it. Intensification of the
gap between the state and the people, between elite and popular culture,

has created serious difficulties for the possibility of both material and symbolic self-realization and self-expression. The imposed assimilation to the West and its value system, and the disruption of any sense of continuity — thanks to the dissemination of these values via the expanding networks of radio and television — have produced a situation of anomie and social anxiety. The interruption of the economic, political, and social life of society has constituted one consequence of this form of cultural and political-economic domination, further subjugating Iranians to dominating foreign power.

As opposed to some Orientalist and neo-Orientalist views, which describe fundamentalism as the result of an antagonism between the traditionalist clergy and a modernist secularist elite, I would say that the growth of fundamentalism directly correlates with the rebellion of the many young men and women who look to such fundamentalism as a source of identity, self-worth, and social action. One example is the creation, after the 1979 revolution in Iran, of many social and political organizations such as the Bassij-e Motazafan (Mobilization of the disempowered), which boasted almost half a million members during the Iran-Iraq war.[37]

The dynamic and tripartite change in social values, institutions, and agents has distorted the development of modernization, rendering necessary a continuous and often fractious dialogue between different social ideologies and worldviews. As a result, the rejection of the cultural and political-economic domination both national and international has found its ideological expression and historical and cultural roots in Islam.

The return to the collective imagination invites a return to Muhammad. This return is quite consonant with the historical identity of Islam, which has always seen itself as the vehicle for creating a better society as a whole, one that is just and conforms to the divine will. As Fatima Mernissi has noted, Islam here becomes a source of reference and a psychological force, and the return to Islam constitutes not simply a return to the religious tenets, but to a meaningful psychology.[38] It is also a return to a materialistic worldview encompassing a set of psychological devices about self-empowerment and making oneself at home everywhere around the globe, regardless of language or cultural differences.

Islam, it was believed, could help rebuild a confident and combative identity via collective self-help and an ideology of egalitarianism that would enable people to organize and control their own communities as well as to resist Western policies of assimilation and repression.

In Iran, the quasi-existence of a civil society, the total control of the cultural sphere, and the hegemony of the state over political culture has resulted in the birth of a counterculture. The failure of the traditional left, as well as of the nationalist movement, allowed room for the growth of a religious countermovement.[39] Among the intelligentsia, a new form of identity started to take hold. Jalal al-e-Ahmad, an influential secularist writer, published a book entitled *Garbzadegi* [Westoxication], in which he rejects the passive absorption of the West and calls for a return to the roots of Islamic tradition as a source of indigenous identity and authentic political action.[40]

This movement toward the Islamic heritage as a source for social action, and the development of a non-Western as well as non-Marxist identity has been elaborated at two sites, one among the intelligentsia, the other among political activists. The ideas propounded by these revivalists inspired increasing numbers of young, educated, and newly urbanized Iranians to organize themselves politically up until the time of the revolution in 1979. Many different groups emerged from this tradition, ranging from the Islamic anarchists to Islamic conservatives.

Shari'ati, a kind of Iranian Fanon, emerged as one of the important figures during those years. On his return to Iran in 1964, after being educated in France, he called for a rethinking of Islam as a sociological phenomenon and a radical interpretation of the Shi'ite school.[41] In his critique of Western capitalism, Shari'ati takes Shi'ism as a resource for social change.[42] In order to divide the social protest movement from the so-called sacred kingship of the Pahlavi regime, he distinguishes between a Safavid Shi'ism, based on the ulama's alliance with the monarchy (the Safavid dynasty), used to "opiate" the masses, and an Alavid Shi'ism exemplified by Imam Hussein's resistance to oppression. He goes on to call for the establishment of a *Jameyeh-e bi tabaghah-e tohidi* (monotheistic classless society), a powerful harking back to the prophet Muhammad.[43]

Many Iranian students enthusiastically received Shari'ati's call for political resistance to despotic rulers, foreign exploiters, greedy capitalists, and law-and-order clergy as well as his emphasis on the role of the young generation in social change. Shari'ati's teachings also became a common source of inspiration for a number of Islamic political organizations, including the Organization of the Mujahideen of the People (Sazeman Mojahedin-e Khalq), a guerrilla organization that helped to spread his ideas far and wide. As a result, Shari'ati was highly popular among young students during the revolution of 1979. His legacy remains omnipresent in political and cultural spheres in Iran today.

In spite of the Islamic revivalism, the pieties, and the scripturalism inherent in his doctrine, Shari'ati's views by no means call for purity and closure. In fact, Shari'ati remained an ever present figure in the political sphere of Iranian society, inspiring groups such as the Islamic nationalists, socialists, and anarchists alike. He still functions as a central figure in the context of the current Iranian reform movement. The Iranian Islamic elite has not only built on Shari'ati's ideas but has also used his legacy to promote an Islamic framework open to the political intervention of Islamic intellectuals. The notion of a religious intellectual (*roushanfikr-e dini*) suggested by Abdolkarim Souroush, and the active presence of such intellectuals in Iranian civil society, has not only legitimized a hermeneutics of Islam based on its temporality and spatiality but also has encouraged a multiplicity of political positions based on various constructions of the Islamic canon and its application in political life.[44]

However, from the point of view of fundamentalists, the idea of *elteghate* (mixture) of Marxist and socialist elements in some Islamic guerrilla movements, or liberal elements in some Muslim nationalist movements, constitutes a sign of impurity and a sellout to the West.[45] Their ideology of nonmixture continues to influence Iranian political ideas and the political scene in general. Various groups concerned about the boundaries of Islam and the West, and about their mutual inclusion or exclusion, repeatedly ask the question "Who are we?" However, the range of responses to this question has thrown the Iranian Islamic Republic into a legitimacy crisis, since religion no longer stands as a unified force behind the state but is divided between a variety of political positions working both within and beyond the state.[46]

A defensive, fundamentalist version of Islamic revivalism continues to exist in the Iranian political sphere. Some authors, by contrasting "Shari'ati" versus "Motahari" tendencies, have tried to see basic differences inside Islamic revivalism in Iran.[47] A detailed analysis of the various tenets of Islamic ideology goes beyond the scope of this paper, but for our purpose here, it is necessary to highlight the core elements of such revivalism as they relate to the construction of a dominated ethnicity. My focus will be on Khomeini's writings and lectures because he has emerged as one of the most influential Islamists, not only in Iran but transnationally.

Fundamentalist Islam: The Identity of a Defensive Ethnicity

The two main elements of Islamic nationalism are the concepts of the individual and of the ummat. These two (very modern) values are related to the assumption that God is the ultimate and absolute sovereign of all creation. God, in this sense, is owner and master of the ummat, or community of believers, in which each individual participates. Indeed, this idea has roots in the early Islamic community as described by Robert Bellah: "The effort of modern Muslims to depict the early community as a very type of egalitarian participant nationalism is by no means entirely an unhistorical ideological fabrication."[48] In his writings, Ayatollah Khomeini constantly refers to this idea. He emphasizes the mutual reciprocity of the two notions: religion must be totally in the service of the individual and, conversely, the individual in the service of religion.[49] An ensemble of interconnected elements characterizes this kind of communalization based on Islamic principles.

The first is the construction of a common past. The cyclical time of myth here becomes the linear time of social and historical struggles.[50] In the Shi'ite reconstruction of the past, two episodes in the history of Islam became especially important: the usurpation of power by illegitimate caliphs and the Karbala uprising. These two episodes create a sense of historicity by connecting an Islamic past to the present. They also allow a sense of agency for Muslims, offering an invitation to rise up against injustice.

The second element refers to the idea of territory. In the context of the Iranian revolution, and on the basis of this idea, different versions of Islamic revivalism engage in the reconstruction of the West and the East as separate but connected entities.

The third element constitutes a reference to the cultural cohesion (Islam as *tassavor,* vision) that would be realized through an Islamic revolution and a commitment to collectivity. The real significance of Islam, according to this schema, is not the subjective religious experience but the acceptance of the collective Islamic life and individual devotion to the cause. Some ideas and concepts related to significant historical events are singled out and applied to the present situation, and Islamic culture is then used to unify the marginalized majority. The fundamentalist version of revivalism thereby hoped to protect itself from the criticism that it concerned only the privileged few.

The polarization of Allah/God and *taghut*/idol, and the constant reference to jihad/holy war, make up the fourth element. Jihad, in this view, constitutes not only a revolt against the ruler but also one against oneself (*jihad-e-nafs*, "worldly asceticism"). Khomeini refers to these two forms of jihad as *akbar* (major) and *asghar* (minor), and as a war against taghut (idolatry).[51] The reference to jihad-e-nafs as akbar underscores the importance and difficulty of a holy war waged against one's individual needs; the self is sacrificed to the will of Allah. The polarity, Allah versus taghut, in the jihad-e-nafs, opens the way to an ongoing cultural and psychological rejection of non-Islamic values and to the affirmation of Islamic values. In order to become a member of Allah's community, one must reject the taghut before proclaiming a new adherence to Allah.[52] The chronology inherent in this case reveals the dialogical structure of the discourse to the extent that one has to identify, know, and reject the taghut before submitting to the rules of Allah.

The fifth element is the myth of a common present. The Islamic ummat had to be constructed as material, historical, and actual. In this sense, the ummat is related to the idea of progress and the turn toward the future. None of the various versions of Islamic revivalism reject the idea of progress; in fact, all of them claim the compatibility of progress and Islam. In this sense *harekat* and *tagiir* (movement and change) are involved in an evolutionary schema of development.[53]

Finally, there exists the concept of a gender-divided community. Islamic fundamentalism emphasizes particularly the participation and politicization of women and men in society, in which they have their designated "proper" places. Fundamentalist discourse reserves a special place for the man as the protector/provider and for the woman as the keeper/reproducer. This last element is particularly significant because of the role it affords women, not only as procreators but also as the main agents of socialization and the transmission of culture and ethnicity.[54]

The example of Karbala holds great importance to an understanding of such forms of communalization. Karbala signifies not only a significant episode in history but also a symbol of self-sacrifice and resistance.[55] Women and men in Karbala both exhibit bravery, but in different ways: men are the warriors and women are the guardians of family ties and kinship. As the main agents of social continuity, mothers, sisters, wives, and daughters serve as role models for the community. The double embrace of "this world" and the "other world" in Karbala has been used to mobilize the disempowered Muslim masses. *Shehadat* (martyrdom) becomes a core element and the final step in making the impossible possible.

The core elements of an identity based on Islamic nationalism during

212 ■ MINOO MOALLEM

and after the revolution were formulated by Khomeini, who successfully combined popular culture, religious texts, and political doctrine in a coherent, exclusive, and antagonistic ideology. Khomeini brings together the local and the global within a single frame of reference. His deployment of the language of identity can only be understood within a dichotomous logic. The antagonism between the two poles calls for constant action and militarism. The friend/foe logic of Khomeini's fundamentalism is effective and simple, and it draws on familiar codes and a collective historical memory. His use of ethnicity is based on a unified we-ness *and* a unified otherness. In this sense, he speaks in a language he shares with his Western adversaries and the pro-West locals: the language of identity and ethnicity.

This dichotomous language is based on boundaries that serve to include and exclude. The West here becomes a global political economy (represented by Zionists and imperialists) as opposed to an Islamic disinherited ummat. The strict boundaries run between two homogenized unities: a positive vision of Islam as opposed to a negative one of taghut; the unity of disinherited people as against the superpowers; the *mostzaf*/poor as opposed to the *mostakbar*/rich; *manaviat*/spiritualism as opposed to *maddiayt*/materialism; and, finally, the veiled as opposed to the unveiled woman. Local and global are intertwined in Khomeini's polar pairs; he constantly shifts from one to the other. Addressing a single history where the local and the global interpenetrate, he is not only able to use populist language but also to present an alternative to the ideology of the dominant bloc. However, in the aftermath of the establishment of an Islamic Republic divided by class, gender, ethnicity, religion, and geographical location, Khomeini's conceptual polarity has fallen into crisis.

In the Community of Oppressed Brothers and Sisters

O oppressed people of my country, all the oppressed people of the world! My HIJAB is an element of the ideology of Islam and heralds the imminent arrival of a society which Islam has promised, a society in which all, as a united Ummah, see God, not wealth and power, nor high position, prestige, pleasure, sex and licentiousness.—Zahra Rahnavard, *The Message of Hijab,* 1990

It is through the two metaphors of blood and veil as signifiers for a hegemonic masculinity and an emphasized femininity that Islamic cultural nationalism and fundamentalism succeeded in reconstructing a community of brothers and sisters located in opposition to the West. By referring to complementary models of masculinity and femininity, both Muslim men and women are invited to participate in their community and its militarism against taghut.

The main responsibility of men and women is jihad-e-nafs. The "warrior brother," by sacrificing his life to the community, shows his commitment and responsibility and revitalizes the masculinity of the emasculated Muslim man. Men must reject dependence on material life, as exemplified in wealth, family, women, and children, say, in order to revitalize their manhood.[56] Martyrdom as a process of re-masculinization enters into the symbolic language of gender identity to reestablish a community both gender-divided and complementary. Urban spaces are conquered by *shohada* (martyrs' memorials). In this way, martyred men repossess the public sphere once dominated by the state. Their pictures as symbolic models of masculinity recapture the sphere of representation. They are ever present figures in contemporary Iran.

Complementing this model of hegemonic masculinity, there exists an emphasized model of femininity, the veiled woman. This does not suggest that women are denied martyrdom, but it is not blood that symbolizes a woman's contribution. The responsibility of the woman is to cover herself in the black chador, a long, all-covering veil. In this context, the veil does not form part of religion or custom, but functions as a signifier in the cultural war of representation. Both blood and the black chador have local and global meaning. They enter the sphere of cultural representation in the form of competing masculinities and femininities in the constant conflict over self-realization and self-expression. These symbols also speak to individuals, reminding them of their responsibility and commitment to their community and of their need to give up their individuality to the will of the latter. They call for total submission to the community of believers and unceasing action toward the goals of the community. It is a mistake to read fundamentalist encouragement of the black chador either as a sign of passivity or as a sign of religiosity; it is rather an invitation to participation and political activity, that is, to take one's life in hand and make meaning out of it. The massive participation of women in the political sphere in postrevolutionary Iran and in the context of the political life in the Islamic Republic exemplifies this call to action.[57]

Competing Patriarchies and the Quest for Cultural Hegemony

The divine essence of womanhood used to be the infinite source of goodness, and morality. You were a mother, a sister, a wife; you personified piety, respect, innocence, chastity, pure love, kindness.—Zahra Rahnavard, *The Message of Hijab,* 1990

Fundamentalist women actively participate in the community, but their proper place is as its mother and keeper.[58] In this context again, the past is mobilized to give meaning to the present, although the present also has a role in the redefinition of the past. I agree with those scholars who claim that a return to Islam includes the reactivation of patriarchy,[59] but I also believe that the inherent contradictions between the present globalist, modern and assimilationist form of patriarchy and the particularistic forms of local patriarchy have caused this reactivation and revitalization.[60] One good example is the way in which the Islamic state in Iran expanded its notion of private patriarchy, originally confined to the Islamic family, in the direction of a more state-regulated public patriarchy.[61] For precisely this reason, the black chador became so important in the construction of an Islamic ethnonationalist identity.

It also explains why the first appearance of fundamentalism in the universities occurred when women started to wear the black chador. This veiling differed inherently from customary veiling because most of the women who wore the chador did so by choice and not in conformity with tradition. Eminently critical of a "universal imperialist model of femininity" and its pursuit of fashion, beauty, and consumerism, many fundamentalist women turned to the veil as a symbol of cultural disapproval.[62] However, considering the role of clothing for the construction of ethnicity, reveiling has constituted an important sign of adherence to an Islamic ethnicity.

There are at least four reasons for the importance of the politics of gender in fundamentalist Islam: (1) the construction of a "coercive community," or a community based on the complementarity of gender, which reproduces itself through the appropriated work of women as procreators, keepers, and socializers; (2) the re-masculinization of Muslim men in the construction of a hegemonic masculinity and an emphasized femininity, which guarantees emasculated Muslim men domination over Muslim women; (3) the dynamic relation of participation between the gendered social agents and the community of believers, where each individual recognizes the needs of the community over their own and so participates in the construction and reconstruction of symbolic boundaries; (4) the reduction of class differences and structural conflicts of interest between unveiled women of the upper and middle classes, and men of the middle and lower middle classes because gender hierarchies prevail over class hierarchies.

The Cultural Politics of Closure and the Crisis of Governmentality

The fundamentalist totalizing view of social reality is based on the supposed homogeneity of the sacred community of ummat and the participation of the individual believer in her or his relation to God as absolute sovereign. Islamic nationalism and fundamentalism bring the individual back to the worldly sphere of political activity. It calls for the social sacrifice and martyrdom of emasculated Muslim men and the black chador of women in a jihad and revolt not only against the ruler but also against oneself. The double embrace — of this world and the other world, inherent in the fundamentalist view and its effective use — mobilizes the Muslim masses formerly disempowered. The blood of the martyred Muslim men and the black chador of Muslim women enter into a cultural war of representation.

In the definition of Islamic fundamentalism as a form of ethnicity in opposition to a global world, we have examined the existence of an interconnected history. This is not to forget specificity and temporality, but rather to offer a framework that connects the local and the global in a single history. In this sense, local and global intervene and interact, not in a unilateral and passive way, but in an active and reciprocal way. I am not suggesting that the ethnographic reality of cultures and societies is unimportant; rather, I am linking different realities so as to bring attention to new constructions. Moreover, it is important to look at the internal contradiction of dominant and dominated ethnicity. Both discourses, which claim homogeneity and coherence, are sites of many antinomies and antagonisms. One way of revealing these is to include issues of diversity and difference.

Neither the dominant ethnicity of the West nor the dominated ethnicity of fundamentalism can free itself of internal contradictions, conflicts, and antagonisms. Different power relations based on gender, class, and ethnicity deconstruct and undermine the claimed homogeneity and coherence of both systems in their discursive intellectual elaborations. In the last few years,

Iranian society has witnessed an intensification of such internal tensions and resulting fragmentation at the level of Islamic identitarian claims and women's place within them. In addition, many Iranian Muslim women, both as participants in the building of an Islamic society and as citizens of an Islamic nation-state, have challenged the patriarchal laws of the state by taking an active role in the development of a more egalitarian interpretation of the religious and legal domains of Islam. Many Iranian Muslim feminists and gender activists have pushed for the reconfiguration of both women's rights and needs in the context of everyday life where the state rules in the name of Islam.[63] In addition, the reliance of the state on the notion of an Islamic nation or ummat defined by the territorial boundaries of Iran has thrown into crisis the internal boundaries of a transnational notion of the Islamic community.

In tracing the politics of difference, we need to investigate, explore, and explain — both theoretically and empirically — the interconnection between gender, class, and ethnicity in distinct layers of social reality. Social realities as particular cultural realities are constructed and reconstructed at the crossroads of such social divisions. Assuming the multiplicity of social relations at a theoretical level, and observing it at an empirical level, will provide a framework that enables a better understanding of the cultural politics of closure expressed and exercised through sexism and racism as well as through the renaissance of religious fundamentalism and new forms of cultural nationalism and essentialism.

Notes

I am grateful to Vasant Kaiwar, Sucheta Mazumdar, and Iain Boal for their feedback and help at various stages of this essay.

1. *Hegemonic masculinity* and *emphasized femininity* are concepts suggested by R. W. Connell, *Gender and Power: Society, the Person, and Sexual Politics* (Stanford, Calif.: Stanford University Press, 1987), to characterize the differentiated power structures of heteronormativity within gender categories.

2. A number of scholarly works have tried to complicate current Islamic movements, including John L. Esposito, *The Islamic Threat: Myth or Reality?* (New York: Oxford University Press, 1992); Bobby S. Sayyid, *A Fundamental Fear: Eurocentrism and the Emergence of Islamism* (London: Zed, 1997); Martin E. Marty and R. Scott Appleby, eds., *Fundamentalisms Observed* (Chicago: University of Chicago Press, 1991); John Stratton Hawley, ed., *Fundamentalism and Gender* (New York: Oxford University Press, 1994). This body of scholarship has helped to diffuse the sole attribution of fundamental-

ism to Islam. Nevertheless, the mainstream media has been consistently using fundamentalism to "otherize" and "racialize" Muslims both in North America and Europe. In the Middle East itself, Islamist groups sometimes employ the term *fundamentalist* to characterize others: for example, the Mohjahedin-e Khalq refers to the Iranian Islamic Republic as fundamentalist, while the Iranian Islamic Republic so referred to the Taliban regime in Afghanistan.

3. For an interesting study of Islamic liberalism, see Leonard Binder, *Islamic Liberalism: A Critique of Development Ideologies* (Chicago: University of Chicago Press, 1988).

4. For a critical review of this sociological literature, see Nader Naderi, "Max Weber and the Study of the Middle East: A Critical Analysis," *Berkeley Journal of Sociology,* 35 (1990): 71–87.

5. As Janet Jakobson and Ann Pellegrini argue: "Recognizing the co-origination of secularism and market-reformed Protestantism unmasks the national and religious particularities that have come to pass as a universal 'secular.' This secularism was linked at its origins to a particular religion and a particular location, and it was maintained through a particular set of practices" ("World Secularisms at the Millennium: Introduction," *Social Text* 18.3 [2000]: 1).

6. Edward W. Said, *Orientalism* (New York: Vintage, 1979).

7. Farhad Khosrokhavar, "Du néo-orientalisme de Badie: Enjeux et méthodes: L'orientalisme interrogations," *Peuples méditerranéens* 50 (1990): 121–48.

8. Ali Behdad, *Belated Travelers: Orientalism in the Age of Colonial Dissolution* (Durham, N.C.: Duke University Press, 1994); Bryan S. Turner, *Orientalism, Postmodernism, and Globalism* (London: Routledge, 1994).

9. Ervand Abrahamian, "Khomeini's Populism," *New Left Review* 186 (1991): 102–19; Hassan Riffat, "The Burgeoning of Islamic Fundamentalism: Toward an Understanding of the Phenomenon," in Norman J. Cohen, ed., *The Fundamentalist Phenomenon: A View from Within; a Response from Without* (Grand Rapids, Mich.: Eerdmans, 1990); Esposito, *The Islamic Threat*; Akbar S. Ahmed and Donnan Hastings, *Islam, Globalization, and Postmodernity* (London: Routledge, 1994).

10. Shayegan's description of "l'idéologisation de la tradition," and Lawrence's distinction between religion and ideology and their interaction, are basic to our understanding of universalistic and particularistic impulses in Islam (Darius Shayegan, *Qu'est-ce qu'une révolution religieuse?* [Paris: Presses d'aujourd'hui, 1982]; Bruce Lawrence, *Defenders of God: The Fundamentalist Revolt against the Modern Age* [New York: Harper Row, 1989).

11. Robert Wuthnow, *Meaning and Moral Order: Explorations in Cultural Analysis* (Berkeley: University of California Press, 1987), 191–92.

12. Stuart Hall, "The Local and the Global: Globalization and Ethnicity," in Anthony D. King, ed., *Culture, Globalization, and the World-System: Contemporary Conditions for the Representation of Identity* (Binghampton, N.Y.: SUNY-Binghampton, Department of Art and Art History, 1991), 35–36.

13. Immanuel Wallerstein, "The Rise and Future Demise of the World Capitalist System," in *The Capitalist World-Economy: Essays* (New York: Cambridge University Press, 1979), 1–36.

14. Theodore Von Laue, *The World Revolution of Westernization: The Twentieth Century in Global Perspective* (New York: Oxford University Press, 1987), 7.

15. Eric R. Wolf, *Europe and the People without History* (Berkeley: University of California Press, 1982); see also, V. G. Kiernan, *The Lords of Human Kind: Black Man, Yellow Man, and White Man in an Age of Empire* (Boston: Little, Brown, 1986).

16. Ella Shohat, "Rethinking Jews and Muslims: Quincentennial Reflections," *Middle East Report*, September-October 1992, 25.

17. Inderpal Grewal, *Home and Harem: Nation, Gender, Empire, and the Cultures of Travel* (Durham, N.C.: Duke University Press, 1996); Anne McClintock, *Imperial Leather: Race, Gender, and Sexuality in the Colonial Context* (New York: Routledge, 1995).

18. See Mona Etienne and Eleanor Leacock, eds., *Women and Colonization: Anthropological Perspectives* (New York: Praeger, 1980); Lourdes Benería, ed., *Women and Development: The Sexual Division of Labor in Rural Societies: A Study* (New York: Praeger, 1982); Maria Mies, *Patriarchy and Accumulation on a World Scale: Women in the International Division of Labour* (London: Zed, 1986); Cynthia H. Enloe, *Bananas, Beaches, and Bases: Making Feminist Sense of International Politics* (Berkeley: University of California Press, 1990); Enloe, *The Morning After: Sexual Politics at the End of the Cold War* (Berkeley: University of California Press, 1993). It is not that I believe that patriarchal gender relations did not exist in the colonies; what I am suggesting is that a globalized patriarchy had to face either particular forms of patriarchal relations or simply different gender relations, which created over time and space a complex set of social formations, relations, and identities.

19. Grewal and Kaplan introduce the notion of *scattered hegemonies* to characterize women's historicized and particular relationship to multiple patriarchies as well as to international economic hegemonies. See Inderpal Grewal and Caren Kaplan, eds., *Scattered Hegemonies: Postmodernity and Transnational Feminist Practices* (Minneapolis: University of Minnesota Press, 1997). See also Minoo Moallem, "The Universalization of Particulars: Civic Body and Gendered Citizenship in Iran," *Citizenship Studies* 3.3 (1999): 319–35, for an analysis of the construction of racialized and gendered bodies in the context of Iranian state formation and gendered citizenship.

20. Englishness and Frenchness were not in reality homogeneous categories. Even in the British Isles the notion of Englishness masked antagonisms and conflicts with the Irish and the Scots. As has been well documented by Martin Bernal, *Black Athena: The Afroasiatic Roots of Classical Civilization* (New Brunswick, N.J.: Rutgers University Press, 1987), the central mythos of Western civilization, that is, classical Greece, is deeply embedded in the self-understanding of the ruling classes of imperial Europe. Bernal argues that the deep roots of classical civilization in Egypt and in the Middle East have been suppressed for racist reasons.

21. See Timothy Mitchell, *Colonising Egypt* (Berkeley: University of California Press,

1991), for an in-depth analysis of such representation of the world in the colonial and postcolonial orders. Also, Guillaumin's monumental research on the juxtaposition of race, gender, and sexuality in colonial discourse provides an important frame for the understanding of the discourses of power as they produce a complex system of domination. Colette Guillaumin, *L'idéologie raciste: Genèse et langage actuel* (La Haye: Mouton, 1972).

22. Ernest Renan, "Islam and Science," quoted in Antonie Wessels, "The So-called Renaissance of Islam," *Journal of Asian and African Studies* 19.3–4 (1984): 193.

23. Sayyid Jamal ad-Din al-Afghani (1838–97) is one of the most dramatic anticolonial figures of nineteenth-century Middle Eastern history. His Islamic revival and his reinterpretation of the Islamic past in modern and nationalist terms became increasingly popular in the Middle East. For an excellent biography and translation of some of his ideas, see Nikki Keddie, *An Islamic Response to Imperialism: Political and Religious Writings of Sayyid Jamal ad-Din al-Afghani* (Berkeley: University of California Press, 1968).

24. Ibid., 84–95.

25. This slogan was also much used to mobilize the Iranian masses during the revolution of 1979.

26. See Malek Alloula, *The Colonial Harem*, trans. Myrna Godzich and Wald Godzich (Minneapolis: University of Minnesota Press, 1986), for an extensive analysis of the visual staging of sexuality and gender, including veiling, in pictorial Orientalism. Also see Reina Lewis, *Gendering Orientalism: Race, Femininity, and Representation* (New York: Routledge, 1996), for a further investigation of gendered Orientalism.

27. Occidentalism is a term used by some scholars to refer to the way in which the "East" (including the Muslim world) has represented the "West." For an extensive discussion of occidentalism, see Laura Nader, "Orientalism, Occidentalism, and the Control of Women," *Cultural Dynamics* 2.3 (1989): 323–55; Mohamad Tavakoli-Targhi, *Refashioning Iran: Orientalism, Occidentalism, and Historiography* (New York: Palgrave, 2001); Couze Venn, *Occidentalism: Modernity and Subjectivity* (Newbury Park, Calif.: Sage Publications, 2000).

28. For a fascinating analysis of such translational and transactional practices, see Mohamad Tavakoli-Targhi's essay in this volume.

29. For a detailed account of Iranian history in the early twentieth century, see Parvin Paidar, *Women and the Political Process in Twentieth-Century Iran* (Cambridge: Cambridge University Press, 1995); and Janet Afary, *The Iranian Constitutional Revolution, 1906–1911: Grassroots Democracy, Social Democracy, and the Origins of Feminism* (New York : Columbia University Press, 1996).

30. Not only is it impossible for the national bourgeoisie to develop in this case but also any attempt at the organization of an autonomous women's movement is repressed. See Eliz Sanasarian, *The Women's Rights Movement in Iran: Mutiny, Appeasement, and Repression from 1900 to Khomeini* (New York: Praeger, 1982).

31. I call it pseudonationalism because of its deep dependence on colonial and external powers. The construction of nationalism in Iran goes beyond Reza Shah. Indeed the nationalist movement was for the most part an adversary force to the Pahlavi regime.

32. For example, J. Arthur de Gobineau, *Essai sur l'inégalité des races humaines* (1853–55; Paris: Belfond, 1967).

33. I take up a detailed discussion of this question in *Between Warrior Brother and Veiled Sister: Islamic Fundamentalism and Cultural Politics of Patriarchy* (Berkeley: University of California Press, forthcoming).

34. Yet the relation between the two was ambivalent since it was based at times on an alliance with some of the ulama and at other times on an antagonism with them.

35. An adequate explanation of the Pahlavi regime, and the sociopolitical and socioeconomic causes of the Iranian revolution, go beyond the scope of this paper, but substantial work has been done in recent years on these issues by, among others, Nikki Keddie, *Roots of Revolution: An Interpretive History of Modern Iran* (New Haven, Conn.: Yale University Press, 1981); Theda Skocpol, "Rentier State and Shi'a Islam in the Iranian Revolution," *Theory and Society* 11 (1982): 266–83; and M. J. Michael Fischer and Mehdi Abedi, *Debating Muslims: Cultural Dialogues in Postmodernity and Tradition* (Madison: University of Wisconsin Press, 1990).

36. Motahari was a student of Khomeini's and a powerful and outspoken religious figure. He was assassinated soon after the revolution by Furqan, an anticlerical guerrilla group. For a careful analysis of Motahari's arguments, see Fischer and Abedi, *Debating Muslims*, 181–221.

37. Both male and female members of these militant squads were mobilized when Khomeini ordered the creation of the notorious "twenty-million member army." With respect to women/sisters (*bassig-e khaharan,* "mobilized sisters"), the squads' responsibilities included military training, medical assistance (*emd gari*), ideological training, and political organizing. See *Zan dar ayeneh-e defay-e moghadass* [Women in the mirror of sacred defense] (Tehran: Sisters Propagation Squad, Islamic Revolutionary Guards, 1990).

38. Fatima Mernissi, *The Fundamentalist Obsession with Women* (Lahore: Women's Resource and Publication Centre, 1987).

39. Here I want to focus on the cultural process, although this is not to deny the economic and political contradictions involved. The failure of the nationalist movement and the left in Iran make for a separate subject of inquiry.

40. Jalal al-e-Ahmad, *Garbzadegi* (Tehran: Ketab, 1962).

41. Shari'ati was arrested and imprisoned for ten months. After this period, he began teaching at the University of Mashad, but the popularity of his radical teachings led to his subsequent dismissal. In 1968 he gave a series of lectures at a newly founded Islamic mosque and lecture hall called Hosseinieh Ershad. In the absence of any open discussion or critical examination, Shari'ati's modernist references to Shi'ism were accepted and followed by hundreds of thousands of young Iranians.

42. Shi'a Twelver Islam constitutes a major branch of Islam. Shi'is emerged as partisans of Ali, the prophet's cousin and son-in-law, holding that he and his descendants should rule the realms of Islam and serve as spiritual guides. Shi'ites believe in the disappearance of the infant twelfth imam who will return as the messianic Mahdi to institute a reign of justice and equity on earth. This belief has been favored historically in the mobilization of Shi'ism as social protest. See Juan R. I. Cole and Nikki R. Keddie, eds., *Shi'ism and Social Protest* (New Haven, Conn.: Yale University Press, 1986), 2–5.

43. See Ali Shari'ati, *Ummat va imamat* (Tehran: Intisharat-i Husayniyah Irshad, 1971).

44. Abdolkarim Souroush, *Razdani, roushanfikri va dindari* (Tehran: Sarat, 1992).

45. This belief became more influential when some important members of this group turned to Marxism while in the shah's prisons. The more fundamentalist groups started to distance themselves from the members of the Mojahedin-e Khalq organization and began to establish their own identity and distinctive mode of action. The openness of the Mojahedin-e Khalq vis-à-vis other political groups, as well as their flexibility vis-à-vis democratic movements, was received with mistrust and suspicion by many fundamentalists. At the time more and more fundamentalist trends were starting to distinguish themselves from the Mojahedin-e Khalq by emphasizing religious activities and by adopting a very rigid and exclusive attitude in relation to other groups. One of the important signs of this distinctiveness emerged when women of the groups opposed to Mojahedin-e Khalq who used to wear a symbolic "scarf"—a sign of their Islamic identity—decided to wear the black chador. Soon after the revolution, the Mojahedin-e Khalq organization became Islamic puritanism's most hated group, and hundreds of thousands of its young members were imprisoned, tortured, and executed by the Islamic Republic. Following this organization's exile from Iran and their relocation in Iraq (especially during the Iran/Iraq war), it gradually lost popularity inside and outside Iran. This derives partly from its adoption of a sectarian and militaristic program, its self-identification as the sole opponents of the Iranian government, and its goal of seizing state power at any price.

46. See Ziba Mir-Hosseini, *Islam and Gender: The Religious Debate in Contemporary Iran* (Princeton, N.J.: Princeton University Press, 1999) for a careful discussion of the religious debate in Iran.

47. See, among others, Farah Azari, ed., *Women of Iran: The Conflict with Fundamentalist Islam* (London: Ithaca, 1983).

48. Robert N. Bellah, *Beyond Belief: Essays on Religion in a Post-traditional World* (New York: Harper and Row, 1970), 151.

49. S. Ruhollah Khomeini, *Islam and Revolution: Writings and Declarations of Imam Khomeini,* trans. Hamid Algar (Berkeley, Calif.: Mizan, 1981), 76–78.

50. Shayegan, *Qu'est-ce qu'une révolution religieuse?,* 139.

51. S. Ruhollah Khomeini, *Hukumat-e islami: Velayat-e faqih* (Tehran: Amir Kabir, 1978), 52.

52. For example, Hadi Gafari, a well-known Iranian fundamentalist leader, makes extensive use of such a dichotomy in his book *Hamd mi-amouzad* (Tehran: Bessat, 1979), 19–30.

53. Ibid., 15, 17.

54. Minoo Moallem, "Pluralité des rapports sociaux: Similarité et différence: Le cas des Iraniennes et Iraniens au Québec" (Ph.D. diss., Université de Montréal, 1989), 356–77.

55. The so-called Karbala parable refers to the story of Hussein, Muhammad's grandson and his family, in their stand against oppressive tyranny and corruption and their subsequent martyrdom. The audience learns to identify with the extreme pain and suffering Hussein and his family experienced in Karbala. Shi'ite myths have a great deal of influence on the daily life of Iranians.

56. Gafari, *Hamd mi-amouzad,* 34.

57. See Moallem, "The Universalization of Particulars," for an extensive analysis of gender dynamism in Islamic nationalism and fundamentalism in Iran.

58. A number of scholars have elaborated on the mobilization of women and their assertive participation in various religious fundamentalist movements. See, for example, Sucheta Mazumdar, "Women, Culture, and Politics: Engendering the Hindu Nation," *South Asia Bulletin* 11.2 (1991): 1–24; Renee Debra Kaufman, *Rachel's Daughters: Newly Orthodox Jewish Women* (New Brunswick, N.J.: Rutgers University Press, 1991); Tanika Sarkar and Urvashi Butalia, eds., *Women and Right-wing Movements: The Indian Experience* (London: Zed, 1995); Brenda E. Brasher, *Godly Women: Fundamentalism and Female Power* (New Brunswick, N.J.: Rutgers University Press, 1998).

59. Susan E. Marshall, "Paradoxes of Change: Culture Crisis, Islamic Revival, and Reactivation of Patriarchy," *Journal of Asian and African Studies* 19.1–2 (1984): 1–17.

60. For example, the dichotomization of family law versus civil law created contradictions and tensions in everyday legal practices and appeals to social justice both in the public and private spheres. This situation was not peculiar to Iran; other colonial and postcolonial societies have had similar experiences. See Marnia Lazreg, *The Eloquence of Silence: Algerian Women in Question* (New York: Routledge, 1994); and Zakia Pathak and Rajeswari Sunder Rajan, "Shahbano," *Signs* 14.3 (1989): 558–82. For an extended study of gender in various social and cultural discourses in the Middle East, see Deniz Kandiyoti, ed., *Gendering the Middle East: Emerging Perspectives* (Syracuse: Syracuse University Press, 1996).

61. Another telling example is the way the Islamic Republic of Iran publicized and triggered "temporary marriage," using it as evidence of the Islamic understanding of matters concerning the regulation of sexuality. For a study of temporary marriage, see Shahla Haeri, *Law of Desire: Temporary Marriage in Shi'i Iran* (Syracuse: Syracuse University Press, 1989).

62. An excellent example, among the many works on this subject by fundamentalist women, is Zahra Rahnavard, *Toloueh zan-e mosalman* [The emergence of the Muslim woman] (Tehran: Mahboubeh, n.d.).

63. See Ziba Mir-Hosseini, *Islam and Gender,* and Afsaneh Najmabadi, "Feminisms in an Islamic Republic: 'Years of Hardship, Years of Growth,'" in Yvonne Yazbeck Haddad and John L. Esposito, eds., *Islam, Gender, and Social Change* (New York: Oxford University Press, 1998), 59–84, for further analysis of such negotiations.

Sucheta Mazumdar

The Politics of Religion and National Origin:

Rediscovering Hindu Indian Identity in the United States

■ It has been suggested that all earlier forms of national identity have given way and that "we are in the process of moving to a new global order in which the nation-state has become obsolete and other formations for allegiance and identity have taken its place."[1] This essay argues that, to the contrary, the perduring power of certain forms of identity politics born alongside the nation-state require closer scrutiny even in the global moment. I am interested in exploring the ways in which the identity politics of immigrants continue to be shaped by homeland nationalist projects and how their own claims to cultural authenticity are articulated through the selective appropriation of nationalist legacies. I focus on two distinctive periods, the 1920s and 1990s, junctures when identity politics in the United States were being reestablished with distinctive trajectories. In the 1920s, renewed nativism, eugenics, and debates about immigration focused on the question of citizenship and the national ethos as a "white" nation.[2] In the 1990s, in a period of major new immigration changing the complexion of America, state-sponsored projects of multiculturalism premised on an unchanging and essentialized ethnicity of the immigrants have sought to define yet another model of the nation: a vision of a people made anew in America even as they remake the nation.[3] Immigrants are, however, very much a people *with* a history. This history and its mythographies shape the politics and consciousness of immigrants long after their arrival, even as they are recast in the processes of relocation. For the majority of the immigrants from India this history has been formulated as "Hindu." Immigrants from this one religious group have successfully appropriated "India" for themselves and become its sole cultural representatives in the United States. What are the implications of this construction of Indian ethnicity as Hindu in America, given the conjuncture of rising Hindu ultranationalism in the homeland?

Indian Immigrants in the United States: Religion and Race

The first immigrants from India were sailors on American ships who stayed on, and young men and women brought in as servants and slaves from Madras, Bombay, Surat, Cochin, and Calcutta via the British-India trade and then direct American trade with India. We do not know how many individuals might have come in this manner. The Pennsylvania Abolitionist Society, the Maryland State Archives, and the Massachusetts Historical Society all have records of "East Indians" and "East India Indians" brought as indentured servants and slaves.[4] Living and working in a country that equated dark skin with unfree status, these immigrants seem to have merged with the African American population, leaving few traces.[5] The records indicate only their Christian names: Thomas Banks, Samuel James, John Ballay, John Dunn, Mary Dove. . . . Sometimes only the first name is given; there was a "Peter" whose daughter Mary Fisher married a "Negro man named Richard Fisher, a slave."[6] These Christian names indicate that the immigrants either converted or were renamed by their American masters just as African slaves were. Or they well may have been Christians prior to arrival, for several of the Indian coastal areas have had Christian communities for centuries. In eighteenth-century America, the Indians' skin color and not their religious affiliation as Christians presented the pertinent factor.

The U.S. census of 1900 reported 2,050 East Indians resident in the United States.[7] Most were listed as students, businessmen, professionals, and religious teachers. Shortly thereafter, starting in 1904, immigrants from peasant backgrounds, predominantly from the province of Punjab, began arriving, initially as a spillover from emigration to Vancouver in Canada. Between 1907 and 1910, approximately 1,000 immigrants entered each year, so that by 1910 between 5,000 and 10,000 Indians resided in the United States.[8] The majority were Sikhs, and well over one-third of the immigrants were Muslim. But the media and federal and state agencies called them "Hindus." For the United States was, by now, far more familiar with India as the land of Hindus.

U.S. trade with India had produced passing fancies for Indian goods, while notions about exotic India at the popular level were promoted alike by Barnum's circus elephants, songs like the "Hindu Girl," and plays such as *The Rajah's Daughter* and *Cataract of the Ganges* performed by the Boston Theater.[9] For the East Coast elites, the first introductions to Indian literature and religions arrived via the work of European Orientalists and their translations of Sanskrit texts. Benjamin Franklin had met William Jones, the noted Orientalist; Jefferson had a couple of translations of Jones's *Sacontala* (*Shakuntala*), a fourth-century drama of love and abandonment, in his library along with *The Cambridge History of the War in India* and a volume on *Indian or Bengali Vocabulary*.[10] By the 1830s, the increased availability of European Orientalist interpretations of Hinduism and Max Müller's translations of the Bhagavad Gita and the Upanishads were familiar to American scholars in the divinity schools of Yale and Harvard and among the Free Religionists. Most relevantly, however, it was Hindu philosophy and Hindu religion, and not the cultural diversity of India or Indian Islam, that had merited American attention.[11]

Along with American evangelical Christians going out to India from 1813 onward, railing against heathen Hindu practices in print and sermon and the publication of works like William Tudor's *Theology of the Hindoos,* which appeared in 1818, interest among American Unitarians in comparative religions led to sympathetic readings of texts on Hinduism. When prominent Indians like Ram Mohan Roy became involved with Unitarianism, his activities and those of his disciples were regularly covered in various Unitarian journals throughout the nineteenth century.[12] The fascination with "oriental religions" among the New England Transcendentalists such as Thoreau and Emerson further introduced "Hindu" India to Americans in the 1840s. Yet other Americans who embraced theosophy in the last quarter of the nineteenth century found aspects of Hinduism and Buddhism appealing.[13] Pantheistic religions had their own attractions for some: Hindu gods like Shiva, Vishnu, and Krishna made their way into the nomenclature of geographical sites of the Grand Canyon in the 1870s, along with Greek and Egyptian gods.[14] By the time Walt Whitman wrote his elegiac "Passage to India" in 1869, and Edwin Arnold his *The Light of Asia* in 1880 (which went through at least eighty-three American editions and sold a million copies by 1900), educated Americans had been exposed to a literary tradition underlining (Hindu) India's ancient exotic spirituality.[15]

But this familiarity with Hinduism perhaps would not have proven enough to create the burst of interest that followed, had it not been for particular conditions within the United States itself. By the 1890s, the United States was entering a period referred to as one of "spiritual crisis." Very rapid changes in the American social fabric had occurred by the 1890s: the huge new immigration from Europe combined with the rash of urbanization and dislocation of people as they moved from farms to cities with industrialization. In addition, Americans faced the intellectual challenges posed by Darwinism and criticism of the Bible, and the deep rift that had emerged between conservative and liberal Christians.[16] By the time the Hindu monk Vivekananda arrived in Chicago in 1893, as one of twenty other Indians invited to participate in the World Parliament of Religions,[17] some Americans were ready to be impressed by elegant saffron-robed swamis and their message of the superior spiritual values of the "East," based on a "pure" Hinduism reclaimed from the ancient Vedas. While Vivekananda's claims of the imminent conversion of thousands of Americans to Hindu Vedanta philosophy and their supposed tumultuous response to his speeches were well-managed self-promotion,[18] his lecture tour secured several wealthy American patrons, predominantly women, who helped set up Vedanta societies in American cities coast to coast, which regularly brought over priests from India.[19] These constituted the first organized transnational Hindu religious institutions in America.

Vivekananda and the order of Hinduism he represented was part of a burgeoning of Hindu religious movements in the last decades of the nineteenth and the early twentieth century, all of which sought to revitalize Hinduism and, through that, the Hindus themselves. These movements thus constituted political projects from their very inception. While some of them can be seen as the second generation of Hindu religious reform movements that had begun in the first half of the nineteenth century when Christianity and Enlightenment thought had first challenged small groups of urban elite Indians, these new Hindu movements surfaced in a very different world. The social order that had emerged in the immediate aftermath of colonization and the end of the wars of colonization was being transformed at the core and, with it, family structures and gender roles. Crucially, Hindu caste hierarchies themselves were in flux even as the colonial state sought to impose and fix religious identities on the populace through its administrative mechanisms, including the census. The full impact of modernization and colonialism had now become manifest in everyday life: visible in the railway system that spread across the country; in the economic and social changes in the rural sector (with its new groups of moneylenders and outsider merchants); in the growth of hundreds of small towns, which gradually added members of the new professional classes of lawyers, doctors, teachers, railway and postal workers; and in the population mix of the port cities of Bombay, Madras, and Calcutta, which expanded with professionals, businessmen, entertainers, service-sector workers, and an emerging working class.[20] Newcomers everywhere had to sort out religious and caste identities, form new alliances, even arrive at a consensual definition of what it meant to be Hindu as belief systems themselves underwent questioning. These challenges came not just from the Christian missionaries and the racial hierarchies fostered by the colonial state but from educated Indian reformers and social activists who interrogated orthodox Hindu religious dogma, criticized practices such as untouchability and child marriage, and, more fundamentally, as nationalists queried the role of religion in the nation-state that was to be the India of the twentieth century.[21]

The spectrum of new Hindu religious movements that emerged in this period spanned fundamental and crucial differences. Issues ranged from differing emphases on ritual and religious practice, selections of textual authorities, social activist agendas on subjects such as women's education, widow remarriage, and the upliftment of untouchables (if not the erasure of the institution altogether), the reconversion of those who had "strayed" into Christianity, the protection of cows, the promotion of vegetarianism as the Hindu way, and the exclusion of Muslims from political and public space. But what all of them had in common was that these new religious movements and their founders saw themselves as nationalists, trying to reclaim political space and power for a reinvigorated Hinduism (of course of their own particular brand) that was to define the Indian polity. As such they were reactionary movements, reacting to experiences of the time, wanting to resuscitate a world that seemed to be slipping away, trying to give shape to the future by reclaiming an authentic past. At the same time, however, the movements represented a new type of modern organization. Interested in political power, all had well-defined leadership hierarchies and structures of authority functioning with articulated sociopolitical agendas, designated officers in charge of fund-raising, voluminous publications in the vernacular languages and English, public outreach programs, conferences and seminars, and, in due course, organized schools and colleges with curricula that reflected the worldview of the organization.[22] And some of them were global in their mission and outreach long before the term *globalization* had become common parlance.

The Ramakrishna movement in Bengal, which Vivekananda reorganized,[23] and the contemporary Arya Samaj movement developed by Dayananda Saraswati in Punjab shared numerous characteristics. They based their philosophical underpinnings on the concept of a golden age of high Hinduism, which they wanted to revive by promoting a unitary notion of the divine by going back to the ancient Vedic texts stripped of all the vulgar accretions of three millennia of idolatry. Simplifying ritual practice and promoting saffron as the color of their reborn Hinduism, these movements took their organizational structures and strategies from the Protestant missionary movements to which they were partly a response. And, like the Christian missionaries, they incorporated a combination of religious and humanitarian activities at home and abroad. However, if the Ramakrishna Mission projected itself as the intellectual legatee of all the various syncretic reform movements of Bengal,[24] and tried to find its base among the established middle and upper classes in the metropolitan centers at home and abroad, the Arya Samaj promoted a more homespun image. It was aggressively critical of all other religions including Reform Hinduism, Saivite Hinduism, and particularly Islam, while reaching out to a large constituency comprised of the newly urbanizing professionals, the petite bourgeoisie, mercantile groups of small-town north India, and even those excluded from orthodox Hinduism, such as untouchables. In addition, the Arya Samaj also sought to integrate into their fold those marginalized by Brahmanical Hinduism, such as the lower-caste immigrants overseas who were converting to Christianity. Throughout the twentieth century, the Arya Samaj proselytized and established educational institutions to recruit adherents among the Indian communities from Fiji, Mauritius, and Uganda to Trinidad and Guyana.

The Arya Samaj was also by far the most articulate of all the new religious movements in its definition of the nation. Dayananda, the founder of the Arya Samaj, in his *Satyartha Prakash* [The light of truth], was the first to elaborate as early as 1872 the notion of *Aryavarta* (land of the Arya) as a synonym for India. The Arya Samaj made Aryavarta the property of all those who were true believers, giving a seemingly universal element of inclusion to this proposed community. But Dayananda also asserted that only one particular belief system entitled one to a membership in this Arya-varta; a primordial loyalty was owed to India because one had partaken of its food and water, and he declared those "inclined to alien faiths" (i.e., Muslims and Christians) treacherous. According to him, only Sanskrit, the Vedas, the *rishis,* and sages of ancient India constituted the fount of all that was worth knowing and preserving.[25] By the twentieth century, the Arya Samaji concept of citizenship had converged on an exclusive and exclusion-ary Hinducentric consciousness: "The consciousness must arise in the mind of each Hindu that he is a Hindu, and not merely an Indian," declared Dayananda's disciple Lal Chand in 1909 in an anticipation of the yet more strident versions of exclusive and militant political Hinduism that were to develop in the 1920s.[26]

The transformation of the word *Arya,* which had once meant "noble one," into its association with peoples and the racial categories of "white and Caucasian" were of late-eighteenth-century origin. As pointed out by Vasant Kaiwar in "The Aryan Model of History and the Oriental Renais-sance," the work of German romantics, Orientalists, and Indologists had given rise to the "Aryan" theory of Indian history, namely, that the struc-tural and linguistic similarities between Sanskrit, Greek, and Latin bespoke a common history of kinship and migration. By the nineteenth century, presumed Aryan as a racial category had become part of the self-definition of upper-caste Hindus. While later European Indologists questioned any congruence between language and race and declared Aryan to refer only to a language group and not a race of people, presumed Aryan racial origin became central to the process of creating a community and a distinct re-ligious identity for the Hindus.[27]

Hindus could now claim ancestral origins similar to those of the Euro-peans by arguing that they descended from superior European Aryans who came in via the north and conquered the indigenous non-Aryan people. In ideal form this "Aryan" was "white." As Vivekananda elaborated for his audience in Detroit in 1894, "To the great tablelands of the high Himalaya mountains first came the Aryans, and there to this day abides the pure type of Brahman, a people which [the Westerners] can but dream of. . . . Their features are regular, their eyes and hair dark, and their skin the color of which would be produced by the drops which fell from a pricked finger into a glass of milk. These are the Hindus in their pure type, untainted and untrammeled."[28] This reading of Aryan, in turn, served to justify the supe-

rior status of Hindus vis-à-vis Muslims. Still based on the Orientalist notions of migration, Aryans were transplanted but superior sons of the soil;
Hindus alone had the right to identify as "Indian."

The formation of new Hindu religious-political organizations continued
to intensify through the 1890s and into the early decades of the twentieth
century. Several Hindu *sabha* (councils or associations) to promote and
defend Hindu rights were formed throughout northern and western India
by orthodox Hindus who felt troubled by even the obliquely articulated
politics of social reform of the Arya Samaj. Most of these organizations
were also acutely aware of the global dimension of their missions. The
Sanathan Dharma Sabha (Council of Eternal Religion), founded in 1895
expressly to defend orthodox Hinduism, became especially involved in
outreach to émigré communities from Fiji to the Caribbean.[29] Hinduism
united the disparate Indian communities, gave the sons and daughters of
indentured laborers a homeland identity, a literary canon, a history, and a
"noble" cultural heritage that set them apart from the "people without
history," the Pacific Islanders and the Afro-Caribbeans.

The Hindu Mahasabha (The Great Assembly of Hindus), founded in
1915, and the Rashtriya Swayamsevak Sangh (RSS, the National Assembly
of Volunteers), founded in 1925, articulated the most strident aspirations
of modern political Hinduism. Their vision of Hinduism wanted to eliminate troublesome sectarianism and the multiplicity of local gods in favor of
a homogeneous national Hinduism to create a uniform ideology and identity. The term *Hindu* acquired a symbiosis with the concept of *Aryan,*
shifting in the process from a religious to a national-racial category. Anti-
miscegenationist notions were incorporated into this racialized view of
history, which drew the boundaries of India at the Indus river:

> On the northwestern side of our nation the commingling of races was
> growing rather too unceremonious to be healthy and our frontiers too
> shifty to be safe. . . . The day on which the patriarchs of our race had
> crossed that stream they ceased to belong to the people they had defi-
> nitely left behind, and laid the foundation of a new nation — were reborn
> into a new people . . . and by expansion to grow into a race and a new
> polity that could only be most fittingly and feelingly described as Sindhu
> or Hindu.[30]

The speeches and writings of the founders and leaders of these movements
— V. D. Savarkar, K. B. Hedgewar, and M. S. Golwalkar — promoted the

notion of an organic, all-encompassing Hinduism and energized the concept of *Hindutva* which embraced a unitary notion of nation: race-people-culture-religion-history-civilization. Savarkar wrote in *Hindutva* (1923), "Let this noble stream of Hindu blood flow from vein to vein . . . till at last the Hindu people get fused and welded into an indivisible whole, till our races get consolidated and strong and sharp as steel."[31] Seven times president of the Mahasabha, Savarkar considered Muslims, for example, treacherous for "the tie of a common Holyland has at times proved stronger [for them] than the chains of a Motherland."[32]

In these religion-as-culture, religion-as-identity Hindu movements, formed in a period when the British colonial repression of the intensifying nationalist movement had stripped the liberal secular model of viability,[33] notions of essentialized differences between "civilizations" that separated "East" and "West" were recast. Vivekananda's nineteenth-century model of a "spiritual East" teaching the "materialist West" had now become a far more acute and essentialized divergence.[34] There was a militant defense of the supposed integral differences that were to be preserved as markers of the nation's civilization; social practices which would blur these civilizational categories had to be rejected aggressively. As Lajpat Rai, involved with both the Arya Samaj and later the Hindu Mahasabha, demanded of the secular reformers in 1904:

> Cannot a revivalist . . . ask the reformers into what they wish to reform us? Whether they want us to be reformed into the particular pattern of the English or the French? Whether they want us to accept the divorce laws of Christian society or the temporary marriages that are now so much in favor in France or America? Whether they want to make men of our women by putting them into those avocations for which nature never meant them? Whether they want us to substitute the legal *niyoga*[35] of the Mahabharata period with the illegal and immoral *niyoga* that is now rampant in European society? Whether they want to reform us into Sunday drinkers of brandy and promiscuous eaters of beef? In short whether they want to revolutionize our society by an outlandish imitation of European customs and manners and an undiminished adoption of European vice?[36]

For Indian immigrants to the United States, many of the Hindu revivalists' ideas proved attractive. As nationalists, some of them were in close sympathy with Lajpat Rai and organizations such as the India Home Rule

League of America, started up by Rai in 1914 when he spent five years in the United States. But, even more importantly, these ideas of India's primordial distinctiveness allowed the immigrants to claim racial lineage that could bypass the biology-based racism dominating the U.S. racial lexicon. Proclaiming their status as Hindu, and equating "high-caste Hindu" with "Aryan ancestry," could help sidestep the thorny question of citizenship rights in America.

Locating the Aryan/Caucasian: White or Non-White?

With Indian immigration to the United States increasing in 1907, West Coast racist organizations such as the Asiatic Exclusion League immediately started agitating for restricting and terminating the migration of this newest of the Asian immigrant groups. As the League stated, "From every part of the [West] Coast complaints are made of the undesirability of the Hindoos, their lack of cleanliness, disregard of sanitary laws, petty pilfering, especially of chickens, and insolence to women."[37] The victims of anti-"Hindu" riots in Bellingham, Washington, in 1907, and Live Oak, California, in 1908, like the majority of the immigrants, were Sikh and Muslim. They worked as farm labor, in lumber yards, and in railroad construction. With few exceptions, the educated professionals and businessmen, mostly Hindus, were located in the cities of the northeast. They did not confront such direct hostility; many married white American women and developed new networks of support. A handful of professionals were involved in the anti-British nationalist struggle, such as the Ghadar movement in California, and worked to raise money through the donations of their compatriots; most, however, had no contact with the agricultural laborers. So when the question of rights to citizenship came up in 1907 from the ranks of the professionals and from those who were wealthy enough to own property, the court battles were taken up on an individual basis. The issue at hand was "race." Were the Indians "white" or "non-white"? More to the point, was a particular Indian an "Aryan," and as such entitled to naturalization as a "white person"?

The Chinese had been the first national group to be denied rights to citizenship through naturalization in 1882 on the basis of the U.S. Naturalization Act of 1790, which limited citizenship by naturalization to "free white aliens" and, by a revision of the law in 1870, to those of African origin and descent.[38] Asians did not fit either category. Without citizenship rights, they could neither freely depart and reenter the United States nor hope to own landed property because of the "alien land laws" enforced in many states. By the 1920s, Japanese immigrants were also fighting legal battles in an attempt to gain naturalized citizenship, using the argument that the Japanese were "white." In 1922, however, the U.S. Supreme Court rejected the test-case appeal for citizenship, citing that although the Japanese American appellant Takao Ozawa was highly educated, and "his family had attended American churches and he had maintained the use of the English language in his home" and that this made him "well qualified by character and education for citizenship," he was nonetheless a member of the "yellow race."[39] That Supreme Court decision did not dissuade Indians from trying to gain citizenship because surely they were Aryan and, by extension, "Caucasian" and therefore "white."

Within the professional groups of Indians no consensus existed on the issue of how to struggle for racial parity; there was, however, consensus on the "purity of blood." The Hindus repeatedly stressed they were members of "high caste(s)," and therefore "of pure blood" or "of the Aryan race." Indians from other religious affiliations used the same types of arguments; Zoroastrians, for example, sought to prove that "Parsees (as people from Persia) belong to the white race."[40] Yet others became vigorous defenders of the caste system and used Orientalist constructions of a rigid caste system as their defense. As one Punjabi writer declared, "The Aryan blood is pure. No inter-marriage and cross-breeding has ever taken place except at the risk of ex-communication. . . . The Punjabis living at present in the Pacific Coast states are as pure Caucasians as the Germans. The people of Punjab are all Aryans, as there are no low-caste Pariahs or aborigines in this section."[41]

Between 1907 and 1923, approximately seventy persons, all of them educated professionals, gained citizenship on the grounds that they (as particular individuals) were members of the "Aryan race" and, as such, "white," that is, of Caucasian origin. The Asiatic Exclusion League obviously got their history from the same sources, namely European theorists of racial vitality such as Arthur Comte de Gobineau, who posited a connection between economic development and racial hierarchies. The league did not deny Hindus membership in the family of Aryans. Instead they argued that while Hindus were "members of the same family as Americans of European ancestry," the distinction was that the "forefathers" of the white Americans "pressed to the west, in the everlasting march of conquest, progress and civilization; . . . the forefathers of the Hindus went east and became enslaved, effeminate, caste-ridden and degraded. . . . And now we the people of the United States are asked to receive these members of a degraded race on terms of equality."[42]

The test case for the Indians developed with the citizenship application of Bhagat Singh Thind, a light-skinned Punjabi and U.S. army veteran of World War I. His brief to the Supreme Court on the subject of race reads in part:

> The people residing in many of the states of India, particularly the north and the northwest, including the Punjab, belong to the Aryan race. The Aryan race is the race that speaks the Aryan language. . . . The Aryan language is indigenous to the Aryan of India as well as to the Aryan of Europe. . . . The high-class Hindu regards the aboriginal Indian Mongoloid in the same manner as the American regards the negro, speaking from a matrimonial standpoint. The caste system prevails in India to a degree unsurpassed elsewhere.[43]

The U.S. Supreme Court did not directly challenge this; the mythical relationship between all Caucasians was allowed to stand. In rejecting Thind's application, Justice Sutherland elaborated that "it may be true that the blonde Scandinavian and the brown Hindu have a common ancestor in the dim reaches of antiquity." However, he ruled that, " 'Caucasian' is a convention word of much flexibility . . . and while it and the words 'white persons' are treated as synonymous . . . they are not of identical meaning and Indians clearly did not qualify as 'white persons' in the 'language of the common man.' "[44] Sutherland noted that, "Aryan has to do with linguistic and not at all [with] physical characteristics, and it would seem reasonably clear that mere resemblance in language, indicating a common linguistic root buried in remote ancient soil, is altogether inadequate to prove common racial origin." Then, perhaps indicating his own categorization of the Indians, he selected the example of African Americans and pointed out that, after all, "millions of Negroes, whose descendants can never be classified racially with the descendants of white persons notwithstanding both may speak a common root language."[45]

Following the Thind decision, the Immigration and Naturalization Service moved to cancel the citizenship of all those Indians who had gained citizenship prior to the Supreme Court ruling. By September 1926, forty-three of them had had their citizenship annulled while the others were to battle in the courts for years to come. The arguments presented in each case show that the defense invariably invoked the "Aryan" status of the immigrant as the justification for naturalization. For the Indian immigrants engaged in this debate, their classification as Aryan and Caucasian had become an integral part of their identity in America, as it had for their relatives back in India.

Several other aspects of this convoluted discussion stand out. Thind clearly hoped to draw on white fears of miscegenation by reminding the court of how "Americans" did not marry "Negroes." Indians, then as now, made valiant efforts not to be confused with blacks. The other is the equation of *Hindu* and *Aryan* with *Indian*. Neither the American courts nor the lawyers challenged the uses of the words *Aryan* and *Hindu*. In the American context it was perhaps easier to distinguish the Indians (Native Americans) and Indians from India by using religion as a reference point for those from India rather than geographical or national origin. Repeatedly, in all sorts of discussions of Asian immigration, one finds references to "Chinese, Japanese and Hindus."[46] Those who were of Hindu origin, predominantly the professionals and members of the middle class, saw no discrepancy in this equation. Muslims and Sikhs, not to mention the Christians, faded from the picture in this construction of India as the land of Hindus, although the vast majority of the 2,405 Indians counted by the U.S. census of 1940 were Sikh, and the half a dozen or so *gurdwaras* (Sikh temples) dotting Imperial Valley and the central California valley formed the sole nucleus of the Indian (including Hindu and Muslim) immigrant community until the 1960s.

Becoming Hindu in Late-Twentieth-Century America

Indians became eligible to apply for U.S. citizenship in 1946, but the quota system of immigration under the Walter-McCarren Act restricted immigration from India as part of the Asia Pacific Triangle to a hundred immigrants each year until 1965. Major new immigration from India started with the passage of the Immigration Act of 1965, which repealed the previous restrictive measures and opened up immigration to the United States to the present level of 750,000 individuals worldwide annually. By 2000, almost 1.7 million individuals of Indian origin had immigrated to the United States. Overall, Indian immigrants form a highly educated group, particularly relative to educational attainments in India: the 1990 census data indicated over 80 percent of the men and 52 percent of the women had college degrees. The census also showed an overwhelmingly white-collar employment profile. With the exception of New York, New Jersey, and some parts of California, where there is a working class, almost 33 percent of the immigrants work in technical, sales, and administrative support, while 44 percent work in managerial positions or in medicine and engineering. By 1990, over 26,000 physicians of Indian origin practiced in the United States.[47] The post-1993 legislation allowing for an additional 65,000 visa slots annually for workers in high-tech fields (increased since 1998 to 115,000) has created a new surge in the immigration of highly trained technical personnel; almost 48 percent of the total slots go to Indian applicants. Others own hotels and motels, while some have become successful entrepreneurs in Silicon Valley during the 1990s. The community can easily raise hundreds of thousands of dollars for causes they believe in; for example, a group of ten couples in California raised $600,000 for the Democratic Party presidential candidate in the course of one evening.[48] Most recent immigrants are devout Hindus, turning patios and bedrooms into Hindu shrines and prayer rooms, starting Hindu versions of Bible studies and Sunday schools, sponsoring priests for functions at home, rushing to temples to witness miracles, and helping build temples.[49] About 200 temples have already been built, and another 1,000 are in various stages of planning and construction.[50]

Many immigrants are also aggressive supporters of political Hinduism. Several have donated extensive funds to Hindu ideological causes both in the United States and in India, notwithstanding the fact that the resurgence of Hindu political activism in India has included the well-known illegal occupation and destruction of a sixteenth-century mosque in 1992, numerous pogroms against Muslims that have escalated into coordinated nationwide killings in the 1980s and 1990s, and anti-Christian activities that have included murders and rapes. The violence of 1992 seems to have taken many commentators by surprise, and the support given to these activities by the overseas communities was seen as unexpected or read as a manifestation of new transnational forms of nationalism.[51] However, a brief sketch of the postindependence history of the Hindu movement may help us better interpret the continuities in the identity politics of the U.S. Indian community. "Long-distance nationalism" may have a longer history than imagined.[52]

While, as Eric Hobsbawm points out, national liberation movements in the colonized world attempted to construct states that were generally the opposite of the ethnically and linguistically homogeneous nation-states of Europe and the Americas,[53] when the dust settled after independence the postcolonial governments turned out not so different after all. The logic of nation-state formation seemingly sets in motion specific processes that have been universal in their reliance on tropes of language, race, and religion. The trajectories of modern identity politics have seldom been linear; Benedict Anderson to the contrary, the "line between the political nation and a putative original ethos"[54] has always been a thin one. In India, the decades since the 1940s have witnessed a combative postcolonial nationalism rearticulating Hindu cultural pride and the ideology of "Hindutva," which is to embrace, as in the vision of V. D. Savarkar, "all departments of thought and activity of the whole Being of our Hindu race . . . the vital spinal cord through our whole body politic."[55]

Immediately after independence in 1948, questions of "who is an Indian" and the equation of the national identity with "Hindu" as vocalized by the Hindu Mahasabha and RSS were very briefly muted when Gandhi was assassinated by a right-wing Hindu activist and a former member of the RSS. But this did not lead to any national soul-searching about Hindu identity politics, even as the brother of the assassin explained that Gandhi was murdered because he was not a good Hindu: "He consistently insulted the Hindu nation and had weakened it by his doctrine of *ahimsa* (nonviolence). . . . We wanted to show the Indians that there were Indians who would not suffer humiliation — that there were still men left among the Hindus."[56]

After a year-long ban, the RSS reemerged as a legal organization in 1951, when some of its well-known cadres joined with the Hindu Mahasabha to form an electoral party, the Jana Sangh. Later reorganizations of this party created the Bharatiya Janata Party (BJP). Today, the BJP is the leading political party, controlling the ruling coalition government of India and holding power in several states. The current Indian prime minister's political career began as a RSS cadre,[57] and the RSS still provides the core ideological leadership of the movement (the writings of Savarkar are still necessary reading), while the Vishwa Hindu Parishad (VHP, World Hindu Congress), established in 1964, has emerged as the aggressive cultural arm of political Hinduism in India and abroad. As a movement it has successfully appropriated not only populist Hindu religious symbols such as Ram, Krishna, Ganesha, and the Bhagavad Gita but also many of the (Hindu) icons made familiar during the Indian nationalist movement: photographs and paintings of Vivekananda, Shivaji, and the like reassuringly decorate office walls. The ethos of the eternal nation recast as Hindutva has made the message a particularly attractive one to the dislocated middle-class emigrants who find themselves suddenly joining the hoi polloi in the land of immigrants. But matters are seldom left to chance in a fraternity that has honed its impressive organizational skills over decades in training loyal cadres.

In 1970 a group of RSS members living in the United States met in New York City to form the VHP of America (VHPA). It was registered as a non-profit organization with the stated goal of bringing "cultural enrichment and cultural awareness to American society, based on time-tested Eternal Hindu values." The first annual conference of the organization was held in Canton, Ohio, with thiry-five delegates. The tenth conference held in New York in 1984 was attended by some 5,000 delegates.[58] The VHP also has numerous branch organizations among the Indian communities in Canada and Britain, as well as in several East African, and Southeast Asian countries.[59] RSS officials and, with the success of the BJP in the national elections, office-holding Indian politicians regularly visit these branches and are feted at public functions with well-coordinated media coverage.

The enormous success of the BJP-RSS-VHP "family" in electoral and cultural politics in postcolonial India and their appeal to the Indian middle and lower middle classes can be attributed to a variety of reasons, but perhaps most importantly to its ability to provide the only organized alternative to secular socialist politics from at least 1947 onward.[60] After all, despite suicidal internal divisions, left-wing parties had managed to win 20 percent of the national vote in the first elections of 1951.[61] Golwalkar of the RSS was undoubtedly speaking for many when he wrote confidently to Home Minister Vallabhai Patel, a senior Congress Party member and one of their supporters, "[If] you with government power and we with organized force combined, we can eliminate this menace of [communism]. I am intensely worried at the waves of victory of that foreign 'ism' which are sweeping our neighbouring countries."[62] Golwalkar also wrote to Prime Minister Nehru, "Rashtriya Swyamsevak Sangh is the only way to meet the challenge of communism and it is the only ideology which can harmonise and integrate the interests of different groups and classes and thus successfully avoid any class war."[63] It is therefore perhaps no accident that the BJP has recently declared a *mahajot* (grand alliance) of political parties hoping to defeat the communists in the two states where these have been elected to power. While the RSS-VHP organizational outreach has taken many forms in postindependence India—targeting constituencies considered particularly susceptible to communist and socialist tendencies, ranging from labor to the women's movement—here I want to focus on the outreach done among university students, precisely the group who were to provide (and continue to provide) potential immigrants to the United States.

Indian universities, even elite ones, have few facilities for extracurricular activities, practically no counseling services, and scant resources for newcomers, many of whom are away from home for the first time. The enormous need for such services, always crucial, was particularly acute when, with the rapid expansion of two- and four-year colleges as well as universities in the 1960s and 1970s, suddenly hundreds of thousands of students entered postsecondary educational structures, many from families that had not had access to university education before. By providing these services, and quite a bit more, the RSS was able to develop a new constituency. Unlike other preexisting campus organizations, such as faculty or student unions, the RSS built a "community" organization, which included faculty and staff in its local Vidyarthi Parishad (Student Association/Council), while each campus branch was linked to the national organization (Akhil Bharatiya Vidyarthi Parishad, or, All-India Student Association). Each campus parishad connected ideologically sympathetic faculty and senior students as mentors of the new arrivals. With activities ranging from student clubs for those interested in sports to the natural sciences, debates, concerts, book banks, tutorial centers, and health clinics, as well as camps and study circles elaborating on the ideological premises of the organization, the RSS and its sympathizers emerged as a major presence on Indian college and university campuses by the late 1960s.[64] By 1974 the Vidyarthi Parishad could claim 160,000 members in 790 branches (campuses) and through student elections had won control of several campus unions at elite universities, including Delhi University.[65]

At the same time, the activities of the Vidyarthi Parishad began to extend into large-scale mobilizations (other than riots against Muslims in which various branches had been active since 1961) on issues that appealed to the lower middle classes, such as state government inertia and corruption, especially since these issues were being taken up by radical communist student groups.[66] By 1983 the national organization could count 250,000 members and 1,100 branch organizations.[67] Many of the graduates from these universities constitute the new immigrants from India, and they include in their number the much touted thousands of computer and software experts. Some of these experts help maintain over five hundred VHP Web sites (www.vhp.org) with their messages of Hindutva, Hindu history, and Muslim-bashing.[68]

Elsewhere I have written in detail about the current political crisis of the South Asians (Indians, Pakistanis, Bangladeshis, Nepalese, and Sri Lankans) in the United States who have sought to distance themselves from the implications of the color of their skin.[69] Some continuities with the 1920s exist: Indian school textbooks still use racial categories, and so do the immigrants. Studies of the recent, highly educated, and affluent Indians suggest that the issue of racial identity has not been reconstructed. For example, a survey of twenty-four individuals carried out by Maxine Fisher in New York City in 1975 asking what "race" they belonged to showed that fifteen of the respondents stated that they were "Aryan" in some measure. Five people replied that Indians were Caucasians, six stated that Indians were not Caucasians, while five others said "some Indians are white."[70] Therefore, while Indians may be ambiguous about their own racial categorization, their familiarity with concepts of race makes them quite unambiguous about accepting and utilizing American racial hierarchies.[71] As in the 1920s, they distance themselves from other minorities. Additionally, core changes in the political-cultural landscape of India itself are recasting notions of race, ethnicity, and citizenship which allow the Indian immigrants of the 1990s to articulate a distinctive version of ethnic identity.

For the majority of contemporary Indians, born or certainly growing up in the post-1947 period, the colonial state's racial categorizations of "white" and "native" ceased to be a fact of daily life. Unlike Vivekananda, who was at pains to argue that the upper-caste Indian was as light-skinned as any European, skin color, while still a yardstick of female beauty, has become merely incidental to identity politics in India. And that is why, perhaps, reiterations by progressive scholars based in the United States of "alternative histories" of Indian racial solidarity with African Americans can do little to shift the immigrants' self-identity. Indo-Americans see themselves as a people who may "look black" but have nothing in common with people who *are* "racially" *black*.[72] Rather, the flexibility of the concept of race has enabled a new configuration: the subsumption of the "Aryan Hindu" to "the essentials of nationality," as Savarkar put it.[73] The category *Hindu* overrides the older racialized histories of the supposedly lighter-skinned north Indian Aryan, who came from somewhere beyond the borders of India, versus the darker-skinned, supposedly aboriginal, lower-caste and south Indian Dravidian. Instead, it has been universalized to embrace both the exclusive ethnic identity of the original peoples of India and the authentic cultural essence of the nation. Political Hindutva, seeking to define the nation and its peoples in all aspects, has resurrected the Orientalist myth of India as the land of the Hindus; being Hindu is the only condition that ensures one the rights of citizenship in India. Muslims and Christians who embrace Hindutva can be allowed to exist as long as they confine their religion and cultural ambitions to private space. As Ashok Singhal, general secretary of the VHP puts it, "The Hindu Rashtra can only be a state where there must be Hindu churches and Hindu mosques for Hinduism is not a religion. . . . In Hindu India, everyone has to call himself a Hindu."[74]

For Indians coming to the United States after the 1960s, these identity politics of Hindutva could survive and, perhaps unexpectedly even thrive, in the political and cultural moment opened up by the civil rights movement. They have benefited directly from myriad changes in the social and political climate that have occurred since the 1960s. They have been protected as visible minorities in ways impossible to conceive of in the 1940s and 1950s. Once included as minorities under the rubric of Asian Americans, they have been able to take advantage of new legislation providing for small-business loans to minorities, antidiscrimination legislation in housing, commissions for tracking hate crimes, affirmative action hiring programs in companies, and so on. There were also unexpected openings of cultural space. In the 1960s, Martin Luther King's oft cited references to Gandhi (with little awareness of Gandhi's own ambivalence and racism toward South African blacks) and King's use of nonviolent protest popularly attributed as originating with Gandhi also gave the new immigrants a certain respectable niche in reiterating their connections with their homeland. Richard Attenborough's film *Gandhi* (1982), romanticizing its protagonist, introduced a sudden burst of interest in India in the universities. This, combined with California and New York fashions in clothing and music, Hare Krishna groups on street corners celebrating their colorful festivals, Rajneesh ashrams, pop divas wearing *mehendi* (henna) and *bindis,* and the proliferation of Indian paraphernalia as counterculture icons have all helped relocate India at the heart of the exotic East. As the United States discovered the new "evil empire" of Islam abroad and contentious black Muslims at home, the late twentieth century has not been a bad time for a Hindu Indian in America. On the contrary, demonstrative re-

ligious affiliation has, in fact, brought space, prestige, and political vis-
ibility in contemporary U.S. climate.

The United States, after all, boasts over 255,000 registered churches
nationwide and many thousands more if one counts the home churches.
Almost 50 percent of the U.S. population holds membership in a church, a
far higher level than any European country.[75] Recent years have witnessed
an increase in overt religiosity in American political life, evidenced by the
plethora of prominent Americans who are "born-again Christians."[76] The
promotion of "family values" by the church-led conservative movement in
America has also provided safe public spaces for Indian immigrants who
want to display their religious beliefs and share these values. This climate
has permitted Hindu temples to proliferate with tax-deductible contributions, become centers of regular weekend social activity for the adults, and
the locus of socialization for the second generation. It has also provided
space and context for the VHP and other Hindutva-related organizations.
Publications like *Hinduism Today,* published by the VHP, are distributed at
the temples. These publications reiterate themes that have played well in
India for the better part of a century in arming the Hindu Religious Right.[77]
Essays, news briefs, and commentaries promote the usual anxieties of
Hindus losing ground, noting that there are more Muslims than Hindus in
America and harping on the perennial worry of greater Muslim assertive-
ness and organization.[78]

The arrival of large numbers of Indians from the mid-1960s on partakes
of the changing pattern of U.S. immigration. The 2000 census counted
close to 1.7 million Asian Indians, making them the third largest group
among the Asian Americans.[79] Unlike the earlier period, however, when
immigration from Europe was the norm and Asian immigration was limited, highly visible, and, in due course, sequentially curtailed, Indians from
the mid-twentieth century on entered the United States along with hundreds of thousands of people coming from Asia and Central America. They
simply constituted one more group of people of color changing the landscape of urban America. The struggles of Latinos, African Americans, and
others in the inner cities passed the majority of Indians by, for their own
entry point into the U.S. economy as highly trained professionals allowed
them to move rapidly to safe suburbia, or at least to middle-class apartments where most of their neighbors are white. For the middle-class Indian
immigrants, the long history of colonialism had led to an acceptance of
Anglo culture as the normative and preferred culture of America, and their

facility with English has eased their way into American economic life. Indo-Americans could elaborate on their identity as Hindu Americans who happened to be "brown-skinned whites."

Most Indians who live and, for the second generation, have grown up in Anglo-American suburbia have not had reason to question or challenge their version of identity politics. The innocence with which one Indo-American student at the University of California at Berkeley declared, "I never really had to deal with being Asian until I got here. It was never an issue with me,"[80] speaks volumes about the kinds of communities most middle-class Indians live in and the political culture they cultivate. Indians, along with other Asians, became the "model minorities" of the Reagan-Bush era of the 1980s. In addition to raising millions for the Republican Party, Indo-Americans became willing partners in managing the politics of diversity. The success of an immigrant bourgeoisie could now be used to discipline the wayward working-class domestic population that demanded resources from the state. Indians and other Asians were anointed the model minority precisely because they would not and did not need to make common cause with African Americans and others experiencing cutbacks, inner-city gang warfare, police brutality, and a serious erosion of the gains of the civil rights movement.

Yet suburbia and affluence could not at all times protect all immigrants from the politics of race. As early as 1976, 44 percent of Indians interviewed in a sample of 159 in Chicago mentioned experiences of discrimination, one-half of which related to being passed over for raises and promotions in corporate America in favor of white Americans, and one-third to refusals to rent houses or apartments clearly on the market.[81] But because they did not understand these examples of discrimination as systemic problems affecting all people of color, the Indian response has again been to develop individual strategies to maneuver around them. Even an extremely wealthy and successful entrepreneur like Paul Jain, who conceded that considerable racial bias in Silicon Valley affected his own upward mobility, nevertheless concluded, "One thing that is great about America is that Americans value skills over color."[82]

The issue of racial politics, however, became more pressing for the Indians by the late 1980s. More Indians had started operating small businesses in the cities and a working class had emerged, forming distinct Indian neighborhoods. These immigrants started facing more overt racial hostilities. In separate incidents in 1987 in Jersey Heights, an Indian man was beaten to death, another beaten into a coma, and two women assaulted at a bus stand. With a sense of disbelief, Indians heard white teenagers joking about the beatings, saying, "It's white people against the Hindus" and "Heights [i.e., Jersey Heights] is for whites." In other incidents in the area, Indian women were spat on, and trash, stones, and obscenities hurled at Indian homes and businesses. In a partially printed letter in *The Jersey Journal,* someone wrote, "We will go to any extreme to get the Indians to move out of Jersey City," signing it "The Dotbusters" (referring to the bindi).[83] During 1987 some fifty incidents of racial violence occurred in the area.[84]

In 1989, in a schoolyard shooting rampage by a white man in Sacramento, California, where five Southeast Asian children were killed and thirty others injured, the killer was identified as having "a deep-seated hatred towards Indians, Pakistanis, Cambodians and Vietnamese."[85] Generally, common vandalism has been replaced since the late 1980s by attacks directed toward people in addition to property.[86] Intimidation and incidents of violence directed toward Indians have continued in numerous towns from Pennsylvania and New Jersey to California, Oregon, and Washington. While we must place this violence against Indians and Pakistanis in the context of increased violence since the Reagan-Bush era — against all visible minorities, between minority groups, and against gays and lesbians[87] — coupled with the rollback in proactive antiracist initiatives, the Indian community has responded by reiterating its distinctive heritage.[88]

Generally, middle-class professionals have simply chosen to deny the politics of race in America, and with their own racialized consciousness, suggest that instead everybody should try harder to assimilate into Anglo-America, learn "the American way to speak English," cook "American foods" so that no offensive curry odors are noticeable, and learn American customs and social graces.[89] But the dominant racial categories are clearly oppressive and labels such as "non-white Caucasians"[90] or "ambiguous nonwhite"[91] are not much help. Mallika Rao, a teenager in Dallas, Texas, may have been speaking for many young Indians when she confided, "when she was small, she dreamed of painting herself white and having white children." "I wanted to fit in," said Mallika.[92] But what has enabled Mallika and her mother, a neurologist, to look optimistically to the future, if not to quite fit in now, is, as they said, "a Hindu renaissance."[93] This response has a long history; from Vivekananda in the 1890s to the VHP in the 1990s, the slogan has remained the same: "Garv se kaho hum Hindu hain" (say with pride that I am a Hindu).[94]

Among the newspaper vendors in New York and the late-night convenience store operators, many of whom have been victims of petty urban violence, identity politics has taken the form of racist politics. With their own petit-bourgeois aspirations, they see the black urban classes in the same way as conservatives do, as people unwilling to work as hard as the new immigrants. Many of them are products of the third-tier institutions of higher education set up throughout India with political patronage that have ill equipped them for white-collar jobs in either India or the United States.[95] Their location in the lower tiers of the urban U.S. economy, however, does not mean that they see themselves as members of the working class. Quite the contrary. For them, as for the professionals, the dominant response to the jarring experiences of racism has been to reiterate a national-cultural identity that would give them "respect" and a claim to a unique cultural heritage. For them, too, Hindutva fits the bill.

In the 1980s and 1990s, state-sponsored projects of multiculturalism, with their superficial celebration of difference and the obfuscation of the politics of class, unequal power, and patriarchal control, have in fact created an environment where the fashioning and sustaining of ethnic-cultural differences is not only feasible but desirable. Although a few individuals, mostly younger and second-generation South Asians, have sought to build cross-ethnic alliances and engage in the broader struggle for social justice in America (e.g., members of the Committee Against Anti-Asian Violence or union organizers in New York and Los Angeles),[96] or have individually taken up issues of discrimination (as in the case of Navjot Singh Nijjar, who filed a joint class-action suit with her African American friends against Denny's restaurant and won a $28 million settlement),[97] these activists are far from representative of the political tendencies of the majority of the 1.7 million Indo-Americans. In an essentialized search for preserving the authentic ethnic in a multicultural society, marking difference has itself become a sign of ethnicity and ethnic pride, for example, wearing the bindi, or dot, when going out, "lest [one] be taken for Puerto Rican."[98] In the wake of the 1992 Los Angeles riots, amidst worries that the Indian community had made no efforts to link up with African Americans and hence could be subject to similar attacks as Korean Americans, an Indian businessman noted that there was little chance of coalition building for, after all, "Blacks or Hispanics don't wear saris. And blacks don't like Indian food."[99] The rhetoric of multiculturalism has further empowered VHPA and related organizations as self-appointed guardians of Hindu culture. For example, protests by over one hundred Hindu organizations—including the Mathura-based World Vaishnava Association, the American Hindu Federation, the Hindu Swayam Sevak Sangh, and the American Hindus Against Defamation, modeled on the Jewish Anti-Defamation League—forced the producers of the popular sci-fi television series *Xena: Warrior Princess* to withdraw an episode for depicting "Lord Krishna as a fictional character."[100]

Hindutva in the United States

While the insecurities of the bourgeoisie have, in many cultures and at different times and places, led to a new religiosity, and while this has certainly contributed to the spate of temple building by Hindus in America, the religio-political movement that has emerged in the overseas Indian communities suggests perhaps two distinct processes at work, one political and the other personal. Both processes have contributed to the empowerment of the Hindutva movement in America. The political dimension of the global alliance articulated in normative religious terms is the more complicated of the two. Since the mid-1980s, segments of the Indian community have aspired to present a more unified image of this community. Electoral and representational politics require certain types of homogeneity. American businesses and local political offices often apportion contracts and distribute resources to "ethnic community leaders." Incessant public arguments and even court battles regarding leadership of community associations, temples, and gurdwaras have proven inimical to these interests. The VHP/RSS model of an ecumenical approach to temple building, first started by Savarkar and then continued by wealthy industrialist supporters such as the Birlas, had already led to the development of a new type of Hindu temple by the 1930s.[101] In Delhi, for example, the Kali temple was placed alongside the Krishna temple (also conveniently located next to the head office of the Hindu Mahasabha). The larger temples built in America, with shrines to Ram and Venkateswara (popular deities from the north and south respectively) placed in one complex, have by and large followed this model. Similarly ecumenical in its approach—and again replicating a model proven very successful in India in bringing together various Hindu sects that can then be recruited to VHP causes—the VHPA regularly sponsors "Dharma Prasar" (religious outreach) events throughout the United States, in which Jain preachers, Hindu swamis of various sects, and large numbers of devotees "join hands in unifying the voice of Hindus in the West."[102] The local sects, sants (religious teachers), and preachers thus selected by the VHPA for the American tours, then also emerge as more influential in India by virtue of having access to larger funds.

Not only do temples have vast sums of money but they also confer social status on those who serve as temple officials and provide the necessary contacts to businessmen in real estate, insurance, immigration, and related services. A version of Hinduism that blurs sectarian differences and projects a unified Indian identity has therefore proven attractive to the upwardly mobile immigrants. It is part of a strategy of the accumulation of political power for a new bourgeoisie, of developing an identity that further legitimates its cultural hegemony both at home and abroad. That coalitions as the one described above have successfully come to dominate community politics, is a result of their affiliations with the BJP and VHP and the increased clout these organizations have in India today. The common goal of building a Hindu *rashtra* (Hindu state) in India is seen as a project that will also empower the Hindu bourgeoisie in America, giving it access to business opportunities and resources both in the United States and in India. The BJP has been more assiduous in courting "Non-Residential Indians" than other political parties by including frequent discussions of dual citizenship and an "orange card" that eliminates the need for single-entry visas for ten years at a time.

The drumbeat of a "strong Motherland" bringing prestige to all its sons and daughters finds a resounding echo particularly among the new immigrants, most of whom are not members of the older, established cosmopolitan Indian bourgeoisie. The vast majority come from small-town backgrounds, and their access to higher technical education in independent India changed family fortunes when they found jobs as doctors and engineers in the United States. Acutely resentful of the exclusionary politics of the older Indian metropolitan bourgeoisie whose class advantages placed them in better universities, their pride is assuaged when heads of major organizations and political parties from India come to visit them for the dollars they control. Overqualified but low-ranked technocrats with foreign-born English accents dealing with native-born Anglo-American arrogance or underappreciated academics teaching at small colleges in remote locations and third-tier universities are all given a voice and feel powerful when affiliated with VHP and BJP organizations like the Overseas Friends of the BJP or The Friends of India Society International. The VHP International links and organizes this new transnational bourgeoisie; the leadership travels back and forth to raise and dispense funds and help smooth the way for political and financial accumulation.

When BJP leader Keshubhai Patel, a longtime RSS activist and the chief minister of Gujarat, came on a tour to attract investments from overseas Indians for industrial development in his state, he could offer "100 percent incentive for the hotel industry," knowing well enough that expatriates from Gujarat dominated the hotel-motel industry in the United States. He could also promise labor control, noting there is "no problem of strikes, violence and unions" in Gujarat.[103] Through hard work and persistence, the U.S.-based leadership can also deliver. For example, the BJP leader L. K. Advani was made an honorary citizen of California and greeted as the "next prime minister of India" by California state officials at one of the series of events organized during his visit in January 1992, years before BJP victory at the polls was assured. Advani returned the favor; a $75.00-per-plate event featuring Advani helped raise more than $30,000 for the Overseas Friends of the BJP in California in the course of an evening.[104]

Supporters can also be mobilized to disrupt the meetings of political rivals; for example, 1995 demonstrators noisily disturbed a meeting of the former prime minister V. P. Singh with the Federation of Hindu Associations, accusing Singh of being "the supporter of pseudo-seculars and the appeasers of minorities" (referring to the Mandal Commission and India's program for affirmative action that the BJP targeted for special criticism).[105] It is indeed ironic that a minority community in the United States would seek to create a religio-cultural homogeneity in their erstwhile homeland and participate in the making of a nation that would not permit the same religious and cultural equality to minorities in India that they themselves enjoy, or would like to enjoy, in their current country of residence.

For most immigrants participating in temple activities has become an essential dimension of social life, for the temple serves both as a community center and a social club. In turn, this brings them into a closer nexus with the VHP vision of Hinduism. And true to the remarkable organizational skills of the group, these well-coordinated events draw a substantial attendance. Several Hindu organizations, grocery stores, and temples all cooperate to sell tickets and ensure a good turnout. It is not unusual in Los Angeles to get a crowd of 8,000 to hear Morari Bapu, a Gujarati preacher known for his political connections with the BJP.[106] The Hindu Ektamata Samiti organized a *mahayagna* (great fire ceremony) in which over 3,000 Indians participated. For the centennial celebrations of Vivekananda's visit to

America, an estimated 5,000 visitors turned out. In June 2001, an event entitled "A Hindu Vision for Human Entitlement" drew 15,000 people and featured RSS leader K. Sudarshan as the keynote speaker. Thirty-five organizations supported the northern California program, including a dozen Hindu religious groups but notably also community associations with secular credentials ranging from the Fiji Group, Prabashi Bengali Association to the Association of the Development of Bihar and Kannada Koota. Three hundred children performed the *Ramayana*.[107] The speakers were "hopeful and optimistic that the next 15 to 20 years will witness a reclaiming of Hindu values, culture and tradition."[108] This event was repeated in Toronto and New York later in 2001. Sudarshan was honored that evening by being given the key of the city of Milipitas (where the event took place) by the local mayor. The mayor of the adjoining city attended the celebration, while the Democratic Party congressman, Mike Honda, also put in an appearance.

The networks that put together these massive events can be mobilized for raising money for U.S. politicians (hence their appearances at these Hindutva events), but also for causes such as the building of Ram temples in India. Any comments critical of these activities are dealt with ferociously and intimidatingly. When Rajan Anand, a longtime editor of a major community newspaper, *India-West,* ventured a brief personal opinion in the "Letters to the Editor" page about the irony of an advertisement in the newspaper for a *puja* that stated, "Shree Ram symbolizes all that is highest, noblest and greatest in the Indian tradition," ignoring the numerous riots and killings in 1992–93 that occurred in the name of preserving this tradition, readers responded for months with angry and vehement accusations against him. Other letters extolled the virtues of the VHP.[109]

With dozens of tax-deductible societies and associations linked directly to the VHP, the VHPA has reached into every temple and community organization throughout the United States, while friends of the VHP can be found in many other types of associations. At secular Indian community events, such as the commemoration of Gandhi's birthday, for example, sponsored by umbrella organizations like the Association of Indians in America, it is not unusual to find a VHP fund-raising pamphlet along with the evening's program.[110]

Hinduism in America, in both its religious and political forms, has yet another function: it serves as a bridge to link the immigrants of Indian origin from Fiji, Guyana, Britain, and Africa. Professionals from these groups and from the subcontinent have little in common except their religious affiliation. Building on the old networks of the Arya Samaj and the new networks of the VHPA allows upwardly mobile immigrants not from the subcontinent cultural linkages that distinguish them from the Afro-Caribbean and African legacies they wish to leave behind. Like ritual purification, there is an effort to promote a more orthodox Hinduism among the 100,000 Caribbean Indians in New York by the priests of the Hindu Federation of Mandirs, "an effort to reconstruct a pristine Bhojpuri past," with strict bans on dancing, drinking, and playing chutney music, "vices" attributed to the Afro-Caribbean influences creeping in along with the musical beats, all of which need to be exorcised.[111]

The VHPA and its affiliate organizations also provide community services directed at the second generation. These activities have further empowered them within the Indian community as avenues for the socialization and acculturation of children. The VHP's comic-book format Hindu epics and Hindu chauvinist tales, the *Amar Chitra Katha* series, were sold everywhere from temples to grocery stores. Now Web sites promote similar themes. The comics, running into well over a hundred titles, narrate the stories of the "approved" versions of the epics and also include "historical tales" which provide a substantial dose of Hindu nationalist lore replete with stories of Muslim treachery. In addition, there are a variety of youth-oriented programs throughout the country. They cover a broad range: essay competitions on the life of Dayananda and Vivekananda; weekend educational events, heritage language classes; summer youth camps with sessions on "Hindu history"; hikes on trails set up with miniature replicas of famous temples with children reciting the saga of each temple; and entertainment programs of dance and film shows.[112] Some programs involve the celebration of festivals that incorporate regional customs: in Houston, with its large Gujarati community, the VHPA holds youth programs for festivals such as Makar Sankranti and Ram Navami and sponsors *ras garba* dancing in addition to the more standard celebrations of Dusshera and Diwali. Few organizations can match the fund-raising capabilities of the VHP, which always seems able to garner substantial resources for projects such as youth summer camps and youth conferences. At their annual event in Houston in 1995 the VHPA managed to raise $75,000 for their projects in the course of an evening.[113]

First-generation immigrants have eagerly turned to these summer camps as a means of socializing their children in Indian Hindu culture in hopes that it will help them preserve institutions such as arranged marriage and keep the children from succumbing to the lures of American-style independence and rebellion. As their daughters reach college age, the frequency of visits to India increases in efforts to impart a more "authentic" culture to their offspring, and sending them to camp is part of the process. The current American focus on family values has touched a raw nerve among the immigrants who experience dislocation, changing gender roles, and fissures within their own families as a result of the experience of immigration. Here, too, the VHPA and RSS are ready to help and promote themselves; as one Hindutva spokesperson put it, "Unless they [the adult immigrants] sharpen their approach to their heritage, they are going to have a lot of problems especially dealing with young people."[114] And at the "Workers Education Camps," organized at mountain retreats for Hindu activists to "rejuvenate the ideological commitment," psychiatrists provide workshops on challenges faced by Indian immigrant families.[115] Multiculturalism has given a sanctity to tradition and heritage that the older assimilationist model denied immigrants. The class insecurities of an immigrant bourgeoisie in fact foment a more aggressive definition of Hinduism as culture, religion, heritage, and tradition; even loyalty to the "motherland" becomes linked in this definition of identity and family.

Second-generation Indo-Americans, brought up on a steady dose of VHP Hindu history in the summer camps and family outings to temples, and without any context for critically understanding the religious and political diversity of India, often construct their ethnic identity and interpretations of heritage on the bedrock of VHP Hinduism. Their early socialization prepares them to say with surety, "Religiously I'm settled, I'd like to follow Hinduism."[116] Over one-half of the 5,000 participants at the VHP-organized Vivekananda celebrations in D.C. were teenagers. Given the vague romanticism about spirituality and Eastern religions found on college campuses in the United States, Hindu identity politics even acquire a certain chic. Wearing T-shirts inscribed with "Save a Cow" or "Udderly Cool" and attending lectures on Hindu vegetarianism are in step with animal rights activism; few recognize the anti-Muslim messages encoded in these very gestures.

The Hindu Student Council (HSC), modeled on the Vidyarthi Parishads of India, organized by RSS and VHPA supporters, has become an active presence on all major U.S. campuses. Outreach among incoming freshmen during the campuswide orientation week is done by pro-VHS-RSS faculty/

staff or graduate students, who then sponsor Sunday Gita classes and lunch. The HSC now has over sixty branches on various campuses, including Harvard, MIT, University of Chicago, Stanford, UC Berkeley, and UCLA. Its leaders claim a membership of 13,000. They have a Web site and run the Hindu Women Talk Net discussion group, which has biographies of BJP-VHP activists as role models.[117] Given the proliferation of religious organizations of all kinds on campuses throughout the United States, from the "Campus Crusade for Christ" to "Bible Study Groups," the Hindu Student Council becomes an innocuous group. For deans of student activities who sign off on these activities, the larger political connections of the HSC remain invisible or even unknown. But as registered student groups, Hindu Student Councils have access to university student-activity funds and campus resources to bring their message to the uninitiated and hold conferences to promote their cause. The VHPA also sends them funds. The political implications of an association with the VHPA and the BJP are by far not clear to the students who see these organizations and events as just upholding Hindu pride.[118] Since the nonstudent VHP-RSS mentors vet the invited speakers, they can make sure that speakers and viewpoints that would challenge the VHP line are not foolishly included by the students.[119] The VHP takes this student outreach very seriously. As Yash Pal Lakra, president of the VHP in 1998, observed, "We look to the HSC as our real hope. We expect that when its members join think tanks, colleges and universities, they will be able to undo the negative propaganda Leftist Indian academics have carried out over many years against the VHP, the RSS, and the BJP."[120]

Proudly declaring Hindu as their ethnic identity that, as such, demands preservation, the second generation can create a cultural space for themselves that does not require them to confront either their skin color or their avid emulation of Anglo-American culture. And the VHP intends to make certain that the next generation stays "Hindu." With plans for a Hindu University of America, an International Foundation of Vedic Education, efforts to have Sanskrit taught at all major universities as a "heritage language," and dozens of radio programs and Internet bulletins, Hindutva supporters make certain that their cultural politics remain the dominant voice of the Indian community in their new homeland. The discourse of multiculturalism, with its token inclusions and instant accreditation of all difference regardless of the political message, has greatly eased the way for adherents of Hindutva. As a member of the University of Michigan chapter of the Hindu Student Council elaborated: "Most students felt that American schools need to incorporate the contributions of non-Western cultures into the curriculum. Hindu contributions to the world are many and diverse, and almost always are unrecognized. HSC is playing a tremendous role in America by making people aware of what Hindus have achieved."[121]

That this vision of Hindu India, and its origin in an idyllic Vedic past, is the product of Orientalist reconstruction, an erasure of the complexities of Indian history, and a product of RSS-VHP mythography seems irrelevant; it is what a "real" Hindu believes. For both the first-generation middle-class immigrants and their children, the VHP's brand of Hinduism, reified as "Indian" culture and tradition, figure as the primordial and sacred symbols of ethnicity and legitimacy in America. They employ this timeless normative practice attributable to a sacred past of Hindus to set themselves apart from all others, be it South Asian Muslims, Sikhs, and Christians, or African Americans, Hispanics, and East Asian Americans. In the United States, with even greater ease than in India, religion is abstracted from the myriad interactions that define social and political life and that permit, by the same token, possibilities of query. For the time being, the class politics of the immigrant bourgeoisie have successfully coagulated around Hindutva and a racial-cultural identity of being Hindu in America.

Notes

Earlier versions of this paper were presented at the University of Michigan, Ann Arbor, Asian American Studies Program, and at the University of Pennsylvania, South Asian Regional Studies. I would like to thank the participants for helpful comments. I would also like to thank Chetan Bhatt for sharing his work with me and sending me the special issue of *Ethnic and Racial Studies* (vol. 23, no. 3, May 2002), edited by him and Parita Mukta, titled "Hindutva Movements in the West." The articles in that issue have been an important resource for my own thinking on the subject.

1. Arjun Appadurai, *Modernity at Large: Cultural Dimensions of Globalization* (Minneapolis: University of Minnesota Press, 1996), 169.

2. George Brown Tindall and David E. Shi, *America: A Narrative History* (New York: Norton, 1996), 679.

3. On essentialized ethnicity, see Michael Omi, "Shifting the Blame: Racial Ideology and Politics in the Post–Civil Rights Era," *Critical Sociology* 18.3 (1991): 77–98.

4. "Indentures of Asiatic Persons," Reel 22, Series 4, Historical Society of Pennsylvania, Philadelphia.

5. My own searches have not yielded much, nor have the efforts of others, such as Vijay

Prashad, *The Karma of Brown Folk* (Minneapolis: University of Minnesota Press, 2000), 71; see also the discussion in Joan Jensen, *From India to America* (New Haven, Conn.: Yale University Press, 1988), 12–13.

6. Francis Assisi, "Indian American Roots: Were Slaves the First Immigrants?" *India-West*, 8 June, 2001, 36.

7. H. Brett Melendy, *Asians in America: Filipinos, Koreans, and East Asians* (New York: Hippocrene, 1981), 186.

8. The total number of South Asians in the United States is a matter of some controversy. The U.S. Immigration Commission estimated that by 1910 there were some 5,000 East Indians in the country. A 1930 Bureau of Census recapitulation of the "minor races" in the United States reported that there were 2,544 "Hindus" in the country in 1910. Carey McWilliams reports that 10,000 immigrants lived in California before World War I. McWilliams, *Factories in the Field: The Story of Migratory Farm Labor in California* (Boston: Little, Brown, 1942), 119.

9. Jensen, *From India to America*, 14.

10. James Gilreath and Douglas L. Wilson, eds., *Thomas Jefferson's Library: A Catalog with the Entries in His Own Order* (Washington, D.C.: Library of Congress, 1989), 26, 117, 122, 127.

11. The few Americans who became interested in Islam in the nineteenth century focused on Sufism and Persia.

12. Carl T. Jackson, *Vedanta for the West: The Ramakrishna Movement in the United States* (Bloomington: Indiana University Press, 1994), 8.

13. Thomas A. Tweed, *The American Encounter with Buddhism, 1844–1902: Victorian Culture and the Limits of Dissent* (Bloomington: Indiana University Press, 1992).

14. Wallace Stegner, *Beyond the Hundredth Meridian: John Wesley Powell and the Second Opening of the West* (Boston, Houghton Mifflin, 1954), 196.

15. Harold R. Isaacs, *Images of Asia: American Views of China and India* (New York: Harper Torchlight, 1972), 249–58. See also Balakrishna Govind Gokhale, *India in the American Mind* (Bombay: Popular Prakashan, 1992). Gokhale's uncritical and hyperbolic Hindu chauvinism detracts from the value of the book.

16. Paul Allen Carter, *The Spiritual Crisis of the Gilded Age* (DeKalb: Northern Illinois University Press, 1971).

17. Other participants included Anagarika Dharmapala from Sri Lanka and Protap Chandra Majumdar (Brahmo Samaj) and Virchand Gandhi (Jain Association) from India.

18. As Narasingha P. Sil, *Swami Vivekananda: A Reassessment* (Selinsgrove, Pa.: Susquehanna, 1997), 159–62, points out, this was the assessment of newspaper reports. But Vivekananda wrote several letters to India telling everybody how brilliant he had been, a story his promoters, for whom this visit was an investment, were all too happy to hear.

19. Jackson, *Vedanta for the West*, 29. Vivekananda's wealthy patrons included Christina Greenstidel, Edith Allan, Sara Bull, Ida Ansell, Mary and Harriet Hale, and the Boston heiress Kate Sanborn. Josephine McLeod (known as Jo Jo) provided him with a "pension" of $50 a month, quite a fortune in those days (Sil, *Swami Vivekananda*, 57). The impressive temple complex in Belur, Calcutta, home of the Ramakrishna Mission, was paid for by an English patron, Henrietta Müller, who gave a whopping Rs. 39,000 (ibid., 49). The West Coast missions were set up in 1899 when Vivekananda returned for a second trip that was unsuccessful and barely caused a ripple in the press.

20. Dharma Kumar and Megnad Desai, eds., *The Cambridge Economic History of India* (Cambridge: Cambridge University Press, 1982), 2:517–21.

21. For example, Pandita Ramabai, Bahramji Malabari, and M. G. Ranade.

22. See, for example, Nita Kumar, "Religion and Ritual in Indian Schools," in Nigel Crook, ed., *The Transmission of Knowledge in South Asia: Essays on Education, Religion, History, and Politics* (Delhi: Oxford University Press, 1996), 135–54; and Krishna Kumar, *Political Agenda of Education: A Study of Colonial and Nationalist Ideas* (New Delhi, Sage, 1991).

23. Vivekananda fundamentally converted what had been a local and eccentric phenomenon based on Ramakrishna's Bengali syncretic mysticism into a well-funded national and international church based on high Hindu philosophy and Vedanta.

24. Its temple structure in Belur, the head office and central monastery, incorporates architectural elements of mosques, Hindu and Buddhist temples, and a Christian church.

25. Dayananda Saraswati, *The Light of Truth: English Translation of Swami Dayananda's Satyartha Prakasha,* trans. Ganga Prasad Upadhyaya (Allahabad: Kala, 1960), particularly 548–49, where he criticizes the Brahmo Samaj and the Prarthana Samaj. First published in 1872, the second expanded edition (1882) included attacks on Muslims and Christians as well as Hindu reformers.

26. Lal Chand, as quoted in Sumit Sarkar, *Modern India, 1885–1947* (Madras: MacMillan India, 1983), 75.

27. Romila Thapar, "Ancient History and the Modern Search for a Hindu Identity," *Modern Asian Studies* 23.2 (1989): 228; Sumit Sarkar, *Modern India,* 72. Sarkar, by placing the blame for Aryan race theories on Max Müller, however, avoids the more fundamental question of why those ideas were so attractive to the upper castes.

28. As quoted in Sil, *Swami Vivekananda,* 61.

29. Richard Forbes, "Arya Samaj in Trinidad" (Ph.D. diss., University of Miami, 1984).

30. Vinayak Damodar Savarkar, *Hindutva: Who Is a Hindu?* (Bombay: Veer Savarkar Prakashan, 1969), 29.

31. Ibid., 139, 141.

32. Ibid., 135.

33. By the first decades of the twentieth century, the British authorities were targeting the educated middle classes, and the frequency with which civil liberties were suspended and activists imprisoned escalated, culminating in the Jallianwallabagh massacre of unarmed civilians in 1919, where at least 379 were killed.

34. Vivekananda's 1894 speech in New York declared, "When the Occident wants to learn about the spirit, about God, about the soul, about the meaning and mystery of this universe, he must sit at the feet of the Orient to learn" (reprinted in Stephen Hay, ed., *Sources of Indian Tradition* [New York: Columbia University Press, 1988], 2:99.

35. Intercourse allowed between a childless widow and her husband's brother or kinsman in order to bear babies who would then be considered the children of the husband.

36. Lajpat Rai, *Writings and Speeches,* reprinted in Hay, *Sources of Indian Tradition,* 164.

37. Asiatic Exclusion League, Proceedings, 16 February 1908, Bancroft Library, University of California at Berkeley, 8–10.

38. Tricia Knoll, "Asian Americans and American Immigration Law," in Hyung-chan Kim, ed., *Dictionary of Asian American History* (New York: Greenwood, 1986), 51.

39. *Takao Ozawa v. United States,* reprinted in Hyung-chan Kim, ed., *Asian Americans and the Supreme Court: A Documentary History* (New York: Greenwood, 1992), 520.

40. Melendy, *Asians in America,* 217.

41. Pardaman Singh, *Ethnological Epitome of the Hindustanees of the Pacific Coast* (Stockton, Calif.: Khalsa Diwan Society, 1922). This was an attempt by the Sikh community of Stockton in 1922 to "prove" that Punjabi Sikhs were of "pure Aryan blood" even if the other Indians, such as the "Dravidians," were not.

42. Ronald Takaki, *Strangers from a Different Shore: A History of Asian Americans* (Boston: Little Brown, 1989), 298.

43. *United States v. Bhagat Singh Thind,* reprinted in Kim, *Asian Americans and the Supreme Court,* 533.

44. Ibid., 535–345.

45. Ibid., 538.

46. For example Paul Scharrenberg of the American Federation of Labor, 1939, quoted in Melendy, *Asians in America,* 224.

47. U.S. Bureau of the Census, *Census of Population, 1990* (Washington, D.C., 1993).

48. "Funds Raised for Vice-President Gore," *India-West,* 29 June, 2000, 1.

49. A religious frenzy spread across the world, starting from India on 20 September, 1995, when idols of Ganesha were supposed to have been found drinking milk. With extensive media coverage across the United States, thousands of Indians, doctors and engineers alike, either flocked to temples to witness the miracle or "fed" their family altars. *India-West,* 29 September, 1995, 1, 12–16. When scientists pointed out that stone, marble, and terra cotta, the materials commonly used to manufacture the idols, were absorbent to a certain degree, and interrogated the suspect political timing of the "miracle" just preceding parliamentary elections, they were angrily dismissed by the BJP.

50. Deborah Caldwell, "A Hindu Renaissance," *News and Observer* (Raleigh, N.C.), March 19, 1999.

51. There has been an enormous body of literature produced, primarily by Indian scholars, in the aftermath of the violence, riots, and killings that followed the destruction of the Babri Mosque in 1992. The overarching thrust of these works, although approaching the issues from very different perspectives, has been to see the rise of right-wing Hindu groups as an anomaly of the 1980s without querying the long-term trajectory of Indian nationalism. See, for example, Ashis Nandy et al., *Creating a Nationality: The Ramajanabhumi Movement and Fear of the Self* (Delhi: Oxford University Press, 1995); Gyanendra Pandey, ed., *Hindus and Others: The Question of Identity in India Today* (New Delhi: Viking, 1993); Tapan Basu et al., *Khaki Shorts and Saffron Flags: A Critique of the Hindu Right* (Delhi: Orient Longman, 1993); Praful Bidwai, "Democracy at Risk in India," *Nation*, 25 January, 1993, 86; Achin Vanaik, *The Furies of Indian Communalism: Religion, Modernity, and Secularization* (London: Verso, 1997); Arvind Rajagopal, "An Unholy Nexus: Expatriate Anxiety and Hindu Extremism," *Frontline*, September 10, 1993, 12–14; Prashad, *The Karma of Brown Folk*, 133–56. Arvind Rajagopal, "Hindu Nationalism in the US: Changing Configurations of Political Practice," *Ethnic and Racial Studies* 23.3 (2000): 467–96, does consider the longer-term history but identifies the Congress Party with secular politics.

52. The term is taken from Benedict Anderson, "Exodus" *Critical Inquiry* 20.2 (1994), 326. While the Internet and e-mail may have provided instant communication and global reach, Anderson overestimates the novelty of such enterprises, videlicet Sinn Fein.

53. E. J. Hobsbawm, *Nations and Nationalism since 1780: Programme, Myth, Reality* (Cambridge: Cambridge University Press, 1990), 164.

54. Anderson, "Exodus," 326.

55. Savarkar, *Hindutva*, 4, 46. The cover of the fifth edition shows a triangular saffron flag with a prominent swastika, which has been used as a symbol of the movement throughout.

56. Quoted in Walter K. Andersen and Shridhar D. Damle, *The Brotherhood in Saffron: The Rashtriya Swayamsevak Sangh and Hindu Revivalism* (Boulder, Colo.: Westview, 1987), 51.

57. Atal Behari Vajpayee joined the RSS in the 1940s after having worked as the general secretary of the Arya Samaji youth organization in Gwalior.

58. Andersen and Damle, *Brotherhood in Saffron*, 136.

59. Ibid., 137.

60. Sucheta Mazumdar, "Women, Culture, and Politics: Engendering the Hindu Nation," *South Asia Bulletin* 12.2 (1992): 14. A cozy relationship with the Congress Party developed at many levels, including official work. For example, the Indian government used Golwalkar of the RSS leadership on a mission to "persuade" the ruler of Kashmir to join India (Andersen and Damle, *Brotherhood in Saffron*, 49, 121, 129).

61. T. J. Nossiter, *Marxist State Governments in India: Politics, Economics, and Society* (London: Pinter, 1988), 17.

62. Quoted in Andersen and Damle, *Brotherhood in Saffron*, 52.

63. Letter in *Organizer*, quoted in B. D. Graham, *Hindu Nationalism and Indian Politics: The Origins and Development of the Bharatiya Jana Singh* (Cambridge: Cambridge University Press, 1990), 47–48.

64. Andersen and Damle, *Brotherhood in Saffron*, 119–21. Many more became sympathizers rather than activists, with approximately one-third of the parishad members taking part in RSS activities (ibid., 148 n. 31).

65. Ibid., 120.

66. For example, the mobilization by Naxalbari groups in Bihar in 1974–75.

67. Ibid., 122.

68. These sites cover the gamut, including references to works on Hindutva, links to speeches of VHP leaders, and so on. For a full discussion, see Vinay Lal, "The Politics of History on the Internet: Cyber-Diasporic Hinduism," *Diaspora* 8.2 (1999): 137–90.

69. Sucheta Mazumdar, "Racist Responses to Racism," *South Asia Bulletin* 9.1 (1989): 47–55; and Mazumdar, "Race and Racism: South Asians in the United States," in Gail M. Nomura et al., eds., *Frontiers of Asian American Studies: Writing, Research, and Commentary* (Seattle: Washington State University Press, 1990), 25–38.

70. Maxine P. Fisher, *The Indians of New York City: A Study of Immigrants from India* (Columbia, Mo.: South Asia Books, 1980), 125.

71. Given this history, it is perhaps disingenuous to suggest a lack of clarity about racial identity among contemporary South Asians. See Rosemary George, "From Expatriate Aristocrat to Immigrant Nobody," *Diaspora* 6.1 (1997): 31–60; and Nazli Kibria, "Not Asian, Black, or White," *Amerasia Journal* 22.2 (1996): 77–86.

72. See, for example, Prashad, *The Karma of Brown Folk,* 157–83. In my earlier essays on this subject, I too, like Prashad here, had considered the possibilities of cross-ethnic alliances. But for the first generation, the foreign-born one, such alliances would seem elusive for the very reasons explored in this chapter.

73. Savarkar, *Hindutva,* 141.

74. VHP of Chicago, *Seventeenth Annual Calendar* (1995).

75. *Yearbook of American and Canadian Churches* (Nashville: Abingdon, 1998). In the South, membership is higher, at 60 percent of the population. Overall, church membership is put at over 158 million, which does not include "home churches," which would raise the total in both categories. By way of comparison, only 12 percent of the French are churchgoers.

76. For example, Al and Tipper Gore. The frequency with which the religion of the presidential candidates is reported on by the media, not to mention the increase in the power of the Religious Right on issues such as abortion and school prayer, is also striking.

77. This rhetoric reached new levels in the 1980s and 1990s, when numerous BJP politicians and RSS activists repeatedly suggested that Hindus were fast becoming an endangered minority (although they form over 80 percent of the population) because the Muslims (12 percent of the population) were having more children. See Christophe Jaffrelot, *Hindu Nationalist Movement in India* (New York: Columbia University Press, 1996), 338–68 for an overview on this subject, although he does not enter into the birth-control issue. VHP/RSS slogans of "hum do hamare do, hum panch, hamare panchis" (we two, our two, we five, our twenty-five) target the birth-control program and the Muslim marriage law, suggesting that the Muslims with four wives are likely to have twenty-five children, in contrast to the Hindus, having married one woman and having two children.

78. As quoted in Caldwell, "A Hindu Renaissance." It is troubling to see these assertions repeated by people such as Diana Eck, director of the Pluralism Project at Harvard University and a scholar of Hinduism, in the interview with Caldwell, without reference to the politics of these ideas.

79. This was probably an undercount because the term *Asian* Indian is a self-identified census category; many of Indian origin who have arrived in the United States from Africa and the Caribbean do not identify themselves as such.

80. Francis Assisi, "Asian American Students Seek Ethnic Identity," *India-West,* August 9, 1991, 49.

81. Fisher, *Indians of New York City,* 130.

82. Richard Springer, "Technocrat Cites Bias in Silicon Valley," *India-West,* August 2, 1991, 61.

83. Michael Marriott, "In Jersey City Indians Face Violence," *New York Times,* October 12, 1987.

84. Ankur Goel, interview, *India-West,* November 10, 1989, 21.

85. *India-West,* November 10, 1989, 21.

86. *New York Times,* October 12, 1987, B1.

87. During 1995–96, there was a reported seventeen-percent increase in hate crimes in California alone ("More than 10,000 Hate Crimes in the U.S. in 1996," *India-West,* January 16, 1998, 28).

88. Vasantha Arora, "People Will Stay Despite Racism, Says *Post* Report," *India-West,* November 27, 1992, 34.

89. Bala K. Srinivas, "Build Bridges Not Fences," *India-West,* September 9, 1988, 4, 22. Srinivas was then mayor of Hollywood Park, Texas.

90. The description used by the Association of Indians in America (AIA) in congressional hearings in 1975. Quoted in Fisher, *Indians of New York City,* 123.

91. Term used by Kibria, "Not Asian, Black, or White," 79.

92. Caldwell, "A Hindu Renaissance," F2.

93. Ibid.

94. Bumper stickers and wall posters with this slogan were particularly numerous all over north India in the early 1990s when the mass mobilization was underway for the assault on the mosque in Ayodhya.

95. Based on interviews carried out me in New York City, in the summers of 1996 and 1997.

96. Undoubtedly, this is a significant coalition, although it seems to have constituted a primarily defensive reaction. See Prashad, *The Karma of Brown Folk,* 196–97. Moreover, the cab drivers are predominantly Sikh and Muslim, both groups recently victimized by the Hindu Right in pogroms. There is little evidence that, barring the few progressive young men and women working with them as organizers, other Hindu Indians are going to rush to emulate this cross-cultural coalition or work with them as models for their own organizations.

97. Viji Sundaram, "San Jose Student to Share Denny's Bias Settlement," *India-West,* June 10, 1994, 47.

98. Fisher, *Indians of New York City,* 124.

99. *India Today,* May 31, 1992, 51.

100. *India-West,* April 9, 1999, A1.

101. Jaffrelot, 22.

102. Archana Dongre, "VHP's Dharma Prasar Yatra Launched with Devotion," *India-West,* August 6, 1999, B1. The organizational reach of the Hindu Right is once again impressive; starting out in Los Angeles, the twelve-member team of speakers and musicians brought from India by the VHP organized programs in San Francisco, Chicago, Detroit, Washington, D.C., Atlanta, Boston, Houston, Philadelphia, New Jersey, and various other locations in Texas.

103. *India-West,* September 29, 1995, B1, B16.

104. *India-West,* January 17, 1992, 1, 24–27.

105. *India-West,* October 20, 1995, 20.

106. *India-West,* August 9, 1991, 49.

107. *India-West,* advertisement, June 15, 2001, B15.

108. *India-West,* July 27, 2001, B1, B32, B33.

109. *India-West,* various fortnightly issues of 1992–93.

110. See, for example, Zia Hasan and Sharmila Roy's letter to the editor, *India-West,* November 4, 1994, 6.

111. Marsha Fernandes, "Chutney: The Spice of Life," *SAMAR* 11 (1999): 61.

112. The Ramayana has been made into a Disney-style animation film called *Ram the Warrior Prince.* See Rajagopal, "Hindu Nationalism," for a rich ethnographic account of these camps.

113. Beth Kulkarni, "VHP's Annual Fundraiser," *India-West,* January 27, 1995, 60.

114. Arthur Pais, "The War of the Worlds," *India Today International,* April 6, 1998.

115. *India-West,* June 4, 1995, 38.

116. Caldwell, "A Hindu Renaissance."

117. See the Web site at http://www.hindunet.org.

118. At Duke University, where the HSC sponsored its annual conference in January 2001, student leaders claimed that they did not know the history of the VHP and its connections with their student organization.

119. When I was invited to speak in Professor Madhulika Khandelwal's class at the University of Massachusetts, Boston, November 22 1999, it created such anxieties that the HSC headquarters at Needham sent out a special speaker to convince [successfully] the Hindu students to stay away.

120. Pais, "The War of the Worlds.

121. *India-West,* January 13, 1995.

Vasant Kaiwar and Sucheta Mazumdar

Race, Orient, Nation in the Time-Space of Modernity

■ Born out of the experience of the constant revolutionizing of the means of production, the massive unsettling and resettling of people, and the continual recasting of global divisions of labor, aspects of modernity do capture a sense of evanescence, of things melting away before they are fully formed, of "everlasting uncertainty" and the cold cash nexus that so characterize the age of capital.[1] However, modernity does not express itself solely through heady visions of rapid change and the alienation born of a commodity economy. In the ideological realm, the principal categories of both popular and "critical" thought have sought to counter this sense of ceaseless movement and the sense of uprootedness that accompanies it. Indeed, political and cultural projects have been at great pains to invent fixities and solidarities spanning large expanses of time and space, a kind of heroic continuity and a sense of belonging in a world of radical discontinuity. The concepts of race, Orient, and nation — categorial innovations of the modern epoch, notwithstanding their appearance to the contrary and claims to antiquity made on their behalf — have been crucial, if not indispensable, in doing so.

Althusser's definition of ideology — "the imaginary representation of the subjects' relationship to his or her Real conditions of existence"[2] — affords a further insight into the workings of modernity. While, as Fredric Jameson notes, Althusser's definition stresses the gap between the "local positioning of the individual" and the "totality of class structures,"[3] we argue that in modern ideologies, the particular and the universal appear thoroughly imbricated with each other. In the spatial dimension, notions of nation, race, and culture break up the global expanse of capitalism into more particular entities and attach themselves to secular versions of fate and destiny, but they do so, as we discuss below, through the development of universalist criteria. At the temporal level, the acute awareness of time that accompanies modernity also perversely creates the notion of an antiquity that presages the present. The "Greek miracle" of "classical antiquity" was widely seen as a presage of modern-day Europe, a lineage that has given us the durable category of the "West." Similarly, the Aryan model of history linked an even further antiquity with the present, and via narratives of the worldwide dispersal of a master race, it posited affinities between widely separated groups of people while asserting the lack thereof between neighboring ones. It constructed, too, lineages of membership and authenticity in Europe and in the Indo-Persian world. Modernity is seemingly inconceivable without antiquity.

One aspect of the modernist mind-set involves the rejection of totalizing categories and explanations, devoid of secular space-time considerations; another involves a seemingly contradictory process, that is the generation of romantic totalities supposed to possess autonomous and timeless explanatory value. The conceptualization and deployment of the categories of race, Orient, and nation partakes of both characteristics, encompassing the physical and human sciences, as well as the discipline of time, to produce a "tissue of scholarly myths."[4] The myths, no less than the sciences and the history, go into the making of modernity.

The battle between the disintegrative forces unleashed by capital and the ideological means to counter them is being constantly renewed, and the never resolved tensions engendered in the process are central to understanding modernity. Even when concepts such as race, Orient, and nation appear successful in forging solidarities and fixities, they are nonetheless forced constantly to reckon with the fallout from the onward march of the economic system. Nor, despite attempts by academics and progressive political activists to cast doubts on their continued salience in the postmodern moment,[5] have the concepts of race, Orient, and nation lost their bite in the "real" world of identity and cultural politics.

It is for this reason that our volume, engaged at the beginning of the twenty-first century with understanding contemporary political culture, nonetheless grapples with these supposedly nineteenth-century concepts. Neither the claim that "globalization" — an awkward and ultimately misleading way of speaking about industrial and postindustrial capitalism — is producing a kind of uniform cosmopolitanism, nor the one that localist movements have a sort of sui generis reality, and that they require to be viewed through entirely novel lenses, have the slightest validity. So-called nineteenth-century concepts have a great and continued vitality, we argue, not because one approves of them, but because they are thoroughly integral to the overall cultural and political economy of the capitalist world system. Fundamentalism, for example, cannot be understood apart from the histories of Orientalism and nationalism. Race, Orient and nation are woven into the seams of modernity and the unfinished battles over the contours of the future, and thus they can be reinvented and constantly resuscitated in new forms, as indeed they were in their heyday. In the pages that follow, we will elaborate on the flexibility and symbolic range of the concepts themselves and their mobilization as part of political and cultural projects of varying scope and success.

Race and Universalism

Race, as one of the formative conceptions to shape the modern consciousness, reflects acutely the tensions inherent in modernity. The concept of race is quintessentially modern in that it does not explain difference in cosmological terms (for instance, the chosen people), but locates it in concrete (historical) time and space.[6] Races have their origins, their migration routes, their points of settlement, and they leave a record that can be studied and evaluated according to the best scientific principles. To be effective, the concept had to ground itself in historical time. On the other hand, historical accounts that used race as a key category often acquired the characteristics of myth (heroic virtue, the manifest destiny of the superior race, etc.). Epic time and space have a mythic quality; impossibly vast areas become the space of racial myth-histories. The story is best told over long epochs during which the protagonists obey some inner law not susceptible to dynamic alterations.[7]

Axial to the universalizing potential of the notion of race is that it can be both rigid and flexible, presenting itself as a set of deterministic characteristics that more or less decide the potentialities and limitations of groups of people fitted to one or another racial category even as, over time, what constitutes the essence of a race keeps changing.[8] The more deterministic versions of racialist thought defined human potentialities by appealing to the notion of polygenesis, the impact of geography, climate or some other "objective" criterion. Less deterministic versions of racism resorted either to an implicitly "biologized" view of culture or a hypostatized view of history.[9] Both cases, however, take the realm of social meaning out of the flux of everyday life and contention and assign it to a category appearing to possess a metahistorical continuity. Paradoxically, while developing in tandem with history—that is, at least claiming to eschew metaphysical speculation in favor of narratives grounded in the "real world"—racism violated the procedural and substantive protocols of history. History as a discipline seeks to elucidate the not easily visible mechanisms that cause social change and provide the basis of conjunctural explanations. Changes could be slow or rapid, in the latter situation transforming socioeconomic hierarchies in short periods. Racist thought, on the other hand, claimed to use visible and verifiable indices to explain relatively permanent differences between social formations.

The seeming durability and mobility of the concept of race arose pointedly from the historical context in which it emerged. Elevating difference to a central position, it surfaced partly as a reaction to the Enlightenment's universal humanism, partly as a pragmatic device to justify colonial rule, and partly also as a response to the more progressive principles of liberalism.[10] A whole slew of considerations enters into any particular manifestation of racism. Gobineau's ideas on cranial forms, facial features and their links to intellectual capacities, for example, cannot wholly explain his views on the Algerians. Rather, as Uday Mehta maintains, and Gobineau's contemporary, Tocqueville, understood, they had much to do with Gobineau's anxieties about the position of France in Europe and the meaning of Europeanness. Similar themes underlay British racism in India or Dutch racism in Indonesia. As George Mosse stresses, "racism . . . was a scavenger ideology, which annexed the virtues, morals, and respectability of the age to its stereotypes and attributed them to the inherent qualities of a superior race."[11]

Universalism and racism are more than complementary; they are "contraries affecting one another from the inside."[12] It is difficult to think of a world-organizing concept like racism without the existence of a global system of material and ideological production. The classifications of race appeared at a certain moment in history to correspond to the uneven geography of economic development. They provided a way to erase the uncertainties of history by substituting for flux and mutability a relatively stable set of hierarchies. And while seeming to ground itself in the "real" world, the notion of race appeared nearly as permanent as the cosmological axes of difference it replaced.[13] This tension between the purported fixity of the notion of race (and racial hierarchies) and its actual fluidity and responsiveness to changing circumstances is crucial to understanding its longevity.[14] It is in many ways an analogue of the world constituted by the dialectical tension of flux and fixity.

RACE AS IDEOLOGY

Race is an ideology in the Marxian sense: it is something that conceals, by distortion, the inner workings of a system; and that through social practice acquires an "almost independent power to mould beliefs, preferences and even identities."[15] In that sense, racism, as a system of social classification, is not passive, that is, simply recording difference already "objectively" in existence in the world, but one that actively creates its subjects.[16] Racism is a way of producing races, rather in the way nationalism creates nations, often turning mutable identities into fixed ones. While claiming consistency and constancy, it enjoys a great deal of mobility, not only shifting the grounds on which it is based — biology, language, geography, culture, flexible combinations of the above — but also integrating a variety of apparently unrelated topics — such as class, morality, sexuality — into its gravitational field.[17]

The classification of humans into racial types originally emerged as part of "a broader enterprise of taxonomy" made possible by the decline of the theological worldview.[18] "The ideal and the fantasy" of eighteenth- and nineteenth-century racial thought was scientific; the reduction of an empirical maze of differences to a few universalizable categories from which general laws could be derived.[19] The division of all humanity into three races (the Caucasoid, Mongoloid, and Negroid) paralleled the classificatory model of botany that Linnaeus developed for plants in the eighteenth century and Cuvier for the "animal kingdom" in the early nineteenth century.[20] Such classifications reduced the complexities of the social world to naturalistic and therefore unchangeable determinants.[21]

The "alluring simplicity" of racism allowed a plethora of "potentialities, dispositions and attitudes to be read off from self-evident physical characteristics or somatic types."[22] The realms of politics, culture, and psychology

—not to mention the capacity for scientific or philosophical thought—
could be "neatly determined along two or three gross physical configurations" corresponding to the racial division of humanity. Visible and measurable indices—the cephalic index, prognathism, or skin color—came to
serve as a proxy for qualities and potentialities that would otherwise remain beyond the reach of quantifiable science. In this view, the contrasting
qualities of the master race versus the subject races—each identifiable by
physical form—helped explain the course of history. This highly economical model could account for both change—attributable to the dynamism
of the master race—and (epochal) continuity associated with the stable
reproduction of races. As far as racist logic was concerned, some things
changed while others did not, and the things that did not change explained
those that did. Over time, as criteria other than physical form—say, language—came to dominate racial classificatory schemes, the same economical model could be mobilized for comparably invidious ends. Indeed, this
whole enterprise is consistent with the recurring tendency of modernity to
link change and continuity to large, unifying categories.

RECASTING OLDER FORMS OF STRATIFICATION

Race and caste appear to have some superficial similarities: a strong sense
of hierarchy not contingent on historical factors but based on relatively
permanent "facts" about human groups. Notwithstanding this, one should
not lose sight of the differences between the original concept of *varna* on
the one hand and race on the other. Racism employed the language of
"science and cultural naturalism," while the original discourse of varna
used cosmology and religion—never science, and not particularly history
as we understand it either.

The flexibility of the concept of race is nowhere better illustrated than in
the ways in which older discourses can be recast in racelike terms. Anthropologists in nineteenth-century India, for example, were extremely productive in devising racial classifications. Each presidency in British India devised its own elaborate "castes and tribes" studies adopting methods of
classifying and organizing populations using craniometric and phrenologi-
cal technologies first pioneered in the study of race.[23] The classic discourse
of caste, with its cosmological determinants infused with a cosmic notion of
time, was recast in secular terms, as spatiotemporal units of identity and
difference linked to racial stories of migrations, conquests, settlement, and
colonization. Caste, like race, could be reinvented so that superior socio-

economic standing in the present could be read off as a reward for having historically occupied a high position on the racial "domination index."[24] India had its Aryans and Dravidians, neatly divided along linguistic and geographic lines, with Indian history written to conform to a model of conquest by a virile white race over an effete dark-skinned one. Theories of subsequent Aryan degeneration in a tropical milieu could then draw on climatological and biological theories employed to portray the study of humanity as scientific.

It is only in this modern context that caste could begin to operate as a social synonym of race, and only a modernizing state with its technologies of representation—among them the census, map, and museum, to echo Benedict Anderson[25]—could redraw the social stratigraphies of precolonial India, consisting of a hodgepodge of local hierarchies of differentiation (*jati*), into an operational universalist scheme. To suggest that varna or, more absurdly, jati somehow prefigure racism is an anachronism; in fact, they in crucial ways expressed the very antithesis of the concept of race.[26] The caste system, like racism, must be understood as liberalism's Other, each needing the opposite one, as it were, to complete itself. If the labeling of humans is more than a "passive system of classification of pre-existing social entities, but a way of producing those subjects who will be so assigned,"[27] colonial anthropology and the census were identifiably active instruments in the racialization of castes and tribes.

If an existing system of hierarchization could not advance the colonial purpose of classifying and rewarding (or punishing/surveilling) sections of the population, racist thought could be exported in its entirety to do so. In India, caste could be remodeled as an adequate functional surrogate of race. In Africa, racist classifications simply found application without much regard for plausibility. Absurdly enough, the vivid colonial imagination populated Africa with Aryans and Semites, in addition, of course, to "Negroes," the former two naturally endowed with greater nobility and capacity for development (self-development as well as external, i.e., economic, development). Thus (racial) identity and (capitalist) economy became fused in one economical model. Entire populations could be recast, their bodies studied, skulls measured, and their potentialities assessed—all of which then became linked to entitlements (or the lack of them).[28]

The nature of the colonial enterprise itself may serve as a partial explanation for the ease of translation. Colonialism needed collaborators, people who would rule themselves and other subordinated indigenous populations on behalf of the overall reproduction of the colonial regime.[29] Tensions arose precisely at this interface between the global imperialist venture and the local articulation of the collaborator ruling elite. The latter should be understood as an emergent, dynamic phenomenon, not ready-made, but, through their participation in the enterprise of imperialism, in the process of becoming. The challenge for the collaborators was to demand a fuller participation (equal rights, representation in the councils of power) in the imperialist venture, while denying others ranking lower, for one reason or another, those same rights.[30] After all, the Enlightenment and racism came to the colonies in the wake of colonialism. In its more radical tendencies the former promoted equality, while the latter dwelt on ascriptive hierarchies cloaked in the language of science. Simultaneously committed to both, the colonized ruling class revealed its split personality.

Orientalism, History, and Time

Orientalism develops in the ambiguous spaces of race, imperialism, and nationalism — in Europe, and also in the world that Europe colonized. It is a "genuinely recent creation," the product of "modern European history that seeks credibility and support by claiming ancient roots and classical origins for itself."[31] As a structured phenomenon and organized movement it could hardly have existed "prior to the rise, consolidation and expansion of modern bourgeois Europe,"[32] and it is, therefore, as integral to modernity as racism and nationalism. Orientalism wrote, or rewrote, "histories of conquest" as "epics of imperial entitlement," in the process creating a mythic discourse "unaware of its own genealogy of historical process and struggle, of its own violence and violation."[33] This amnesia perhaps permitted thinking about the roots of the power hierarchies of the world — conqueror and conquered — in terms of a causal relationship between race (potential) and culture (achievement).

Like racist thought, Orientalism was not a mere classification, but an active constitution of peoples and cultures unthinkable outside the resources afforded by modernity.[34] There are, accordingly, continuities between the less biologically deterministic versions of racism and Orientalism. The crucial issue here is not which came first, or which was the more powerful, generative ideology. Suffice it that at different moments one or the other exerted an influence on the (at that instance) less significant ideology.

First-generation Orientalists were concerned to identify the defining moment of a particular civilization, wishing to mark the instance when its lineaments were clearly etched for the first time and which defined its subsequent development through long epochs. To this end, they developed a discipline of time called philology, combining history, literature, philosophy, linguistics, textual analysis, and the like. As Max Müller put it: "The object and aim of philology, in the highest sense, is but one — to learn what man is, by learning what man has been."[35] In this exercise, not just any stretch of a "civilization's" past would do; the philologist had to zero in on a crucial defining period. Antiquity became the preferred period of study, and within this, "the first moment of true civilization."[36] If this moment could be understood through an exhaustive study of its definitive texts, then the unfolding of a civilization, nation, race, people was a matter of following the clues for an essence that manifested itself early at a moment that we might call classical antiquity. The study of Vedic India and the "classical" period (roughly 2000 B.C.E. to the early second century C.E.), for instance, was not just about the defining qualities of Indic civilization, but about those of the entire Indo-European civilization itself; Sanskrit took on a momentous quality. As Max Müller wrote:

> In little more than a century, Sanskrit has gained its proper place in the republic of learning, side by side with Greek and Latin. . . . But, no one . . . who desires to study the history of that branch of mankind to which we ourselves belong and to discover in the first germs of that language, the religion, the mythology of our forefathers, the wisdom of Him who is not the God of the Jews only . . . can dispense with some knowledge of the language and ancient literature of India.[37]

Unlike the "Greek miracle," which was taken as a sign of future European greatness, the study of ancient India for the Orientalists indicated some anterior greatness, the ur-culture of Indo-Europeans in their global diaspora. Max Müller's comments illustrate the marriage of Romanticism, racism (note the quote's explicit anti-Semitism), and the blurring of lines between language, religion, and mythology so definitive of Orientalist thought.

Over time, Orientalist discourse itself changed and acquired a life vastly beyond anything its originators could have imagined.[38] In little more than half a century or so, its center of gravity had shifted from literature, philology, and philosophy to social Darwinism and scientific racism. Grounded in anthropology, biology, and the historical narrativization of both, it straddled the worlds of scholarship and administrative technologies requiring the collection and processing of vast amounts of "data."[39] In this sense, Orientalism, like racism, constitutes a highly mobile set of ideas that, at any one moment, hides its own mobility behind a dogmatic facade.

But Orientalism is more than a set of mere prejudices. Like racism, it is a relationship of power. Its power, however, stems not only from the fact of conquest and subsequent "pacification" of conquered populations, but also from its association with modern technologies of representation and with methods of research, collection, and presentation of data, all of which transpired to produce an impressive body of "knowledge" that hegemonized the colonizer and the colonized. A double amnesia is implicated here: one about the agency involved in the construction of this knowledge and one about the historicity of the construction of institutions framing the subsequent production of knowledge. Institutionalized by science and politics, Orientalism served as a template for "knowing an Oriental other in contradistinction to European capitalism, rationality, historicity, modernity and powers of self-transformation."[40] Using the disciplines of time and space, European modernity constructed its Other, which supposedly lacked precisely rationality, history, modernity, and the powers of self-transformation.

All of this would probably have seemed odd to one of the so-called founders of Orientalism, William Jones. As Jones wrote in his *Speeches of Isaeus* (1779):

> In the course of his [the legal scholar's] enquiries he will constantly observe a striking similarity among all nations, whatever seas or mountains may separate them, or how many ages soever may have elapsed between the periods of their existence, *in those great and fundamental principles*, which being clearly deduced by *natural reason, are equally diffused over all mankind*, and are not subject to alteration by any change in *place or time*. Nor will he fail to remark as striking a diversity in those laws, which proceeding merely from *positive institution* are consequently as various as the wills and fancies of those who enact them.[41]

This is a very Burkean kind of conservatism — all civilizations have some deep affinity for each other, and mere innovation proves dangerous as it threatens the equilibrium of the natural law — and it stands in contrast to what Abdel Malek, Edward Said, and others have characterized as Orientalism.[42] Indeed, Jones appears to be an archaic conservative universalist, and between his non-Whiggish attitude and that of latter-day Orientalists like James Mill and Thomas Macaulay, we find the yawning gulf of modernity. Raymond Schwab's insight that the "Oriental Renaissance" of the late eighteenth and early nineteenth century was associated with the threat of rapid changes, initiated by the French Revolution, is borne out by the revitalization of a conservative universalism that valued stability, which it ostensibly found in the "Orient."[43] However, as the radical ideas of the French Revolution became domesticated in the course of the nineteenth century, with radical Jacobin tendencies exhausted after 1848 and the European drive to acquire colonies intensified, the production of knowledge shifted from philosophers and philologists to the budding social scientists, not to mention the practical "men of action."[44] This later version of Orientalism was founded on an exact anti-Jonesian assumption — that of a *permanent* cleavage between the "Occident" and the "Orient."

There is, as Al-Azm points out, great economy involved in this model:

> In Orientalist thought, the primordial — "mind," "psyche," "essence" — shines through the events, circumstances and accidents forming the history of such a people as, e.g. the Arabs. The primordial reveals its potency, genius and distinguishing characteristics through the flux of historical events and the accidents of time, *without either history or time ever biting into its intrinsic nature.* Conversely, one can work backward through history and time to the unchanging Arab "mind," "psyche," or "essence."[45]

With minor variations, this model could be extended to India or, for that matter, China. Orientalist thought rests on three rather circular assumptions: (1) that social development is caused by characteristics internal to a society; (2) that historical development of a society is either an evolutionary progress or a gradual decline; (3) and that society is an "expressive totality" in the sense that all institutions of a society are the expressions of a primary essence.[46] More empirically minded social scientists could embellish this foundation through demonstrations of lacunae in the societies under question. To them, development did not occur in the Middle East or India because these societies lacked something, a middle class, autonomous cities, civil society, revolutions.[47] The critical point is the existence in the modern epoch of societies fundamentally impervious to either history or time — literally, therefore, "people without history"[48] — though paradoxically one can locate this immunity to history itself in time and space, in keeping with the historicist and social-scientific concerns of Orientalism. The "Islamic world" and "Hindu India" have boundaries, beyond which lies something else. And, most important of all, at some geographic point the Orient itself is replaced by the West, with all the qualities that the Orient lacks.

The "economy" of the Orientalist model should not suggest that it was in any sense simple. Orientalism involved a series of complex articulations not only to other powerful ideologies of the time, namely racism and nationalism, but also, by subsumption of even the "most instrumental knowledge produced to sustain technologies of colonial rule," to the Enlightenment, under the rubric of its scientific pretensions.[49] It was, as Al-Azm notes, connected to a "whole set of progressively expanding institutions, a cumulative body of theory and practice, a suitable ideological superstructure with an apparatus of complicated assumptions, beliefs, images, literary productions, and rationalizations, not to mention the underlying foundation of commercial, economic, and strategic vital interests."[50] This institutional Orientalism was intrinsically linked to a cultural-academic Orientalism that generated a vast repertoire of images and stereotypes with claims to the "disinterested pursuit of the truth" via the application of supposedly impartial scientific methods and value-free techniques in studying the peoples, cultures, religions, and languages of the "Orient."[51] Orientalism ultimately drew sustenance from the political-economic projects of colonialism that sought to map the colonized world as exhaustively as possible, as well as from the technologies developing autonomously in a Europe undergoing rapid internal transformations. In due course, under the sheer inertial weight of the volumes of material produced by the colonial writing factories and the various social sciences, Orientalism could float free from its original moorings in the colonial enterprise and become objectified — reified even — as a set of "factualized statements about a reality that existed and could be known independent of any subjective, colonizing will."[52] This detachment from politics both required and reinforced a culture that "objectivized the world as a collection of scientific observations with universal validity."[53]

The transformation of general philosophical precepts into a body of law, or of a hodgepodge of local customary practices into a thirty-year revenue policy as in India, was the very stuff of Orientalist empiricism, except that this empiricism involved the preemptive use of general, indeed universal, principles. Technically, they could therefore easily be applied to any society, even metropolitan ones, and they sometimes were, even before finding application in the colonies.[54] If, in practice, the English countryside, for example, was not subject to the same procedures as the Indian countryside, the *differentiae specificae* lay in the historical relationship between state power, social organization, and economic development over a long historical epoch rather than in the ontological peculiarity of colonial society itself.[55]

There is a paradox involved. Administrative or institutional Orientalism may have been directed toward proving the irreducible specificity of the colonies; but, in fact, the principles that activated it were universal. "Knowledge" about India, and the colonized world in general, was part and parcel of both political economy and world history.[56] What appear as empirically based discussions of the potentialities and limitations, virtues and shortcomings of a particular civilization, contributed signally to the development of the social sciences themselves[57]—to modeling the conditions that produce poverty and wealth, social welfare, government policies, and so on. Orientalism's procedures involved smoothing out the bumps of history so as to frame a supposed cultural particularism (of the "Orient") within the scientific universalism (of the "West").

ORIENTALISM AND THE UNIVERSAL ABSTRACTION

Does the mere placement of, say, India and Europe side by side in "universal theories of history" constitute Orientalism?[58] Why should comparative history, sociology, or political economy—or even treating one region as "typical" or normative—be Orientalist?[59] Said implies that a relationship of power resides at the core of this optic. But, as we have tried to theorize it, it is the peculiar and particular way in which this power finds expression that ties it to Orientalism.

Orientalism, we argue, is not just one case among many of the general historical tendency of a culture to portray others as lacking some desirable qualities—a variation on the barbarian syndrome. Orientalism partakes crucially of one of the key properties of capitalist modernity: the attribution to the hegemonic subject of the notion of exchange value, pure exchangeability—value in the abstract. In mundane terms, the "Orient" might be portrayed as lacking important qualities ("civil society," "individuality," "secondary structures,"[60] notions of freedom, and so on); by a rhetorical strategy, the "Orient" might be pushed back in time and constructed as "primitive" or "backward."[61]

However, this is hardly the crux of the matter. Orientalism relies on an axis that endows the self-constituted hegemonic subject — the Western bourgeois male, for example — with "unlimited properties," whose universality is a matter of *"literal indifference . . .* [a] consequence of *being able to take anyone's place, of occupying any place, of a pure exchangeability."*[62] Beside this hegemonic subject, the others represent so many particularities, remaining incapable of self-transformative action and hence the transcendence of their particularities, so as to partake of the former's universality. The hegemonic subject occupies a position abstracted from all such limitations, and the development that places the universal subject in the position of abstraction is "normal" development, shorn of all the absences or lacunae that cripple the others.[63] That the self-appointed universal subject and the others (irreducibly particular in their evolution or nonevolution) are equally artifacts of imperialist power becomes the subject of historical amnesia. Thus colonial states could remove themselves from any causal account of the economic, political, and social conditions in the colonies. India is a classic case. In report after official report, the state portrayed itself as a neutral arbiter among the subcontinent's warring religious, caste, and tribal communities. In this welter of peculiarities, the colonial state could represent itself as the "perfect, disinterested judge formed for and by the public sphere."[64] This notion of the hegemonic subject's autonomy and freedom from particularism that allows it to act as the "perfect disinterested judge" in a diversity of contexts constitutes the nub of the Orientalist spatialization of difference.

It is only with the advent of capitalism that the concept of universal exchangeability acquires the force of a social abstraction. When everything is particular and there is no mechanism, such as the market imperative,[65] to render the particularities commensurable, the universal as pure exchangeability is inconceivable. Orientalism as one paradoxical expression of this type of universality is, without question, entirely an artifact of modernity. If modernity represents the coexistence in global time/space of the premodern and modern (i.e., capitalist) economy and community, then Orientalism effects a decisive spatial separation of the two: the projection of the premodern onto the non-Western Other, accompanied by the configuration of the West as the pure space of development and transformation of universal history and the universal subject.

To the extent that anticolonial nationalisms aspired to transcend their particularity, and "eccentricity," they often reversed the signs of Orientalism, while retaining its grammar, thereby claiming a universal significance without vacating their locational specificity.[66] Their main task was to construct nation-states based simultaneously on universalistic principles of citizenship and on some unique cultural properties undissolvable into some larger, or smaller, entity. Orientalism was a crucial resource for anti-imperialist nationalism, for it allowed nationalists to speak simultaneously in both universalist and particularist registers via a transvaluation of the values of Orientalism.

For nationalists, discovering the truth of their "Orient" proved crucial to the development of a nationalist ideology. The latter applied the "readily available structures, styles and ontological biases of Orientalism upon themselves and upon others."[67] Orientalism's diagnoses of deficiencies became nationalism's positive virtues; the recovery of the truth of the Orient from the misrepresentations of Orientalism was a vital part of the construction of a new-model community. Not surprisingly, the Romantic-rejectionist register has tended to dominate this aspect of the nationalist discourse, with the rejection of the twin symbols of European modernity — the French and the Industrial Revolutions — being central to this aspect of anti-colonial nationalism. For example, as Ben Bella, the Algerian nationalist and one of the founders of the Algerian liberation movement, the Front de Libération National (FLN), declared: "It's an error to believe our nationalism is the nationalism of the French Revolution. Ours is a nationalism fertilized by Islam. . . . All our political formulation is Koranic formulation. . . . Thus Algerian nationalism and Arab nationalism is a cultural nationalism essentially based on Islam."[68] Ben Bella linked this cultural nationalism to the fact that the peasants, not the workers, gave Algeria its freedom fighters. The rejection of the French Revolution, and the working class, is linked not to a reaction to colonialism, but to a discourse of authenticity. The Islamic elements of cultural nationalism are anchored to the peasants — the *Volk*, the salt of the earth as it were — and not to the political calculations of the nationalist leadership. An even more obscurantist strand of nationalism, à la Gandhi in the Indian case, rejected the Industrial Revolution and its results, again in the name of authenticity and cultural continuity:

> It is not that we did not know how to invent machinery, but our fore-fathers knew that, if we set our hearts after such things, we would become slaves and lose our moral fibre. They therefore, after due delib-eration, decided that we should do what we could with our hands and

feet. . . . They further reasoned that large cities were a snare and a useless encumbrance. . . . They were therefore satisfied with small villages. . . . A nation with a constitution like this is fitter *to teach others than to learn from others.*[69]

Once the twin revolutions of the modern world had been rejected, the way opened for the most exaggerated neo-Orientalist fantasies, holding fast, however, to the linguistic method pioneered by Orientalism. Al-Azm gives the example of a Syrian scholar who tries to derive some essential characteristics of the "Arabic mind" from a linguistic analysis of the Arabic word for "man," and he goes on to comment: "The exaggerated value placed upon Arabic as a language permits the Orientalist to make the language equivalent to mind, society, history and nature. For the Orientalist, *the language speaks the Arab Oriental,* not vice versa."[70] In a similar vein, Sanskrit became central to Hindu nationalism in North India, as did Tamil to a "Dravidian" nationalism in South India.[71]

Religion occupied an equally important role, reversing the dissociation between nationalism and religion in the Creole nationalism of the Western hemisphere and that of Europe.[72] The causes of this historical reversal lie in the operations of colonialism. The British posited something they called Hinduism as the essence of Indianness; and the French, for their part, made Islam into the essence of, for instance, Algerianness. In the period of high colonialism, both colonial powers focused their cultural critique on the sociocultural shortcomings of societies held hostage by defective or degenerate faiths. Emergent nationalism responded by turning Hinduism and Islam, respectively, into the instruments of a nationalist "renaissance," revivalism, and reformation. While formerly high Brahmanism or Sunni Islam were merely one element among many — with a multitude of smaller sects having their own legitimate spheres of operation — they became, in the course of resistance to colonialism, the core around which "all other signifiers condensed."[73]

The fastening of national symbols onto the body of the "colonized woman" accompanied this reactive nationalism. The veil and the *chechia,* which had been "in the traditional [North African] context, mere vestimentary details endowed with an almost forgotten significance, simple elements of an unconsciously devised system of symbols,"[74] not to mention the sari in India, grew to acquire an exaggerated political significance in the anticolonial culture wars. In the colonial situation, such symbols expressed not only resistance to the foreign order and foreign values, but also "fidelity to their own system of values."[75] This type of anticolonial traditionalism became the core of nationalist identity politics in India and Africa.

In this discourse of Orientalism-in-reverse, the figure of the "West" has become a convenient, if by now purely formalistic, target of attack. Orientalism's real legacy for nationalist projects was that it afforded "rich ground for invention, wide ground for maneuver and opposition, [a] versatile component of national discourse."[76] The key words are *unity, autonomy,* and *permanence,* applicable with equal indifference to "Indian civilization," the "Arabic Orient," or some other idealized space in the imaginary of Orientalism-in-reverse.

If this were the only register in which anti-imperialist nationalism spoke or acted, the matter would be simple. But, since anti-imperialist nationalism was involved in an intimate dance with the "enemy," it also adopted the other, more civic-universal register of colonial Orientalism. The colonizers' Orientalism — if not the academic-romantic variety — was, after all, implicated in a centrally contradictory enterprise. On the one hand, colonial subjects were exoticized both vis-à-vis the West and vis-à-vis each other. That is, the Orient was composed, in the colonizers' imagination, of communities exhibiting a radical internal cultural/racial commonalty and an equally radical external cultural/racial difference. Thus, even if they lived in the same space, different caste groups or sects, or more severely Hindus and Muslims, were thought of as engaging in foreign relations with each other while being internally self-contained. This, as Appadurai remarks, seems to be the "critical marker of the colonial twist in the politics of the modern nation-state."[77] On the other hand, the exotic body of the colonial subject — "fasting, feasting, hook-swinging, abluting, burning, bleeding" — had to be made suitable for modernity by being counted, classified, and generally cleaned up for such "humdrum projects as taxation, sanitation, education, warfare and loyalty."[78]

The colonizers' Orientalism, therefore, rested simultaneously on two pillars: the perduring exoticism of the colonial subject requiring the permanent disciplinary agency of Western rule; and the potentiality of their becoming modern citizens of a secular state, in which an unprecedented degree of civic uniformity would prevail. Colonialism might create, via the census, separate "communities," but it could not, in everyday life, create as many separate entrances and exits, so to speak, in the civic arena. Appadurai is entirely right to note that while certain components of the colonial state were "active propagators of discourses of group identity," others, such as those involved with law, education, and moral reform, were implicated in the creation of what might be called *"a colonial bourgeois subject, conceived as an 'individual.'"* [79]

And sometimes these bourgeois subjects came in oddly composite shapes. After all, the same Ben Bella, who praised the peasants for their adherence to Islam cultivated the resolutely atheistic and communistic Fidel Castro; stressed "national" education, but also developed cultural and economic relations with France. And Gandhi, while condemning the railroad as one of the most notorious, poisoned gifts of industrial civilization, was nonetheless using it incessantly to construct a mass nationalist movement. And along with decrying "Western individualism," he continuously urged individual moral responsibility as the basis of social reform. [80] The exigencies of modernity — the construction of new-model polities and communities — ultimately limit the room for a purely exoticist vision of societal reconstruction.

Nations and Nationalism

Neither the notion of race in its "scientific" guise nor Orientalism in its Aryanist version would appear to be appropriate categories for incorporation into nationalist thought. After all, the boundaries of the "races" far transcended those of actually existing nations or those in the process of formation in the late nineteenth and the first half of the twentieth century. However, the notion of race became one of the underpinnings of nationalist discourse, revealing not only the flexibility of the concept itself but also the characteristic tension between larger, universal categories and particular movements that create identity and locality. Race, as we have seen, was a strategic concept as well, one that could be mobilized for class and national purposes. It assumed an important position at the same time that nationalism was becoming a powerful global ideological and political force. These two concepts, apparently irreconcilable in scalar ambition and political application, were brought together into a rough symbiosis via the development of racialized histories of nations, in which antiquity became the key to an understanding of modernity.

Orientalism, with its ontological essences and vast generalizations about civilizations, explicitly creates its "Orients" as either a motley collection of local, ascriptive communities or as a form of generalized slavery controlled by despots. In either version the "Orient" supposedly lacks the sense of history, vitality, organization, or altruism needed to construct genuine national communities. Perversely, the sense of a timeless Orient becomes integrally linked to the historic constitution of nation-states in the colonized world of the nineteenth century. This, in turn, replays an enduring theme of nationalism — that is, the link between modern community formation and histories or myths of antiquity. A notion of epic time, located in, yet still beyond history, is crucial to creating a notion of "classical antiquity," when the genius of a Volk, or race, explodes in a plenitude of creativity.

THE NATION AS COMMUNITY

Why should the transformations and dislocations associated with modernity — the uprooting of people from rural occupations and the corporate ties of feudal and early modern life, the destruction of small face-to-face communities, with their members being cast adrift into migratory and urban patterns of life[81] — have brought about the specific type of community that one associates with nation-states? Partly, no doubt, because in this unprecedented and transitional moment capitalism reworked society as a whole. Capitalism, unlike previous epochs of production, does not leave local social and productive arrangements more or less alone, merely removing the surplus as revenue for redistributive purposes. It is, as Marx pointed out in the *Grundrisse* and in *Capital*, a global system of self-expanding value that transforms the labor process and ways of producing material wealth and, over time, decisively terminates the autonomy of small, relatively self-sufficient rural communities.

The conquest of space through time — a central feature of capitalism — the removal of people from agrarian ways of life, the spatial separation of production and consumption, and the overthrow of ancien régime modes of legitimization combine to produce a crisis (in the sense of the closure of a way of life) that opens up possibilities for the emergence of a new type of state form capable of both mobilizing and domesticating uprooted people.[82] The legitimacy of the new state comes to rest on the creation of a new identity and a new set of boundaries: identities based on "universal," that is, nonparticularistic, criteria for membership of a community, while preserving the boundaries of each new state thus formed against others.[83] This is not to say that powerful interests engaged in this transformation in the earliest instances were themselves preemptively nationalist, although some of them might have been. It is to argue that inchoate popular aspirations for community—in conditions of fairly severe alienation induced by the new socioeconomic realities—have been given shape as an actual historical community by precisely those powerful interests. The emergence of nations (as a specific form of community) and nationalism (as a body of thought) combined slow antecedent processes with explosive new needs generated by the social and economic transformations of the late eighteenth and early nineteenth century.[84]

With the powers of absolutist rulers eroded by movements from below, the question, "Who are the people?" in whose name these movements claimed to be acting, became "unavoidable."[85] Nationalism took shape by positing the existence of a community linked by language, culture, and history, whose sovereignty was thwarted by absolutist or imperialist tyranny. As an interstate system matured in early modern and modern times in Europe—the new nationalist movements sometimes inherited these states, sometimes overthrew them—the principle of nationality appeared to provide the only widely accepted legitimization to order life within the state and to regulate relationships between states. By conferring citizenship without regard to particularist criteria—gradually developing the civic space in which otherwise destructive struggles might be smoothed over[86] and making the nation-state the arena in which stable solidarities could evolve, offsetting the "agonistic individualism" associated with modernity[87]—the nation-state becomes a historical subject in its own right, over and above competing classes, ethnic groups, and their identity politics.

Nationalism is, in this sense, an important ideology for the reconciliation of capitalism and a stable social order—in articulating the particular shape of modernity as we have experienced it.[88] Once in place, it is arguable that the demonstration effect of the success in the modern world of those regions that had effectively staked a claim to nation-statehood, and, in the case of late arrivals, resistance to the encroachment of earlier established, more powerful nation-states (for example, in the colonial context), all served to generalize the appeal of the idea of nation-states as the basis of collective life.

However, one is not free to conceive of an "imagined community" in any arbitrary form; imagination is constrained by the historical circumstances of the national formation and decides, if only for the moment, whether civic-universal or ethnic particular forms will be hegemonic. As Hobsbawm points out after Pierre Vilar, in revolutionary moments ethnicity was not of the essence of claims to membership of a national community.[89] The claim of the "nation-people from below" was precisely that it represented "the common interest against particular interests, the common good against privilege." Arguably, therefore, for the radical "nation-people from below," ethnic group differences were, "from this revolutionary-democratic point of view, as secondary as they later seemed to socialists."[90]

Only the cauldron of revolutionary activity seems to generate such universalist sentiments. More often, the ethnic-particular becomes the common denominator for establishing citizenship and membership of a national community, even if it means creating fictional unities and excluding some long-term residents of a particular country from full cultural membership of the imagined community. Even demands for rights seem to undergo an "ethnicization" process, that is, become exclusive with regard to membership in any particular (national) community. This suggests that the process of reconstruction, following the winding-down of the revolutionary imperative, takes as a central concern the particularization of the universal. Universal aspirations — democracy, human rights, equality, fraternity, and the like. — become confined within the cramped spatial range of the nation-as-ethnic-group-writ-large. One finds a contradictory movement of dual spatialization here: even the smallest nation is larger than the ethnic communities of the period preceding the full impact of capitalism; but even the largest nation is smaller than the planetary ecumene of revolutionary thought.

It takes the modern state, so to speak, to create an ethnic nation as the basis of a nation-state. As Hegel, acutely observing its unfolding, noted: "Those heroes [the ancient heroes of their countries' history] do not live solely in their nations' imagination; their history, the recollection of their deeds is linked with public festivals, national games, with many of the state's domestic institutions or foreign affairs, with well-known houses and districts, with public memorials and temples."[91] All of these activities make up ethnic memory and customs — even, perhaps, create ethnic memories and customs that can then be naturalized as part of a durable structure of institutionalized myths. This is not to imply a cynical manipulation of the "truth" or simply getting history wrong, but to refer to a large-scale structure of belief and identity that is part and parcel of the way these historically new communities work.[92] Concurrently, however, the modern state, while emerging from the destruction of particularistic ethnic communities and the radical alienation caused by market forces, nonetheless must at least appear to confer on people organized into political communities "a higher sphere of ethical life, historical personality and collective agency."[93]

"The completed bourgeois state" has to found a community stripped of all particularistic vestiges associated with the ancien régime, and therefore "universal" in its criteria of citizenship, though the coexistence of similar units in the larger space-time of world politics limits its universality.[94]

These secular considerations are, in part, integral to the nature of membership in a modern community, which, as Habermas points out, is always "spelt out in a double code": on the one hand, in legal and political terms, for example, civil rights, guaranteed by a revisable constitution and won through struggles of which exist copious written records (the "voluntary nation of citizens"); on the other hand, in terms of inherited or ascriptive membership in a national community (a "culturally [or ethnically] defined community").[95] One might add to this Benedict Anderson's insight that "in the twentieth century, it was becoming clear that it was impossible to *think* about nationalism except comparatively and globally. But it was also very difficult to *feel* it and *act politically* on it, in any but particular terms."[96] The nation's secular legitimacy involves an immensely complex dialectical unfolding of the civic/universal and the ethnic/particular.[97]

The immanent universalism of the capitalist mode of production cannot operate unhindered. Its necessary mediation through class and political interest, the uneven geographies of development, popular alienation from and the very crises of the capitalist system, the transformation, even creation, of ethnic memories by the touch of radical activism from below and political "entrepreneurship" from above—all combine to create powerful deflections. It is in this sense that the operation of the capitalist world system has not produced a "flat cosmopolitanism."[98] The productive powers of society, including telecommunications, may increase the density of contact between members of particular states, while simultaneously limiting movement across state boundaries with checkpoints, passports, and visas.[99] They both free people of particularist identities and dissolve them into larger ones, and in the same breath stridently demarcate the newly "imagined" ones from others across the borders of neighboring nation-states.[100] The larger political and cultural economy of modernity arguably generates out of its internal tensions and contradictions the basis of national cultures.

In premodern times fuzzy boundaries were the rule, with large "march" areas separating the core political hegemonies of neighboring polities. The process of modernization has generated new technologies of communication and representation (including novel mapping techniques) that supersede these fuzzy boundaries. By an odd twist, the time of nationalism inverts the causal relationship between modernization and the drawing of boundaries, securing for the space of modern polities an uncontestable imaginative reality going "back" to the mist-enveloped regions of antiquity beyond history. The nation-state comes to rest on the precision of temporal and spatial boundary marking that only modern academic disciplines and technology can provide, while simultaneously exploiting the amorphousness of mythic time and space.

HISTORY AND THE NATION

Nationalism is quintessentially a modern project of state and community building which hides its innovations under the guise of continuity. It has an ambivalent relationship to history and is, in actuality, "either hostile to the real ways of the past, or arises on its ruin."[101] Not surprisingly, when the modern discipline of history came to be practiced with all its scientific pretensions, it was often written in the form of "biographies of nations."[102] Bounded time that marks the temporal twists and turns of the fate of a people, the timelessness of the nation, and the immortality of the favored people come together in this telling.

Anthony Smith and Benedict Anderson stress the religion-like, ontological elements in national formation and nationalism as "an anthropological constant of organized social life."[103] Without this anthropological constant, the peculiar power of nationalism — its pathos, so to speak — would be inexplicable. Smith suggests that a global culture "seems unable to offer the qualities of collective faith, dignity and hope that only a 'religion surrogate,' with its promise of a territorial culture community across the generations, can provide."[104] Thus, beyond any "political or economic benefits" that nationalism can offer, it holds out to its members the "promise of collective but *terrestrial immortality* outfacing death and oblivion."[105]

Nationalism taps certain archaic themes: drawing on older myths of "ethnic election," that is, the notion of a chosen group which may fulfill its destiny and find salvation on its "ancestral soil," and satisfying a "more general craving for immortality," no longer via divine providence but through secular multigenerational continuity.[106] Nationalist histories marry ethnic memories with a notion of collective destiny. While Smith concedes the importance of the activities of intellectuals in vastly enhancing the scope of popular traditions, he suggests that the mobilization of the "fundamental symbolic components of ethnicity" must be placed in a longer historical and cultural context in which "the aims and activities of intellectual, professional and other elites" must be interrelated with "the mass sentiments and memories of the common people."[107] However, and this is crucial to Smith's argument, the power of nationalism does not stem merely from its immersion in popular culture; it draws its power from providing, via an imagined community of immense flexibility and symbolic range, answers to the "ultimate issues of mortality and oblivion."[108]

This quasi-religious tone, which seemingly marks nationalism out from other ideologies of the modern world, has allowed nationalism, in some cases, to link up with world historical religions like Islam, Judaism, Buddhism, and Hinduism; in others to substitute itself for declining religious traditions, as happened in Western Europe.[109] An essentially secular ideology of culture and politics reveals a transcendental dimension, "one that raises the individual above the earthly round and out of immediate time."[110]

However, while the nation may be an "anthropological formation" in the senses spelt out above, it is also the source, for most people, of historical consciousness.[111] Under the relentless pressure of capitalist demands for productivity, time itself is broken down into tiny, discrete units, and individuals mostly experience it as an immediate pressure, either as a deadline against which to finish a quantity of work, or a social measure of ongoing productive activity, "socially-necessary labor time," in Marx's phrase.[112] The sense of time as objective systemic pressure does not in itself spontaneously produce a historical consciousness; on the contrary, it seems inimical to the emergence of such a consciousness. Most people experience time in its longer duration, and as historical consciousness, through their membership in a national community.[113]

This imbrication of historical consciousness and nationalism is grounded in the fact that the nation, as a secular community, secures its pedigree and legitimacy by using time in the modern sense to construct its myths of origin and growth.[114] "Nations," as Hobsbawm points out, "do not make states and nationalism but the other way around."[115] It is precisely this inversion in popular consciousness of the causal sequence of nation and nationalism — of power, process, and intersubjectivity — that underpins the nationalist claim to power. Nationalist discourse is also, as Abbas Vali notes, a "misconception and misrepresentation of the real . . . a historicization of a fictitious subject."[116] Nationalist genealogies, therefore, have a political purpose: "The rediscovery of the past in order to lay claim to the (national) present."[117]

Historical consciousness emerges in the seams of the modern and the premodern — and in the fantastic contortions of causality that nationalism produces — rather than merely as a spontaneous function of the precision with which recent centuries have marked time. A national community — as the synthesis of a premodern notion of a community of ethnic election, with its quasi-religious overtones, and a modern notion of a secular civic society expressing a momentary "general will" — appears in the consciousness of its members as both transcendental and historical. In its most typical expression in the nationalist discourse, the former is attached to an ethnic or protonational identity not subject to external determination. The nationalist claim asserts that the identity in question has always existed; there is no point in recorded history without or before its existence — a condition of freedom from external determinants of any kind.[118] The task of modern nationalism is to give this transcendental identity a political body. The latter, in turn, acts as a guarantor of the former.[119] Nationalist histories, particularly in their textbook and museumized versions, are not only concerned to spell out the antiquity and continuity of the nation, but also to hide its crises and ruptures — or present the latter as part of a triumphal progression from small beginnings to imperial glory, slavery to freedom, or variations on those themes. In their more politically conservative forms, these histories serve to reinforce reactionary humanism and cultural integralism. In their more neutral versions, for most people, they provide the means to think of community, time, and the future.[120] However, any attempt to understand nations and nationalism outside a historical framework grounded in modernity runs the risk of primordialism, of taking literally the ideological claims of its proponents and thereby mystifying a relatively recent phenomenon associated with the necessity for establishing a new type of state and community in the face of upheavals produced by the breakdown of ancien régimes and the concomitant growth of capitalism.

Conclusion

Ultimately, modernity cannot escape history. If the ideas of modernity as captured, say, in the radical Enlightenment, appear revolutionary compared to those of a later period, then history — not race, culture, or any other timeless construct — must be a prominent part of the explanation. In Western Europe, for example, modernity expressed itself in a radical idiom from the seventeenth through the late eighteenth century. This development arose at the junction of two revolutionary movements: the struggles of an emerging bourgeoisie against the ancien régime, and their simultaneous efforts to hegemonize the radical aspirations of the working poor, including the artisanate.[121] The struggles to remove the ancien régime from effective power and to contain the artisanate's struggle for rights within the new order account for the radical elements of bourgeois ideology. These include, among other qualities, the incorporation of a scientific worldview that had been developing among the upper reaches of the artisanate and the bourgeoisie,[122] and innovative ideas of community and representation that became the basis of nationalism and democracy, respectively. Rapid economic transformation added to the sense of movement and turmoil in which revolutionary ideas could take root and reshape humans' understanding of the material world and social relations.[123]

On the other hand, modernity in the world that came to be colonized during the mid-eighteenth to the early twentieth century developed in decidedly different circumstances. In those situations, the actions of a conquering imperialism removed the ancien régimes. Modernity itself was imposed by the colonial regime within the enclosures of Orientalism and racism. When a bourgeoisie did emerge within the ranks of the colonized, it was limited by colonial rule but protected from the classes above and, more so, from the classes below them by the paternalism of the colonial state. The bourgeoisie in the colonies did not actively have to develop a new set of radical ideas to deal with the removal of the ancien régime. Nor did it have to work to contain the radical demands of the lower-ranked orders of society until the nationalist movement took full shape in the early twentieth century, by which time the principal opposition had become crystallized in spatial terms — for instance, of India to the West, a clear indication of the organizing power of Orientalism. The remnants of the princely elite could be portrayed as tools of British imperialism, and the lower orders of society could be co-opted by pointing to the external rulers as the source of their problems.[124] Moreover, the broad thrust of colonial rule was to strengthen, if not create, all kinds of conservative social institutions that produced an enviable degree of social, if not economic, security for the bourgeoisie in colonized countries.

Economic development under colonialism was, for the most part, too slow to produce in the consciousness of the colonized people the sense of evanescence that Marx captured so well in *The Communist Manifesto*.[125] Here, the very potentiality for development was arrested or skewed, leaving the colonized bourgeoisie with a very limited horizon of hope. At the elite level, the modern consciousness took the form of a sharp dichotomy between the inner life (religious/spiritual "revival" and renovation; experience of modernization not as a transformative reality but as an academic experience) and the outer life (gross economic underdevelopment; the coexistence, in revamped form, of the institutions and practices of a previous epoch).[126]

Whereas the discourse of the colonizers took the form of racism — a superior "us" and an inferior "them" — which was then projected into the far reaches of the epic imagination,[127] the discourse of the colonized took the form of an interior life of development that contrasted sharply with the exterior life of underdevelopment. The lacuna between the inner and outer life expresses the historical juncture of much colonial modernity.[128]

The uneven geography of capitalist development has also produced in our times a deep rift between the advocates of globalization and facile universalism — often conservative apologists of capitalism — and neopopulist advocates of small-scale appropriate technologies, opponents of science, technological innovation, and complex organization.[129] These localists, so to speak, have taken on the mantle of new-age radicalism and present themselves as critics of a triumphalist modernity. Historical amnesia on the part of the former has enabled them to avoid the real differences through which modernity is elaborated over time and space. Universalism has, not surprisingly, come to be associated with the hegemonic ideology of the ruling elite. As for the latter (the localist, new-age radicals), Berman is surely right to say that for their ideas to become anything more than wishful thinking would involve the most "radical redistribution of economic and political power," and he points to a paradox of modern times whereby only the "most extravagant and systematic thinking big" can open up channels for "thinking small."[130] That there might be progressive forms of universalism has become, in fact, something of a minority position.

The possibility of articulating a transformative politics — which would involve challenging the hegemony of capitalism — requires us to be aware of the spatiotemporal dimensions and elaboration of modernity. Neither universalism nor particularism, or localism, are per se emancipatory.[131] To understand why those exist in dialectical tension is a precondition for going beyond "conservative" universalism and "radical" particularism toward a transformation of both, and indeed therefore of modernity itself. The latter's antinomies must become part of a critical reevaluation of politics in our time.

Notes

1. Karl Marx, *The Communist Manifesto* (1848; London: Verso, 1998), 37–38.

2. Quoted in Fredric Jameson, "Cognitive Mapping," in Cary Nelson and Lawrence Grossberg, eds., *Marxism and the Interpretation of Culture* (Urbana: University of Illinois Press, 1988), 353.

3. Ibid.

4. Maurice Olender, *The Languages of Paradise: Race, Religion, and Philology in the Nineteenth Century,* trans. Arthur Goldhammer (Cambridge: Harvard University Press, 1992), ix–x.

5. For our definition of the postmodern, see note 13 of the introduction to this volume.

6. This space is geopoliticized. See the excellent essay by Immanuel Wallerstein, "Social Conflict in Post-Independence Black Africa: The Concepts of Race and Status-Group Reconsidered," in Etienne Balibar and Wallerstein, *Race, Nation, Class: Ambiguous Identities* (London: Verso, 1991), 187–203, esp. 199–200.

7. Martin Bernal analyzes this tendency in the construction of the Aryan model of ancient Greek history in *Black Athena: The Afroasiatic Roots of Classical Civilization* (New Brunswick, N.J.: Rutgers University Press, 1987). See the essay by Kaiwar in this collection.

8. Ann Laura Stoler, "Racial Histories and Their Regimes of Truth," *Political Power and Social Theory* 11 (1997): 199. This last point is made somewhat differently by Michael Adas, *Machines as the Measure of Men: Science, Technology, and Ideologies of Western Dominance* (Ithaca, N.Y.: Cornell University Press, 1989). Somewhat perversely, Adas uses this internal inconsistency in the definition of race to deny its importance in the constitution of modern difference.

9. Uday Mehta, "The Essential Ambiguities of Race and Racism," *Political Power and Social Theory* 11 (1997): 236.

10. The last point was originally made by E. J. Hobsbawm, *The Age of Capital, 1848–1875* (1975; New York: Vintage, 1996), 268.

11. George Mosse, *Towards the Final Solution: A History of European Racism* (Madison: University of Wisconsin Press, 1985), 234.

12. Etienne Balibar, "Racism as Universalism," in Balibar, *Masses, Classes, Ideas: Studies on Politics and Philosophy before and after Marx,* trans. James Swenson (New York: Routledge, 1994), 199.

13. Hence, too, the paranoia about "miscegenation."

14. One should, however, avoid an unnecessarily instrumentalist view of racist thought: that is, that it employs decoys, talking about one thing while actually referring to another. Racism must express the "reality" of something, at least as seen from within a certain ideological perspective. People who employ(ed) racist ideas do (did) not need to be aware of using decoys.

15. Mehta, "Essential Ambiguities," 238.

16. Ann Laura Stoler, "On Politics, Origins, and Epistemes," *Political Power and Social Theory* 11 (1997): 250.

17. Stoler, "Racial Histories," 194; see also Victor Kiernan, *The Lords of Humankind: Black Man, Yellow Man, White Man in an Age of Empire* (Boston: Little, Brown, 1969), for a discussion of the way in which class stereotypes became racial stereotypes in the course of the nineteenth century.

18. Loïc Wacquant, "For an Analytic of Racial Domination," *Political Power and Social Theory* 11 (1997): 231 n. 5; Benedict Anderson, *Imagined Communities: Reflections on the Origin and Spread of Nationalism* (London: Verso, 1991), chs. 2–3.

19. This particular definition of race, as nothing more than the classification of humanity by the use of certain physical indices and the attachment of relatively unalterable qualities to them, is, as the foregoing pages note, only a small part of a much more elusive situation.

20. Carl von Linnaeus, *The "Critica Botanica" of Linnaeus*, translated by the late Sir Arthur Hort (London: The Ray Society, 1938); Georges Cuvier, *The Animal Kingdom Arranged in Conformity with Its Organization*, trans. H. MacMurtrie (New York: G. and C. and H. Carvill, 1831).

21. Since biological change is glacially slow compared to social and economic change, the notion of *race* was probably soothing to sections of the ruling class made uncomfortable by the rapid changes of the eighteenth and nineteenth century. See Mehta, "Essential Ambiguities," 236.

22. Ibid.

23. These classifications then became a way of organizing entitlements, and also of surveilling certain "criminal" tribes.

24. Thus Brahmans were not just high castes because they performed functions highly valued by, for example, the state, but also because they were the descendants of the conquering Aryans. Victor Courtet de l'Isle (1813–67) put forth these ideas in *La science politique fondée sur la science de l'homme* (Paris, 1835), especially the conclusion, "Mémoire sur les races humaines," quoted in Léon Poliakov, *The Aryan Myth: A History of Racist and Nationalist Ideas in Europe*, trans. Edmund Howard (New York: Basic Books, 1974), 228.

25. Anderson, *Imagined Communities*, ch. 10.

26. This point was made with great polemical vigor by Oliver Cromwell Cox, *Caste, Class, and Race: A Study in Social Dynamics* (New York: Monthly Review, 1948), 91.

27. Stoler, "On Politics, Origins, and Epistemes," 250.

28. Sub-Saharan Africans were considered unfit for higher education. Only belatedly was technical education introduced in parts of East Africa (Daniel R. Headrick, *The Tentacles of Progress: Technology Transfer in the Age of Imperialism, 1850–1940* [New York: Oxford University Press, 1988], ch. 9).

29. See the essay by Andrew Barnes, "Aryanizing Project, African 'Collaborators,' and Colonial Transcripts," in this volume.

30. As Sumit Sarkar demonstrates, Indian nationalists in the late 1930s, while fighting for emancipation from colonial rule, were quick to punish strikers who demanded fair wages and working conditions. *Modern India, 1885–1947* (Madras: Macmillan India, 1983), 362.

31. Sadik Al-Azm, "Orientalism and Orientalism in Reverse," *Khamsin* 8 (1981): 6.

32. Ibid.

33. Nicholas Dirks, "Colonial Histories and Native Informants: Biography as an Archive," in Carol A. Breckenridge and Peter van der Veer, eds., *Orientalism and the Postcolonial Predicament: Perspectives on South Asia* (Philadelphia: University of Pennsylvania Press, 1993), 311. Among other virtues, this collection of essays is immensely valuable for illustrating our point that though the categories of modernity come under scrutiny in this postmodern moment and may no longer be used in their classic forms, they are nonetheless indispensable in constituting the discursive media in and through which new projects are formulated.

34. In this sense, we think it irrelevant if some institution or practices of the conquered regions — varna, jati, slavery, the veil, and so on — afforded the imperialists/Orientalists the "raw materials" for their classifications. The latter could be produced from any indigenous institution at hand. When Orientalists could not rely on caste or castelike hierarchies, they would focus on tribalism; if not polytheism and idol worship, then the veil and the harem, and so on. Recent attempts at discovering deep, that is, precolonial, indigenous roots for oppressive institutions therefore prove somewhat quixotic, to say the least.

35. Quoted in Vinay Dharwadker, "Orientalism and the Study of Indian Literatures," in Breckenridge and van der Veer, *Orientalism and the Postcolonial Predicament,* 175.

36. Ibid.

37. F. Max Müller, *A History of Ancient Sanskrit Literature, so Far as It Illustrates the Primitive Religion of the Brahmans* (1859; London: Williams, 1956), 2–3.

38. An excellent point variously made in Dharwadker, "Orientalism and the Study of Indian Literatures," 168; and David Ludden, "Orientalist Empiricism: Transformations of Colonial Knowledge," in Breckenridge and van der Veer, *Orientalism and the Postcolonial Predicament,* 251, 268.

39. Ludden, "Orientalist Empiricism," 251. Orientalism thus served as something of a portmanteau for all kinds of disciplinary developments, political concerns, anxieties, and the like. This is rather similar to the point Uday Mehta makes in relation to racist thought. Orientalism, like racism, could become a convenient idiom for the expression of thoughts perhaps otherwise impossible to articulate — a characteristic transposition of modernity, given its uneasy antinomies.

40. Ludden, "Orientalist Empiricism," 265.

41. A. M. Jones, ed., *The Works of Sir William Jones,* vol. 4 (London: G. G. and J. Robinson, R. H. Evens, 1799), 9–10, quoted in Javed Majeed, *Ungoverned Imaginings: James Mill's The History of British India and Orientalism* (Oxford: Clarendon, 1992), 45. Emphasis added.

42. The critical point here is that Orientalism is not just a mélange of provincial prejudices but a world-organizing triumphalist ideology, hegemonic in its time. It seems banal to project Orientalism back to the "Europe" of classical Greece, as Edward Said is sometimes wont to do, or even more vacuous to find progenitors for it in the Sanskrit texts of the first millennium A.D., as Sheldon Pollock attempts to do in "Deep Orientalism: Notes on Sanskrit and Power beyond the Raj," in Breckenridge and van der Veer, *Orientalism and the Postcolonial Predicament, 96.* As Edith Hall in *Inventing the Barbarian: Greek Self-Definition through Tragedy* (New York: Oxford University Press, 1989) shows through her close reading of various Greek texts, the Hellenes attributed to the "barbarians" many characteristics that were the very opposite of what latter-day Orientalism would ascribe to the "Orient." For example, the barbarians gave power to their women, even military command and leadership.

43. Raymond Schwab, *The Oriental Renaissance: Europe's Rediscovery of India and the East, 1680–1880,* trans. Gene Patterson-Black and Victor Reinking (New York: Columbia University Press, 1984), 23.

44. A point well made by Dharwadker, "Orientalism and the Study of Indian Literatures," 170. Thomas R. Trautmann, *Aryans and British India* (Berkeley: University of California Press, 1997), for example, notes the tension between the Jonesian version of Orientalism and the Saidian definition of it, but fails to follow up the implications.

45. Al-Azm, "Orientalism and Orientalism in Reverse," 20. Emphasis added.

46. Bryan S. Turner, *Marx and the End of Orientalism* (London: Allen and Unwin, 1978), 81. Emphasis added.

47. Ibid.

48. The title, of course, of Eric R. Wolf's magisterial work, *Europe and the People without History* (Berkeley: University of California Press, 1982).

49. Ludden, "Orientalist Empiricism," 252.

50. Al-Azm, "Orientalism and Orientalism in Reverse," 5.

51. Al-Azm rightly credits Edward Said with showing how "cultural-academic" Orientalism is "shot through and through with racist assumptions, barely camouflaged mercenary interests, reductionist explanations, and anti-human prejudices." And further: "This image, properly scrutinized, can hardly be the product of genuinely scientific investigation and scholarly discipline." Al-Azm, "Orientalism and Orientalism in Reverse," 5. See, for example, Edward Said, *Orientalism* (new York: Pantheon, 1978), 42.

52. Ludden, "Orientalist Empiricism," 252.

53. Ibid.

54. See, for example, Michel Foucault, *The Birth of the Clinic: An Archaeology of Medical Perception,* trans. A. M. Sheridan Smith (1973; New York: Vintage, 1994); Foucault, *Discipline and Punish: The Birth of the Prison,* trans. Alan Sheridan (1977; New York: Vintage, 1995).

55. A very important observation by Al-Azm, "Orientalism and Orientalism in Reverse," 18. Al-Azm goes on to note that the epistemological implications of this notion of ontological difference, "the conceptual instruments, scientific categories, sociological concepts, political descriptions, and ideological distinctions employed to understand and deal with Western societies remain [in the Orientalist schema], in principle, inapplicable to Eastern ones." This is true up to a point, but we think it important to remember that even these epistemological implications have to be located within disciplines of inquiry whose rules (of evidence, for example) required a universal validity. Thus what could be admitted as evidence — in theory, at any rate — necessitated, in all social milieus, the same recourse to "primary sources," source criticism if texts were involved, collation, comparison, and systematic documentation. Techniques developed in one area could be applied to another.

56. Ludden, "Orientalist Empiricism," 258.

57. As others have pointed out, Karl Marx's understanding of the peculiarity of feudalism, and the transition from feudalism to capitalism, is worked out through a global arrangement of the different modes of production, including the so-called Asiatic mode of production. While this enterprise may not have been central to Marx, it nonetheless informed his overall structure of comparative sociology. On this point, see E. J. Hobsbawm's introduction to Karl Marx, *Pre-Capitalist Economic Formations,* trans. Jack Cohen, ed. Hobsbawm (New York: International Publishers, 1977), 9–65. More explicitly, Max Weber's introduction to *The Protestant Ethic and the Spirit of Capitalism,* trans. Talcott Parsons (1930; London: Harper Collins, 1977) is a compact collection of the principal Orientalist stereotypes. Earlier on, James Mill's *The History of British India* (New York: Chelsea House, 1968) served as an extended exposition of the universal validity of utilitarian principles and served as a critique of Jonesian/Burkean conservatism (Majeed, *Ungoverned Imagining,* 200; Ludden, "Orientalist Empiricism," 264–65). The point is that even someone as suspicious of culturalist arguments and explanations as Marx was, did, to some extent, get drawn into the gravitational field of Orientalism. Mill's argument illustrates the value of an "outside" source to underline the need for "internal" reforms along rational-universal lines.

58. This is Ludden's contention, "Orientalist Empiricism," 265.

59. Samir Amin is absolutely correct to point out that social inquiry is implicitly comparative and, as we near our present epoch, that comparisons are inevitably global. Such inquiry, in itself, thus does not constitute Orientalism. Unfortunately, Amin fails to investigate fully the necessity, indeed imperative, of a particular kind of spatialization for an Orientalist comparative exercise. See Samir Amin, *Eurocentrism,* trans. Russell Moore (New York: Monthly Review, 1989). For an extended review of this work, see Vasant Kaiwar, "On Provincialism and 'Popular Nationalism': Reflections on Samir Amin's *Eurocentrism,*" *South Asia Bulletin* 11.1/2 (1991): 69–78.

60. Meyda Yegenoglu, *Colonial Fantasies: Towards a Feminist Reading of Orientalism* (Cambridge: Cambridge University Press, 1998), 6.

61. Ibid.

62. David Lloyd, "Race under Representation," *Oxford Literary Review* 13.1/2 (1991): 70. Emphasis added.

63. Joan Scott, "Multiculturalism and the Politics of Identity," *October* 61 (1992): 14–15.

64. Yegenoglu, *Colonial Fantasies,* 103.

65. For an illuminating discussion of the market imperative, see Ellen Meiksins Wood, *The Origin of Capitalism* (New York: Monthly Review, 1999), 67–104. Wood tends to separate capitalism and modernity rather sharply, associating the former with the social-property transformation of rural England during the course of the seventeenth century and the latter with the universalist impulses of the eighteenth-century Enlightenment and the French Revolution. However separated capitalism and modernity might have been at their inception, it seems somewhat excessive to insist that they did not comingle over time. Surely, the Girondin faction of the French Revolution, and their successors, were not opposed to capitalism; and some apologists of capitalism were more than willing to take on the more "bourgeois" aspects of universalism. We have insisted throughout this essay that ideologies do transform themselves over time, and capitalism is so powerful that it could hardly fail to impose some of its logic of operation over systems of thought that may have originated outside the realm of the capital relation.

66. Sarvepalli Radhakrishnan's statement—"The Vedanta is not a religion, but religion itself in its *most universal and deepest significance*"—represents a fairly typical attempt to turn a romantic cliché about Indian spirituality into a higher universalism. In this sense the grammar of Orientalism—in one or the other of its guises—was indispensable to the construction of colonial modernity. Radhakrishnan is quoted in Wilhelm Halbfass, *India and Europe: An Essay in Understanding* (Albany: State University of New York Press, 1988), 409; emphasis added.

67. Al-Azm, "Orientalism and Orientalism in Reverse," 19, refers to this as "ontological Orientalism in reverse."

68. Quoted in Yegenoglu, *Colonial Fantasies,* 141.

69. M. K. Gandhi, *Hind Swaraj and Other Writings,* ed. Anthony J. Parel (Cambridge: Cambridge University Press, 1997), 69; emphasis added. *Hind Swaraj* was originally composed in Gujarati and translated into English by Gandhi himself. The formative influences on the text, as Parel notes, were a variety of Euro-American late romantic and postromantic writers whose disillusion with the Industrial Revolution took the form of a yearning for an earlier form of community, shorn of all its sociopolitical contradictions and apotheosized as community par excellence.

70. Al-Azm, "Orientalism and Orientalism in Reverse," 20.

71. See, for example, A. R. Venkatachalapathy's essay in this volume.

72. The historical reasons for this disassociation are convincingly argued in Benedict Anderson, *Imagined Communities,* esp. 9–66.

73. Yegenoglu, *Colonial Fantasies,* 137; see also Marnia Lazreg, "Gender and Politics in Algeria: Unravelling the Religious Paradigms," *Signs* 15.4 (1990): 759.

74. Pierre Bourdieu, *The Algerians* (Boston: Beacon, 1961), 156.

75. Ibid.

76. Ludden, "Orientalist Empiricism," 272. There is an ironic universalism here in that the same reversal of Orientalism's signs could be applied to China, India, or Morocco.

77. Arjun Appadurai, "Number in the Colonial Imagination," in Breckenridge and van der Veer, *Orientalism and the Postcolonial Predicament,* 330. One might note, however, that the colonizers denied their colonies the makings of modern nation-states, lacking as they were said to civil society and similar qualities.

78. Appadurai, "Number in the Colonial Imagination," 334.

79. Ibid., 335; emphasis added.

80. Seemingly influenced by his reading of Ralph Waldo Emerson.

81. Jürgen Habermas, "The European Nation-State—Its Achievements and Its Limits: On the Past and Future of Sovereignty and Citizenship," in Gopal Balakrishnan, *Mapping the Nation* (London: Verso, 1996), 284–85.

82. Derek Sayer, *Capitalism and Modernity: An Excursus on Marx and Weber* (London: Routledge, 1991), 72–82.

83. Karl Marx, "On the Jewish Question," in Robert C. Tucker, *The Marx-Engels Reader,* 2d ed. (New York: Norton, 1978), 33.

84. Nationalism fulfills a number of the definitions of ideology that Terry Eagleton spells out. To select the most obvious ones, nationalism is: "a conjuncture of discourse and power"; "the indispensable medium in which individuals live out their relations to a social structure"; "the medium in which conscious social actors make sense of their world"; "the process whereby social life is converted to a natural reality"; "socially necessary illusion." Terry Eagleton, *Ideology: An Introduction* (London: Verso, 1991), 2. Anthony Smith (*Nations and Nationalism in a Global Era* [Cambridge: Polity Press, 1995], 160) and Benedict Anderson (*Imagined Communities,* 17–19) stress the religion-like, ontological elements in nation formation and nationalism, the so-called ultimate issues of "mortality and oblivion." Both the labyrinthine complexity of nationalist historiography and consciousness and the attachment of nation-states to real material interests suggest why that might be so. This does not mean it is not an ideology, although Balakrishnan maintains in his discussion of Benedict Anderson that the latter does not hold nationalism to be an ideology on the grounds that it is neither a "coherent doctrine" nor "a form of false consciousness" (Balakrishnan, "The National Imagination," 204).

85. Anthony D. Smith, *Nations and Nationalism,* 154.

86. For example, via the recognition of labor unions, the right to strike, the rights of national minorities to cultural autonomy, and a certain modicum of respect for human rights, the modern nation-state has contained popular struggles while giving nationalist claims of community a semblance of plausibility.

87. Balakrishnan, "The National Imagination," 203.

88. This is our single most serious reservation against Marshall Berman's otherwise excellent work, *All That Is Solid Melts into Air: The Experience of Modernity* (New York: Simon and Schuster, 1982). After all, the nineteenth century—when many of the institutions we take for granted as ensuring the stability of social life were still somewhat inchoate—was a time of intense engagement in constructing the basis of "national" institutions and life, and so the experiments of writers and thinkers were not merely Dionysian expenditures of energy, but also attempts at engagement with and the construction of a stable modernity.

89. Eric Hobsbawm, *Nations and Nationalism since 1780: Programme, Myth, Reality* (Cambridge: Cambridge University Press, 1990), 169. Which came first is not a chicken-and-egg question. Nigel Harris, *National Liberation* (Harmondsworth: Penguin, 1990), is clear about the historic priority of the state, which then pushed through projects of nationalism in the interests of the new bourgeois ruling class. Abbas Vali, "The Kurds and Their 'Others': Fragmented Identity and Fragmented Politics," *Comparative Studies of South Asia, Africa, and the Middle East* 18.2 (1998): 82–95, has argued that the Kurds — 30 million strong — are the "largest stateless nation" in the contemporary world (82). This suggests that the modern projects of nation building tend to enclose more than one "nationality," indeed may create nationalities where none existed. This argument would appear to hold with most Marxists, who would contend that most states are multinational. For an interesting demurral on this in the case of India, see Achin Vanaik, *The Painful Transition: Bourgeois Democracy in India* (London: Verso, 1990), 118.

90. Hobsbawm, *Nations and Nationalism since 1780,* 20.

91. Quoted in Balakrishnan, "The National Imagination," 202.

92. It would be unnecessarily romantic to imply that face-to-face communities did not require myths to create their sense of community; nor that a future community — that transcends by transforming today's form of the nation-state — will not create its own. One only has to look critically at the activism of socialists, past and present, to know that "scientific" socialism came with its own sets of myths, not least of all those about the Soviet Union and later about the Peoples Republic of China.

93. Balakrishnan, "The National Imagination," 201, referring to Hegel's *Philosophy of Right.*

94. In speaking of the universalization of the particular, we refer to the multiplication of nation-states founded on more or less identical principles. And as to the particularization of the universal, we have in mind the way in which notions of human rights, equality, and the like have been domesticated to the realm of particular nation-states. The point is well made by Balakrishnan, "The National Imagination," 201, drawing on Marx's "On the Jewish Question."

95. Habermas, "The European Nation-State," 286–87.

96. Benedict Anderson, introduction to Balakrishnan, *Mapping the Nation,* 2.

97. Habermas, "The European Nation-State," 286.

98. Anderson, introduction, 4.

99. Of course, such "internal" intensification and "external" attenuation were made possible by the development of the productive forces (and communications) associated with capitalist development: the drawing of clear and exclusive boundaries and the establishment of border checkpoints, passports, and visas, all of them associated with the development of nation-states.

100. Anderson, introduction, 4.

101. Hobsbawm, *Nations and Nationalism since 1780,* 169.

102. A point made by Martin Bernal, *Black Athena,* vol. 1.

103. For a very incisive review of Anderson's book, see Balakrishnan, "The National Imagination." The quote is from p. 205.

104. Smith, *Nations and Nationalism in a Global Era,* 160. This argument, without further qualification, is impossible to accept. Perhaps a medieval person would have thought it absurd that such an insubstantial imagined community as the nation could ever replace the real face-to-face oral communities of his or her time. Accepting the nation as both timeless and irreplaceable is part of the ideological apparatus of nationalism.

105. Ibid.

106. Ibid., 157, 159.

107. Ibid., 80.

108. Ibid., 183. One supposes that the family does the same to an extent. Yet the nation as imagined community performs this function on an immensely larger scale, corresponding to the greater scalar demands of modernity.

109. Ibid., 159.

110. Ibid.

111. Benedict Anderson, for example, approvingly cites Miroslav Hroch to the effect that nations are "real anthropological formations," in the process being critical of Ernest Gellner (Anderson, introduction, 10). See also Miroslav Hroch, *Social Preconditions of National Revival in Europe: A Comparative Analysis of the Social Composition of Patriotic Groups among the Smaller European Nations,* trans. Ben Fowkes (Cambridge: Cambridge University Press, 1985); and Ernest Gellner, *Nations and Nationalism* (Oxford: Blackwell, 1983).

112. Marx defines "socially necessary labor-time" as "the labor-time required to produce any use-value under the conditions of production normal for a given society and with the average degree of skill and intensity of labor prevalent in that society" (Karl Marx, *Capital: A Critique of Political Economy,* vol. 1, trans. Ben Fowkes [New York: Vintage, 1976], 129). The social process that links the individual labor of an immediate producer with that of all others is, as Moishe Postone, quoting Marx, remarks, a process that goes on "behind the backs of the producers." Marx, *Capital,* vol. 1, 135, quoted in Moishe Postone, *Time, Labor, and Social Domination: A Reinterpretation of Marx's Critical Theory* (Cambridge: Cambridge University Press, 1993), 191.

113. Most of the history one learns at school, or through the mass media, has to do with more or less fanciful versions of the nation's past and present.

114. A selective history in which amnesia, no doubt, proves as important as remembrance. See, for example, Ernest Renan, *Qu'est que c'est une nation?* trans. Wanda Romer Taylor (1882; Toronto: Tapir, 1996). However, it is also important to stress that this process should be read noninstrumentally, that is, as not simply the manipulation of facts or a distortion of the truth. The "manipulation" and "distortion" have to be related to larger structuring conditions in which their "truth" appears as almost commonsense to suitably socialized subjects. Since arguably the "truth" itself is a dialectical societal project, the process of its formation and its necessarily open-ended formative/constitutive relationship with broader social processes of economic and political transformations needs to be underlined.

115. Hobsbawm, *Nations and Nationalism since 1780,* 10.

116. Abbas Vali, "Nationalism and Kurdish Historical Writing," *New Perspectives on Turkey* 14 (1996): 25.

117. Ibid., 34.

118. In discussing Kurdish historical writing, particularly of the romantic-reactionary type, Vali notes that Kurdish identity is "intrinsically linked to a *transcendental concept of freedom*" (ibid., 43; emphasis added).

119. In the more conservative versions of nationalism that have come to dominate the postcolonial world order, anything that weakens this political body—class struggles, radical and "foreign" ideologies like Marxism or feminism—must be disciplined or destroyed.

120. It is therefore somewhat pointless to complain that the national form imprisons most histories. This is how a general sense of historical time emerged. It is not to argue, however, that its original matrix of the national community somehow traps history. Once a sense of time depth and temporal discipline emerges, it can be put to more critical uses. We would assume that Renan was aware of the irony involved in his statement that "getting history wrong is an essential part in the formation of a nation." Renan, *Qu'est que c'est une nation?* 7–8.

121. See, for example, Christopher Hill, *The World Turned Upside Down: Radical Ideas during the English Revolution* (London: Temple Smith, 1972); and Albert Soboul, *A Short History of the French Revolution, 1789–1799,* trans. Geoffrey Symcox (Berkeley: University of California Press, 1977).

122. This group, in many respects, was continuous with the lower ranks of the bourgeoisie. With the acceleration of Western European economic growth in the early modern period, there may have been some movement of artisans into bourgeois ranks.

123. See, for example, the excellent discussion in E. J. Hobsbawm, *The Age of Revolution, 1789–1848* (1962; New York: Vintage, 1996), 277–96.

124. Of course, the nationalist leadership had enormous problems convincing working people that this was exclusively the case. When propaganda failed, violence was always at hand. Sumit Sarkar develops this theme in his *Modern India.*

125. Much of the dislocation in India was associated with famine, and that, we believe, creates a rather different mind-set from the headlong rush of economic forces characteristic of nineteenth-century England, for example. Both produce nostalgist visions, but the Indian version has been immeasurably stronger, rooted as it is in myths of a golden age, brought to a sad end by invading external forces.

126. Partha Chatterjee makes much of this distinction in *The Nation and Its Fragments: Colonial and Postcolonial Histories* (Princeton, N.J.: Princeton University Press, 1993). He focuses almost exclusively on the emergence of nationalism in India and rather marginalizes the uneven globalization of capitalism as a moment in the emergence of this dichotomy of the inner and the outer. In fact, uneven spatial development—and therefore the experience of being on the periphery of the global system of expanded reproduction —so succinctly captured in nationalist writings from R. C. Dutt to Jawaharlal Nehru, suggest the importance of the peculiar colonial experience of modernity to the specific dichotomies and archaisms of Indian nationalism.

127. Adas, *Machines as the Measure of Men,* makes this very clear.

128. The anti-Enlightenment posturing of Indian writers and most of the subaltern school of historians, for example, is quite consistent with Indian nationalism and the development of bourgeois ideology in India. There is nothing radical about it. It has been quite unambiguously the ideology of the propertied classes in colonial and postcolonial India.

129. Berman, *All That Is Solid Melts into Air*, 83.

130. Ibid.

131. Given the dire economic, ecological, and social conditions in which most of the world's population finds itself after more than two centuries of industrial capitalism, we do not think it necessary to provide a special argument in favor of transformative politics that will simultaneously address, en route to overcoming, the limits of capitalism and modernity.

Select Bibliography

Aarslef, Hans. *The Study of Language in England, 1780–1860*. Minneapolis: University of Minnesota Press, 1983.

Abrahamian, Ervand. "Khomeini's Populism." *New Left Review* 186 (1991): 102–19.

Adam, Heribert. "Nationalism, Nation-Building and Non-racialism." In Rhoodie and Liebenberg, eds., *Democratic Nation-Building in South Africa*.

Adas, Michael. *Machines as the Measure of Men: Science, Technology, and Ideologies of Western Dominance*. Ithaca, N.Y.: Cornell University Press, 1989.

Afary, Janet. *The Iranian Constitutional Revolution, 1906–1911: Grassroots Democracy, Social Democracy, and the Origins of Feminism*. New York: Columbia University Press, 1996.

Ahmed, Akbar S., and Donnan Hastings. *Islam, Globalization, and Postmodernity*. London: Routledge, 1994.

Aiyangar, M. Srinivasa. *Tamil Studies: Essays on the History of the Tamil People, Language, Religion, and Literature*. Madras: Guardian Press, 1914.

Al-Azm, Sadik. "Orientalism and Orientalism in Reverse." *Khamsin* 8 (1981): 5–26.

Al-e-Ahmad, Jalal. *Garbzadegi*. Tehran: Ketab, 1962.

Alexander, Neville. "Approaches to the National Question in South Africa." *Transformation* 1 (1986): 63–95.

———. "Capitalism and Democracy in South Africa." In Marxist Theory Seminar (UWC, *The Limits of Capitalist Reform in South Africa*. Cape Town: University of the Western Cape, 1993.

———. "Comment on Liebenberg by Neville Alexander." In Rhoodie and Liebenberg, eds., *Democratic Nation-Building in South Africa*.

————. "Core Culture and Core Curriculum in South Africa." In Jackson and Solis, eds., *Beyond Comfort Zones in Multiculturalism.*

————. *Education and the Struggle for National Liberation in South Africa.* Johannesburg: Skotaville, 1990.

————. "Language and the National Question." In Maharaj, ed., *Between Unity and Diversity.*

————. *Sow the Wind: Contemporary Speeches.* Johannesburg: Skotaville, 1985.

Ali, Rahman. *Tazkarah-'i 'Ulama-yi Hind.* Lucknow: Matba'-i Munshi Niwal Kishur, 1914.

Allami, Abu al-Fazl. *The A-in-i Akbari.* Trans. H. Blochman. Delhi: Low Price Publications, 1989.

Allen, Theodore W. *The Invention of the White Race.* London: Verso, 1994.

Alloula, Malek. *The Colonial Harem.* Trans. Myrna Godzich and Wald Godzich. Minneapolis: University of Minnesota Press, 1986.

Ambler, Charles. "Alcohol, Racial Segregation, and Popular Politics in Northern Rhodesia." *Journal of African History* 31.2 (1990): 295–313.

Amin, Samir. *Eurocentrism.* Trans. Russell Moore. New York: Monthly Review, 1989.

Anaimuthu, Ve., ed. *Periyar Ee.Ve.Ra. Chinthanaigal.* Tiruchi: Sinthanaiyalar Kazhagam, 1974.

Andersen, Walter, and Shridhar Damle. *The Brotherhood in Saffron: The Rashtriya Swayamsevak Sangh and Hindu Revivalism.* Boulder, Colo.: Westview, 1987.

Anderson, Benedict. "Exodus." *Critical Inquiry* 20.2 (1994): 314–27.

————. *Imagined Communities: Reflections on the Origin and Spread of Nationalism.* London: Verso, 1991.

Anderson, Perry. "Modernity and Revolution." In Nelson and Grossberg, eds., *Marxism and the Interpretation of Culture.*

————. *The Origins of Postmodernity.* London: Verso, 1998.

Anquetil-Duperron, Abraham-Hyacinthe. *The Parsis: Essays on Their Sacred Language, Writings, and Religion.* New Delhi: Cosmo, 1978.

————. *Zend-Avesta.* New York: Garland, 1984.

————, trans. *Ouenek'hat: Id est, secretum tegendum.* Argentorati: Levrauet, 1801–2.

Appadurai, Arjun. *Modernity at Large: Cultural Dimensions of Globalization.* Minneapolis: University of Minnesota Press, 1996.

————. "Number in the Colonial Imagination." In Breckenridge and van der Veer, eds., *Orientalism and the Postcolonial Predicament.*

Arberry, A. J. *Oriental Essays: Portraits of Seven Scholars.* London: Allen and Unwin, 1960.

Arooran, K. Nambi. *Tamil Renaissance and Dravidian Nationalism, 1905–1944.* Madurai: Koodal, 1980.

Arora, Vasantha. "People Will Stay Despite Racism, Says *Post* Report." *India-West,* November 27, 1992, 34.

Arzu, Saraj al-Din Khan. *Chiraq-i Hidayat.* Ed. Mansur Sirvat. Tehran: Amir Kabir, 1984.

——. *Dad-i Sukhan*. Ed. Sayyid Muhammad Akram. Rawalpindi: Iran Pakistan Institute of Persian Studies, 1974.

——. *Muthmir*. Ed. Rehana Khatoon. Karachi: The Institute of Central and West Asian Studies, 1991.

Assisi, Francis. "Asian American Students Seek Ethnic Identity." *India-West,* August 9, 1991, 49.

——. "Indian American Roots: Were Slaves the First Immigrants?" *India-West,* June 8, 2001, 36.

Ayandele, E. A. *Holy Johnson: Pioneer of African Nationalism, 1836–1917*. New York: Humanities Press, 1970.

——. "The Missionary Factor in Northern Nigeria, 1870–1918." In Kalu, ed., *The History of Christianity in West Africa*.

——. *The Missionary Impact on Modern Nigeria, 1842–1914: A Political and Social Analysis*. London: Longmans, 1966.

Azad, Muhammad Husayn. *Ab-i Hayat*. 1907. Lucknow: Uttar Pradesh Urdu Akademi, 1982.

Azari, Farah, ed. *Women of Iran: The Conflict with Fundamentalist Islam*. London: Ithaca, 1983.

Balakrishnan, Gopal, ed. *Mapping the Nation*. London: Verso, 1996.

Balibar, Etienne. *Masses, Classes, Ideas: Studies on Politics and Philosophy before and after Marx*. Trans. James Swenson. New York: Routledge, 1994.

Balibar, Etienne, and Immanuel Wallerstein. *Race, Nation, Class: Ambiguous Identities*. London: Verso, 1991.

Ballard, J. A. " 'Pagan Administration' and Political Development in Northern Nigeria." *Savanna* 1.1 (1972): 1–14.

Barnes, Andrew E. "Catholic Evangelizing in One Colonial Mission: The Institutional Evolution of Jos Prefecture, Nigeria, 1907–1954." *Catholic Historical Review* 84.2 (1999): 242–64.

——. " 'Evangelization Where It Is Not Wanted': Colonial Administrators and Missionaries in Northern Nigeria during the First Third of the Twentieth Century." *Journal of Religion in Africa* 25.4 (1995): 412–41.

Barth, Auguste. *Les religions de l'Inde*. Paris: Fischbacher, 1879.

Basham, A. L. "Aryan and Non-Aryan in South Asia." In Deshpande and Hook, eds., *Aryan and Non-Aryan in India*.

——. *The Wonder That Was India: A Survey of the Culture of the Indian Subcontinent before the Coming of the Muslims*. New York: Grove, 1959.

Basu, Tapan, et al. *Khaki Shorts and Saffron Flags: A Critique of the Hindu Right*. Delhi: Orient Longman, 1993.

Bayly, C. A. "Knowing the Country: Empire and Information in India." *Modern Asian Studies* 27.1 (1993): 3–43.

Behdad, Ali. *Belated Travelers: Orientalism in the Age of Colonial Dissolution*. Durham, N.C.: Duke University Press, 1994.

Behera, Navnita Chadha. "End of History." *HIMAL* 9 (1996): 41–2.

Bellah, Robert N. *Beyond Belief: Essays on Religion in a Post-traditional World*. New York: Harper and Row, 1970.

Benería, Lourdes, ed. *Women and Development: The Sexual Division of Labor in Rural Societies: A Study*. New York: Praeger, 1982.

Bergaigne, Abel. *Les dieux souverains de la religion védique*. Paris: Viewig, 1877.

Bergaigne, Abel, and Paul Lehugeur. *Sacountala: Drame en sept actes mêlés de prose et de vers*. Paris: Librairie de bibliophiles, 1884.

Berman, Marshall. 1982. *All That is Solid Melts into Air,* New York: Viking Penguin.

Bernal, Martin. *Black Athena: The Afroasiatic Roots of Classical Civilization*. New Brunswick, N.J.: Rutgers University Press, 1987.

———. *Black Athena Writes Back*. Durham, N.C.: Duke University Press, 2001.

Bernier, François. *Travels in the Moghul Empire*. Delhi: Chand, 1968.

Bhabha, Homi. "The Other Question. . . ." *Screen* 24.6 (1983): 18–36.

Bhandarkar, Devadatta Ramakrishna. *Lectures on the Ancient History of India in the Period from 630 to 326 B.C*. Calcutta: University of Calcutta Press, 1919.

Bhargava, P. L. *India in the Vedic Age: A History of Aryan Expansion in India*. Lucknow: Upper India Publishing House, 1956.

Bidwai, Praful. "Democracy at Risk in India." *Nation,* January 2, 1993, 86.

Binder, John, and David Wellbery, eds. *The End of Rhetoric: History, Theory, and Practice*. Stanford, Calif.: Stanford University Press, 1990.

Binder, Leonard. *Islamic Liberalism: A Critique of Development Ideologies*. Chicago: University of Chicago Press, 1988.

Bingham, Roland K. "Seven Sevens of Years and a Jubilee: The Story of the Sudan Interior Mission." In Carpenter, ed., *Missionary Innovation and Expansion*.

Blaut, J. M. *The Colonizer's Model of the World: Geographical Diffusion and Eurocentric History*. New York: Guilford, 1993.

Boer, Jan Harm. *Missionary Messengers of Liberation in a Colonial Context: A Case Study of the Sudan United Mission*. Amsterdam: Rodopi, 1979.

Bohm, David. *Wholeness and the Implicate Order*. London: Routledge and Kegan Paul, 1980.

Bopp, Franz. *A Comparative Grammar of the Sanskrit, Zend, Greek, Latin, Lithuanian, Gothic, German, and Slavonic Languages*. Trans. Lieutenant Eastwick. 3 vols. London: Madden and Malcolm, 1845–53.

———. *Grammaire comparée des langues indo-européennes*. 5 vols. Paris: Imprimerie impériale, 1866–74.

Boroujerdi, Mehrzad. "Westoxication and Orientalism in Reverse." *Iran Nameh* 8.3 (1990): 375–90.

Bose, Sugata, and Ayesha Jalal. *Modern South Asia: History, Culture, Political Economy*. New York: Routledge, 1998.

Bourdieu, Pierre. *The Algerians*. Boston: Beacon, 1961.

———. *Outline of a Theory of Practice.* Trans. Richard Nice. Cambridge: Cambridge University Press, 1977.

Boyce, Mary. *Zoroastrians: Their Religious Beliefs and Practices.* London: Routledge and Kegan Paul, 1979.

Brantlinger, Patrick. *Rule of Darkness: British Literature and Imperialism, 1830–1914.* Ithaca, N.Y.: Cornell University Press, 1988.

Brasher, Brenda E. *Godly Women: Fundamentalisms and Female Power.* New Brunswick, N.J.: Rutgers University Press, 1998.

Braudel, Fernand. "History and the Social Sciences: The Longue Durée." In *On History,* trans. Sarah Matthews. Chicago: University of Chicago Press, 1980.

Breckenridge, Carol A., and Peter van der Veer, eds. *Orientalism and the Postcolonial Predicament: Perspectives on South Asia.* Philadelphia: University of Pennsylvania Press, 1993.

Brown, Edward G. *A Literary History of Persia: From the Earliest Times until Firdawsi.* New York: Scribner's, 1902.

Budge, E. A. T. W. *The Gods of the Egyptians: Or, Studies in Egyptian Mythology.* 2 vols. London: Methuen, 1904.

Bunnens, Guy. *L'expansion phénicienne en méditerrannée: Essai d'interprétation fondé sur une analyse des traditions littéraires.* Brussels: Institut historique Belge de Rome, 1979.

Burnet, James. *Of the Origin and Progress of Languages.* Menston: Scholar Press, 1967.

Burnouf, Emile. *The Science of Religion.* Trans. J. Liebe. London: S. Sonnenschein, Lowrey, 1888.

Burnouf, Eugène. *Le lotus de la bonne loi.* Ed. Theodore Pavie. Paris: A. Maisonneuve, 1852.

Bury, J. B. *A History of Greece to the Death of Alexander the Great.* London: Macmillan, 1902.

Caldwell, Deborah. "A Hindu Renaissance." *News and Observer* (Raleigh, N.C.), March 19, 1999.

Callaway, Helen, and Dorothy O. Helly. "Crusader for Empire: Flora Shaw/Lady Lugard." In Chaudhuri and Strobel, eds., *Western Women and Imperialism.*

Callinicos, Alex, ed. *Between Apartheid and Capitalism: Conversations with South African Socialists.* London: Bookmarks, 1992.

Cannon, Garland Hampton. *Oriental Jones: A Biography of Sir William Jones, 1746–1794.* New York: Asia Publishing House, 1964.

———. "Sir William Jones's Persian Linguistics." *Oriental Society* 78 (1958): 262–73.

Capricorn Africa Society. *Capricorn Africa.* London: Newman Neame, 1953.

Carpenter, Joel A., ed. *Missionary Innovation and Expansion.* New York: Garland, 1988.

Carter, Paul Allen. *The Spiritual Crisis of the Gilded Age.* DeKalb: Northern Illinois University Press, 1971.

Chabert, J-M. *La Société des missions africaines de Lyon en Afrique: L'islam chez les sauvages et les cannibales de la Nigerie du nord*. Lyon: Impr. des Missions Africaines, 1926.

Chardin, Jean. *Voyages de chevalier Chardin en Perse, et autres lieux de l'orient*. Ed. L. Langlés. Paris: Normant Imprimeur Libraire, 1811.

Chatterjee, Bankim Chandra. *The Abbey of Bliss: A Translation of Bankim Chandra Chatterjee's Anandamath*. Trans. Nares Chandra Sen-Gupta. Calcutta: Neogi, 1906.

Chatterjee, Partha. *Nationalist Thought and the Colonial World: A Derivative Discourse*. London: Zed, 1986.

———. *The Nation and Its Fragments: Colonial and Postcolonial Histories*. Princeton, N.J.: Princeton University Press, 1993.

Chattopadhyaya, Haraprasad. *Indians in Africa: A Socio-Economic Study*. Calcutta: Bookland, 1970.

Chaudhuri, Nupur, and Margaret Strobel, eds. *Western Women and Imperialism: Complicity and Resistance*. Bloomington: Indiana University Press, 1992.

Childe, V. Gordon. *The Aryans: A Study of Indo-European Origins*. New York: Knopf, 1926.

Cole, Juan R. I., and Nikki Keddie, eds., *Shi'ism and Social Protest*. New Haven, Conn.: Yale University Press, 1986.

Connell, R. W. *Gender and Power: Society, the Person, and Sexual Politics*. Stanford, Calif.: Stanford University Press, 1987.

Cook, S. A. "The Semites." *The Cambridge Ancient History*. 1st ed. Cambridge: Cambridge University Press, 1924.

Cowan, M. *An Anthology of Writings of Wilhelm von Humboldt: Humanist without Portfolio*. Detroit: Wayne State University Press, 1963.

Cox, Oliver Cromwell. *Caste, Class, and Race: A Study in Social Dynamics*. New York: Monthly Review, 1948.

Crampton, E. P. T. *Christianity in Northern Nigeria*. London: Chapman, 1979.

Creighton, T. R. M. *Southern Rhodesia and the Central African Federation: The Anatomy of a Partnership*. New York: Praeger, 1960.

Crocker, Walter R. *Nigeria: A Critique of British Colonial Administration*. London: Allen and Unwin, 1936.

Crone, Patricia. *Pre-Industrial Societies*. Oxford: Blackwell, 1989.

Crook, Nigel, ed. *The Transmission of Knowledge in South Asia: Essays on Education, Religion, History, and Politics*. Delhi: Oxford University Press, 1996.

Curtius, Ernst. *History of Greece*. Trans. Adolphus William Ward. 5 vols. New York: Scribner's, 1886.

Curtius, Georg. *Principles of Greek Etymology*. Trans. Augustus S. Wilkins and Edwin B. England. 5th ed. London: Murray, 1886.

Cuvier, Georges. *The Animal Kingdom arranged in Conformity with Its Organization*. Trans H. MacMurtrie. New York: G. and C. and H. Carvill, 1831.

Dalmia, Vasudha. *The Nationalization of Hindu Traditions, Bharatendu Harischandra, and Nineteenth-Century Banaras*. Delhi: Oxford University Press, 1999.

Das, A. C. *Rigvedic India*. Calcutta: University of Calcutta Press, 1921.

Davidson, Basil. *The Lost Cities of Africa*. Rev. ed. Boston: Little, Brown, 1987.

Degenaar, Johan. "Beware of Nation-Building Discourse." In Rhoodie and Liebenberg, eds., *Democratic Nation-Building in South Africa*.

——. "The Myth of a South African Nation." Idasa occasional paper 40, 1991.

Deshpande, Madhav M., and Peter Edwin Hook, eds. *Aryan and Non-Aryan in India*. Ann Arbor: Center for South and Southeast Asian Studies, University of Michigan, 1979.

Dharwadker, Vinay. "Orientalism and the Study of Indian Literatures." In Breckenridge and van der Veer, eds., *Orientalism and the Postcolonial Predicament*.

Dirks, Nicholas. "Colonial Histories and Native Informants: Biography as an Archive." In Breckenridge and van der Veer, eds., *Orientalism and the Postcolonial Predicament*.

Dirlik, Arif. "The Postcolonial Aura: Third World Criticism in the Age of Global Capitalism," *Critical Inquiry* 20.2 (1994): 328–56.

Dongre, Archana. "VHP'S Dharma Prasar Yatra Launched with Devotion." *India-West*, August 6, 1999, B1.

Dotson, Floyd, and Lillian O. Dotson. "Indians and Coloureds in Rhodesia and Nyasaland." *Race* 5.1 (1963): 61–75.

——. *The Indian Minority of Zambia, Rhodesia, and Malawi*. New Haven, Conn.: Yale University Press, 1968.

Drake, St. Clair. *Black Folk Here and There: An Essay in History and Anthropology*. Los Angeles: Center for Afro-American Studies, University of California, 1987.

Drew, Allison. "Political Representation and the Indian Question in South African Politics." *South Asia Bulletin* 12.2 (1992): 57–69.

Dunbuli, Adb al-Razzaq Maftun. *Ma'a-ir-i Sultaniyah*. Tehran: Ibn Sina, 1972.

Eagleton, Terry. *Ideology: An Introduction*. London: Verso, 1991.

Echeruo, Michael J. C. *Joyce Cary and the Novel of Africa*. New York: Africana, 1973.

Edwards, Paul, ed. *Encyclopedia of Philosophy*. 3 vols. New York: MacMillan, 1967.

Enloe, Cynthia H. *Bananas, Beaches, and Bases: Making Feminist Sense of International Politics*. Berkeley: University of California Press, 1990.

——. *The Morning After: Sexual Politics at the End of the Cold War*. Berkeley: University of California Press, 1993.

Enthoven, R. E. *The Tribes and Castes of Bombay*. Bombay: Government Printing Office, 1922.

Esposito, John L. *The Islamic Threat: Myth or Reality?* New York: Oxford University Press, 1992.

Etienne, Mona, and Eleanor Leacock, eds. *Women and Colonization: Anthropological Perspectives*. New York: Praeger, 1980.

Fabian, Johannes. *Time and the Other: How Anthropology Makes Its Object*. New York: Columbia University Press, 1983.

Fafunwa, A. Baba. *History of Education in Nigeria*. London: Allen and Unwin, 1974.

Fasa'i, Hasan Husayni. *Farsnamah-'i Nasiri*. Ed. Mansur Rastigar Fasa'i. Tehran: Amir Kabir, 1988.

Featherstone, Mike, ed. *Global Culture: Nationalism, Globalization, and Modernity*. London: Sage, 1990.

Fernandes, Marsha. "Chutney: The Spice of Life." *SAMAR* 11 (1999): 60–61.

Fischer, M. J. Michael, and Mehdi Abedi. *Debating Muslims: Cultural Dialogues in Postmodernity and Tradition*. Madison: University of Wisconsin Press, 1990.

Fisher, Maxine P. *The Indians of New York City: A Study of Immigrants from India*. Columbia, Mo.: South Asia Books, 1980.

Fisher, Michael. "The Office of Akhbar Nawis: The Transition from Mughal to British Forms." *Modern Asian Studies* 27.1 (1993): 45–82.

Forbes, Richard. "Arya Samaj in Trinidad." Ph.D. diss., University of Miami, 1984.

Forgacs, David. "National-Popular: Genealogy of a Concept." In *Formations of Nation and People*. London: Routledge and Kegan Paul, 1984.

Foster, Malcolm. *Joyce Cary. A Biography*. Boston: Houghton Mifflin, 1968.

Foucault, Michel. *The Birth of the Clinic: An Archaeology of Medical Perception*. Trans. A. M. Sheridan Smith. 1973. New York: Vintage, 1994.

———. *Discipline and Punish: The Birth of the Prison*. Trans. Alan Sheridan. 1977. New York: Vintage, 1995.

Fraser, James Baillie. *Narrative of the Residence of the Persian Princes in London, in 1835 and 1836*. London: Bentley, 1838.

Frederikse, Julie. *The Unbreakable Thread: Non-racialism in South Africa*. Bloomington: Indiana University Press, 1990.

Freund, Bill. *Capital and Labour in the Nigerian Tin Mines*. London: Longman, 1981.

Gafari, Hadi. *Hamd mi-amouzad*. Tehran: Bessat, 1979.

Gandhi, M. K. *Hind Swaraj and Other Writings*. Ed. Anthony J. Parel. Cambridge: Cambridge University Press, 1997.

Gann, L. H. *A History of Southern Rhodesia: Early Days to 1934*. London: Chatto and Windus, 1965.

Gellner, Ernest. *Nations and Nationalism*. Oxford: Blackwell, 1983.

George, Rosemary. "From Expatriate Aristocrat to Immigrant Nobody." *Diaspora* 6.1 (1997): 31–60.

Ghate, V. S. "Persian Grammar in Sanskrit." *The Indian Antiquary* (1912): 4–7.

Ghose, Aurobindo. *Speeches*. Calcutta: Arya, 1948.

Gilreath, James, and Douglas L. Wilson, eds. *Thomas Jefferson's Library: A Catalog with the Entries in His Own Order*. Washington, D.C.: Library of Congress, 1989.

Gobineau, J. Arthur de. *Essai sur l'inégalité des races humaines*. Paris: Belfond, 1967.

———. *Oeuvres*. Paris: Pléiades, 1983.

Goel, Ankur. Interview. *India-West*, November 10, 1989, 21.

Gokhale, Balkrishna Govind. *India in the American Mind*. Bombay: Popular Prakashan, 1992.

Golwalkar, M. S. *We, or, Our Nationhood Defined*. Nagpur: Bharat Prakashan, 1939.

Graham, B. D. *Hindu Nationalism and Indian Politics: The Origins and Development of the Bharatiya Jana Singh*. Cambridge: Cambridge University Press, 1990.

Grant, Michael. *The Ancient Mediterranean*. 1969. New York: Meridian, 1988.

Gray, Richard. *The Two Nations: Aspects of the Development of Race Relations in the Rhodesias and Nyasaland*. London: Oxford University Press, 1960.

Greenstein, Ran. "Racial Formation: Towards a Comparative Study of Collective Identities in South Africa and the United States." *Social Dynamics* 19.2 (1993): 1–29.

Gregory, Robert G. "Co-operation and Collaboration in Colonial East Africa: The Asians' Political Role, 1890–1964." *African Affairs* 80.319 (1981): 259–73.

——. *South Asians in East Africa: An Economic and Social History, 1890–1980*. Boulder, Colo.: Westview, 1993.

Grewal, Inderpal. *Home and Harem: Nation, Gender, Empire, and the Cultures of Travel*. Durham, N.C.: Duke University Press, 1996.

Grewal, Inderpal, and Caren Kaplan, eds. *Scattered Hegemonies: Postmodernity and Transnational Feminist Practices*. Minneapolis: University of Minnesota Press, 1994.

Grimm, Jakob. *Geschichte der deutschen Sprache*. 3d ed. Leipzig: S. Hirzel, 1868.

Guillaumin, Colette. *L'idéologie raciste: Genèse et langage actuel*. La Haye: Mouton, 1972.

Habermas, Jürgen. "The European Nation-State—Its Achievements and Its Limits: On the Past and Future of Sovereignty and Citizenship." In Balakrishnan, ed., *Mapping the Nation*.

Haeri, Shahla. *Law of Desire: Temporary Marriage in Shi'i Iran*. Syracuse, N.Y.: Syracuse University Press, 1989.

Halbfass, Wilhelm. *India and Europe: An Essay in Understanding*. Albany: State University of New York Press, 1988.

Halhed, Nathaniel Brassey. *A Code of Gentoo Laws: Or, Ordinations of the Pundits, from a Persian Translation, Made from the Original, Written in the Shanscrit Language*. London: n.p., 1776.

Hall, Edith. *Inventing the Barbarian: Greek Self-Definition through Tragedy*. New York: Oxford University Press, 1989.

Hall, Stuart. "The Local and the Global: Globalization and Ethnicity." In Anthony D. King, ed., *Culture, Globalization, and the World-System*.

——. "Old and New Identities." In Anthony D. King, ed., *Culture, Globalization, and the World-System*.

Hancock, Ian. *White Liberals, Moderates, and Radicals in Rhodesia, 1953–1980*. London: Croom Helm, 1984.

Hannaford, Ivan. *Race: The History of an Idea in the West*. Baltimore: Johns Hopkins University Press, 1996.

Harris, Nigel. *National Liberation*. Harmondsworth: Penguin, 1990.

Harvey, David. *The Condition of Postmodernity: An Enquiry into the Origins of Cultural Change*. Oxford: Blackwell, 1990.

Hasan, Zia, and Sharmila Roy. Letter to the editor. *India-West*, 4 November, 1994, 6.

Haug, Martin. *The Parsis: Essays on Their Sacred Language, Writings, and Religion.* 1878. New Delhi: Cosmo, 1978.

Hawley, John Stratton, ed. *Fundamentalism and Gender*. New York: Oxford University Press, 1994.

Hay, Stephen, ed. *Sources of Indian Tradition*. New York: Columbia University Press, 1988.

Headrick, Daniel R. *The Tentacles of Progress: Technology Transfer in the Age of Imperialism, 1850–1940*. New York: Oxford University Press, 1988.

Herbert, Thomas. *Travels in Persia, 1627–1629*. 1634. New York: Books for Libraries, 1972.

Heussler, Robert. *The British in Northern Nigeria*. London: Oxford University Press, 1968.

——. *Yesterdays Rulers: The Making of the British Colonial Service*. Syracuse: Syracuse University Press, 1963.

Hill, Christopher. *The World Turned Upside Down: Radical Ideas during the English Revolution*. London: Temple Smith, 1972.

Hillebrand, Karl. "De la philologie en Allemagne dans la première moitié du siècle: L'école historique." *Revue moderne* 33 (1865): 239–68.

Hobsbawm, E. J. *The Age of Capital, 1848–1875*. 1975. New York: Vintage, 1996.

——. *The Age of Revolution, 1789–1848*. 1962. New York: Vintage, 1996.

——. Introduction to Karl Marx, *Pre-capitalist Economic Formations*. Trans. Jack Cohen. New York: International Publishers, 1977.

——. *Nations and Nationalism since 1780: Programme, Myth, Reality*. Cambridge: Cambridge University Press, 1990.

Holm, A. *History of Greece*. London: Macmillan, 1894.

Howe, Stephen. *Anticolonialism in British Politics: The Left and the End of Empire, 1918–1964*. Oxford: Clarendon, 1993.

Hroch, Miroslav. *Social Preconditions of National Revival in Europe: A Comparative Analysis of the Social Composition of Patriotic Groups among the Smaller European Nations*. Trans. Ben Fowkes. Cambridge: Cambridge University Press, 1985.

Irigaray, Luce. *This Sex Which Is Not One*. Trans. Catherine Porter. Ithaca, N.Y.: Cornell University Press, 1985.

Irschick, Eugene. *Dialogue and History: Constructing South India, 1795–1895*. Berkeley: University of California Press, 1994.

Isaacs, Harold R. *Images of Asia: American Views of China and India*. 1958. New York: Harper Torchlight, 1972.

Isichei, Elizabeth. *A History of Nigeria*. London: Longman, 1983.

Iyer, A. V. Subramania. *Tharkala Tamil Ilakkiyam*. 1942. Madras: Makkal veliyeedu, 1985.

Jackson, Carl T. *Vedanta for the West: The Ramakrishna Movement in the United States*. Bloomington: Indiana University Press, 1994.

Jackson, Sandra, and José Solis, eds. *Beyond Comfort Zones in Multiculturalism: Confronting the Politics of Privilege.* Westport, Conn.: Bergin and Garvey, 1995.

Jaffrelot, Christophe. "The Genesis and Development of Hindu Nationalism in the Punjab: From the Arya Samaj to the Hindu Sabha, 1875–1910." *Indo-British Review* 21.1 (1989): 3–40.

———. *The Hindu Nationalist Movement in India.* New York: Columbia University Press, 1996.

Jakobson, Janet, and Ann Pellegrini. "World Secularisms at the Millennium: Introduction." *Social Text* 18.3 (2000): 1–27.

Jameson, Fredric. "The Antinomies of Postmodernity." In *The Seeds of Time.* New York: Columbia University Press, 1994.

———. "Cognitive Mapping." In Nelson and Grossberg, eds., *Marxism and the Interpretation of Culture.*

———. *Postmodernism, or, The Cultural Logic of Late Capitalism.* Durham, N.C.: Duke University Press, 1991.

Jensen, Joan. *From India to America.* New Haven, Conn.: Yale University Press, 1988.

Jones, E. L. *The European Miracle: Environment, Economies, and Geopolitics in the History of Europe and Asia.* Cambridge: Cambridge University Press, 1981.

Jones, William. *A Grammar of the Persian Language.* Menston, U.K.: Scholar Press, 1969.

———. *Lettre à A*** du P***, dans laquelle est compris l'examen de sa traduction des livres attribués à Zoroastre.* London: Chez P. Elmsly, 1771.

———. *The Letters of Sir William Jones.* Ed. Garland Hampton Cannon. Oxford: Clarendon, 1970.

Juteau-Lee, Danielle. "La production de l'ethnicité, ou la part réelle de l'idéal." *Sociologie et société enjeux ethniques: Production des nouveaux rapports sociaux* 15.2 (1983): 39–54.

Kaempfer, Engelbert. *Amonitatum exoticarum politico-physico-medicarum fasciculi V.* Lemgoviate: Meyer, 1712.

Kaiwar, Vasant. "On Provincialism and 'Popular Nationalism': Reflections on Samir Amin's *Eurocentrism.*" *South Asia Bulletin* 11.1–2 (1991): 69–78.

———. "Racism and the Writing of History." *South Asia Bulletin* 9.2 (1989): 32–56.

Kalu, O. U., ed. *The History of Christianity in West Africa.* London: Longman, 1980.

Kandiyoti, Deniz, ed. *Gendering the Middle East: Emerging Perspectives.* Syracuse: Syracuse University Press, 1996.

Kaplan, Caren, Norma Alarcon, and Minoo Moallem, eds. *Between Woman and Nation: Nationalisms, Transnational Feminisms, and the State.* Durham, N.C.: Duke University Press, 1999.

Kassim, Mohammed. "Reflections on the Indian Dilemma." *Dissent* 28 (1960): 15–17.

Kaufman, Renee Debra. *Rachel's Daughters: Newly Orthodox Jewish Women.* New Brunswick, N.J.: Rutgers University Press, 1991.

Kaunda, Kenneth D. *Zambia Shall Be Free: An Autobiography.* London: Heinemann, 1962.

Keddie, Nikki R. *An Islamic Response to Imperialism: Political and Religious Writings of Sayyid Jamal ad-Din al-Afghani*. Berkeley: University of California Press, 1968.

———. *Roots of Revolution: An Interpretive History of Modern Iran*. New Haven, Conn.: Yale University Press, 1981.

Khan, Ghulam Husayn. *Siyar al muta'akhirin*. Published as *A Translation of the Seir-mutagherin*. 1789. Lahore: Sheikh Mubarak Ali, 1975.

Khomeini, S. Ruhollah. *Hukumat-e islami: Velayat-e faqih*. Tehran: Amir Kabir, 1978.

———. *Islam and Revolution: Writings and Declarations of Imam Khomeini*. Trans. Hamid Algar. Berkeley, Calif.: Mizan, 1981.

———. *Simay-e Zan dar Kalam-e Imam Khomeini*. Tehran: Vezarat-e Ershad-e Islami, 1986.

Khosrokhavar, Farhad. "Du néo-orientalisme de Badie: Enjeux et méthodes: L'orientalisme interrogations." *Peuples méditerranéens* 50 (1990): 121–48.

Kibria, Nazli. "Not Asian, Black, or White." *Amerasia Journal* 22.2 (1996): 77–86.

Kiernan, Victor. *The Lords of Humankind: Black Man, Yellow Man, White Man in an Age of Empire*. Boston: Little, Brown, 1969.

Kim, Hyung-chan, ed. *Asian Americans and the Supreme Court: A Documentary History*. New York: Greenwood, 1992.

———. *Dictionary of Asian American History*. New York: Greenwood, 1986.

King, Anthony D., ed. *Culture, Globalization, and the World-System: Contemporary Conditions for the Representation of Identity*. Binghamton, N.Y.: SUNY Binghampton, Department of Art and Art History, 1991.

King, Kenneth James. "The Nationalism of Harry Thuku: A Study in the Beginnings of African Politics in Kenya." *Transafrican Journal of History* 1.1 (1971): 39–59.

———. *Pan-Africanism and Education: A Study of Race Philanthropy and Education in the Southern States of America and East Africa*. Oxford: Clarendon, 1971.

Knox, Robert. *The Races of Men: A Philosophical Enquiry into the Influence of Race over the Destinies of Nations*. London: Renshaw, 1862.

Kosambi, Damodar Dharmanand. *An Introduction to the Study of Indian History*. Bombay: Popular Books, 1956.

Kosmin, B. A. " 'Freedom, Justice, and Commerce': Some Factors Affecting Asian Trading Patterns in Southern Rhodesia, 1897–1942." *Rhodesian History* 6 (1975): 15–32.

Kristeva, Julia. *Language, the Unknown: An Initiation into Linguistics*. Trans. Anne M. Menke. New York: Columbia University Press, 1989.

Kuklick, Henrika. *The Imperial Bureaucrat: The Colonial Administrative Service in the Gold Coast, 1920–1939*. Stanford, Calif.: Hoover Institution Press, 1979.

———. *The Savage Within: The Social History of British Anthropology, 1885–1945*. Cambridge: Cambridge University Press, 1991.

Kulkarni, Beth. "VHP's Annual Fundraiser." *India-West*, January 27, 1995.

Kumar, Dharma, and Meghnad Desai, eds. *The Cambridge Economic History of India*. Cambridge: Cambridge University Press, 1982–83.

Kumar, Krishna. *Political Agenda of Education: A Study of Colonialist and Nationalist Ideas*. New Delhi: Sage, 1991.

Kumar, Nita. "Religion and Ritual in Indian Schools." In Crook, ed., *The Transmission of Knowledge in South Asia*.

Lahuri, Abu al-Barakat Munir. *Karnamah*. Ed. Sayyid Muhammad Akram. Islamabad: Iran Pakistan Institute of Persian Studies, 1977.

Lal, Vinay. "The Politics of History on the Internet: Cyber-Diasporic Hinduism." *Diaspora* 8.2 (1999): 137–90.

Lauer, Jean-Philippe. *Observations sur les pyramides*. Cairo: Institut Français d'Archéologie Orientale, 1960.

Lawrence, Bruce B. *Defenders of God: The Fundamentalist Revolt against the Modern Age*. New York: Harper Row, 1989.

Lazreg, Marnia. *The Eloquence of Silence: Algerian Women in Question*. New York: Routledge, 1994.

——. "Gender and Politics in Algeria: Unravelling the Religious Paradigms." *Signs* 15.4 (1990): 755–80.

Leach, Edmund. "Aryan Invasions over Four Millennia." In Ohnuki-Tierney, ed., *Culture through Time*.

Lefkowitz, Mary R., and Guy MacLean Rogers, eds. *Black Athena Revisited*. Chapel Hill: University of North Carolina Press, 1996.

Lewis, Bernard. *Islam and the West*. New York: Oxford University Press, 1993.

——. *The Muslim Discovery of Europe*. New York: Norton, 1982.

Lewis, Reina. *Gendering Orientalism: Race, Femininity, and Representation*. New York: Routledge, 1996.

Linden, Ian, with Jane Linden. *Catholics, Peasants, and Chewa Resistance in Nyasaland, 1889–1939*. Berkeley: University of California Press, 1974.

Linnaeus, Carl von. *The "Critica Botanica" of Linnaeus*. Trans. Arthur Hort. London: Ray Society, 1938.

Liverani, Mario. "The Bathwater and the Baby." In Lefkowitz and Rogers, eds., *Black Athena Revisited*.

Lloyd, David. "Race under Representation." *Oxford Literary Review* 13.1–2 (1991): 62–94.

Ludden, David. "Orientalist Empiricism: Transformations of Colonial Knowledge." In Breckenridge and van der Veer, eds., *Orientalism and the Postcolonial Predicament*.

Lugard, Frederick John Dealtry. *The Dual Mandate in British Tropical Africa*. Edinburgh: Blackwood, 1922.

Ma'ani, Ahmad Gulchin. *Karvan-i Hind: Dar ahval va asar-i sha'iran-i 'asr-i Safavi kah bah Hindustan raftahand*. Mashhad: Intisharat-i Astan-i Quds-i Razavi, 1369/1990.

Macfarlane, Alan. *Marriage and Love in England: Modes of Reproduction, 1300–1840*. Oxford: Blackwell, 1986.

Maharaj, Gitanjali, ed. *Between Unity and Diversity: Essays on Nation-Building in Post-Apartheid South Africa*. Cape Town: Idasa, 1999.

Mahood, M. M. *Joyce Cary's Africa*. Boston: Houghton Mifflin, 1965.

Majeed, Javed. *Ungoverned Imaginings: James Mill's The History of British India and Orientalism*. Oxford: Clarendon, 1992.

Makambe, E. P. "The Asian Labour Solution in Zimbabwe, 1898–1904: Labour Practices and Racial Attitudes in a Colonial Society." *Transafrica Journal of History* 13 (1984): 110–45.

Malcolm, John. *Sketches of Persia: From the Journals of a Traveller in the East*. Philadelphia: Carey, Lea, and Carey, 1828.

Mallory, J. P. *In Search of Indo-Europeans: Language, Archaeology, Myth*. London: Thames and Hudson, 1989.

Mangat, J. S. *A History of the Asians in East Africa, c. 1886 to 1945*. Oxford: Clarendon, 1969.

Manifesto of the All-India Bharatiya Jana Sangh. New Delhi: Jana Sangh Publication, 1951.

Mann, Michael. *The Sources of Social Power*. Vol. 1, *A History of Power from the Beginning to* A.D. 1760. Cambridge: Cambridge University Press, 1986.

Marriott, Michael. "In Jersey City Indians Face Violence." *New York Times*, October 12, 1987.

Marshall, Susan E. "Paradoxes of Change: Culture Crisis, Islamic Revival, and Reactivation of Patriarchy." *Journal of Asian and African Studies* 19.1–2 (1984): 1–17.

Marty, Martin E., and R. Scott Appleby, eds. *Fundamentalisms Observed*. Chicago: University of Chicago Press, 1991.

Marx, Karl. *Capital: A Critique of Political Economy*. Vol. 1. 1867. Trans. Ben Fowkes, London: Vintage, 1976.

———. *The Communist Manifesto*. 1848. London: Verso, 1998.

———. "On the Jewish Question." In Robert C. Tucker, *The Marx-Engels Reader*. 2d ed. New York: Norton, 1978.

Mashkur, Muhammad Javad. *Farhang-i Huzvarish ha-yi Pahlavi*. Tehran: Bunyad-i Farhang-i Iran, 1967.

Mason, Michael. "The History of Mr. Johnson: Progress and Protest in Northern Nigeria." *Canadian Journal of African Studies* 272 (1993): 196–217.

Maspero, G. *Etudes de mythologie et d'archéologie égyptiennes*. Paris: Leroux, 1893–1916.

Mazumdar, Sucheta. "Race and Racism: South Asians in the United States." In Nomura et al., eds., *Frontiers of Asian American Studies*.

———. "Racist Responses to Racism." *South Asia Bulletin* 9.1 (1989): 47–55.

———. "Women, Culture, and Politics: Engendering the Hindu Nation." *South Asia Bulletin* 12.2 (1992): 1–24.

McClintock, Anne. *Imperial Leather: Race, Gender, and Sexuality in the Colonial Context*. New York: Routledge, 1995.

McWilliams, Carey. *Factories in the Field: The Story of Migratory Farm Labor in California*. Boston: Little, Brown, 1942.

Meek, C. K. *The Northern Tribes of Nigeria: An Ethnographical Account of the North-*

ern Provinces of Nigeria together with a Report on the 1921 Decennial Census. 2 vols. London: Oxford University Press, 1925.

——. A Sudanese Kingdom: An Ethnographical Study of the Jukun-speaking Peoples of Nigeria. London: Paul, Trench, Trubner, 1931.

Meer, Fatima. Portrait of Indian South Africans. Durban: Avon House, 1969.

Meerza, Najaf Khoolee. Journal of a Residence in England, and of a Journey from and to Syria of their Highness Reeza Koolee Meerza, Najaf Koolee Meerza, and Taymoor Meerza, of Persia. To Which Are Prefixed Some Particulars Respecting Modern Persia and the Death of the Late Shah. Trans. Assaad Y. Kayat. 2 vols. London: Tyler, 1839.

Mehta, Uday. "The Essential Ambiguities of Race and Racism." Political Power and Social Theory 11 (1997): 235–46.

Melendy, H. Brett. Asians in America: Filipinos, Koreans, and East Asians. New York: Hippocrene, 1981.

Mernissi, Fatima. The Fundamentalist Obsession with Women. Lahore: Women's Resource and Publication Centre, 1987.

Metcalf, Thomas R. Ideologies of the Raj. The New Cambridge History of India, pt. 3, vol. 4. Cambridge: Cambridge University Press, 1994.

Michelet, Jules. Sélections. Comp. Lucien Fèbvre. Geneva: Traits, 1946.

Mies, Maria. Patriarchy and Accumulation on a World Scale: Women in the International Division of Labour. London: Zed, 1986.

Mignolo, Walter. The Darker Side of the Renaissance: Literacy, Territoriality, and Colonization. Ann Arbor: University of Michigan Press, 1995.

Mill, James Stuart. The History of British India. 1817. New York: Chelsea House, 1968.

Miller, Walter. Audu: A Hausa Boy (A True Story). London: Church Missionary Society, 1904.

——. Yesterday and To-Morrow in Nigeria. London: Student Christian Movement Press, 1938.

Mir-Hosseini, Ziba. Islam and Gender: The Religious Debate in Contemporary Iran. Princeton, N.J.: Princeton University Press, 1999.

Mitchell, Timothy. Colonising Egypt. Berkeley: University of California Press, 1991.

Moallem, Minoo. "Pluralité des rapports sociaux: Similarité et différence: Le cas des Iraniennes et Iraniens au Québec." Ph.D. diss., Université de Montréal, 1989.

——. "Transnationalism, Feminism, and Fundamentalism." In Kaplan, Alarcon, and Moallem, eds., Between Woman and Nation.

——. "The Universalization of Particulars: Civic Body and Gendered Citizenship in Iran." Citizenship Studies 3.3 (1999): 319–35.

Modeen, Mirza Itesa. Shigurf Namah I Velaët; or, Excellent Intelligence Concerning Europe: Being the Travels of Mirza Itesa Modeen, in Great Britain and France. Trans. James Edward Alexander. London: Parbury, Allen, 1827.

Modi, Jivanji Jamshedji. "Anquetil Du Perron of Paris — India as Seen by Him (1755–60)." In Anquetil Du Perron and Dastur Darab. Bombay: Times of India, 1916.

———. "Notes on Anquetile Du Perron (1755–61), on King Akbar, and Dastur Meherji Rana." In B. P. Ambashthya, ed., *Contributions on Akbar and the Parsees*. Patna: Janaki Prakashan, 1976.

Moghadam M., Valentine, ed. *Identity Politics and Women: Cultural Reassertions and Feminisms in International Perspective*. Boulder, Colo.: Westview, 1994.

Money, R. C. *Journal of a Tour in Persia during the Years 1824 and 1825*. London: Teape, 1928.

Mookerji, Radhakumud. *The Fundamental Unity of India*. New York: Longmans, Green, 1914.

Moreland, W. H., and A. C. Chatterjee. *A Short History of India*. 1936. London: Longman, 1953.

Morier, James Justinian. *A Second Journey through Persia, Armenia, and Asia Minor, to Constantinople, between the Years 1810 and 1816 With a Journal of the Voyage by the Brazils and Bombay to the Persian Gulf*. London: Longman, Hurst, Rees, Orme, and Brown, 1818.

Mosse, George L. *Toward the Final Solution: A History of European Racism*. Madison: University of Wisconsin Press, 1985.

Muhammad, Mirza Khan ibn Fakhr al-Din. *Tuhfat al-Hind*. Ed. Nur al-Hasan Ansari. Tehran: Bunyad-i Farhang-i Iran, 1975.

Mujtabai, Fathullah. *Aspects of Hindu Muslim Cultural Relations*. New Delhi: National Book Bureau, 1978.

Müller, F. Max. *A History of Ancient Sanskrit Literature, So Far as It Illustrates the Primitive Religion of the Brahmas*. London: Williams, 1859.

———. *India: What Can It Teach Us? A Course of Lectures Delivered before the University of Cambridge*. New York: Funk and Wagnalls, 1883.

———. "Preface to the Sacred Books of the East." In *The Upanishads*. Delhi: Motilal Banarsidass, 1965.

———. *The Sacred Languages of the East Translated by Various Oriental Scholars*. Delhi: Motilal Banarsidass, 1965.

Müller, Johann, Nico Cloete, and Shireen Badat, eds. *Challenges of Globalisation: South African Debates with Manuel Castells*. Cape Town: Maskew Miller Longman, 2001.

Muthusamy, E. S. *Tamil Perumpulavar Ee. Mu. Subramania Pillai*. Madras: Pari Nilayam, 1984.

Nader, Laura. "Orientalism, Occidentalism, and the Control of Women." *Cultural Dynamics* 2.3 (1989): 323–53.

Naderi, Nader. "Max Weber and the Study of the Middle East: A Critical Analysis." *Berkeley Journal of Sociology* 35 (1990): 71–87.

Najmabadi, Afsaneh. "Feminisms in an Islamic Republic: 'Years of Hardship, Years of Growth.'" In Yazbeck Haddad and Esposito, eds., *Islam, Gender, and Social Change*.

Nandy, Ashis, et al. *Creating a Nationality: The Ramjanmabhumi Movement and Fear of the Self*. Delhi: Oxford University Press, 1995.

Needleman, Jacob and George Baker, eds. *Understanding the New Religions*. New York: Seabury 1978.

Nehru, Jawaharlal. *The Discovery of India*. Garden City, N.Y.: Anchor, 1960.

Nelson, Cary, and Lawrence Grossberg, eds. *Marxism and the Interpretation of Culture*. Urbana: University of Illinois Press, 1988.

Nicolson, I. F. *The Administration of Nigeria, 1900–1960: Men, Methods, and Myths*. Oxford: Clarendon, 1969.

Nkomo, Joshua. *Nkomo: The Story of My Life*. London: Methuen, 1984.

Nomura, Gail M., et al., eds. *Frontiers of Asian American Studies: Writing, Research, and Commentary*. Seattle: Washington State University Press, 1989.

Norton, Robert. "The Tyranny of Germany over Greece? Bernal, Herder, and the German Appropriation of Greece." In Lefkowitz and Rogers, eds., *Black Athena Revisited*.

Nossiter, T. J. *Marxist State Governments in India: Politics, Economics, and Society*. London: Pinter, 1988.

Nyagumbo, Maurice. *With the People: An Autobiography from the Zimbabwe Struggle*. London: Allison and Busby, 1980.

Nyangoni, Wellington W. *African Nationalism in Zimbabwe (Rhodesia)*. Washington, D.C.: University Press of America, 1977.

Ohnuki-Tierney, Emiko, ed. *Culture through Time: Anthropological Approaches*. Stanford, Calif.: Stanford University Press, 1990.

Olender, Maurice. *The Languages of Paradise: Race, Religion, and Philology in the Nineteenth Century*. Trans, Arthur Goldhammer. Cambridge: Harvard University Press, 1992.

Oliver, Roland, and Gervase Matthew, eds. *History of East Africa*. Oxford: Clarendon, 1963–1976.

O'Malley, Kierin. "A Neglected Dimension of Nation-Building in South Africa: The Ethnic Factor." In Rhoodie and Liebenberg, eds., *Democratic Nation-Building in South Africa*.

Omi, Michael. "Shifting the Blame: Racial Ideology and Politics in the Post-Civil Rights Era." *Critical Sociology* 18.3 (1991): 77–98.

Ouseley, William. *Travels in Various Countries of the East*. London: Rodwell and Martin, 1819–23.

Ozigi, Albert, and Lawrence Ocho. *Education in Northern Nigeria*. London: Allen and Unwin, 1981.

Paidar, Parvin. *Women and the Political Process in Twentieth-Century Iran*. Cambridge: Cambridge University Press, 1995.

Pais, Arthur. "The War of the Worlds." *India Today International*, April 6, 1998.

Palmer, Herbert Richmond. *The Bornu, Sahara, and Sudan*. London: J. Murray, 1936.

Pandey, Gyanendra. "The Civilized and the Barbarian: The 'New' Politics of the Late Twentieth Century India and the World." In Pandey, ed., *Hindus and Others*.

———. "Which of Us Are Hindus?" In Pandey, ed., *Hindus and Others*.

———, ed. *Hindus and Others: The Question of Identity in India Today*. New Delhi: Viking, 1993.

Pandian, M. S. S. "Notes on the Transformation of 'Dravidian' Ideology, Tamil Nadu, c. 1900–1940." *Social Scientist* 252–53 (1994): 84–104.

Patel, Hasu. "Changing Asian Politics." *Central African Examiner* (Salisbury), August 27, 1966, 14–15.

———. "The Indian Dilemma." *Dissent* (Salisbury), February 18, 1960.

Pathak, Zakia, and Rajeswari Sunder Rajan. "Shahbano." *Signs* 14.3 (1989): 558–82.

Phimister, Ian. *An Economic and Social History of Zimbabwe, 1890–1948: Capital Accumulation and Class Struggle*. London: Longman, 1988.

Pictet, Adolphe. *Les origines indo-européennes, ou les Aryas primitifs: Essai de paléontologie linguistique*. 3 vols. Paris: Sandoz et Fischbacher, 1877.

Pillai, S. Vaiyapuri. *Tamil chudaramanigal*. Madras: Tamil Puthakalayam, 1949.

Poliakov, Léon. *The Aryan Myth: A History of Racist and Nationalist Ideas in Europe*. Trans. Edmund Howard. New York: Basic Books, 1974.

Pollock, Sheldon. "Deep Orientalism: Notes on Sanskrit and Power beyond the Raj." In Breckenridge and van der Veer, eds., *Orientalism and the Postcolonial Predicament*.

Postone, Moishe. *Time, Labor, and Social Domination: A Reinterpretation of Marx's Critical Theory*. Cambridge: Cambridge University Press, 1996.

Powell, Avril. "Perceptions of the South Asian Past: Ideology, Nationalism, and School History Textbooks." In Nigel Crook, ed., *The Transmission of Knowledge in South Asia*.

Prasad, Mahesh. "The Unpublished Translation of the Upanishads by Prince Dara Shikoh." In Darab Peshotan Sanjana et al., eds., *Dr. Modi Memorial Volume: Papers on Indo-Iranian and Other Subjects*. Bombay: Fort Printing Press, 1930.

Prashad, Vijay. *The Karma of Brown Folk*. Minneapolis: University of Minnesota Press, 2000.

Price, William. *A Grammar of the Three Principal Oriental Languages, Hindoostani, Persian, and Arabic on a Plan Entirely New, and Perfectly Easy; to Which Is Added, a Set of Persian Dialogues Composed for the Author, by Mirza Mohammed Saulih, of Shiraz*. London: Kingsbury, Parbury, and Allen, 1823.

———. *Journal of the British Embassy to Persia: Embellished with Numerous Views Taken in India and Persia; Also, a Dissertation upon the Antiquities of Persepolis*. 2 vols. London: Thorpe, 1832.

Rahnavard, Zahra. *The Message of Hijab*. London: Al-Hoda, 1990.

———. *Toloueh zan-e Mosalman*. Tehran: Mahboubeh, n.d.

Rajagopal, Arvind. "Hindu Nationalism in the US: Changing Configurations of Political Practice." *Ethnic and Racial Studies* 23.3 (2000): 467–96.

———. "An Unholy Nexus: Expatriate Anxiety and Hindu Extremism." *Frontline*, September 10, 1993, 12–14.

Rajagopalachari (Rajaji), C. *Katturaigal*. Karaikkudi: Pudumai Pathippagam, 1944.

Ralston, Richard D. "Political Change in Colonial African Leadership (ca. 1914–ca. 1945): American and Afro-American Influences." *Ufahamu* 4.2 (1973): 78–110.

Ranger, T. O. "African Politics in Twentieth-Century Southern Rhodesia." In Ranger, ed., *Aspects of Central African History.*

——, ed. *Aspects of Central African History.* Evanston, Ill.: Northwestern University Press, 1968.

Renan, Ernest. *Etudes d'histoire religieuse.* Paris: M. Lévy frères, 1857.

——. *Oeuvres complètes.* Ed. Henriette Psichari. 10 vols. Paris: Calmann-Lévy, 1947–61.

——. *Qu'est-que c'est une nation?* 1882. Trans. Wanda Romer Taylor. Toronto: Tapir, 1996.

Rhoodie, Nic, and Ian Liebenberg, eds. *Democratic Nation-Building in South Africa.* Pretoria: Human Sciences Research Council Publishers, 1994.

Richardson, John. *Dictionary, Persian, Arabic, and English.* London: Cox, 1829.

Richardson, Peter. *Chinese Mine Labour in the Transvaal.* London: Macmillan, 1982.

Riffat, Hassan. "The Burgeoning of Islamic Fundamentalism: Toward an Understanding of the Phenomenon." In Norman J. Cohen, ed., *The Fundamentalist Phenomenon: A View from Within; a Response from Without.* Grand Rapids, Mich.: Eerdmans, 1990.

Robertson, R., and F. Lechner. "Modernization, Globalization, and the Problem of Culture in World System Theory." *Theory, Culture, and Society* 2.3 (1985): 103–18.

Robertson, Roland. "Mapping the Global Condition: Globalization as the Central Concept." In Featherstone, ed., *Global Culture.*

Robertson, Roland, and JoAnn Chirico. "Humanity, Globalization, and Worldwide Religious Resurgence: A Theoretical Exploration." *Sociological Analysis* 46.3 (1985): 219–42.

Rocher, Rosane. *Orientalism, Poetry, and the Millennium: The Checkered Life of Nathaniel Brassey Halhed, 1751–1830.* Delhi: Motilal Banarsidass, 1983.

Rodinson, Maxime. *Europe and the Mystique of Islam.* Trans. Roger Veinus. Seattle: University of Washington Press, 1987.

Roediger, David R. *The Wages of Whiteness: Race and the Making of the American Working Class.* London: Verso, 1991.

Rotberg, Robert I. *The Rise of Nationalism in Central Africa: The Making of Malawi and Zambia, 1873–1964.* Cambridge: Harvard University Press, 1965.

Rubin, Isaak Illich. *Essays on Marx's Theory of Value.* Trans. Miloš Samardžija and Fredy Perlman. Montreal: Black Rose, 1973.

Rushdie, Salman. *In Good Faith.* New York: Granta, 1990.

Sadiq, Muhammad. *A History of Urdu Literature.* Delhi: Oxford University Press, 1984.

Saghal, Gita, and Nira Yuval-Davis, eds. *Refusing Holy Orders: Women and Fundamentalism in Britain.* London: Virago, 1992.

Said, Edward W. *Covering Islam: How the Media and the Experts Determine How We See the Rest of the World.* New York: Pantheon, 1981.

——. *Orientalism.* New York: Pantheon, 1978.

Saine, Thomas P. *Georg Forster*. New York: Twayne, 1972.

Samkange, Stanlake. *Newsletter*, January 27 1961, 3–4.

Sanasarian, Eliz. *The Women's Rights Movement in Iran: Mutiny, Appeasement, and Repression from 1900 to Khomeini*. New York: Praeger, 1982.

Sandys, John Edwin. *A History of Classical Scholarship*. 3 vols. Cambridge: Cambridge University Press, 1903–8.

Sanson, Nichola. *Voyage, ou relation de l'etat présent du royaume de Perse: Avec une dissertation curieuse sur les moeurs, religion et gouvernement de cet état*. Paris: Cramoisi, 1695.

Saraswati, Dayananda. *The Light of Truth: English Translation of Swami Dayananda's Satyartha Prakasha*. Trans. Ganga Prasad Upadhyaya. Allahabad: Kala, 1960.

Sarda, Har Bilas. *Life of Dayananda Saraswati, World Teacher*. Ajmer: P. Bhagwan Swarup, 1946.

Sarkar, Sumit. *Modern India, 1885–1947*. Madras: Macmillan India, 1983.

Sarkar, Tanika. "Educating the Children of the Hindu Rashtra: Notes on RSS Schools." *South Asia Bulletin* 14.2 (1994): 10–15.

Sarkar, Tanika, and Urvashi Butalia, eds. *Women and Right-Wing Movements: The Indian Experience*. London: Zed, 1995.

Savarkar, Vinayak Damodar. *Hindutva: Who is a Hindu?* Bombay: Veer Savarkar Prakashan, 1969.

Sayer, Derek. *Capitalism and Modernity: An Excursus on Marx and Weber*. London: Routledge, 1991.

Sayyid, Bobby, S. *A Fundamental Fear: Eurocentrism and the Emergence of Islamism*. London: Zed, 1997.

Schreiner, Olive. *Thoughts on South Africa*. London: T. Fisher Unwin, 1923.

Schwab, Raymond. *The Oriental Renaissance: Europe's Rediscovery of India and the East, 1680–1880*. Trans. Gene Patterson-Black and Victor Reinking. New York: Columbia University Press, 1984.

Scott, James C. *Domination and the Arts of Resistance: Hidden Transcripts*. New Haven, Conn: Yale University Press, 1990.

Scott, Joan. "Multiculturalism and the Politics of Identity." *October* 61 (1992): 12–19.

Sebeok, Thomas F. *Portraits of Linguists: A Biographical Source Book for the History of Western Linguistics, 1746–1963*. Bloomington: Indiana University Press, 1966.

Sen, Keshub Chunder. "Philosophy and Madness in Religion." In *Keshub Chunder Sen's Lectures in India*. London: Cassell, 1901.

Shamuyarira, Nathan M. *Crisis in Rhodesia*. London: Deutsch, 1965.

Shari'ati, Ali. *Fatemeh Fatemeh Ast*. Tehran: Hussainiyya Irshad, 1971.

———. *On The Sociology of Islam: Lectures*. Trans. Hamid Algar. Berkeley, Calif.: Misan, 1979.

———. *Ummat va imamat*. Tehran: Husainiyya Irshad, 1971.

Sharma, Shriram. *A Descriptive Bibliography of Sanskrit Works in Persian*. Hyderabad: Abul Kalam Azad Oriental Research Institute, 1982.

Shaw, Flora Louisa. *A Tropical Dependency: An Outline of the Ancient History of the Western Soudan, with an Account of the Modern Settlement of Northern Nigeria.* London: Nisbet, 1905.

Shayegan, Darius. *Qu'est-ce qu'une révolution religieuse?* Paris: Presses d'aujourd'hui, 1982.

Shelley, Percy Bysshe. *Hellas: A Lyrical Drama.* London: C. and J. Ollier, 1822.

Shipley-Jones, Anna Maria, ed. *The Works of Sir William Jones.* 6 vols. London: G. G. and J. Robinson, R. H. Evens, 1799.

Shirazi, Mir Jamal al-Din Husayn Inju. *Farhang-i Jahangiri.* Ed. Rahim 'Afifi. Mashhad: Danishgah-i Mashhad, 1351 A.H. 1972.

Shirazi, Mirza Salih. "Safar Namah-'i Isfahan, Kashan, Qum, Tihran." In *Majmu'ah-'i Safar namah-hayi Mirza-alih Shirazi.* Tehran: Nashr-i Tarikh-i Iran, 1364 A.H. 1985.

Shohat, Ella. "Rethinking Jews and Muslims: Quincentennial Reflecions." *Middle East Report,* September–October 1992, 25–29.

Shukla, N. S. "Persian Translations of Sanskrit Works." *Indological Studies* 3 (1974): 175–91.

Shukuh bin Shahjahan, Muhammad Dara. *Sirr-i Akbar-Sirr al-Asrar.* Ed. Tara Chand and Muhammad Riza Jalali Na'ini. Tehran: Taban, 1961.

Shushtari, Mir 'Abd al-Latif. *Tuhfat al-'Alam va Zil al-Tuhfah.* Ed. S. Muvvahid. Tehran: Tahuri, 1984.

Sil, Narasingha P. *Swami Vivekananda: A Reassessment.* Selinsgrove, Pa.: Susquehanna, 1997.

Singh, K. S. *The Scheduled Tribes.* In *People of India.* National Series 3. Delhi: Oxford University Press, 1994.

Singh, Pardaman. *Ethnological Epitome of the Hindustanees of the Pacific Coast.* Stockton, Calif.: Khalsa Diwan Society, 1922.

Sizwe, No. *One Azania, One Nation: The National Question in South Africa.* London: Zed, 1979.

Skocpol, Theda. "Rentier State and Shi'a Islam in the Iranian Revolution." *Theory and Society* 11 (1982): 266–83.

Smith, Anthony D. *Nations and Nationalism in a Global Era.* Cambridge, Mass.: Polity, 1995.

Smith, Vincent Arthur. *The Oxford History of India.* Ed. Percival Spear. 3d ed. Oxford: Clarendon, 1958.

Soboul, Albert. *A Short History of the French Revolution, 1789–1799.* Trans. Geoffrey Symcox. Berkeley: University of California Press, 1977.

Solway, J. "From Shame to Pride: Politicized Ethnicity in the Kalahari, Botswana." *Canadian Journal of African Studies* 28.2 (1994): 254–75.

Souroush, Abdolkarim. *Razdani, Roushanfikri va Dindari.* Tehran: Sarat, 1992.

Springer, Richard. "Technocrat Cites Bias in Silicon Valley." *India-West,* August 2, 1991.

Srinivas, Bala K. "Build Bridges Not Fences." *India-West,* September 9, 1988.

Stegner, Wallace. *Beyond the Hundredth Meridian: John Wesley Powell and the Second Opening of the West*. Boston: Houghton Mifflin, 1954.

Stigger, P. "Asians in Rhodesia and Kenya: A Comparative Political History." *Rhodesian History* 1 (1970): 1–8.

Stoler, Ann Laura. "On Politics, Origins, and Epistemes." *Political Power and Social Theory* 11 (1997): 247–55.

———. "Racial Histories and Their Regimes of Truth." *Political Power and Social Theory* 11 (1997): 183–206.

Suleri, Sara. *The Rhetoric of English India*. Chicago: University of Chicago Press, 1992.

Sundaram, Viji. "San Jose Student to Share Denny's Bias Settlement." *India-West,* June 10, 1994, 47.

Sutton, J. E. G. *Early Trade in Eastern Africa*. Nairobi: East African Publishing House, 1973.

Tagore, Rabindranath. "The Call of Truth." *Modern Review* 30 (1921): 4.

Takaki, Ronald. *Strangers from a Different Shore: A History of Asian Americans*. Boston: Little, Brown, 1989.

Talageri, Shrikant G. *The Aryan Invasion Theory: A Reappraisal*. New Delhi: Aditya Prakashan, 1993.

Tavakoli-Targhi, Mohamad. "Contested Memories: Narrative Structures and Allegorical Meanings of Iran's Pre-Islamic History." *Iranian Studies* 29.1–2 (1996): 149–75.

———. "Imagining Western Women: Occidentalism and Euro-Eroticism." *Radical America* 24.3 (1993): 73–87.

———. "Orientalism's Genesis Amnesia." *Comparative Studies of South Asia, Africa, and the Middle East* 16.1 (1996): 1–14.

———. "The Persian Gaze and Women of the Occident." *South Asia Bulletin* 11.1–2 (1991): 21–31.

———. "Refashioning Iran: Language and Culture during the Constitutional Revolution." *Iranian Studies* 23.1–4 (1992): 77–101.

———. *Refashioning Iran: Orientalism, Occidentalism, and Historiography*. New York: Palgrave, 2001.

Temple, Charles Lindsey. *Native Races and Their Rulers: Sketches and Studies of Official Life and Administrative Problems in Nigeria*. 1918. London: Cass, 1968.

Thapar, Romila. "Ancient History and the Modern Search for a Hindu Identity." *Modern Asian Studies* 23.2 (1989): 209–31.

Tilak, Bal Gangadhar. *The Arctic Home*. 1903. Poona: Tilak, 1956.

———. *The Orion, or Researches into the Antiquity of the Vedas*. 1893. Poona: Tilak, 1955.

———. *Srimad Bhagavadgita Rahasya*. Trans. Bhalchandra Sitaram Sukthankar. 2 vols. Poona: Tilak, 1935–36.

Tindall, George Brown, and David E. Shi. *America: A Narrative History*. New York: Norton, 1996.

Trautmann, Thomas R. *Aryans and British India*. Berkeley: University of California Press, 1997.

——. "Hullabaloo about Telugu." *South Asia Research* 19.1 (1999): 53–70.

Turner, Bryan S. *Marx and the End of Orientalism*. London: Allen and Unwin, 1978.

——. *Orientalism, Postmodernism, and Globalism*. London: Routledge, 1994.

Tweed, Thomas A. *The American Encounter with Buddhism, 1844–1902: Victorian Culture and the Limits of Dissent*. Bloomington: Indiana University Press, 1992.

Ubah, C. N. "Christian Missionary Penetration of the Nigerian Emirates, with Special Reference to the Medical Missions Approach." *Muslim World* 77.1 (1987): 16–27.

——. "Problems of Christian Missionaries in Muslim Emirates of Nigeria." *Journal of African Studies* 3.3 (1976): 351–71.

Vali, Abbas. "The Kurds and Their 'Others': Fragmented Identity and Fragmented Politics." *Comparative Studies of South Asia, Africa, and the Middle East* 18.2 (1998): 82–95.

——. "Nationalism and Kurdish Historical Writing." *New Perspectives on Turkey* 14 (1996): 23–52.

Vambe, Lawrence. *From Rhodesia to Zimbabwe*. Pittsburgh: University of Pittsburgh Press, 1976.

Vanaik, Achin. *The Furies of Indian Communalism: Religion, Modernity, and Secularization*. London: Verso, 1997.

——. *The Painful Transition: Bourgeois Democracy in India*. London: Verso, 1990.

Van Sertima, Ivan, and Runoko Rashidi, eds. *African Presence in Early Asia*. New Brunswick, N.J.: Transaction, 1988.

Venkatachalapathy, A. R. *Andha kalathil kappi illai muthalana aivu katturaigal*. Nagercoil: Kalachuvadu, 2000.

——. *Dravida iyakkum vellalarum*. Madras: South Vision, 1994.

——. "The Dravidian Movement and the Saivites, 1927–1944." *Economic and Political Weekly* 30.14 (1995): 761–68.

Venn, Couze. *Occidentalism: Modernity and Subjectivity*. Newbury Park, Calif.: Sage, 2000.

Vermeil, Edmond. *L'Allemagne: Essai d'explication*. Paris: Gallimard, 1940.

Vivekananda, Swami. *The Complete Works of the Swami Vivekananda*. 9 vols. Calcutta: Advaita Ashrama, 1964–97.

Von Laue, Theodore. *The World Revolution of Westernization: The Twentieth Century in Global Perspective*. New York: Oxford University Press, 1987.

Wacquant, Loïc. "For an Analytic of Racial Domination." *Political Power and Social Theory* 11 (1997): 221–33.

Wadia, Ardaser Sorabjee N. *The Romance of Rhodesia*. London: Dent, 1947.

Waite, Gloria. "East Indians and National Politics in the Caribbean." *South Asia Bulletin* 2.2 (1982): 16–28.

——. "The Role of Black Consciousness in the South African Liberation Struggle: An Interview with Saths Cooper." *South Asia Bulletin* 7.1–2 (1987): 112–22.

Waley, Arthur D. "Anquetil Duperron and Sir William Jones." *History Today* 2 (1952): 23–33.

Wallerstein, Immanuel. "Culture as the Ideological Battleground of the Modern World-System." In Featherstone, ed., *Global Culture*.

——. "The Rise and Future Demise of the World Capitalist System." In *The Capitalist World-Economy: Essays*. New York: Cambridge University Press, 1979.

——. "Social Conflict in Post-Independence Black Africa: The Concepts of Race and Status-Group Reconsidered." In Balibar and Wallerstein, eds., *Race, Nation, Class*.

Weber, Max. *The Protestant Ethic and the Spirit of Capitalism*. 1930. Trans. Talcott Parsons. London: Harper Collins, 1977.

Weiss, John. *Ideology of Death: Why the Holocaust Happened in Germany*. Chicago: Dee, 1996.

Wessels, Antonie. "The So-called Renaissance of Islam." *Journal of Asian and African Studies* 19.3–4 (1984): 190–201.

West, Michael O. " 'Equal Rights for all Civilized Men': Elite Africans and the Quest for 'European' Liquor in Southern Rhodesia, 1924–1961." *International Review of Social History* 37.3 (1992): 376–97.

——. "Indian Politics in South Africa: 1860 to the Present." *South Asia Bulletin* 7.1–2 (1987): 97–111.

——. "The Tuskegee Model of Development in Africa: Another Dimension of the African/African-American Connection." *Diplomatic History* 16.3 (1992): 371–87.

Wheeler, Robert Eric Mortimer. *Civilizations of the Indus Valley and Beyond*. London: Thames and Hudson, 1966.

Williams, Raymond. *Keywords: A Vocabulary of Culture and Society*. London: Fontana, 1983.

Wills, Alfred John. *An Introduction to the History of Central Africa*. London: Oxford University Press, 1964.

Wilson-Haffenden, J. R. *The Red Men of Nigeria: An Account of a Lengthy Residence among the Fulani, or "Red Men," and Other Pagan Tribes of Central Nigeria, with a Description of their Headhunting, Pastoral, and Other Customs, Habits, and Religion*. 1930. London: Cass, 1967.

Wolf, Eric R. *Europe and the People without History*. Berkeley: University of California Press, 1982.

Wolpert, Stanley A. *Tilak and Gokhale: Revolution and Reform in the Making of Modern India*. Berkeley: University of California Press, 1962.

Wood, Ellen Meiksins. *The Origin of Capitalism*. New York: Monthly Review, 1999.

Wood, J. R. T. *The Welensky Papers: A History of the Federation of Rhodesia and Nyasaland*. Durban: Graham, 1983.

Wright, Denis. *The English amongst the Persians: During the Qajar Period, 1787–1921*. London: Heinemann, 1977.

Wurgaft, Lewis D. *The Imperial Imagination: Magic and Myth in Kipling's India*. Middletown, Conn: Wesleyan University Press, 1983.

Wuthnow, Robert. *Meaning and Moral Order: Explorations in Cultural Analysis*. Berkeley: University of California Press, 1987.

——. "Religious Movements and the Transition in World Order." In Needleman and Baker, eds., *Understanding the New Religions.*

——. *The Restructuring of American Religion: Society and Faith since World War II.* Princeton, N.J.: Princeton University Press, 1988.

Yazbeck Haddad, Yvonne, and John L. Esposito, eds. *Islam, Gender, and Social Change.* New York: Oxford University Press, 1998.

Yearbook of American and Canadian Churches. Nashville: Abingdon, 1998.

Yegenoglu, Meyda. *Colonial Fantasies: Towards a Feminist Reading of Orientalism.* Cambridge: Cambridge University Press, 1998.

Zan der ayeneh-e defay-e moghadass. Tehran: Sisters Propagation Squad, Islamic Revolutionary Guards, 1990.

Zend-Avesta. 1880. Trans. James Darmesteter and Lawrence H. Mills. Westport, Conn.: Greenwood, 1972.

Contributors

Neville Alexander is currently director of the Project for the Study of Alternative Education in South Africa (PRAESA), a research unit in the Faculty of Humanities at the University of Cape Town. He is the author of *English Unassailable but Unattainable: The Dilemmas of South African Language Policy in Education* (PRAESA, 2000), and "A Very Ordinary Country: The Transition from Apartheid to Democracy in South Africa," a manuscript forthcoming with the University of Natal Press in Durban, South Africa.

Andrew Barnes teaches African and European history in the History Department at Arizona State University. In African history, he has forthcoming chapters on "African Intellectual Life during the Colonial Era" and "Western Education in Colonial Africa" in Toyin Falola, ed., *Africa: Colonial Africa, 1885–1939*. In European history his most recent publication is "Church and Society," in Peter Stearns, ed., *Encyclopedia of European Social History*. At present he is writing a study of the European effort to introduce Western civilization in colonial northern Nigeria.

Vasant Kaiwar teaches modern South Asian and world history in the History Department at Duke University. He founded and edited, with Sucheta Mazumdar, the journals *South Asia Bulletin* (1981–93) and *Comparative Studies of South Asia, Africa, and the Middle East* (1993–2002). Educated at the University of Oxford and at UCLA, he has published articles on the socioeconomic history of western India, Marxist theory, and globalization. He is currently completing a book on globalization and the agrarian question: historical perspectives on the industrialization of agriculture and the agro-food industry.

Sucheta Mazumdar teaches Chinese history and Asian American history at Duke University. Co-founder and co-editor with Vasant Kaiwar of the journals *South Asia Bulletin* and *Comparative Studies of South Asia, Africa, and the Middle East,* her teaching and research interests focus on the development of capitalism, globalization, and gender. Her publications include *Sugar and Society in China: Peasants, Technology, and the World Market* (Harvard University Press, 1998). She is currently working on *A Global History of Women in the Long Twentieth Century* (Norton, forthcoming).

Minoo Moallem is Associate Professor and Chair of Women's Studies at San Francisco State University. She is the co-editor (with Caren Kaplan and Norma Alarcon) of *Between Woman and Nation: Nationalisms, Transnational Feminisms, and the State* (Duke University Press, 1999), and she is currently writing a book entitled *Between Warrior Brother and Veiled Sister: Islamic Fundamentalism and the Cultural Politics of Patriarchy* (University of California Press, forthcoming). Trained as a sociologist, she writes on feminist theory, gender and fundamentalism, globalization, and Iranian cultural politics and diasporas.

Mohamad Tavakoli-Targhi is Associate Professor of Historiography and Middle Eastern History at the Illinois State University and editor of *Comparative Studies of South Asia, Africa, and the Middle East.* He is the author of *Refashioning Iran* (St. Anthony's/Palgrave, 2001) and, in Persian, *Tadaddud-i Bumi* [Vernacular modernity] (Tehran: Nashr-i Tarikh-i Iran, 2002). He is also co-editor (with Reza Sheikoleslami) of *The Emergence of Modernity and Nationalism in Iran,* a special issue of *Comparative Studies of South Asia, Africa, and the Middle East* (1998–99).

A. R. Venkatachalapthy took his Ph.D. from Jawaharlal Nehru University, New Delhi, and is on the faculty of the Madras Institute of Development Studies, Chennai. He has held research/teaching assignments in London,

Paris, and Chicago. His most recent publications include a collection of essays on the cultural history of Tamilnadu, titled: *Antha Kalathil Kaappi Illai* (Nagercoil: Kalachuvadu, 2000). He has also edited a chronological and variorum edition of Pudumaippithan's short stories, the first volume of his collected works.

Michael O. West teaches in the Department of Sociology at the State University of New York at Binghamton. His research encompasses southern Africa and pan-Africanism. He is co-editor, with William Martin, of *Out of One, Many Africas: Reconstructing the Study and Meaning of Africa* (Indiana University Press, 1999), and he is finishing a book entitled *The Rise of an African Middle Class: Colonial Zimbabwe, 1898–1965* (Indiana University Press, forthcoming).

Index

Library of Congress Cataloging-in-Publication Data

Antinomies of modernity : essays on race, orient,
nation / edited by Vasant Kaiwar and Sucheta Mazumdar.
p. cm.   Includes bibliographical references and index.
ISBN 0-8223-3011-3 (cloth : alk. paper)
ISBN 0-8223-3046-6 (pbk. : alk. paper)
1. Civilization, Modern. 2. South Asia — Civilization.
3. Middle East — Civilization. 4. Africa — Civilization.
5. East and West. 6. North and south. 7. Imperialism —
History. 8. Capitalism — Social aspects — History.
9. Race relations — History. 10. Orientalism — History.
I. Kaiwar, Vasant. II. Mazumdar, Sucheta
CB358 .A59 2003   950.4′2 — dc21   2002014629